100 Greatest Cult Films

100 Greatest Cult Films

Christopher J. Olson

ROWMAN & LITTLEFIELD
Lanham • Boulder • New York • London

Published by Rowman & Littlefield
An imprint of The Rowman & Littlefield Publishing Group, Inc.
4501 Forbes Boulevard, Suite 200, Lanham, Maryland 20706
www.rowman.com

Unit A, Whitacre Mews, 26-34 Stannary Street, London SE11 4AB

British Library Cataloguing in Publication Information Available

Library of Congress Cataloging-in-Publication Data

Names: Olson, Christopher J. author.
Title: 100 greatest cult films / Christopher J. Olson.
Other titles: One hundred greatest cult films
Description: Lanham : Rowman & Littlefield, 2018. | Includes bibliographical references
    and index.
Identifiers: LCCN 2017047078 (print) | LCCN 2017054104 (ebook) | ISBN 9781442211049
    (electronic) | ISBN 9781442208223 (cloth : alk. paper)
Subjects: LCSH: Cult films—History and criticism. | Sensationalism in motion pictures.
Classification: LCC PN1995.9.C84 (ebook) | LCC PN1995.9.C84 O47 2018 (print) | DDC
    791.43/653—dc23
LC record available at https://lccn.loc.gov/2017047078

♾️™ The paper used in this publication meets the minimum requirements of
American National Standard for Information Sciences—Permanence of Paper
for Printed Library Materials, ANSI/NISO Z39.48-1992.

Printed in the United States of America

For Joe,
my cult movie soul brother

Contents

Appendixes

Acknowledgments

First and foremost, I need to thank my devoted partner (and most loyal proof-reader), CarrieLynn Reinhard, for all her help and support during the writing of this book. Thank you so much for always believing in me, and for sticking by me through the good times and the bad. I love you, Princess, and could not have done this without you. I also need to thank Bob Batchelor for helping set up this project in the first place. Without your guidance and encouragement, I never would have gotten the opportunity to write this book. Thanks also to Stephen Ryan at Rowman & Littlefield for giving me the chance to write an entire tome about one of my favorite subjects. In addition, Jim Barg, Joe Belfeuil, Frank Beno Jr., Sheela Cheeong, Jennifer Dunn, Keith Fordyce, Tyler Foster, Chris Loseke, Jimmy Manning, Gabe Powers, Patrick Ripoll, Lara Stache, Clelia Sweeney, and Kathleen Turner all deserve my gratitude, because they each offered valuable feedback throughout the writing process. Finally, I want to thank everyone involved in the creation of the cult films discussed in this book, because without them the world would have missed out on hundreds of hours of outrageous entertainment.

Introduction

What is a cult film? This question has no easy answer, because *cult* means different things to different people. For some, the term conjures up images of offbeat and/or gory movies like *Eraserhead* or *The Evil Dead*. For others, it refers to films that developed a passionate and devoted following in the years after their release. While the term is difficult to define, the truth is that any movie can inspire devotion among audiences and thereby become a cult film. At the time of this writing, *Wikipedia*'s entry on cult cinema links to a crowdsourced list of nearly 1,750 films, which continues to grow as more cult movies are released or discovered. More importantly, the list demonstrates the various ways that people define *cult*, because it includes everything from well-regarded classics like *2001: A Space Odyssey* and *Double Indemnity* to little-seen oddities like *Meet the Feebles* and *Pulgasari*. In any event, this broad definition of *cult* and the wide array of films to which the term applies makes compiling a list of the 100 greatest cult films quite difficult.

Yet this was the task I set for myself when I embarked on this project. As a lifelong film fanatic with a deep and abiding love of cult cinema, I jumped at the chance to write a book about one of my favorite subjects. Despite (or perhaps because of) my enthusiasm for the project, I found putting together my final list much more difficult than I initially expected; the standard definition of *cult* remains so vague and encompasses such a wide variety of films that I had a hard time deciding which movies to include and which ones to leave out. Therefore, I had to come up with my own working definition of *cult film* that would guide my choices and provide readers with a clear understanding of why some films made the cut and others did not. To accomplish this, I looked at how others had defined *cult* throughout history to understand why some movies inspired such rabid devotion from audiences.

The term *cult film* first emerged in the 1970s and was used to describe midnight movies and underground film culture.[1] Since then, scholars, critics, and film fans have come up with several definitions of *cult*, each one different from the last, and they have applied these definitions to a broad spectrum of films. For some people, a movie only needs to acquire a loyal cult following to qualify as cult. Others, meanwhile, focus on obscure or transgressive films ignored by conventional audiences, and exclude major studio releases and films that gain acceptance with mainstream audiences and critics. Still others reject prefabricated cult movies (such as *Snakes on a Plane* or *Sharknado*). Even this small sampling should give you an idea of the difficulty of defining the term *cult*, which becomes compounded by the fact that so many different types of movies have earned reputations as cult films.

As mentioned earlier, cult films include everything from major studio releases—particularly notorious box office bombs like *Dune* or *Heaven's Gate*—to lesser-known independent efforts that challenge or subvert mainstream sensibilities, such as *Flesh for Frankenstein* and *Nekromantik*. Other times, so-called bad movies might develop a rabid cult of viewers who appreciate the film ironically, like *Samurai Cop* and *Birdemic: Shock and Terror*. Regardless of why people enjoy them, cult films tend to resonate with fans because they include memorable characters, shocking scenes, and quotable dialogue, as in films like *Monty Python and the Holy Grail* ("Run away!") and *Mommie Dearest* ("No . . . wire . . . hangers!"). Finally, while some genres are more prone to develop cults than others—for instance, horror, science fiction, and comedy films often earn cult followings to a much greater degree than other types of movies—cult films encompass all genres, and they frequently mix several different genres in a single movie, such as *Miracle Mile* (action, drama, romance, science fiction, thriller) and *Near Dark* (action, crime, drama, horror, romance, thriller, western). This means there are many different types of cult films that appeal to a wide variety of tastes.

Whatever their origin, cult films usually attract a small but passionate audience, like the one that grew up around *The Rocky Horror Picture Show*. This limited appeal likely explains why cult films inspire such devotion among audiences; viewers sometimes see these films as a form of rebellion against mainstream society and culture, and use them to connect with other members of a like-minded community. Cult film fans tend to see themselves as outsiders and nonconformists, and as such they gravitate toward unconventional or controversial films that challenge or disrupt traditional understandings of narrative and technical conventions. In addition, cult films are often flawed or unusual in a way that sets them apart from the more technically proficient films that dominate the mainstream box office in the United States and elsewhere. Many cult films seem revolutionary because they include the sort of shocking characters, offbeat sensibilities, and subversive content that major studio productions tend to ignore. Also, as previously stated, cult films sometimes use gore and other shocking elements to upset or challenge the somewhat delicate sensibilities of conventional audiences.

For the purposes of this book, I drew on the descriptions discussed earlier to develop my own working definition of *cult* that I would use to determine the 100 greatest cult films. First and foremost, a cult film must have a devoted following, preferably among people who consider themselves outsiders and reject prevailing cultural norms. Next, cult films should challenge mainstream sensibilities in some way and transcend typical ideas about good and bad taste. Finally, cult films ought to defy conventional notions of cinematic storytelling and feature outrageous characters, dialogue, situations, and so on. To be included in this list, a film needed to exhibit one or more of these criteria, which can apply to anything from high-profile blockbusters to microbudget indie flicks, but still narrowed the field a bit and helped to inform my choices.

As with any list, mine is incredibly subjective (to paraphrase Jeffrey "The Dude" Lebowski, it's just, like, my opinion, man), and therefore I should include at least one paragraph explaining why I chose certain films over others. First, given the sheer number of cult films produced around the world, I decided to focus on United States productions or coproductions. Even then, I had numerous films to choose from, so from there I opted to include only feature-length movies, which disqualified great short cult films like *Superstar: The Karen Carpenter Story* and *Scorpio Rising*. I then concentrated on films that developed a legacy or in some way left an imprint on cult cinema (or the culture at large) in the years after their release. Thus, *The Thing* and *The Big Lebowski* warranted inclusion because they developed reputations as bona fide cult classics in the years after their release and remain beloved even now. Meanwhile, movies like *Faster, Pussycat! Kill! Kill!* and *Pink Flamingos* made the list because they were directed by prolific cult icons (not to mention, they are great films). Finally, I excluded movies like *Bride of Frankenstein, Casablanca, It's a Wonderful Life*, and others that have become so thoroughly canonized as classic films that they no longer qualify as cult. Leaving these films off the list allowed me to highlight some lesser-known cult films and to include a few that I believe deserve more attention from cult film fans. Of course, given these criteria, one could argue against the inclusion of films like *Blade Runner, The Thing, Pulp Fiction*, or even *Lebowski*, all of which have developed reputations as classic films. Yet these films maintain their cult status because they do not hold the same widespread audience appeal as those previously listed and therefore deserve a spot on this list.

I also included spotlights on certain creators or institutions as a way of highlighting their contributions to cult cinema. While conceiving this project, I chose to include only one film per director to prevent any single individual from dominating the list. At the same time, prolific cult auteurs like Roger Corman, Brian De Palma, Lloyd Kaufman, David Lynch, John Waters, and others have profoundly influenced cult cinema and therefore warrant special consideration. The same goes for boutique home video labels such as Drafthouse Films and television shows like *Mystery Science Theater 3000*, because these institutions are dedicated to exposing audiences to the trashy charms of cult favorites like *Miami Connection* and *Manos: The Hands of Fate*.

In addition, I decided to include five appendixes that focus on other noteworthy cult films that failed to make the final list for one reason or another. These appendixes highlight ten great international cult films, ten great camp classics, ten great midnight movies, ten great exploitation films, and the ten worst cult films of all time. Like the main list, these inventories are entirely subjective and based on my opinion alone, so I hope readers keep that in mind if their favorite movie appears on the "worst" list. I included these appendixes to draw attention to other movies that cult film fans should seek out (or avoid, in the case of the worst list), because while they failed to qualify for the main list, they nevertheless merit some recognition.

Lastly, rather than assign numbered rankings, the films are presented in alphabetical order. As with cult cinema in general, the films included in this book encompass several different genres and styles, and therefore it becomes difficult to compare them against one another, much less rank them. Furthermore, I dislike numbered lists, largely because I consider such efforts to quantify art reductive (not to mention pointless). Compiling the list in alphabetical order allowed me to highlight those cult films I consider the 100 greatest without falling into the trap of trying to determine which ones are better than others.

I hope this book serves as guide for both longtime fans and those just starting to dip their toes into the waters of cult cinema, and that it helps readers discover great films they might have missed or ignored. I want each entry to remind folks why they fell in love with movies like *Night of the Living Dead* and *Fight Club* in the first place. I want others to enjoy *Speed Racer* and *Drive* as much as I do, and to recognize *Clue* and *UHF* as two of the funniest comedies ever made. I want readers to understand that John Waters not only changed the face of American cinema with *Pink Flamingos,* but American culture as well. More importantly, I want people to enjoy reading this book and to realize that they are not alone in loving some obscure film. That is ultimately what cult cinema is all about: enjoyment and establishing a sense of community. I hope you find both within the pages of this book.

One final note: I did my best to avoid spoilers, but there were times when it proved difficult to refrain from including them. Therefore, readers who have yet to see the films discussed within and wish to watch them completely unspoiled may want to tread lightly, especially when reading the entries on *American Psycho, A Clockwork Orange, Crank, Donnie Darko, The Iron Giant, Love Streams, Memento, Pink Flamingos, Reefer Madness, The Shawshank Redemption, Shock Corridor,* and *Trick 'r Treat.* Consider this your one and only spoiler warning.

Chronological List of Films

Freaks (1932)
Reefer Madness (1936)
Invasion of the Body Snatchers (1956)
Plan 9 from Outer Space (1959)
The Little Shop of Horrors (1960)
Carnival of Souls (1962)
Shock Corridor (1963)
Faster, Pussycat! Kill! Kill! (1965)
Manos: The Hands of Fate (1966)
Night of the Living Dead (1968)
Putney Swope (1969)
A Clockwork Orange (1971)
Harold and Maude (1971)
Sweet Sweetback's Baadasssss Song (1971)
Pink Flamingos (1972)
Ganja & Hess (1973)
Bring Me the Head of Alfredo Garcia (1974)
Foxy Brown (1974)
Phantom of the Paradise (1974)
The Texas Chain Saw Massacre (1974)
Death Race 2000 (1975)
The Rocky Horror Picture Show (1975)
Grey Gardens (1976)
Eraserhead (1977)
Sorcerer (1977)
Phantasm (1979)
Rock 'n' Roll High School (1979)
The Warriors (1979)
The Blues Brothers (1980)
Ms .45 (1981)
Blade Runner (1982)
The Thing (1982)
Strange Brew (1983)
The Adventures of Buckaroo Banzai across the 8th Dimension (1984)
Love Streams (1984)
Repo Man (1984)

Pootie Tang (2001)
Wet Hot American Summer (2001)
Dog Soldiers (2002)
The Room (2003)
Mean Girls (2004)
Brick (2005)
V for Vendetta (2005)
Crank (2006)
The Assassination of Jesse James by the Coward Robert Ford (2007)
Hot Rod (2007)
Trick 'r Treat (2007)
Walk Hard: The Dewey Cox Story (2007)
Punisher: War Zone (2008)
Speed Racer (2008)
Scott Pilgrim vs. the World (2010)
Drive (2011)
Fateful Findings (2013)

A

THE ADVENTURES OF BUCKAROO BANZAI ACROSS THE 8TH DIMENSION (1984)

Director: W. D. Richter
Screenplay: Earl Mac Rauch
Cast: Peter Weller (Buckaroo Banzai), John Lithgow (Lord John Whorfin/Dr. Emilio Lizardo), Ellen Barkin (Penny Priddy), Jeff Goldblum (New Jersey), Christopher Lloyd (John Bigboote), Lewis Smith (Perfect Tommy), Pepe Serna (Reno Nevada), Clancy Brown (Rawhide), Robert Ito (Professor Hikita), Carl Lumbly (John Parker), Vincent Schiavelli (John O'Connor), Dan Hedaya (John Gomez)
Specs: 103 minutes; color
Genre: adventure, comedy, romance, science fiction
Availability: Blu-ray (Shout! Factory)

Plot

With the help of his trusted allies, a brilliant physicist/neurosurgeon/rock musician battles evil alien invaders from another dimension.

Background

In 1974, writer Earl Mac Rauch moved to Los Angeles at the behest of his friend W. D. Richter.[1] Shortly after arriving, Rauch mentioned that he had an idea for a screenplay inspired by the martial arts films of the 1970s.[2] Richter and his wife encouraged Rauch to write the script and to change the lead character's name from Buckaroo Bandy to Buckaroo Banzai. A few years later, Richter and producer Neil Canton formed a production company, and they decided to make *Buckaroo Banzai* their first film.[3] Rauch wrote a sixty-page treatment that Richter and Canton shopped around Hollywood, but most production executives rejected the project as too weird.[4] However, Sidney Beckerman at Metro-Goldwyn-Mayer/United Artists (MGM/UA) liked the idea, and he helped Richter and Canton set up a development deal with studio chief David Begelmen.[5]

Rauch spent the next year and a half working on the screenplay, but the 1981 Writers Guild of America strike derailed the project.[6] Meanwhile, Begelmen departed MGM/UA after several of his films failed at the box office, leaving *Bucka-*

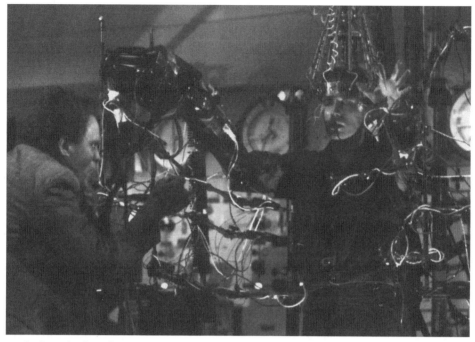

Lord John Whorfin (John Lithgow, left) tortures Buckaroo Banzai (Peter Weller). *20th Century Fox / Photofest © 20th Century Fox*

roo Banzai in limbo.[7] Shortly afterward, Begelmen formed his own production company, Sherwood Productions, and he purchased the *Buckaroo Banzai* script from MGM/UA.[8] He then convinced executives at 20th Century Fox to produce the film under the title *The Adventures of Buckaroo Banzai across the 8th Dimension*, which commenced shooting in September of 1983.[9]

Originally scheduled for June 8,[10] *Buckaroo Banzai* opened on August 15, 1984, and received mixed reviews from confused critics.[11] The film grossed just over $6 million in North America against a $12 million budget,[12] but it became quite popular on home video and soon developed a loyal cult following. *Buckaroo Banzai* is now recognized as a bona fide cult classic that influenced directors such as Kevin Smith, Richard Kelly, Edgar Wright, and Wes Anderson (who includes a direct reference to the film at the end of *The Life Aquatic with Steve Zissou*).[13]

Commentary

Buckaroo Banzai draws inspiration from various influences (including superhero comic books, pulp novels, 1950s sci-fi films, and the *War of the Worlds* radio broadcast) but presents a wildly original story that feels unlike anything made before or since. The dated fashions and somewhat clunky effects mark the film as a product of its time, yet the unconventional storytelling and dynamic filmmaking ensure that *Buckaroo Banzai* still feels fresh and innovative even now. At the same time, the central conflict between the Red and Black Lectroids functions as a pointed commentary on Reagan-era race relations, even as the film inundates the viewer with silly dialogue ("Remember . . . no matter where you go, there you are") and nonsensical imagery (including the title character's charmingly nerdy red glasses, a Lectroid henchman wearing bright red boxing gloves for no apparent reason, and the appearance of a random watermelon). *Buckaroo Banzai* is at once a funny homage to the pop culture of the past that still feels way ahead of its time more than thirty years on, and a smart satire that remains depressingly relevant well into the twenty-first century.

The film also features great performances from the game and talented cast. Peter Weller makes for a convincing (if slightly unusual) leading man thanks to a combination of corny sincerity and lanky handsomeness that evokes the square-jawed, two-fisted scientists of Cold War–era sci-fi flicks like *This Island Earth* and *The War of the Worlds*. Meanwhile, John Lithgow delivers a brilliantly over-the-top performance as Emilio Lizardo (a.k.a. Lord John Whorfin), and he spends the entire film chewing every bit of scenery he can find, spitting out the chunks, and then shoving them back in his mouth so he can chew them up all over again. As female love interest Penny Priddy, Ellen Barkin turns in a solid performance even though the character exists mainly to fall into the bad guys' clutches and spur the hero to action. Christopher Lloyd steals the film as a put-upon Lectroid henchman named John Bigbooté, who becomes increasingly frustrated by the repeated mispronunciation of his name, and Jeff Goldblum shines as Dr. Sidney Zweibel (a.k.a. New Jersey), a gifted neurosurgeon who sings, dances, and dresses like a cowboy.

Buckaroo Banzai offers viewers a weird but enjoyably humorous science fiction adventure that boasts a vivacious mix of spirited performances and energetic filmmaking. The sensational characters, memorable dialogue, and transgressive narrative qualities establish it as perhaps the quintessential cult film.

See also *Repo Man* (1984), *Big Trouble in Little China* (1986), *Earth Girls Are Easy* (1988), *The Life Aquatic with Steve Zissou* (2004).

AMERICAN PSYCHO (2000)

Director: Mary Harron
Screenplay: Mary Harron, Guinevere Turner
Cast: Christian Bale (Patrick Bateman), Justin Theroux (Timothy Bryce), Josh Lucas (Craig McDermott), Bill Sage (David Ban Patten), Chloë Sevigny (Jean), Reese Witherspoon (Evelyn Williams), Samantha Mathis (Courtney Rawlinson), Matt Ross (Luis Carruthers), Jared Leto (Paul Allen), Willem DaFoe (Donald Kimball)
Specs: 102 minutes; color
Genre: drama, horror
Availability: DVD and Blu-ray (Lionsgate Films)

Plot

A handsome, young, upwardly mobile New York investment banker has difficulty separating reality from his violent, hedonistic fantasies.

Background

In 1992, producer Edward R. Pressman optioned the film rights to Bret Easton Ellis's controversial novel *American Psycho*.[14] Pressman and coproducer Chris Hanley then met with several directors, including Stuart Gordon, the man behind such cult films as *Re-Animator* and *From Beyond*.[15] Unfortunately, Gordon envisioned *American Psycho* as a highly faithful adaptation of the book shot in black and white,[16] essentially guaranteeing an X rating and diminished profits. Pressman and Hanley then turned to director David Cronenberg, who asked Ellis to write the script,[17] with Brad Pitt to star,[18] but the project fell apart soon afterward.

American Psycho languished in limbo for a few years until Hanley's wife told him about director Mary Harron's 1996 film *I Shot Andy Warhol*. After watching it, Hanley and Pressman hired Harron to write and direct *American Psycho*.[19] Harron cowrote the screenplay with Guinevere Turner, and then set about finding someone to play lead character Patrick Bateman. She auditioned several actors, but none seemed quite right until she met Christian Bale.[20] Around the same time, Pressman and Hanley set up a distribution deal with independent Canadian distributor Lionsgate, but executives there wanted Leonardo DiCaprio to play Bateman.[21] DiCaprio took the gig, prompting Harron to leave the project out of frustration.[22] Lionsgate replaced her with Oliver Stone.[23] Unfortunately, DiCaprio left to star in *The Beach* for director Danny Boyle (legend has it that feminist activist Gloria Steinem convinced him to pass on *American Psycho*), and Stone abandoned the project.[24] Lionsgate rehired both Harron and Bale on the condition that the budget would stay below $10 million.[25]

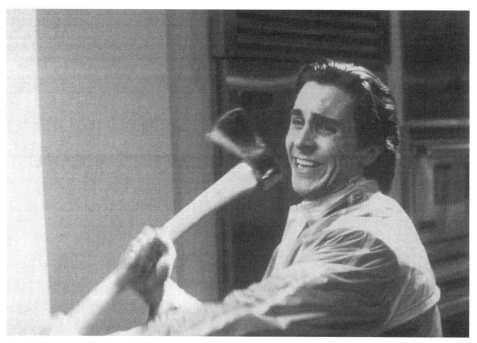

Patrick Bateman (Christian Bale) prepares to assault one of his unsuspecting victims. *Lionsgate Films / Photofest © Lionsgate Films*

Filming commenced in Toronto, Canada, in March 1999, but the production almost immediately faced protests from an organization called Canadians Concerned about Violence in Entertainment.[26] Nevertheless, Harron completed *American Psycho* a few months later, and it premiered to great acclaim at the Sundance Film Festival on January 21, 2000,[27] before entering wide release on April 14, 2000.[28] The film initially received an NC-17 rating, but producers managed to obtain an R rating after they cut eighteen seconds of explicit footage (mostly from a sequence in which Bateman has sex with two prostitutes).[29] *American Psycho* met with mixed critical reception and mediocre box office during its initial theatrical run, but it has since earned a reputation as one of the decade's top horror films.

Commentary

American Psycho is a bloody and cartoonish black comedy that features gorgeous cinematography and a coolly antiseptic mise-en-scène that reflects the lead character's carefully constructed persona. *American Psycho* accurately re-creates the minimalist-yet-extravagant design aesthetic favored by yuppies in the 1980s, and Andrzej Sekula's confident camerawork lovingly captures every single detail of Bateman's sterile apartment and the dirty, rain-slicked streets that exist outside the protagonist's hermetically sealed environment. At the same time, the immaculate surroundings ensure that the blood spilled throughout the film becomes even more shocking, because it stands in stark contrast to the otherwise spotless settings. Meanwhile, Bale delivers an intensely creepy performance, turning Bateman into the embodiment of Reagan-era ideals, complete with his slicked-back hair, pin-striped business suits, and pristine off-white business cards. When judged solely on the filmmaking and the acting, *American Psycho* offers viewers a coldly beautiful horror film that features some incredible compositions and startling juxtapositions.

Unfortunately, the film proves every bit as empty as its main character, and the humor often falls flat while the satire feels toothless and heavy-handed throughout. *American Psycho* covers a lot of the same thematic ground as *American Beauty*, *Fight Club*, *Office Space*, and about a dozen other films that tackle the subject of professional male malaise, but far less successfully than any of them. The film occasionally offers frustrating glimpses of the smart satire that it aspires to be, most notably during the humorous and effective sequence in which Bateman seemingly dispatches his arrogant rival Paul Allen (played with oily confidence by Jared Leto) while extolling the virtues of prototypical 1980s rockers Huey Lewis and the News. This sequence remains one of the few times *American Psycho* truly comes alive and lives up to its promise as a vicious sendup of corporate America. Sadly, the joke wears thin long before the halfway point, and the film fails to sustain its own premise. Much like the main character, *American Psycho* presents a pretty surface that betrays a totally hollow core.

The incredible central performance and striking visuals fail to compensate for the film's thematic emptiness, and the entire enterprise feels like a classic case of style over substance. *American Psycho* never manages to find the right balance between the humor and the horror. It also goes on way too long and quickly overstays its welcome. In the end, *American Psycho* remains worthwhile thanks to the slick filmmaking and Bale's star-making performance, but anyone expecting a substantive cinematic experience may come away disappointed.

See also *A Clockwork Orange* (1971), *Last House on the Left* (1972), *Fight Club* (1999), *The Rules of Attraction* (2002).

THE ASSASSINATION OF JESSE JAMES BY THE COWARD ROBERT FORD (2007)

Director: Andrew Dominik
Screenplay: Andrew Dominik
Cast: Brad Pitt (Jesse James), Casey Affleck (Robert Ford), Sam Shepard (Frank James), Sam Rockwell (Charley Ford), Jeremy Renner (Wood Hite), Garret Dillahunt (Ed Miller), Paul Schneider (Dick Liddil), Mary-Louise Parker (Zee James)
Specs: 160 minutes; color
Genre: biography, crime, drama, history, western
Availability: DVD and Blu-ray (Warner Bros.)

Plot

Brothers Robert and Charley Ford hatch a plan to kill famous outlaw Jesse James, but they soon learn that their actions come with a heavy price.

Background

In March 2004, Warner Bros. and Plan B Entertainment announced plans to adapt Ron Hansen's 1983 novel *The Assassination of Jesse James by the Coward Robert Ford*. The studio hired Andrew Dominik (director of the critically acclaimed *Chopper*) to write and direct the film, which would star Brad Pitt as Jesse James.[30] Dominik chose Casey Affleck for the role of Robert Ford because he felt Affleck knew what it was like to be in a celebrity's shadow due to being Ben Affleck's younger brother.[31] Filming commenced on August 29, 2005, with Calgary, Alberta, Canada, standing in for the town of Creede, Colorado.[32] Principal photography wrapped in December of 2005, and throughout postproduction Dominik clashed with studio executives, who had a fundamentally different vision for the finished film.[33] Dominik set out to make a somber movie that functioned as a bleak meditation on the price of fame. Warner Bros., meanwhile, wanted an exciting, action-packed Western, and they balked at the film's languid pace and extreme length (the original cut was nearly four hours long).[34] Test audiences also disliked this cut of the film, leading to multiple edits.[35]

The resulting two-hour-and-forty-minute cut of *Jesse James* was originally scheduled for release on September 15, 2006.[36] That date came and went, yet the film remained on the shelf. *Jesse James* finally opened in just five theaters throughout the United States on September 21, 2007,[37] and it grossed nearly $150,000 during its opening weekend.[38] The film earned rave reviews and won several awards, but general audiences had difficulty finding it due to the limited release and half-

Robert Ford (Casey Affleck, left) shares an awkward moment with his hero, Jesse James (Brad Pitt). *Warner Bros. / Photofest © Warner Bros.*

hearted advertising campaign. *Jesse James* eventually expanded to 301 screens and played for nineteen weeks before closing on January 31, 2008,[39] with a worldwide gross of just over $4 million.[40] A few weeks later, Warner Home Video somewhat unceremoniously dumped the film on DVD and Blu-ray, but this still allowed a wider audience to at last discover *Jesse James*. The film has since become recognized as one of the best of 2007, as well as one of the finest Westerns ever made.

Commentary

Jesse James is a graceful, elegiac Western that contains haunting imagery and powerful performances and offers up a thoughtful and provocative deconstruction of the frontier myth. Ten years on, it remains one of the most criminally underrated films ever made, and stands as a masterpiece of form and function that serves up a dazzling blend of lyrical filmmaking, captivating performances, and profound thematic significance. The film boasts elegant direction, as well as some of the most gorgeous cinematography ever put to film, courtesy of veteran cinematographer Roger Deakins. *Jesse James* contains a wealth of striking visuals (such as the shot of Jesse standing on the tracks and silhouetted by an oncoming train's headlamp) and quietly beautiful compositions (like the one in which Jesse and Robert sit together on Jesse's front porch lit by a lamp on a table between them). The film also features fantastic production design (particularly in terms of the sets and costumes), and it nails the period details (for instance, characters wear bowlers and stovepipe hats rather than Stetsons). In addition, it features a haunting, melancholy score by Australian singer/songwriter Nick Cave, who also makes an appearance late in the film. All in all, *Jesse James* is an evocative, languorous, and meticulously directed Western that provides viewers with plenty of awesome splendor.

The film also features an incredible cast but hinges almost entirely on the intense lead performances from Pitt and Affleck. Pitt delivers a mesmerizing turn as Jesse James, and he brings the full force of his charisma and star power to bear, making it easy to see why this notorious outlaw inspires such devotion in others. Of course, the film belongs to Affleck, who has become something of a controversial figure in recent years but nevertheless turns in an outstanding and unforgettable performance in *Jesse James*. He infuses Robert Ford with a great deal of nuance and depth, turning the character into a pathetic but captivating young man consumed by obsession and insecurity. Affleck uses his creepy smile and piercing stare to render the character's every glance and hollow attempt at camaraderie completely unnerving. As embodied by Affleck, Ford inspires pity and revulsion in equal measure, but by the end of the film the viewer comes to sympathize with this sniveling kid even as they recoil from him in disgust. The performances also reinforce the film's weighty thematic content, and help turn *Jesse James* into a thoroughly hypnotic meditation on the nature of celebrity and the desire for fame. Additionally, the film deconstructs the Western myth by showing the terrible physical effects of violence and revealing the emotional and psychological toll suffered by the people who commit such deeds. In the end, the stylish filmmaking, magnetic performances, and deep subtext make *Jesse James* one of the most exquisite and thought-provoking Westerns ever made.

See also *I Shot Jesse James* (1949), *No Country for Old Men* (2007), *There Will Be Blood* (2007).

B

BEING JOHN MALKOVICH (1999)

Director: Spike Jonze
Screenplay: Charlie Kaufman
Cast: John Cusack (Craig Schwartz), Cameron Diaz (Lotte Schwartz), Catherine Keener (Maxine Lund), John Malkovich (John Horatio Malkovich), Orson Bean (Dr. Lester), Mary Kay Place (Floris)
Specs: 112 minutes; color
Genre: comedy, drama, fantasy
Availability: DVD and Blu-ray (The Criterion Collection)

Plot

A down-on-his-luck puppeteer takes a job as a file clerk in an anonymous office building, where he discovers a hidden portal that leads directly into the mind of renowned actor John Malkovich.

Background

In 1994, writer Charlie Kaufman wrote a spec script that would eventually become the screenplay for *Being John Malkovich*.[1] Initially conceived as a story about a man who falls in love with someone other than his wife,[2] the script gradually grew into something far weirder and more inventive. Kaufman's script generated a lot of positive buzz around Hollywood, but most studio executives rejected it as too strange.[3] Eventually, Spike Jonze read the script and brought it to Single Cell Pictures (a production company co-owned by Michael Stipe, lead singer of the band R.E.M.), who purchased the screenplay and teamed with Propaganda Films to produce *Being John Malkovich*.[4] Jonze's father-in-law, Francis Ford Coppola, convinced actor John Malkovich to play himself in the film.[5] The rest of the cast fell into place soon afterward.

Principal photography commenced on July 20, 1998, and lasted forty-three days.[6] Jonze shot the film in and around Los Angeles with a crew comprised mainly of people he knew from his days directing music videos and commercials, including cinematographer Lance Acord.[7] The finished film opened in limited release on October 29, 1999,[8] and it instantly became a critical smash, with many

Craig Schwartz (John Cusack, right) clumsily hits on his icy coworker, Maxine Lund (Catherine Keener). *USA Films / Photofest © USA Films*

reviewers hailing it as the best film of the year.[9] Four weeks later, *Being John Malkovich* entered wide release and became a modest hit with general audiences, grossing nearly $23 million against an estimated $13 million budget.[10] *Being John Malkovich* currently enjoys a well-deserved reputation as one of the best and most original films of the 1990s.

Commentary

Nearly twenty years after it first came out, *Being John Malkovich* remains an audacious and thought-provoking work that confronts viewers with an unconventional existentialist tale marked by manic energy and a subversive sense of humor that fluctuates between witty and weird. The film is a darkly comic extravaganza that messes around with gender roles and sexual identity as it contemplates the nature of celebrity and tackles a variety of metaphysical issues (such as the universal desire to become someone else). *Being John Malkovich* boasts exceptionally elegant filmmaking, particularly in terms of the direction and cinematography, but its greatest strength lies with Kaufman's screenplay, which features acerbic dialogue ("Behind the stubble and the too-prominent brow and the male-pattern baldness, I sensed your feminine longing . . . and it just slew me.") and poetically surreal touches (like floor 7 1/2 of the Mertin Flemmer building). Meanwhile, Jonze's daring direction combines with Acord's fanciful cinematography to turn Kaufman's words into an imaginative and sumptuous visual feast. The highly original script and endlessly creative filmmaking ensure that *Being John Malkovich* will stand as a funny and oddly beautiful film for years to come.

The film also shows off the talents of its incredibly gifted cast, starting with John Cusack, who turns lead character Craig into a desperate and pathetic sad sack who yearns for people to recognize his artistic talents. Catherine Keener, meanwhile, puts in a fantastic star-making turn as Maxine, a brash ice queen who becomes the object of Craig's misguided affection, and Cameron Diaz plays wonderfully against type as Craig's long-suffering wife, Lotte. John Malkovich appears to be having a ton of fun as he gleefully sends up his own star persona (the sequence in which he enters his own head remains a masterpiece of demented absurdity), and Charlie Sheen pops up briefly to deliver a performance that plays on his highly publicized reputation as a bad boy. Along with the brilliant screenplay and stylish filmmaking, the immensely talented cast help turn *Being John Malkovich* into a boldly original and highly enjoyable film that rewards multiple viewings and remains completely engrossing as it careens toward a devastatingly bittersweet finale.

See also *Adaptation* (2002), *Eternal Sunshine of the Spotless Mind* (2004), *Synechdoche, New York* (2008), *Where the Wild Things Are* (2009).

SPOTLIGHT: CHARLIE KAUFMAN (1958–)

Charlie Kaufman studied film at New York University, where he met Paul Proch. The two wrote several unproduced scripts together, but went their separate ways after college. In 1991, Kaufman moved to Los Angeles and scored a gig writing for the quirky, short-lived Fox television series *Get a Life*. Over the next few years, Kaufman wrote for several different sitcoms and sketch comedy shows but failed to find steady work. His fortunes changed when he sold the screenplay for *Being John Malkovich*, an ingenious comedy that generated a great deal of positive buzz for both Kaufman and director Spike Jonze. From there, Kaufman wrote and directed several idiosyncratic and highly original films, such as *Human Nature*; *Adaptation*; *Eternal Sunshine of the Spotless Mind*; *Synecdoche, New York*; and *Anomalisa*.

SPOTLIGHT: SPIKE JONZE (1969–)

Director Spike Jonze (formerly Adam Spiegel) moved to Los Angeles at age seventeen and immersed himself in the skateboarding and BMX scene. While there, he codirected a thirty-minute documentary about the renowned Blind Skateboards team, and this led to a gig directing industrial films for MPR, a ship-building firm in Marina Del Rey. From there, Jonze transitioned into directing music videos for artists like Sonic Youth, Daft Punk, Fatboy Slim, Weezer, the Beastie Boys, and Björk. In 1999, Jonze made his feature-length directorial debut with the quirky existential comedy *Being John Malkovich*. The following year, he served as executive producer on the MTV television series *Jackass*, which he co-created with Johnny Knoxville and Jeff Tremaine. In the years since, he has directed a handful of acclaimed feature films, including *Adaptation*, *Where the Wild Things Are*, and *Her*.

BETTER OFF DEAD... (1985)

Director: Savage Steve Holland
Screenplay: Savage Steve Holland
Cast: John Cusack (Lane Meyer), David Ogden Stiers (Al Meyer), Kim Darby (Jenny
   Meyer), Curtis Armstrong (Charles De Mar), Diane Franklin (Monique Junot),
   Demian Slade (Johnny Gasparini), Dan Schneider (Ricky Smith), Laura Waterbury
   (Mrs. Smith), Amanda Wyss (Beth Truss)
Specs: 97 minutes; color
Genre: comedy, romance
Availability: DVD and Blu-ray (Paramount Pictures)

Plot

After his girlfriend leaves him for the captain of the ski team, a suicidal teenager faces a series of increasingly bizarre situations on the way to finding romance with a cute foreign exchange student.

Background

As a teenager, Savage Steve Holland unsuccessfully attempted to kill himself after his high school girlfriend left him for the captain of the ski team.[11] This incident later became the basis for his first feature-length screenplay, *Better Off Dead....* A few years later, Holland's first animated short film, *My 11-Year-Old Birthday Party*, played at the Los Angeles Film Festival, where he met actor/producer Henry Winkler.[12] Holland told Winkler about his idea for *Better Off Dead...*, and Winkler helped the young hopeful set up a production deal with A&M Films and CBS Theatrical Films. Winkler also suggested John Cusack for the lead role, but studio executives wanted someone else because they did not consider Cusack leading man material.[13] Holland fought for Cusack, however, and the studio eventually relented.

Better Off Dead... entered production in November 1984, and filming wrapped the following month. While the production ran smoothly, the film's release caused some drama. Cusack apparently hated *Better Off Dead...* because he thought it made him look foolish.[14] (Years later, however, Cusack clarified that he had nothing against Holland; he just wished the film had turned out better.[15]) In addition, people protested the film's original tagline of "Sometimes . . . you're Better Off Dead," prompting the studio to change it to "Relax . . . you're never Better Off Dead."[16] Despite all this, *Better Off Dead...* opened in wide release on October 11, 1985, and while critics lambasted it, the film became a minor hit, grossing over $10 million in the United States against an estimated $3.5 million dollar budget.[17] Yet the studio considered it a flop because it made much less than *Fast Times at Ridgemont High*.[18] It has since achieved cult status thanks to its hilarious catchphrases, crazy characters, and painfully relatable situations, many of which remain relevant and recognizable today.

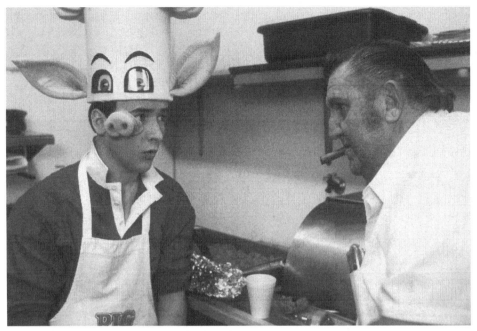

Heartbroken teenager Lane Meyer (John Cusack, left) meets his new boss Rocko (Chuck Mitchell). *Warner Bros. / Photofest © Warner Bros.*

Commentary

Better Off Dead... opens with a humorous animated credits sequence that gives the viewer a pretty good idea of what to expect from the film itself, which often feels like a live-action cartoon (this makes sense given Holland's background as an animator). *Better Off Dead...* boasts plenty of absurdist comedy and nonsensical situations, and it includes numerous silly digressions (such as the "Everybody Wants Some" sequence, in which lead character Lane Meyer daydreams about Claymation hamburgers singing Van Halen tunes) and dozens of iconic lines (most notably, "I want my two dollars!"). At the same time, the film offers a rather accurate (though highly farcical) depiction of high school, that awkward time in everyone's life when everything feels incredibly important and even the smallest setback signals the end of the world. *Better Off Dead...* frequently plays Lane's heartbreak for laughs, but his anguish becomes agonizingly familiar to anyone who has ever faced a similar situation. The film is frantic and funny, but it also contains some genuinely sweet moments that tap into fairly universal experiences.

Of course, *Better Off Dead...* suffers from a few problems. The character of Monique (Diane Franklin) feels a bit undercooked (the viewer learns little about her other than her nationality and her love of baseball and cars), and she mainly serves to provide the main character with a new lease on life (she conforms to pop culture critic Nathan Rabin's conceptualization of a Manic Pixie Dream Girl). She is a blatant wish fulfillment figure who becomes little more than a damsel in distress by the end of the film. *Better Off Dead...* also contains some ever-so-slightly racist humor ("Which is better—speaking no English at all, or speaking Howard Cosell?") and homophobic jokes ("Buy yourself another leotard and I'll be back in a minute, OK?") that mark it as a relic of its era. In addition, the film portrays Lane's nerdy neighbor Ricky Smith (played by actor-turned-writer/ producer Dan Schneider) as an outright sex criminal whose overbearing behavior now comes off as creepy and gross rather than funny. Nevertheless, *Better Off Dead...* stands as an endlessly inventive spoof of teen angst and high school films that contains bizarre characters, uproarious dialogue, larger-than-life situations, and an excess of heart.

See also *Sixteen Candles* (1984), *Real Genius* (1985), *Teen Wolf* (1985), *Weird Science* (1985), *One Crazy Summer* (1986), *How I Got into College* (1989).

SPOTLIGHT: SAVAGE STEVE HOLLAND (1960–)

After studying animation at the California Institute of the Arts, Savage Steve Holland applied his offbeat sensibilities to writing and directing feature films starting with *Better Off Dead...*, a darkly comic tale of young love based on his own teenage years. Despite receiving mostly poor reviews, the film became a minor commercial hit and inspired a devoted cult following. Holland followed it with *One Crazy Summer*, a goofy romantic comedy that similarly flopped with critics but found an audience on home video. Holland then made the forgettable *How I Got into College* before turning his attention to various TV projects. In addition to co-creating and executive producing the cartoon series *Eek! The Cat* for Fox Television, he directed episodes of several television shows like *Encyclopedia Brown*; *Honey, I Shrunk the Kids*; and *Shasta McNasty*, as well as the TV movies *Santa Hunters*, *Bound & Babysitting*, and *Rufus-2*.

THE BIG LEBOWSKI (1998)

Director: Joel Coen, Ethan Coen (uncredited)
Screenplay: Ethan Coen, Joel Coen
Cast: Jeff Bridges (Jeffrey "The Dude" Lebowski), John Goodman (Walter Sobchak), Julianne Moore (Maude Lebowski), Steve Buscemi (Theodore Donald "Donny" Kerabatsos), David Huddleston (The Big Lebowski), Philip Seymour Hoffman (Brandt), Tara Reid (Bunny Lebowski), Peter Stormare (Uli Kunkel), Flea (Kieffer), John Turturro (Jesus Quintana), Sam Elliot (the Stranger)
Specs: 117 minutes; color
Genre: Comedy, Crime
Availability: DVD and Blu-ray (Universal Studios)

Plot

After a case of mistaken identity leads to the soiling of his favorite rug, an easy-going stoner becomes drawn into a confusing world of intrigue and deception.

Background

In the late 1980s, Joel and Ethan Coen attended a dinner party hosted by Peter Exline, a script consultant they met while raising funds for their debut feature *Blood Simple*.[19] During the party, Exline joked that his ratty fake Persian rug really tied the room together and told his guests about the time he tracked down a fourteen-year-old car thief after discovering the kid's homework stuffed into the back seat of his own recently recovered vehicle.[20] This incident served as the inspiration for *The Big Lebowski*, the Coens' comedic homage to Raymond Chandler's hardboiled detective stories.[21]

They based the lead character on their eccentric and jovial friend Jeff Dowd, a former member of the Seattle Seven whom they met during their first trip to Los Angeles.[22] The Coens believed it would be funny to place an individual like Dowd—that is, the man least capable of understanding and untangling a complex situation—at the center of a labyrinthine mystery.[23] They populated their story with other quirky characters inspired by acquaintances and people they admired; for instance, they based the character of Walter Sobchak partly on conservative director John Milius,[24] while Maude Lebowski resembled 1960s avant-garde performance artist Carolee Schneemann.[25]

The Coens wrote *Lebowski* and *Fargo* while shooting *Barton Fink*,[26] but they made *Fargo* first because they wanted to wait until their preferred actors became available before starting *Lebowski*.[27] In the meantime, they asked Jeff Bridges to play main character Jeffrey "The Dude" Lebowski (a.k.a. His Dudeness, Duder, or El Duderino, if you are not into the whole brevity thing). He initially refused[28] but changed his mind once he realized that he shared many similarities with

The Dude (Jeff Bridges, left), Walter (John Goodman, center), and Donny (Steve Buscemi) at the bowling alley. *Gramercy Pictures / Photofest © Gramercy Pictures*

The Dude.[29] With their cast secured, the Coens took the project to Polygram and Working Title Films, and the two studios gave them a $15 million budget.[30] Following several weeks of rehearsal, production commenced on January 27, 1997, and wrapped on April 24, 1997 (one day ahead of schedule).[31]

Lebowski opened on March 6 in the United States and grossed just over $17 million in six weeks.[32] Most critics dismissed the film as lackluster, particularly when compared to the critical and commercial hit *Fargo*.[33] Yet, *Lebowski* thrived in the years after its initial release, becoming a huge hit on the midnight movie circuit and developing a fervent cult audience like the one that grew up around *The Rocky Horror Picture Show*. In 2002, fans in Louisville, Kentucky, organized the First Annual Big Lebowski What-Have-You Fest, a yearly event that continues to this day.[34] *Lebowski* even inspired a religion (the Church of the Latter-Day Dude, or Dudeism),[35] making it perhaps the ultimate cult film.

Commentary

Lebowski offers viewers a sidesplitting subversion of film noir, serving up a shambling, convoluted mystery that unfolds via stylish, laid-back direction and takes its time to reach any sort of resolution. The intricate narrative follows the same sort of complex structure found in classic films noir such as *The Maltese Falcon* or *Double Indemnity*. At the same time, *Lebowski* tweaks the formula and pokes some good-natured fun at overly complicated detective movies like *The Big Sleep* and *The Long Goodbye*. Along the way, the film generates lots of laughs via smart but juvenile humor and occasional bursts of surreal nonsense. *Lebowski* boasts an endlessly quotable and incredibly filthy script that contains dozens of iconic lines like "That rug really tied the room together," "I mean, say what you want about the tenets of National Socialism, Dude, at least it's an ethos," and the immortal and oft-repeated "Shut the fuck up, Donnie!" It also features loads of lively absurdist comedy, most notably during The Dude's amusing dream sequences, one of which includes an appearance by former Iraqi dictator Saddam Hussein (or a reasonable facsimile thereof). Throw in an eclectic soundtrack and an abundance of shaggy charm, and *Lebowski* emerges as one of the grooviest cult films of all time, and if you disagree, well that is just, like, your opinion, man.

The film also benefits from an incredible cast led by Bridges, who delivers an instantly iconic performance as The Dude. With his doughy figure, lackadaisical attitude, and thrift store style, the character becomes the personification of laziness as he ambles through the film with an adult beverage always in hand. Meanwhile, Coen regulars Goodman, Buscemi, and Turturro all deliver memorable performances (particularly Goodman as boisterous Vietnam veteran Walter Sobchack and Turturro as convicted pederast Jesus Quintana). Julianne Moore holds her own as the humorously deadpan Maude Lebowski, and Sam Elliot joins in on the fun as the Stranger, a wizened old cowboy who narrates the film and even pops up in a couple of scenes to impart wisdom to The Dude (and admire his style). In addition, *Lebowski* features excellent supporting turns from Tara Reid, Peter Stormare, David Huddleston, and the late, great Phillip Seymour Hoffmann (who steals the show as toadying sycophant Brandt). The great cast, unforgettable dialogue, and sophisticated direction all come together to ensure that The Dude abides even after more than two decades.

See also *The Long Goodbye* (1973), *Kiss Kiss Bang Bang* (2005), *Inherent Vice* (2014), *The Nice Guys* (2016).

BLADE RUNNER (1982)

Director: Ridley Scott
Screenplay: Hampton Fancher, David Webb Peoples
Cast: Harrison Ford (Rick Deckard), Rutger Hauer (Roy Batty), Sean Young (Rachael), Daryl Hannah (Pris), Edward James Olmos (Gaff), M. Emmet Walsh (Bryant), William Sanderson (J. F. Sebastian), Brion James (Leon Kowalski), Joe Turkel (Dr. Eldon Tyrell), Joanna Cassidy (Zhora), James Hong (Hannibal Chew)
Specs: 117 minutes; color
Genre: science fiction, thriller
Availability: Blu-ray (Warner Bros.)

Plot

Bounty hunter Rick Deckard comes out of retirement to hunt down four synthetic humans who escaped from an off-world colony and returned to Earth in search of their creator. However, Deckard begins to question his own humanity when he falls in love with one of his targets.

Background

In the early 1970s, producer Herb Jaffe optioned the film rights to Philip K. Dick's 1968 short novel *Do Androids Dream of Electric Sheep?*[36] Jaffe's son, Robert, penned a screenplay, but Dick hated it and the project fell apart soon after.[37] In 1975, writer Hampton Fancher wrote his own screenplay based on Dick's novel, and three years later his friend Brian Kelly took it to producer Michael Deeley, who rejected it as too simplistic.[38] Fancher then wrote a new draft that emphasized the same sort of ecological and environmental concerns found in the novel.[39] Deeley liked this version and decided to produce it under the title *Dangerous Days*, though he eventually changed it to *Blade Runner*, the title of a William S. Burroughs novel he had read years earlier.[40]

In February of 1980, Filmways Pictures put up a $13 million budget and hired Ridley Scott to direct *Blade Runner*.[41] Unfortunately, the company was in dire financial trouble and on the verge of collapse, so Deeley brought the film to his friend Alan Ladd Jr., who had a distribution deal with Warner Bros. Ladd liked the script, and he convinced Warner Bros. to invest an additional $7 million in the project.[42] The studio teamed with Tandem Productions, which put up another $7 million.[43] Meanwhile, Fancher argued with Scott and the producers over the film's tone (they wanted an edgier, more explicit film),[44] and he left the project on

Rachael (Sean Young, right) tells grizzled blade runner Rick Deckard (Harrison Ford) about her childhood. *Warner Bros. / Photofest © Warner Bros.*

December 21, 1980, after learning they had brought David Webb Peoples on board to do rewrites (Fancher later returned to contribute additional rewrites).[45]

Casting the film became an adventure unto itself. While Fancher originally wrote the lead role with Robert Mitchum in mind, Deeley and Scott wanted Dustin Hoffman.[46] However, the actor had a radically different vision for the film. The producers decided to go with Harrison Ford, who clashed with Scott throughout the production.[47] Meanwhile, Scott's perfectionism frustrated both cast and crew, because he demanded significant changes to the completed sets and insisted on shooting several takes of each scene.[48] The tumultuous production wrapped after four months,[49] and the finished film opened on June 25, 1982.[50] It received mixed reviews[51] and failed to earn back its $27 million budget during its initial theatrical run.[52] Nevertheless, *Blade Runner* eventually emerged as a cult classic, and it is now considered one of the finest science fiction films ever made. In 2017, Warner Bros. released a belated sequel called *Blade Runner 2049*, directed by Denis Villeneuve and starring Ryan Gosling.

Commentary

As mentioned, *Blade Runner* has developed a reputation as one of the all-time great science fiction films, and it lives up to that distinction thanks to its stunning futuristic visuals and profound thematic content. The film uses fantastic cyberpunk elements to probe the very nature of humanity and raise questions about the role technology plays in people's lives. *Blade Runner* pushes viewers to think about issues like corporatization, environmental degradation, and mankind's relationship to advanced technologies. Granted, the ontological questions often take a back seat to the production design, and the revelation hinted at during the film's conclusion makes little sense given everything that came before. Nonetheless, *Blade Runner* succeeds in creating a bleak but believable future world that raises a variety of metaphysical issues.

In addition, *Blade Runner* emerged as one of the most influential science fiction films ever made due to its detailed production design and splendid visual effects, both of which hold up today. The film's signature visual style impacted science fiction films for years afterward, and its legacy lives on in movies like *The Fifth Element*, *Dark City*, and *Ghost in the Shell* (both versions). The spectacular images never feel flashy or extraneous, and everything onscreen serves to build the world of the film. At the same time, the visuals establish a grim mood, which has since become a hallmark of the genre. The effects and the production design create a dreary dystopian world collapsing under the weight of unchecked capitalism and corporate greed. This dark vision of the future has only become more relevant in the twenty-first century as society scrambles to keep up with new technologies and multinational corporations push back against environmental regulations and government oversight.

Like all great science fiction stories, *Blade Runner* depicts a plausible, technologically advanced future world and uses it to pose deep philosophical questions about the human condition. Entire books have been written about this seminal film, which features meticulous production design, striking visual effects, and a profound (if somewhat muddled) message about human nature. In the end, *Blade Runner* remains a cult classic because it offers viewers an uncompromising vision of the future that is guaranteed to linger in their hearts and minds long after the end credits roll.

See also *Total Recall* (1990), *Ghost in the Shell* (1995), *Strange Days* (1995), *The Fifth Element* (1997), *Dark City* (1998), *The Matrix* (1999), *Minority Report* (2002), *Ghost in the Shell* (2017).

THE BLUES BROTHERS (1980)

Director: John Landis
Screenplay: Dan Aykroyd, John Landis
Cast: John Belushi ("Joliet" Jake Blues), Dan Aykroyd (Elwood Blues), James Brown (Reverend Cleophus James), Cab Calloway (Curtis), Ray Charles (Ray), Aretha Franklin (Mrs. Murphy), Carrie Fisher (Mystery Woman)
Specs: 133 minutes; color
Genre: action, comedy, crime, musical
Availability: Blu-ray (Universal Studios)

Plot

Two blues musicians with shady pasts set out to reunite their old band and raise the $5,000 needed to save the Catholic orphanage where they grew up.

Background

In 1973 John Belushi traveled to the Second City in Toronto, Canada, to recruit talent for the National Lampoon Radio Hour.[53] While there, he visited the 505 Club and approached fellow comedian Dan Aykroyd, who was making good money and therefore refused Belushi's request.[54] Nevertheless, the two comics spent the night bonding over old blues records, and they hatched an idea for a band called The Blues Brothers.[55] In 1975, the comics joined *Saturday Night Live* (*SNL*) and began working on the characters and their performances.[56] Later, while filming *Animal House*, Belushi met Curtis Salgado, a harmonica player for the Robert Cray Band, and this meeting inspired his musical and character performances.[57]

Backed by members of the Saturday Night Live Band, the Blues Brothers initially opened for established blues acts and comedians such as Steve Martin.[58] From there, Aykroyd; Belushi; Belushi's wife, Judy; and friend Mitch Glazer came up with fictional histories for the Blues brothers,[59] and Aykroyd developed several stories featuring the characters.[60] He took his ideas to producer Sean Daniel, a producer on *Animal House*,[61] who helped Aykroyd set up a movie deal with Universal Pictures. The studio put up a $17.5 million budget and hired John Landis to direct.[62] Aykroyd immediately set to writing the script but found the process difficult due to his inexperience. His first draft came in at 324 pages, though Landis trimmed it down to a more manageable 120 pages.[63] Production commenced shortly after.

Jake (John Belushi, left) and Elwood (Dan Aykroyd) make a daring getaway. *Universal Pictures / Photofest © Universal Pictures*

Filming took place in Chicago between July and October 1979.[64] While things ran smoothly for the most part,[65] *The Blues Brothers* still ended up going $10 million over budget[66] due to Belushi's struggles with sobriety[67] and the climactic car chase sequence, which resulted in the destruction of 103 cars (a world record at the time).[68] Further problems arose during the editing phase; the first cut of the film came in at just under three hours, and producer Lew Wasserman ordered twenty minutes shaved off the run time.[69] *The Blues Brothers* finally opened on June 20, 1980, nearly a year after both Aykroyd and Belushi had left *SNL* (and just a few months after Belushi appeared in Steven Spielberg's notorious flop *1941*).[70] It received generally positive reviews and went on to become the tenth highest grossing film of the year.[71] Over time, the film developed a rabid cult following, and in 1998 it spawned a belated (and vastly inferior) sequel called *Blues Brothers 2000*.

Commentary

The Blues Brothers offers up an effective mix of sarcastic wit and cartoonish humor, and serves as the perfect showcase for its two leads. As the title characters, Aykroyd and Belushi deliver deadpan performances (Belushi in particular goes from pokerfaced to manic at the drop of a black fedora hat), and they turn Jake and Elwood into gleeful agents of chaos who cause all sorts of commotion and conflict. These two vulgar conmen delight in messing with people, and their antics often recall those perpetrated by Bugs Bunny (one could easily imagine a version of the Chez Paul sequence that featured Bugs and Daffy Duck tormenting an increasingly exasperated Elmer Fudd). Indeed, the film frequently resembles the silly mayhem of the Looney Tunes, particularly during a climactic chase sequence in which cars defy the laws of physics. Overall, the sardonic humor, frenzied physical comedy, and brilliant performances ensure that *The Blue Brothers* remains one of the funniest comedies ever made.

The film also boasts a fantastic soundtrack and features an array of cameos and supporting turns from music legends like Cab Calloway, James Brown, Ray Charles, Aretha Franklin, and more. *The Blues Brothers* also includes some lively musical numbers (Franklin's "You Better Think" remains a standout). On top of that, the film showcases incredible stunt work and contains not one but two of the most chaotic car chases ever committed to film. Meanwhile, the legendary supporting cast includes the likes of Carrie Fisher, John Candy, Henry Gibson, and Charles Napier, all of whom deliver riotously comic performances. These elements make *The Blues Brothers* an exciting, joyous, and altogether hilarious musical that pays loving homage to the history of both music and comedy.

On the downside, *The Blues Brothers* drags in spots (the Bob's Country Bunker sequence overstays its welcome by quite a bit), and even the theatrical cut could stand to lose about thirty or forty minutes from the total run time. Moreover, the whole thing feels like a collection of skits rather than a cohesive narrative, which makes sense given its origins but still renders the humor a bit scattershot. It also becomes easy to accuse *The Blues Brothers* of cultural appropriation, as the film situates two white guys at the center of a musical genre traditionally associated with African American culture (though the cameos help to somewhat counter that criticism). Nevertheless, *The Blues Brothers* is an enjoyably raucous comedy that doubles as a glorious celebration of rhythm-and-blues music, even as it skirts some potentially thorny issues.

See also *Strange Brew* (1983), *Wayne's World* (1992).

BRICK (2005)

Director: Rian Johnson
Screenplay: Rian Johnson
Cast: Joseph Gordon-Levitt (Brendan), Lukas Haas (the Pin), Nora Zehetner (Laura), Noah Fleiss (Tugger), Matt O'Leary (the Brain), Emilie de Ravin (Emily), Noah Segan (Dode), Richard Roundtree (Assistant V.P. Trueman), Meagan Good (Kara), Brian White (Brad Bramish), Jonathan Cauff (Biff)
Specs: 100 minutes; color
Genre: action, crime, drama, mystery, thriller
Availability: DVD and Blu-ray (Universal Studios Home Entertainment)

Plot

When his ex-girlfriend turns up dead, a teenage outsider sets out to find her killer but becomes entwined in a complex web of drugs and deceit.

Background

Brick grew out of Rian Johnson's obsession with Dashiell Hammett's detective novels,[72] which he discovered after listening to the Coen brothers talk about the author's influence on their film *Miller's Crossing*.[73] Inspired by Hammett's writings, Johnson set out to make *Brick*, a hardboiled crime thriller that takes place inside a high school. In 1997, one year after graduating from USC's School of Cinematic Arts, the twenty-three-year-old Johnson wrote the first draft of the screenplay.[74] He then spent seven years pitching it to various studios, but none wanted to take a chance on such an unconventional film from a first-time director.[75] Finally, in 2003, Johnson decided to make the film independently, and managed to secure a nearly $450,000 budget via donations from family and friends.[76]

Johnson cast former *Third Rock from the Sun* star Joseph Gordon-Levitt as lead character Brendan based on his performance in the film *Manic*.[77] Johnson then assembled the rest of the cast, and after a three-month rehearsal period, *Brick* finally entered production. Principal photography lasted twenty days,[78] and filming took place largely in Johnson's hometown of San Clemente, California.[79] Johnson shot *Brick* on weekends with the help of students from his alma mater, San Clemente High School, with Steve Yedlin, one of Johnson's USC classmates, handling the cinematography.[80] Johnson edited the film himself[81] with the assistance of Philip Harrelson and Tod Lautenberg, both of whom remained uncredited. The young director then submitted *Brick* to the Sundance Film Festival.[82]

Brendan (Joseph Gordon-Levitt) meets with The Pin (Lukas Haas, not pictured) and his goons. *Focus Features / Photofest © Focus Features*

Brick opened in limited release in the United States on April 7, 2006.[83] It played in theaters for a total of fifteen weeks, and while critics praised the film, the limited release prevented many viewers from seeing it during its initial theatrical run. Nevertheless, *Brick* grossed nearly $4 million worldwide[84] and earned a cult following shortly after it debuted on home video on August 8, 2006. The film has since emerged as a cult classic, and many fans now regard it as one of the best films noir of all time.

Commentary

Best described as John Hughes by way of Raymond Chandler, *Brick* is a playful mash-up of film noir tropes and high school movie clichés that shows off some tight direction and an outstanding lead performance from Gordon-Levitt. Johnson imbues the film with a great deal of style and includes several amusing nods to the films that inspired him (for instance, *Brick* shares some DNA with *Three O'Clock High*, and it explicitly references movies like *The Maltese Falcon*, *Rififi*, and *Chinatown*). *Brick* also contains allusions to anime (Johnson cites *Cowboy Bebop* as a primary influence) and spaghetti westerns (the narrative follows the basic structure of Sergio Leone's *A Fistful of Dollars*, which was itself inspired by Akira Kurosawa's *Yojimbo*, as well as the Dashiell Hammet novels *Red Harvest* and *The Glass Key*). Yet Johnson's confident direction guarantees that *Brick* looks and feels like nothing else. Of course, he receives a lot of help from Yedlin, whose striking cinematography gives the film a distinctive appearance and presents viewers with a wealth of breathtaking images (such as the remarkable shot of a flock of birds flying over the football field). *Brick* also features a whimsical score that evokes the hardboiled films of the past and some charmingly contrived dialogue comprised of an invented slang a la *A Clockwork Orange*, all of which ensures that the film remains absorbing throughout.

Brick adopts a winking tone but the actors play everything straight, which feels appropriate given the setting and the deadly serious subject matter. Gordon-Levitt anchors *Brick* as Brendan, a classic noir antihero who comes across as cynical, obsessive, brooding, menacing, sardonic, and insecure all at once. Gordon-Levitt makes for a believable tough guy as he swaggers through the film and snarls out the unnatural dialogue with ease. He also conveys the character's vulnerability and weariness, and turns Brendan into a complex individual who remains likable even while roughing up his female classmates. His cast mates all deliver fine performances, particularly Lukas Haas as notorious twenty-six-year-old drug lord the Pin (who still lives with his mother), and the acting contributes mightily to *Brick's* success. Every member of the young cast strikes the exact right tone, and the heightened performances feel entirely appropriate, since teenagers often take themselves a bit too seriously.

Brick favors mood over story, and some viewers might find the overly complicated dialogue confusing and alienating. Furthermore, the film goes on a bit too long and could stand to lose about fifteen or twenty minutes from the total run time. In addition, the novelty wears off well before the halfway point, and there are times when the whole thing feels a bit too clever for its own good. Nevertheless, *Brick* stands as a fun and engaging (if unconventional) film noir thanks to a thrilling combination of dynamic filmmaking and enthusiastic performances.

See also *Three O'Clock High* (1987), *The Big Lebowski* (1998), *Memento* (2000), *Cowboy Bebop: The Movie* (2001), *Winter's Bone* (2010), *Looper* (2012).

BRING ME THE HEAD OF ALFREDO GARCIA (1974)

Director: Sam Peckinpah
Screenplay: Gordon T. Dawson, Sam Peckinpah, Frank Kowalski (story)
Cast: Warren Oates (Bennie), Isela Vega (Elita), Robert Webber (Sappensly), Gig Young (Quill), Helmut Dantine (Max), Emilio Fernández (El Jefe), Kris Kristofferson (Biker)
Specs: 112 minutes; color
Genre: action, crime, drama, thriller, western
Availability: Blu-ray (Twilight Time)

Plot

An American expatriate living in Mexico sets out with his lover to collect the bounty offered for the head of a dead gigolo.

Background

During production of *The Ballad of Cable Hogue*, screenwriter Frank Kowalski approached director Sam Peckinpah with an idea for a movie in which a Mexican crime boss orders a hit on a dead man.[85] Peckinpah liked the idea and started working on the script while shooting *Straw Dogs*, though he eventually asked Gordon T. Dawson to cowrite the screenplay under the title *Bring Me the Head of Alfredo Garcia*.[86] Peckinpah took the first twenty-five pages to producer Martin Baum, who convinced United Artists to fund the film.[87] Peckinpah initially offered the lead role of Bennie to James Coburn and Peter Falk before turning to his friend and longtime collaborator Warren Oates.[88] Peckinpah then cast Mexican actress Isela Vega as Bennie's girlfriend, Elita, even though she had only appeared in one other English language film prior to starring in *Alfredo Garcia*.[89] Production commenced near the end of September 1973 with an almost entirely Mexican crew that included renowned cinematographer Álex Phillips Jr.[90]

Peckinpah shot the film in and around Mexico City. Production proved physically and mentally demanding for both cast and crew because of Peckinpah's alcohol and drug abuse, which increased due to his notoriously difficult relationship with Mexican actress Begoña Palacios.[91] The shoot proved so miserable that Dawson refused to work with Peckinpah ever again.[92] At one point, the famously

Bennie (Warren Oates) sets out to collect the bounty on Alfredo Garcia. *United Artists / Photofest*
© *United Artists*

combative director stirred up trouble when he publicly announced that Mexico af-forded him greater freedom than Hollywood.[93] This declaration angered members of the Motion Picture and Television Unions, who threatened to boycott *Alfredo Garcia*.[94] Peckinpah tried to smooth things over by claiming that the magazine had misquoted him, and this seemed to work because the unions ultimately aban-doned the boycott.[95]

Principal photography wrapped just before Christmas,[96] and the finished film opened in limited release in August of 1974. *Alfredo Garcia* became a critical and commercial disaster,[97] though it received some accolades from critics like Roger Ebert.[98] Meanwhile, Vega earned a Best Actress nomination at Mexico's Ariel Awards in 1975.[99] Yet none of this praise stopped Harry Medved and Randy Lowell from including *Alfredo Garcia* in their 1978 book, *The Fifty Worst Films of All Time (and How They Got That Way)*. Moreover, the film proved highly contro-versial, and countries like Sweden, Germany, and Argentina banned it outright.[100] Over time, *Alfredo Garcia* developed a reputation as one of Peckinpah's best films, and this critical reassessment helped it garner a devoted cult following.

Commentary

Right from the start, *Alfredo Garcia* strikes a grim and altogether brutal tone, as it opens with vicious mobsters breaking the arm of their boss's pregnant teenage daughter when she refuses to reveal the identity of the man who impregnated her. Things get even gloomier from there, and *Alfredo Garcia* spends its nearly two-hour run time confronting viewers with an unrelenting sense of hopelessness and some aggressively muscular filmmaking. The film advances a bleak view of humanity, and as the grimy, masculine narrative unfolds, it soon becomes clear that Peckinpah seeks to expose the ugliness that lies deep within every man.

Alfredo Garcia moves at a glacial pace but remains compelling throughout, largely due to Oates's laconic but lusty performance as Bennie, a despicable char-acter who nevertheless lives by a strict code of honor. Opposite him, Vega uses her prodigious talents and defiant attitude to turn Elita into perhaps the strongest and most complex female character in Peckinpah's entire oeuvre (even though she serves little purpose other than to die at the halfway point and give the hero a reason to confront the bad guys during the film's bloody finale). *Alfredo Garcia* also features some stunning cinematography that alternates between the sweaty, cramped spaces of rundown cities and the breathtaking, wide-open vistas of the Mexican countryside. As such, the film recalls classical western narratives, which often explore the tension between civilization and the expansive frontier. Peckinpah uses both locations to reinforce the lead characters' insignificance, and show that they have become trapped by their own desires and ambitions. No one wins in *Alfredo Garcia*, because ultimately death waits for everyone. The powerful performances, dreary outlook, and spare but spectacular filmmaking turn *Alfredo Garcia* into a highly existential action flick that takes viewers on a grueling but exciting journey through the dark side of human nature.

The tagline featured in the film's trailer perfectly sums up its unrelentingly dour worldview: "This man will become an animal. This woman's dreams of love will be destroyed. Innocent people will suffer. Holy ground will be desecrated. 25

people will die." *Alfredo Garcia* lives up to that somewhat overwrought description; the film assaults the audience with despair, and some viewers will understandably find the whole thing off-putting (not to mention more than a bit sexist). Nevertheless, *Alfredo Garcia* remains a captivating and electrifying excursion into unpleasantness, and it deserves recognition as one of Peckinpah's finest films as well as one of the greatest cult movies ever made.

See also *Straw Dogs* (1971), *Two-Lane Blacktop* (1971), *Cockfighter* (1974), *Drive* (2010).

BUFFY THE VAMPIRE SLAYER (1992)

Director: Fran Rubel Kuzui
Screenplay: Joss Whedon
Cast: Kristy Swanson (Buffy), Donald Sutherland (Merrick), Paul Reubens (Amilyn), Rutger Hauer (Lothos), Luke Perry (Pike), Michele Abrams (Jennifer), Hilary Swank (Kimberly)
Specs: 86 minutes; color
Genre: action, comedy, fantasy, horror
Availability: DVD and Blu-ray (20th Century Fox)

Plot

A flighty high school cheerleader teams with a wizened mentor and a dreamy rebel to protect Los Angeles from an evil vampire king and his horde of vicious bloodsuckers.

Background

After a brief stint writing for the hit sitcom *Roseanne*, twenty-five-year-old Joss Whedon sold the screenplay for *Buffy the Vampire Slayer* to Sandollar Productions in late 1991.[101] The company shopped the script around Hollywood, but all the major studios passed.[102] Producer Howard Rosenman eventually offered to coproduce the film, and he raised $6 million from foreign investors and set up a distribution deal with Kuzui Enterprises.[103] Co-owner Fran Rubel Kuzui—who previously helmed the critical hit *Tokyo Pop*—loved the script and asked to direct. Rosenman agreed, and Kuzui and her husband, Kaz, cast *Beverly Hills 90210* heartthrob Luke Perry as male lead Oliver Pike.[104] At that point, 20th Century Fox purchased the distribution rights and ordered the film ready for release by the following summer, leaving Kuzui and her team just five weeks to prepare and six weeks to shoot.[105] Filming took place throughout the Los Angeles area, with the cast and crew working mainly at night. Unlike most first-time screenwriters, Whedon remained involved throughout the shoot,[106] though Kuzui made the film much lighter in tone.[107] Unfortunately, Whedon frequently quarreled with actor Donald Sutherland,[108] whose constant demands that the script be rewritten eventually drove the young writer off the set.[109] Meanwhile, lead actress Kristy Swanson developed a

Buffy Summers (Kristy Swanson, left) and Pike (Luke Perry, center) come face to face with the wicked vampire Lothos (Rutger Hauer). *20th Century Fox / Photofest © 20th Century Fox*

contentious relationship with veteran actor Rutger Hauer, who also clashed with Kuzui (though she managed to keep him in line).[110]

Buffy opened on July 31, 1992, and grossed just over $16 million against a $9 million production budget.[111] Whedon complained that the finished film strayed from his original vision, even though it features many of his trademarks, including a deep mythology, a strong feminist subtext, and witty dialogue, all of which might explain why *Buffy* developed a cult following in the years after its release. It also inspired a much-loved television show that spawned comic books, video games, and a popular spinoff series, as well as a wealth of scholarship.

Commentary

Though it has since become eclipsed by the TV series it spawned, the sole cinematic outing of Buffy Summers remains an affably dopey comedy that mostly succeeds despite some flat direction and lifeless performances. The film draws inspiration from a wide variety of pop culture, including superhero comic books, Hammer horror films, and *Scooby-Doo, Where Are You!* Yet it carves out its own unique identity thanks to Whedon's screenplay, which only hints at the intricate lore later explored in depth on the *Buffy* TV show but nevertheless injects the film with his trademark wit and vitality. *Buffy* also benefits from a standout performance by Paul Reubens, whose prolonged death scene remains the film's funniest moment. In addition, the film does a decent job of subverting traditional gender roles, positioning Buffy as the ass-kicking hero while Pike fills the role of damsel in distress. *Buffy* the movie never reaches the same heights as *Buffy* the series, but it offers viewers a lighthearted comic confection that features clever humor and a handful of laugh-out-loud moments.

At the same time, *Buffy* fails to strike the right balance between humor and horror, and the low stakes (no pun intended) make it difficult to develop any sort of emotional investment in the characters or their plight. *Buffy* also suffers a bit from Kuzui's leaden direction, which lacks any sort of flair or distinctiveness. The film screeches to a halt during the dull and poorly staged action scenes, and aside from Reubens, the performances feel listless and the actors' disinterest remains noticeable throughout. Meanwhile, the fashions and slang mark *Buffy* as a relic of its era, and these days the film feels more like a quaint artifact rather than a fresh and exciting genre mash-up that generated a beloved TV series that essentially changed the face of popular culture. Overall, *Buffy* the movie (which features early appearances from future stars Hillary Swank, Ben Affleck, Thomas Jane, and Ricki Lake) remains noteworthy more for its cultural footprint than its entertainment value.

See also *Teen Wolf* (1985), *The Lost Boys* (1987), *Monster Squad* (1987), *Earth Girls Are Easy* (1988), *The Craft* (1996).

SPOTLIGHT: JOSS WHEDON (1964–)

In the late 1980s, Joss Whedon relocated to Los Angeles and landed a gig writing for *Roseanne*. From there, he served as a writer and coproducer on the television show *Parenthood*. During this time, Whedon wrote the screenplay for *Buffy the Vampire Slayer*, which he sold to Sandollar Productions in 1991. This led to subsequent screenwriting jobs on films like *Toy Story* and *Alien: Resurrection*. He also worked as a script doctor throughout the 1990s, doing uncredited work on films like *Speed*, *The Quick and the Dead*, *Waterworld*, *Twister*, and *X-Men*. In 1997, Whedon developed a *Buffy the Vampire Slayer* television series for the fledgling WB Network. The show ran for several seasons and spawned the spin-off series *Angel*. Whedon developed other beloved but short-lived TV series such as *Firefly* and *Dollhouse*. His other projects include the web series *Dr. Horrible's Sing-Along Blog*, and the films *Serenity*, *The Cabin in the Woods*, and *Much Ado about Nothing*. Whedon also contributed to the Marvel Cinematic Universe, writing and directing *The Avengers* and its sequel *Avengers: Age of Ultron*.

C

THE CABLE GUY (1996)

Director: Ben Stiller
Screenplay: Lou Holtz Jr.
Cast: Jim Carrey (the Cable Guy), Matthew Broderick (Steven M. Kovacs), Leslie Mann (Robin Harris), Jack Black (Rick), George Segal (Steven's Father), Diane Baker (Steven's Mother), Ben Stiller (Sam Sweet/Stan Sweet)
Specs: 96 minutes; color
Genre: comedy, thriller
Availability: DVD and Blu-ray (Sony Pictures)

Plot

A man finds his life turned upside down when he forges a tenuous friendship with an emotionally disturbed cable installer who was raised on television.

Background

Los Angeles prosecutor Lou Holtz Jr. came up with the idea for *The Cable Guy* when he saw a cable technician hanging out in the hallway of his mother's apartment building late one evening.[1] Holtz decided to take a chance and write the screenplay, even though he had never written one before. His decision paid off, because Columbia Pictures purchased the script for $1 million.[2] The studio then offered Jim Carrey a record-setting $20 million to star in the film,[3] and hired Ben Stiller to direct based on a suggestion from producer Judd Apatow (the two had worked together on *The Ben Stiller Show* a few years earlier).[4]

Apatow, Stiller, and Carrey liked Holtz's initial idea about a lovable loser intruding on someone else's life in a comical way,[5] but wanted to turn the film into a parody of psychological thrillers like *Cape Fear*, *Unlawful Entry*, *Single White Female*, and *The Hand That Rocks the Cradle*.[6] Holtz rewrote the script four times, making each draft darker than the last.[7] Unfortunately, the producers remained unsatisfied, and Holtz finally left the project. At that point, Apatow took over writing duties,[8] and he worked with Stiller and Carrey to refine the script and tailor it to Carrey's comedic voice.[9] Despite all their hard work, Columbia disliked Apatow's final draft, and studio executives complained about so many scenes that

An unsuspecting Steven (Matthew Broderick, left) meets the Cable Guy (Jim Carrey). *Columbia Pictures / Photofest © Columbia Pictures*

Stiller finally decided to shoot two versions of every scene, one darker in tone and the other lighter.[10]

The Cable Guy opened in the United States on June 14, 1996,[11] and it left most viewers confused because it seemed much more mean-spirited than Carrey's other films.[12] Nevertheless, *The Cable Guy* grossed over $100 million worldwide during its initial theatrical run, though the studio still considered it a flop because it fell short of the expected box office numbers.[13] The film has since become a cult favorite among fans who hail it as one of the funniest black comedies ever made.

Commentary

The Cable Guy takes viewers on a darkly comic excursion into loneliness and obsession, all while offering up a vicious satire of media and the culture at large. *The Cable Guy* riffs on movies like *Fatal Attraction* and *Play Misty for Me* (a clip of which plays on TV during one of the title character's childhood flashbacks), with Carrey as the jilted lover and Matthew Broderick as the object of his warped obsession. The film subverts Carrey's comic persona, twisting the lovable goofiness of characters like Ace Ventura and Lloyd Christmas into something far more sinister and noxious. Carrey engages in his usual shtick, but this time out his antics feel desperate and needy rather than silly and fun. In fact, the title character becomes downright scary as he latches on to mopey sad sack Steven (played to uptight perfection by Broderick) and refuses to let go. As such, *The Cable Guy* becomes an exercise in the sort of awkward cringe comedy found in television programs like *The Office* or *Curb Your Enthusiasm*.

However, whereas the characters in those shows come off as slightly annoying weirdos or charming cranks, the titular cable guy remains creepy and menacing thanks to Carrey's bold performance. *The Cable Guy* features loads of goofy gags and cartoonish physical comedy, but it nevertheless leaves viewers feeling uncomfortable even as they laugh at all the wacky hijinks.

The film also feels prescient in a lot of ways, particularly because it anticipates the Internet age and the rise of trolls and cyberstalking. At one point, Carrey's character declares, "Soon every American home will integrate their television, phone, and computer. You'll be able to visit the Louvre on one channel, or watch female wrestling on another. You can do your shopping at home, or play Mortal Kombat with a friend from Vietnam." With that one line, *The Cable Guy* paints a fairly accurate portrait of the modern world, a time when television has splintered into hundreds of niche channels and streaming services, and gamers wage online campaigns with friends located around the globe. At the same time, Carrey's character feels like a pre-Internet troll due to his overbearing behavior and constant refrain of "I'm just jokin' with ya." Thus, the character resembles 4chan users who spend their days messing with others solely "for the lulz." While the media landscape has changed drastically in the more than twenty years since *The Cable Guy* came out, the film continues to resonate.

The satire occasionally becomes a bit heavy-handed, and the compromised ending feels like a cop-out, but overall *The Cable Guy* remains a solid dark comedy that balances absurdist humor with some keen and oddly prophetic social commentary. The delightfully unhinged central performance and some unforgettable dialogue ("There were no utensils in medieval times, hence there are no utensils at Medieval Times. Would you like a refill on that Pepsi?") turn *The Cable Guy* into one of the best cult films of all time.

See also *Me, Myself & Irene* (2000), *Death to Smoochy* (2002).

CANNIBAL! THE MUSICAL (1993)

Director: Trey Parker
Screenplay: Trey Parker, Matt Stone (uncredited)
Cast: Trey Parker (Alferd Packer), Matt Stone (James Humphrey), Dian Bachar (George Noon), Toddy Walters (Polly Pry), Ian Hardin (Shannon Bell), Jon Hegel (Isreal Swan), Andrew Kemler (Preston Nutter), Jason McHugh (Frank Miller), Robert Muratore (Frenchy Cabazon), Edward Henwood (O.D. Loutzenheiser/the Cyclops), Masao Maki (Indian Chief)
Specs: 95 minutes; color
Genre: biography, comedy, horror, musical, western
Availability: DVD (Troma Entertainment)

Plot

In 1873, a group of miners traveling from Utah to Colorado Territory become lost in the mountains, where they descend into madness and cannibalism.

Background

Cannibal! The Musical began life in 1992 as a three-minute trailer made by Trey Parker, Matt Stone, Jason McHugh, and Ian Hardin for a film class at the University of Colorado at Boulder (UCB).[14] The trailer earned the group a great deal of attention, so they decided to expand it into a feature film.[15] Parker and Stone wrote a screenplay based mainly on the legend of confessed Colorado cannibal Alferd Packer, though Parker also drew inspiration from his messy breakup with his fiancée, Lianne Adamo.[16] After completing the script, Parker and his friends raised $125,000, which they used to produce the film with the help of a cast and crew that consisted of friends, family, local performers, and UCB faculty members (including legendary experimental filmmaker Stan Brakhage).[17]

Shooting took place in and around Loveland Pass toward the end of winter,[18] and everyone involved endured harsh weather and freezing temperatures.[19] Production wrapped later that spring, though reshoots lasted well into the summer.[20] Parker and Hardin then spent several weeks editing the film.[21] Originally titled *Alferd Packer: The Musical*,[22] the finished film premiered on October 31, 1993, at a theater near the campus.[23] Taking a cue from Ed Wood, Parker and his friends hired a limousine to circle the block and bring the cast and crew to the theater's entrance. Afterward, Parker sent a copy of the film to the organizers of the Sundance Film Festival along with the fifty-dollar entrance fee, but he received no response.[24] Undaunted, the group rented a conference room in a nearby hotel and showed the film on their own. This stunt prompted MTV to produce a short news segment about the film, which in turn allowed Parker and his friends to make several connections within the industry.[25]

Alferd Packer (Trey Parker) has some friends for dinner. *Troma Entertainment / Photofest © Troma Entertainment*

Despite all this, nearly every major distribution company rejected the film (executives at Showtime reportedly dismissed it as "unwatchable"). Eventually, Troma Entertainment founder Lloyd Kaufman purchased the film and released it on home video under the title *Cannibal! The Musical*.[26] Unfortunately, many video stores refused to carry it. That all changed when *South Park* premiered and became a big hit for Comedy Central;[27] at that point, copies of the film practically flew off the shelves. Today, *Cannibal!* remains a beloved cult film, and Parker and Stone have found continued success with both *South Park* (in its twenty-first season at the time of this writing) and the popular Broadway musical *The Book of Mormon*.

Commentary

Though amateurish from a technical standpoint, *Cannibal!* quickly establishes itself as a masterpiece of absurdist humor thanks to Parker and Stone's unique comedic sensibilities; they both possess an uncanny ability to craft juvenile dialogue and situations that contain lots of wit and intelligence, and they use this skill to transform their debut film into a crude but clever musical comedy that transcends its low-budget origins. Though they seem nonsensical at first, Parker's brilliantly funny and insanely catchy songs (prepare to have "Shpadoinkle" stuck in your head for days after watching the film) soon reveal themselves as pitch-perfect parodies of the sort of overblown tunes regularly featured in musical theater. At the same time, these cheerful ditties provide a nice contrast to the film's dark themes and extreme gore. Thus, while it initially appears idiotic and poorly made, *Cannibal!* works because the filmmakers manage to strike the exact right balance between smart humor and extreme silliness.

Parker and Stone usually receive all the accolades, but other members of the cast and crew helped turn *Cannibal!* into a cult classic and therefore deserve

SPOTLIGHT: TREY PARKER (1969–) AND MATT STONE (1971–)

Trey Parker and Matt Stone met while attending the University of Colorado at Boulder. While there, they collaborated on the feature-length musical comedy *Cannibal! The Musical*, which became a cult classic and earned the duo a small amount of recognition. Parker and Stone later moved to Los Angeles and spent years pitching various projects to different studios. During this time, Parker wrote and directed *Orgazmo*, a film about a Mormon missionary who becomes a successful porn star. Released in 1997, the film received an NC-17 rating from the Motion Picture Association of America and subsequently failed at the box office. That same year, however, Parker and Stone found great success with *South Park*, an adult animated sitcom produced for Comedy Central. The show became a massive hit, spawning soundtrack albums, video games, and the big-screen adaptation *South Park: Bigger, Longer & Uncut*. The long-running series has garnered numerous awards and remains one of Comedy Central's highest-rated programs. In addition, Parker and Stone collaborated on the film *Team America: World Police*, appeared in cult favorites like *BASEketball* and *Terror Firmer*, produced the short-lived sitcom *That's My Bush*, and teamed with Robert Lopez to develop the hugely successful Broadway show *The Book of Mormon*.

recognition. Dian Bachar stands out as sexually frustrated young miner George Noon, and he displays excellent comedic chops throughout the film. Toddy Walters, meanwhile, delivers a nuanced performance as intrepid reporter Polly Pry and uses her lovely singing voice to imbue the song "This Side of Me" with heartfelt emotion. Additionally, while the film often looks cheap, the effects crew still managed to create some spectacular gore that often looks disturbingly real. Ultimately, anyone looking for a goofy, gory musical about cannibalism should seek out *Cannibal!* (and if you get your hands on a copy of the DVD, make sure to listen to the drunken commentary).

See also *Orgazmo* (1997), *BASEketball* (1998), *South Park: Bigger, Longer & Uncut* (1999).

CARNIVAL OF SOULS (1962)

Director: Herk Harvey
Screenplay: John Clifford
Cast: Candace Hilligoss (Mary Henry), Frances Feist (Mrs. Thomas), Sidney Berger (John Linden), Art Ellison (Minister), Stan Levitt (Dr. Samuels), Herk Harvey (the Man)
Specs: 78 minutes; black and white
Genre: fantasy, horror, mystery
Availability: DVD and Blu-ray (The Criterion Collection)

Plot

After surviving a deadly car accident, a young woman takes a job as a church organist in Utah. Once there, she finds herself drawn to an abandoned carnival pavilion that holds the secret to her tragic past and uncertain future.

Background

In 1952, Herk Harvey quit his job as an instructor in the University of Kansas theater department to work for the Centron Corporation, the foremost industrial and educational film production company in the United States.[28] Over the next decade, Harvey wrote, directed, and produced over thirty-five shorts for the Centron Corporation. When fellow industrial filmmaker Robert Altman scored a surprise hit in 1957 with the low-budget exploitation film *The Delinquents*, Harvey decided to direct his own feature film.[29] He developed the story while driving past the abandoned Saltair Pavilion in Utah on his way home from a film shoot in California.[30] Excited by the possibilities offered by the eerie location, Harvey convinced his Centron colleague John Clifford to write a screenplay.[31] Despite his lack of experience, Clifford agreed, and he spent the next three weeks writing *Carnival of Souls*.[32]

Meanwhile, Harvey set out to raise funds for the production. He initially secured $17,000 from local investors, but later managed to get his hands on an additional

$13,000.[33] As this was happening, Clifford continued working the script, tailoring the story to fit the locations available to the production.[34] For instance, the Reuter Organ Company in Lawrence offered a distinctive setting, so Clifford made the lead character an organist, and this in turn provided the motivation for her to move to Utah and explore the Saltair Pavilion.[35] Upon completing the script, Harvey took a working vacation from Centron to make the film, which he shot in just three weeks.[36] He first cast University of Kansas theater student Sidney Berger,[37] who then traveled to New York and convinced professionally trained actress Candace Hilligoss to play lead character Mary Henry.[38]

Harvey shot part of the film in Lawrence, Kansas, before moving the production to Salt Lake City, Utah.[39] After principal production wrapped, Harvey negotiated a distribution deal with a small company called Herts-Lion and then flew to South America to shoot some geography shorts for Centron.[40] He returned home to discover that the distributor's check had bounced.[41] Nevertheless, *Carnival of Souls* opened in theaters on September 26, 1962, only to bomb at the box office. In the years after its initial release, the film aired frequently on late-night television, at which point it gained a devoted cult following. In 1989, Panorama Entertainment restored *Carnival of Souls* and screened it at festivals and art houses throughout the United States,[42] allowing an even wider audience to rediscover and reevaluate Harvey's sole foray into feature filmmaking. Afterward, *Carnival of Souls* gained a reputation as a milestone in psychological horror, and its spirit lives on in the work of directors like George A. Romero, David Lynch, Peter Jackson, and more.

Mary Henry (Candace Hilligoss) finds herself trapped in a waking nightmare. *Herts-Lion Intl / Photofest © Herts-Lion Intl*

Commentary

Carnival of Souls is an abstract, atmospheric, and amateurish film that often feels obtuse and incoherent. The low budget remains apparent throughout and the seams tend to show, particularly in terms of editing and sound. Yet these weaknesses double as some of the film's greatest strengths; the out-of-sync sound, unconventional editing choices, and weird pacing create an oppressively unsettling ambiance that will leave viewers feeling anxious from beginning to end. While not as technically polished as major studio productions, *Carnival of Souls* succeeds because it rises above its shortcomings and re-creates the moody feeling of Gothic horror on a shoestring budget.

From a purely visual standpoint, *Carnival of Souls* looks fantastic thanks to Maurice Prather's stunning black-and-white cinematography. Throughout the film, Prather employs some unusual compositions and intriguing aesthetic choices, both of which imbue *Carnival of Souls* with a look and feel all its own. Harvey drew inspiration from European directors like Ingmar Bergman and Jean Cocteau,[43] and these stylistic inspirations manifest on-screen in the form of deep shadows, frequent close-ups, and an altogether dreamlike tone. By evoking such highbrow fare, Harvey infused *Carnival of Souls* with an ethereal, disturbing beauty that set it apart from other low-budget horror films of the time. When combined with Gene Moore's haunting organ score, the film establishes a mood and tone all its own.

Virtually ignored upon release, *Carnival of Souls* has emerged as one of the most well-regarded horror films of all time thanks to its atmospheric style and thematic depth. While not for everyone (the film is a bit of an acquired taste), *Carnival of Souls* stands as an unforgettably evocative horror film that looks and feels like nothing else.

See also *Night of the Living Dead* (1968), *The Sixth Sense* (1999), *The Others* (2001), *Insidious* (2010), *Haunter* (2013).

CLERKS (1994)

Director: Kevin Smith
Screenplay: Kevin Smith
Cast: Brian O'Halloran (Dante Hicks), Jeff Anderson (Randal Graves), Marilyn Ghigliotti (Veronica), Lisa Spoonauer (Caitlin Bree), Jason Mewes (Jay), Kevin Smith (Silent Bob)
Specs: 92 minutes; black and white
Genre: comedy
Availability: DVD and Blu-ray (Miramax Lionsgate)

Plot

Called in to work on his day off, a pessimistic convenience store clerk deals with annoying customers, romantic entanglements, rooftop hockey games, and his equally cynical coworker.

Background

After watching Richard Linklater's indie smash *Slacker*,[44] twenty-one-year-old Kevin Smith sold his comic book collection, solicited donations from family members, and maxed out over a dozen credit cards to raise more than $27,000 for his own debut film, *Clerks*.[45] Based on his own experiences working at a convenience store in Leonardo, New Jersey,[46] Smith filmed the ultra-low-budget black-and-white film for twenty-one consecutive nights at a Quick Stop in 1993.[47] The following year, Miramax head honcho Harvey Weinstein purchased *Clerks* for $227,000 after seeing it at the Sundance Film Festival.[48] Miramax released the film into theaters in late 1994,[49] and it became a critical and commercial success, earning over $3 million during its initial run.[50]

Over the years, *Clerks* has earned a reputation as both a landmark of independent cinema and a beloved cult classic. It has appeared on numerous "best of" lists, including *Entertainment Weekly*'s lists of the best cult films produced since 1983 and the funniest movies of the past twenty-five years.[51] In addition, the film helped challenge mainstream perceptions of art house cinema as pretentious and dull, opening doors for other independent filmmakers (though many found themselves relegated to the direct-to-DVD market).[52] *Clerks* also spawned a lucrative franchise that includes an animated TV series, numerous comic books, and two sequels. Furthermore, it serves as the foundation for Kevin Smith's vast multimedia empire, which includes the thriving SModcast network of podcasts.

Randal (Jeff Anderson, left) and Dante (Brian O'Halloran) gab about pop culture while shirking their duties yet again. *Miramax Films / Photofest © Miramax Films*

Commentary

From the hip, "alternative" soundtrack to the grungy style (which features perfectly trimmed goatees, flannel shirts, and Doc Martin boots), *Clerks* serves up a wickedly funny time capsule of the mid-1990s cultural zeitgeist. It also announced the debut of a major new talent who would have a profound impact (for better or worse) on popular culture. Though visually dull, the film features outrageously witty dialogue that more than makes up for any filmic shortcomings. Smith's script is littered with funny but tasteless conversations about everything from the moral quandaries faced by the independent contractors who built the Death Star to the yearly salary of the average jizz mopper. While some viewers might find such jokes offensive, *Clerks* nevertheless remains a treasure trove of insanely quotable lines.

Clerks also captures the sense of aimlessness that afflicted many members of Generation X, those disaffected individuals born between the early 1960s and the mid to late 1970s. Gen Xers were often depicted as apathetic slackers (a label inspired by Linklater's film), and this stereotype absolutely applies to Dante and Randal, the sardonic heroes of *Clerks*. Both men seem content to just sit around talking about pop culture or bitching about their menial, low-paying jobs. In *Fight Club*, Tyler Durden refers to such men as "the middle children of history" and accuses them of having "no purpose or place." Dante and Randal exemplify this notion, and as such, *Clerks* reflects the central tension of the age. Thus, the film becomes much more than a scatological comedy filled with dick and fart jokes; it also functions as an important document of a specific historical period.

Unfortunately, after peaking with this auspicious debut, Smith refused to grow as a filmmaker, and these days he seems more concerned with developing his brand than with producing good movies. The film also features some unfortunate homophobic jokes and a rather icky interlude that mines humor from a young woman's emotional trauma. Nevertheless, *Clerks* stands as a fantastic and

SPOTLIGHT: KEVIN SMITH (1970–)

Like Quentin Tarantino, Kevin Smith found success when he transitioned from convenience store counter jockey to filmmaker. After making a splash in 1994 with his debut film *Clerks*, Smith hit a sophomore slump the following year with the vulgar romantic comedy *Mallrats*, a critical and commercial flop that proved more successful on home video. Smith rebounded in 1997 with *Chasing Amy*, which earned several awards and much critical praise (as well as some debate, sparked by its stereotypical portrayal of lesbians). His next film, *Dogma*, triggered a great deal of controversy in 1999 when the Catholic League denounced it as blasphemous and organized protests to delay its release. Nevertheless, *Dogma* became the third-highest-grossing film during its opening weekend. After a brief foray into television with the *Clerks* animated series, Smith returned to directing films that increasingly appeal to his army of loyal fans, including *Jay and Silent Bob Strike Back*, *Jersey Girl*, *Clerks II*, *Tusk*, and *Yoga Hosers*. In addition to filmmaking, Smith writes comic books, manages a New Jersey comic book store, directs episodes of *The Flash* TV series, and oversees a successful multimedia empire.

hilarious first film that presents viewers with a loving send-up of white, disillusioned, suburban twenty-somethings who have no room to complain about their comfortable lives, but do so anyway.

See also *Slacker* (1991), *Mallrats* (1995), *Chasing Amy* (1997), *Dogma* (1999), *Jay and Silent Bob Strike Back* (2001), *Clerks II* (2006).

A CLOCKWORK ORANGE (1971)

Director: Stanley Kubrick
Screenplay: Stanley Kubrick
Cast: Malcolm McDowell (Alex), James Marcus (Georgie), Warren Clarke (Dim), Michael Tarn (Pete), Michael Bates (Chief Guard), Patrick Magee (Mr. Alexander), Adrienne Corri (Mrs. Alexander), Miriam Karlin (Catlady), Aubrey Morris (Deltoid)
Specs: 136 minutes; color
Genre: crime, drama, science fiction
Availability: Blu-ray (Warner Bros.)

Plot

In a near-future dystopia, a charismatic young sociopath embarks on a crime spree that lands him in prison. While there, he volunteers for an experimental, government-sponsored aversion therapy that curbs his violent tendencies at the expense of his free will.

Background

While working together on the film *Dr. Strangelove*, writer Terry Southern gave director Stanley Kubrick a copy of Anthony Burgess's novella *A Clockwork Orange*.[53] Southern thought it might make a good film, but Kubrick rejected the project because he believed the invented slang used throughout the book would alienate viewers.[54] However, the director changed his mind when he saw just how popular youth films had become during the late 1960s and early 1970s.[55] At that point, Kubrick decided to make his own film about youthful rebellion, and after finishing *2001: A Space Odyssey* he turned his attention to developing an adaptation of *A Clockwork Orange*.[56]

Warner Bros. gave Kubrick just over $2 million to make the film,[57] and hired Burgess himself to write the screenplay.[58] However, Kubrick disliked the author's script so he threw it out and simply used the book instead, though he dialed back the language somewhat.[59] Due to the low budget, Kubrick shot the film mainly on locations he found by looking through architectural magazines.[60] He also remained heavily involved in all aspects of the film, from cinematography to editing to sound to casting.[61] Originally, the studio wanted Mick Jagger for the central role of Alex DeLarge, with the rest of the Rolling Stones as his gang (a.k.a. his "droogs").[62] However, after seeing Lindsay Anderson's 1968 film *If....*, Kubrick felt that Malcolm McDowell would be a perfect fit for the character.[63] Luckily, the studio agreed with

Alex (Malcolm McDowell, center) and his droogs set out to commit a bit of the old ultraviolence. *Warner Bros. / Photofest © Warner Bros.*

this choice, because Kubrick later stated that he would have left the project if the studio refused to let him cast McDowell.[64] The young actor suffered throughout filming; for instance, he scratched his cornea while shooting the aversion therapy sequence[65] and endured freezing temperatures while being dunked headfirst into a trough filled with foul-smelling water.[66] Nevertheless, McDowell gamely withstood these hardships and delivered a career-defining performance.

Upon the film's release, critics disparaged *A Clockwork Orange* while general audiences routinely misunderstood it, with many viewers at the time claiming they enjoyed the violence portrayed on-screen.[67] This might explain why the press blamed *A Clockwork Orange* for inspiring several violent youth crimes, including an incident in which a group of young men sexually assaulted a young Dutch woman while crooning "Singin' in the Rain" (as Alex does in the film).[68] In response to these allegations, Kubrick asked the studio to pull the film from British theaters.[69] Despite this controversy, *A Clockwork Orange* became a substantial hit in the United States, grossing over $26 million and earning critical acclaim as well as several award nominations.[70] These days, *A Clockwork Orange* has many detractors, but it has also earned a well-deserved reputation as one of Kubrick's best films and regularly appears on lists of the best movies ever made.

Commentary

With *A Clockwork Orange,* Kubrick serves up a dazzlingly original vision of the future that still feels dangerous and subversive decades later. The film establishes a confrontational atmosphere with the opening shot of protagonist Alex gazing intently at the viewer as narration comprised of an impenetrable slang unfolds on the soundtrack over Wendy Carlos's eerie synth music. From there, *A Clockwork*

Orange follows Alex and his three droogs (that is, Pete, Georgie, and Dim) as they embark on a series of criminal activities that include beating an old homeless man, battling a rival gang, stealing a car, and raping a woman in front of her helpless husband while belting out "Singin' in the Rain." Alex then returns home to listen to Beethoven and fantasize about even more atrocities. These first 20 minutes introduce audiences to the film's world and make clear that Alex is rotten to the core. At the same time, *A Clockwork Orange* positions Alex as its hero, and spends the rest of its 136-minute run time making the viewer sympathize with this thoroughly horrid young man. The film accomplishes this via Kubrick's expert direction and McDowell's mesmerizing performance, both of which combine to create a vicious social satire that balances exaggerated ultraviolence with brutally funny dark humor.

A Clockwork Orange features heightened performances throughout, and McDowell uses his charisma and lopsided grin to ensure that the audience remains firmly on Alex's side even as he performs completely despicable acts. The film also boasts creative visuals and gloriously self-indulgent production design developed by Kubrick and John Barry, and it features unforgettable dialogue, much of it straight out of the book. Additionally, *A Clockwork Orange* offers up some thrilling violence and mischievous comedy that will leave audiences laughing and cringing all at once. In addition, the film presents viewers with a darkly comic meditation on violence and free will that also serves as a wicked send-up of authority and government institutions. In doing so, *A Clockwork Orange* manipulates the audience into siding with Alex, thereby implicating them in his violence and suggesting that anyone with free will could potentially act in such a manner. Such provocative subject matter and graphic violence will no doubt alienate some viewers, but *A Clockwork Orange* remains a thrilling and altogether important cult film that still feels every bit as unsettling and outrageous as the day it came out.

See also *Eraserhead* (1977), *The Warriors* (1979), *Blade Runner* (1982), *Fight Club* (1999), *American Psycho* (2000).

CLUE (1985)

Director: Jonathan Lynn
Screenplay: Jonathan Lynn, John Landis (story)
Cast: Eileen Brennan (Mrs. Peacock), Tim Curry (Wadsworth), Madeline Kahn (Mrs. White), Christopher Lloyd (Professor Plum), Michael McKean (Mr. Green), Martin Mull (Colonel Mustard), Lesley Ann Warren (Miss Scarlet), Colleen Camp (Yvette), Lee Ving (Mr. Boddy)
Specs: 94 minutes; color
Genre: comedy, crime, mystery, thriller
Availability: DVD and Blu-ray (Paramount Pictures)

Plot

Six strangers blackmailed into attending a dinner party become entangled in a complicated and increasingly silly murder mystery.

Background

Toward the end of 1983, Jonathan Lynn met with Hollywood producer Peter Guber, who wanted Lynn to write an adaptation of the board game *Clue* for director John Landis and producer Debra Hill.[71] Despite some initial reluctance, Lynn flew to Los Angeles to meet with Landis and Hill. By that point, Landis had developed a rough outline of the film's plot, but he failed to come up with a satisfying resolution even after consulting five other writers (including Tom Stoppard and Stephen Sondheim).[72] Landis decided to seek Lynn's help after watching *Yes Minister*.[73] Despite some misgivings about Landis's story (or lack thereof), Lynn agreed and took some tentative ideas to Landis, who asked Lynn to write the screenplay.[74]

Lynn returned to England and spent the next six months working on the script.[75] He incorporated several elements from the board game, including the color-based names and the various murder weapons.[76] He also came up with four endings, each of which needed to jive with the rest of the movie while still revealing a different character as the culprit.[77] Landis thought that playing these different endings in different theaters would encourage audiences to attend multiple screenings, but Lynn worried this tactic might confuse viewers.[78] He did as he was told, however, and finished the screenplay by the middle of 1984.[79] Unfortunately, by then Landis had agreed to direct *Spies Like Us* and could no longer direct *Clue*.[80] Instead, he decided to serve as executive producer, and convinced Lynn to direct the adaptation himself.[81]

Production commenced on November 15, 1984, and wrapped a month later.[82] During filming, Lynn exercised a great deal of control over his script and worked

Wadsworth (Tim Curry, second from right) and the rest of the party guests work to solve the mystery of who killed Mr. Boddy (Lee Ving, not pictured). *Paramount / Photofest © Paramount Pictures*

hard to ensure that the actors followed it to the letter.[83] *Clue* opened in the United States on December 13, 1985, and disappointed both critics and audiences.[84] Theaters around the country received one of three endings (Lynn abandoned the fourth ending because he disliked it).[85] Unfortunately, this marketing gimmick simply bewildered audiences, as Lynn had feared.[86] *Clue* quickly disappeared from theaters, but it hit home video soon after, at which point it found an enthusiastic audience.[87] The film has since become a beloved cult favorite and earned a second life as a midnight movie akin to *The Rocky Horror Picture Show*.[88]

Commentary

Lynn's assured direction and the cast's considerable comedic talents transform *Clue* into a charmingly goofy yet slyly intelligent comedy. The film features an effective combination of inspired wordplay ("In fact the double negative has led to proof positive!") and superb physical comedy (such as Tim Curry unsuccessfully attempting to break down the lounge door). *Clue* captures the spirit of classic British farce (which makes sense given Lynn's pedigree), serving up dozens of silly situations that become progressively more preposterous as the film charges ahead toward its three climaxes.

The brilliant and game (no pun intended) cast deliver deadpan but exaggerated performances, and they transform every line and gesture into comedy gold as they race about the set shouting their lines with wild abandon. Lynn provided an excellent script, but the performers elevate the material and turn it into something truly special (for instance, the funniest and most famous line emerged during an amazing bit of improvisation in which Madeline Kahn's Mrs. White declares her fiery hatred of Yvette, the sexy French maid played by Colleen Camp). Furthermore, the actors convey much of the humor through their facial expressions alone (such as when Eileen Brennan's Mrs. Peacock reacts with visible disgust to Yvette's rather ample cleavage). The confident direction, fantastic performances, and silly script ensure that *Clue* works incredibly well, despite its origins as a board game with just the barest hint of a plot.

The relentless slapstick and nonsensical dialogue often threaten to become tedious, and contemporary viewers might find the film a bit dull and humorless (as did audiences in 1985). *Clue* also remains a product of its time, and some of the humor has aged poorly. Furthermore, the gimmick of the different endings feels superfluous, and none of them makes much sense. Nevertheless, *Clue* remains a charming romp that showcases some talented performers giving it their all to turn a simple board game adaptation into a genuine cult classic.

See also *Murder by Death* (1976).

> # *COMMANDO* (1985)
>
> *Director*: Mark L. Lester
> *Screenplay*: Steven E. de Souza, Jeph Loeb (story), Matthew Weisman (story)
> *Cast*: Arnold Schwarzenegger (John Matrix), Rae Dawn Chong (Cindy), Dan Hedaya (Arius), Vernon Wells (Bennett), James Olson (Major General Franklin Kirby), David Patrick Kelly (Sully), Alyssa Milano (Jenny Matrix), Bill Duke (Cooke)
> *Specs*: 90 minutes; color
> *Genre*: action, crime, thriller
> *Availability*: DVD and Blu-ray (20th Century Fox)

Plot

A former Black Ops commando teams with a resourceful flight attendant to save his kidnapped daughter from a gang of dastardly South American criminals.

Background

In the early 1980s, screenwriter (and later author of such classic comic books as *Batman: The Long Halloween* and *Daredevil: Yellow*) Jeph Loeb had an idea for a film about a former commando trying to come to terms with his violent past.[89] Loeb wrote a spec script that languished in development hell for years.[90] Some time later, Barry Diller of 20th Century Fox was searching for a project for Arnold Schwarzenegger, who was on the verge of becoming the biggest action star in the world.[91] Diller settled on *Commando*, and he hired Mark L. Lester to direct and tasked Steven E. de Souza with rewriting Loeb's screenplay. In the original story, an Israeli soldier emigrates from Israel to the United States to escape the violence of his homeland but is forced back into action to rescue his kidnapped daughter.[92] De Souza heavily revamped the script, tailoring it to fit Schwarzenegger's larger-than-life persona.[93] Schwarzenegger liked de Souza's take on the material and saw the film as an opportunity to play something other than a monosyllabic robot or barbarian.[94]

Commando entered production on April 22, 1985, and Lester shot the film on location in California,[95] with the Pacific coast at San Simeon standing in for San Nicolas Island.[96] Aside from one notable incident in which Schwarzenegger sliced his hand with a knife and had to be rushed to the hospital,[97] the production ran smoothly and wrapped about forty-five days later.[98] *Commando* opened in the United States on October 6, 1985,[99] and instantly became a phenomenon, debuting at number one and remaining there for three weeks.[100] By the time the film ended its theatrical run, it had grossed well over $57 million against a $10 million budget.[101] *Commando* became a certified cult classic in the years after its release, inspiring parodies, pastiches, and a wave of macho action films. Rumors of a remake surfaced in 2010, but have yet to amount to anything.[102]

John Matrix (Arnold Schwarzenegger) sets out to rescue his daughter from a vicious Latin American dictator and his henchmen. *Twentieth Century Fox Film Corp. / Photofest © Twentieth Century Fox Film Corp.*

Commentary

Commando balances delirious action with self-aware humor as it builds toward an explosive and insanely violent climax. The film offers up ninety minutes of bloody, brainless fun backed by a totally 1980s score comprised almost entirely of saxophones, synthesizers, and steel drums. *Commando* features exhilarating action and hard-hitting fight scenes, but it soon becomes clear that the film refuses to take itself too seriously. While it contains plenty of mindless destruction and tough-guy posturing, *Commando* punctuates all the mayhem with lots of knowing wit and slapstick comedy. The film takes a thoroughly postmodern approach to the action/adventure genre, using Rae Dawn Chong's character to comment on the ridiculousness of everything that happens on-screen ("I can't believe this macho bullshit!"). *Commando* contains all the hallmarks of a 1980s action film but adopts a winking tone that leaves the whole thing feeling like an aggressively masculine live-action cartoon.

Of course, everything in the film takes a back seat to Schwarzenegger, who puts his abundant charm and ridiculous physique to good use as a former Black Ops commando turned doting dad who sets out to retrieve his daughter from a group of colorful villains. Schwarzenegger first appears carrying a massive log slung over one shoulder, his bulging biceps glistening in the noonday sun in a hilarious and awesome moment that serves as a fantastic introduction to both the character and the film itself. From there, Schwarzenegger spends the rest of the film tossing the baddies about and speaking almost entirely in tough guy clichés ("I eat Green

Berets for breakfast, and right now, I'm very hungry!") and one-liners ("Let off some steam, Bennett"). He delivers an instantly iconic performance that elevates *Commando* from a run-of-the-mill action flick to one of the best ever made. Admittedly, the film remains an acquired taste, and the excessive jingoism and rampant machismo will likely leave some viewers cold. Nevertheless, *Commando* offers up plenty of audacious spectacle and idiotic fun, and remains one of the most purely entertaining cult films of all time.

See also *Cobra* (1986), *Predator* (1987), *Robocop* (1987), *The Running Man* (1987), *Hard Target* (1993), *Last Action Hero* (1993).

CRANK (2006)

Director: Mark Neveldine, Brian Taylor
Screenplay: Mark Neveldine, Brian Taylor
Cast: Jason Statham (Chev Chelios), Amy Smart (Eve), Jose Pablo Cantillo (Verona), Efren Ramirez (Kaylo), Dwight Yoakim (Doc Miles), Carlos Sanz (Carlito), Reno Wilson (Orlando)
Specs: 88 minutes; color
Genre: action, crime, thriller
Availability: DVD and Blu-ray (Lionsgate Films)

Plot

A hitman learns that he has been injected with a poison that works faster whenever his heart slows down. Now he must keep his adrenaline pumping while he searches for the antidote and his would-be killer.

Background

Prior to directing *Crank*, Mark Neveldine and Brian Taylor codirected a series of action-packed commercials for companies like Nike, Powerade, and Motorola.[103] Eventually, the duo decided they wanted to direct feature films, and they worked together to come up with the high-concept scenario that eventually became their debut film, *Crank*. Drawing inspiration from films such as *D.O.A.* and *Speed*, they hatched an idea about a man who learns he has been poisoned and must keep moving to survive. After raising an estimated $12 million budget[104] (though some reports have it at over $14 million),[105] they set about casting the film. While writing the script, Neveldine and Taylor envisioned an American actor as lead character Chev Chelios, but they failed to find anyone cool enough or tough enough for the role.[106] Then they met British actor Jason Statham, star of films like *Lock, Stock, and Two Smoking Barrels* and *The Transporter*. He impressed the duo with his presence and athleticism,[107] and they hired him on the spot. Production commenced soon after on October 27, 2005.

Neveldine and Taylor shot *Crank* in and around downtown Los Angeles, filming on location in places like Beverly Hills, Boyle Heights, Inglewood, and

Chev Chelios (Jason Statham) battles for his life high above the city of Los Angeles. *Lionsgate Films / Photofest © Lionsgate Films*

Chinatown.[108] To keep things flexible and spontaneous, the duo operated the cameras themselves,[109] though they had help from cinematographer Adam Biddle and several assistant cameramen. Meanwhile, Statham performed many of his own stunts, including riding a motorcycle at top speeds while wearing only a hospital gown and dangling from a helicopter over 3,000 feet above the city.[110] This decision took a physical toll on the actor, who injured his ankles, wrists, and shoulders.[111]

   Crank opened on September 1, 2006,[112] and it grossed over $10 million at the North American box office during its opening weekend.[113] The film left most critics confused, though some reviewers did praise its inventiveness and gleeful excess.[114] Lionsgate released *Crank* to DVD on January 9, 2007, at which point it developed a rabid cult audience. In 2009, Neveldine and Taylor unleashed an even more outrageous sequel called *Crank: High Voltage*, in which Chelios receives an artificial heart that runs on electricity and requires constant recharging.[115]

Commentary

   Crank opens with brightly colored 32-bit video game graphics backed by Quiet Riot's blistering hair metal tune "Bang Your Head (Metal Health)." This brash title sequence lets the audience know exactly what to expect from the rest of the film, which rocks hard and boasts an invigorating mix of delirious action and post-modern humor. *Crank* features frantic cinematography and hyperkinetic editing, and the whole thing feels like a live-action version of the *Grand Theft Auto* games. Throughout the film, Neveldine and Taylor employ a frenetic handheld aesthetic that imbues *Crank* with a feeling of restless agitation that perfectly reflects the character's urgent race against time. The film punctuates the insane mayhem with lots of cartoonish humor and self-aware jokes, and it steadfastly refuses to take itself too seriously as it skewers standard action tropes and repeatedly breaks the fourth wall. For example, late in the film, an Asian businessman speaks Japanese complete with English subtitles that Chev can read and which also appear backward and slightly out of focus whenever the camera points at Chev. Similarly, just before the film's blood-soaked finale, a news reporter covering Chev's rampage warns viewers to send their children out of the room. The energetic action and self-reflexive humor turn *Crank* into one of the most inventive and purely enjoyable action films of the early twenty-first century.

The film also achieves the perfect synthesis between actor and character, and it serves as a prime showcase for Statham, who throws himself into the role entirely and proves up for anything. As Chelios, Statham displays considerable charm while he darts from one bizarre situation to the next, such as parading through the streets of Los Angeles with a visible erection while dressed in a hospital gown and sneakers, or engaging in rough sex with his girlfriend Eve (Amy Smart) in the middle of a crowded Chinatown intersection. He also puts his tough-guy persona to good use and makes for a totally believable action hero as he beats up the bad guys and snarls out ridiculous one-liners like "Don't pop a blood vessel, you little penis" and "I wonder how many steaks I could make out of you?" in his thick cockney accent. Statham even manages to look cool while getting his butt kicked by other gangsters or crashing a stolen police motorcycle into an outdoor restaurant. His abundant charisma ensures that Chev remains likable throughout the film, even when tossing out homophobic or racist insults. In the end, Statham seems like he was born to play Chelios, and his knowing but straight-faced performance is a big part of why *Crank* succeeds as well as it does.

Potential viewers should know that *Crank* is also aggressively offensive, and it frequently thumbs its nose at the very notion of political correctness. There are several times when it appears as though Neveldine and Taylor specifically set out to offend viewers because the film frequently indulges in broad stereotypes and gleefully insensitive humor. At the same time, *Crank* offers up plenty of bloody fun from beginning to end, and it provides an adrenaline-charged rush of slick action and outrageous humor that is guaranteed to delight even the most jaded action fan.

See also *Punisher*: *War Zone* (2008), *Crank 2*: *High Voltage* (2009), *Gamer* (2009), *Scott Pilgrim vs. the World* (2010), *Ghost Rider*: *Spirit of Vengeance* (2011).

D

DEATH RACE 2000 (1975)

Director: Paul Bartel
Screenplay: Robert Thom, Charles B. Griffith
Cast: David Carradine (Frankenstein), Sylvester Stallone ("Machine Gun" Joe Viterbo), Simone Griffeth (Annie Smith), Mary Woronov (Calamity Jane), Roberta Collins (Matilda the Hun), Martin Kove (Nero the Hero), Louisa Moritz (Myra), Don Steele (Junior Bruce), Joyce Jameson (Grace Pander), Carle Bensen (Harold), Harriet Medin (Thomasina Paine)
Specs: 80 minutes; color
Genre: action, comedy, science fiction
Availability: Blu-ray (Shout! Factory)

Plot

In the year 2000 a totalitarian regime rules the United States and distracts the populace with a brutal cross-country automobile race in which contestants run down innocent pedestrians for points. Yet there are those who oppose the race and work to stop it at all costs.

Background

To capitalize on the advance publicity for *Rollerball*, prolific writer/director/producer Roger Corman decided to make his own futuristic sports film.[1] He optioned the rights to Ib Melchior's short story *The Racer* because he thought it might lend itself to a satirical comedy in the vein of *Dr. Strangelove*.[2] He tapped Robert Thom to write the screenplay and hired Paul Bartel to direct.[3] However, Bartel disliked the script Thom came up with, so Corman asked his frequent collaborator Charles B. Griffith to rewrite the screenplay.[4] From there, Corman hired an automotive designer to sketch out the different themed cars that would appear in the film.[5] Corman then brought these drawings to an executive at United Artists who liked them so much he greenlit the film with a $300,000 budget.[6]

With financing secured, Corman and Bartel set about assembling their cast. For the lead character, Corman wanted David Carradine, star of the TV series *Kung Fu*. Meanwhile, Bartel brought Sylvester Stallone in to read for the role of

Frankenstein (David Carradine, right) and his navigator Annie Smith (Simone Griffeth) try to win the Transcontinental Road Race. *New World Pictures / Photofest © New World Pictures*

the villain, "Machine Gun" Joe Viterbo.[7] Corman loved Stallone's audition and hired him on the spot.[8] They filled out the rest of the cast with a mix of young unknowns and members of Corman's stock players.[9] Corman then turned his attention to building the cars. To save money, he purchased several used Volkswagens with rear-mounted engines and had the bodies stripped off and replaced with new fiberglass bodies based on the early designs.[10] Principal photography proved quite difficult, and both the cast and crew worked under a great deal of pressure. The weather remained uncooperative throughout the production, and Corman and Bartel frequently argued about the film's tone (Corman wanted less comedy, while Bartel wanted more).[11] Stallone refused to do nude scenes, which caused tension between him and Corman.[12] At one point, the production ran out of money for stunt drivers, so Corman decided to drive the cars himself.[13]

Despite the troubles on set, *Death Race 2000* became a smash hit upon release on April 1, 1975.[14] While most critics dismissed it as violent trash, such as Roger Ebert,[15] general audiences flocked to the film. In the years after its release, *Death Race 2000* developed a reputation as a cult classic that spawned video games, comic books, and an inferior remake (which was itself followed by two direct-to-video sequels). In 2016, Corman produced *Death Race 2050*, an official sequel/remake directed by G. J. Echternkamp.

Commentary

In interviews, Griffith has claimed that audiences of the 1970s failed to comprehend that *Death Race 2000* was intended as a satire and that the film's ironic humor only became apparent in the years after its release. This claim appears at least partially true, given that many critics at the time lambasted the film for its violent content and widespread appeal among children. Since that time, *Death Race 2000* has earned a well-deserved reputation as a potent spoof of American culture, and one that becomes more relevant with each passing year. Indeed, the rise of reality competition shows, the never-ending debate over violent media, and the increased absurdity of the American political process all ensure that *Death Race 2000* still feels fresh and funny long after its initial release.

At the same time, it becomes somewhat difficult to believe that audiences misunderstood that *Death Race 2000* was intentionally funny because Bartel keeps things light and silly throughout while still injecting the film with plenty of smart social commentary (he also gives the film a sense of scope that belies its low budget, and proves himself adept at directing kinetic action sequences). Meanwhile, the actors all deliver hilarious performances that range from deadpan to excessively wacky. Even Stallone's more serious-minded acting style is rendered campy within the context of the rest of the film and thus adds to the humor. Regardless of whether viewers grasped the satire or merely enjoyed the film as violent spectacle, Griffith's assertion that the humor in *Death Race 2000* became more evident over time has proved true. If anything, the film feels even more vital and important than at the time of its release, particularly as much of the Western world once again struggles with authoritarianism.

See also *The Tenth Victim* (1965), *The Running Man* (1987), *Death Race* (2008), *Death Race 2050* (2017).

THE DECLINE OF WESTERN CIVILIZATION
PART II: THE METAL YEARS (1988)

Director: Penelope Spheeris
Cast: Joe Perry, Steven Tyler, Gene Simmons, Paul Stanley, Alice Cooper, Lemmy
  Kilmister, Ozzy Osbourne, Bret Michaels, Rikki Rockett, Bobby Dall
Specs: 93 minutes; color
Genre: documentary
Availability: Blu-ray (Shout! Factory)

Plot

In this documentary, director Penelope Spheeris shines a harsh light on the decadent Los Angeles heavy metal scene of the mid- to late-1980s.

Background

Penelope Spheeris attended UCLA film school and eventually earned a master of fine arts degree in theater arts.[16] From there, she worked as a film editor and a cinematographer before starting her own music video production company, Rock 'N Reel, in 1974.[17] During this time, she also collaborated with comedian Albert

Brooks on several short films that were featured on the first season of *Saturday Night Live*.[18] In 1981, Spheeris made her feature film debut with *The Decline of Western Civilization*, a documentary about the Los Angeles punk scene. The film received a great deal of critical praise[19] and opened the door for Spheeris to direct a series of narrative features about disaffected young people dealing with the dissolution of the American dream.[20]

In 1988, Spheeris returned to documentary filmmaking with *The Decline of Western Civilization Part II: The Metal Years*, an uncompromising look at the depraved Los Angeles heavy metal scene. With the help of producers Valerie Faris and Jonathan Dayton, Spheeris gained access to high-profile metal acts like Ozzy Osbourne, Aerosmith, and KISS. She also interviewed several up-and-coming groups such as London, Odin, and Seduce. She talked to band members and groupies, all of whom discussed their excessive lifestyles in great detail.[21] In addition, Spheeris gathered footage at the home of one of the film's producers, including an infamous sequence in which a fully clothed and visibly intoxicated Chris Holmes (lead guitarist of the band W.A.S.P.) floats in a pool while his disapproving mother sits quietly at poolside.[22]

The Decline of Western Civilization Part II opened in the United States on June 17, 1988, and immediately struck a chord with critics, some of whom compared it to *This Is Spinal Tap* (which Spheeris declined the opportunity to direct).[23] Unfortunately, the film bombed at the box office, earning just over $373,000 against a reported $500,000 budget.[24] For years, a copyright issue made it difficult to find, except for bootleg copies.[25] The film has since become a cult classic, and it remains a fascinating and funny document of a specific moment in time.

Dave Mustaine (center) and his band Megadeth perform a blistering set in front of hundreds of adoring fans. *New Line / Photofest © New Line Cinema*

Commentary

The Decline of Western Civilization Part II reveals the ridiculousness that lies beneath the surface of heavy metal's shallow celebration of excess. The film lays bare the unchecked egos and libidos driven by a need to fulfill every hedonistic desire. It also exposes the fear and emptiness that often fuels such overindulgence. Throughout the film, Spheeris trains her camera on shallow individuals who long to become famous and adored, but cannot hide the anxiety and self-loathing that propels their quest for notoriety. Spheeris's subjects pose and posture while extolling the virtues of sex, drugs, and rock and roll, but they often come across as sad and oblivious rather than cool and mysterious. By allowing her subjects to reveal their innermost yearnings and doubts in this way, Spheeris offers a fascinating look at a scene that had become bloated to the point of ridiculousness and was teetering on the edge of collapse.

The film sometimes feels slight because it presents only a surface-level exploration of heavy topics like sexism and drug abuse, but that was likely by design. The people interviewed want nothing more than to rock out and get laid while making obscene amounts of money, and *The Decline of Western Civilization Part II* reflects this lack of substance. A frat boy attitude permeates the film; alcohol flows freely, and women with big hair parade around in tiny underwear. Such imagery only accentuates the metal scene's seedy underbelly because the darkness that hides behind the delirious extravagance becomes increasingly apparent during each interview. Spheeris's subjects paint vivid portraits of self-hatred and self-delusion, most notably during the scene in which W.A.S.P. guitarist Chris Holmes drunkenly admits that he hates himself in front of his clearly anguished mother. Even more heartbreaking is the parade of heavy metal hopefuls who long to become rock stars and refuse to acknowledge that they might fail, because these scenes illustrate how wishful thinking fuels the heavy metal scene more than anything else.

The Decline of Western Civilization Part II also serves as an exhilarating concert film, because it features exciting footage of bands like London, Odin, and Faster Pussycat performing in front of crowds of adoring fans. Thus, while the film exposes the scene's dark side, it also offers a triumphant celebration of the alluring power of metal music. Ultimately, *The Decline of Western Civilization Part II* provides viewers with plenty of campy fun without shying away from the gloomier aspects of heavy metal.

See also *This Is Spinal Tap* (1984), *Metallica: Some Kind of Monster* (2004), *Anvil: The Story of Anvil* (2008), *I Am Thor* (2015).

DOG SOLDIERS (2002)

Director: Neil Marshall
Screenplay: Neil Marshall
Cast: Sean Pertwee (Sgt. Harry G. Wells), Kevin McKidd (Pvt. Cooper), Emma
   Cleasby (Megan), Liam Cunningham (Capt. Ryan), Thomas Lockyer (Cpl. Bruce
   Campbell), Darren Morfitt ("Spoon" Witherspoon), Chris Robson (Pvt. Joe Kirk-
   ley), Leslie Simpson (Pvt. Terry Milburn)
Specs: 105 minutes; color
Genre: action, fantasy, horror
Availability: DVD and Blu-ray (Shout! Factory)

Plot

While on a routine training exercise in the Scottish Highlands, British soldiers run into a pack of werewolves and must use all their skills to survive the encounter.

Background

While working on director Bharat Nalluri's *Killing Time* in 1995, Neil Marshall and Keith Bell conceived the idea for *Dog Soldiers*, a film about a ragtag group of soldiers battling a pack of vicious werewolves.[26] The script eventually found its way to producers Brian Patrick O'Toole and Christopher Figg of Kismet Entertainment Group, and they decided to produce the film.[27] The duo traveled to the American Film Market and raised a budget of over $5 million from different investors.[28] Marshall then assembled his cast, and filming commenced in 2001. Marshall shot *Dog Soldiers* mainly in Luxembourg to take advantage of various tax credits,[29] but he traveled to Scotland to gather footage of a helicopter landing.[30] Production ran smoothly for the most part, though Kevin McKidd suffered an injury early on and Marshall reportedly brought Jason Statham in to serve as a stand-in while McKidd recovered.[31]

Dog Soldiers opened in the United Kingdom on May 10, 2002, and became a smash hit during its opening weekend.[32] In the United States, however, the film played for one week at the Egyptian Theater in Los Angeles before premiering on the Sci-Fi Channel in July of 2002.[33] *Dog Soldiers* hit home video a few months later and instantly became a cult sensation, and horror aficionados now consider it one of the best werewolf movies ever made.

Commentary

Dog Soldiers wears its influences on its sleeve; the film openly cribs from genre classics like *Night of the Living Dead* and *Aliens*, and it resembles well-regarded siege movies like *Straw Dogs* and *Assault on Precinct 13*. At the same time, *Dog Soldiers* carves out its own identity thanks to a winning combination of distinctive dialogue and inventive filmmaking. The characters all speak in a rapid-fire patter that consists of stale tough-guy clichés and obscure pop culture references ("When we blow that fuse that place is gonna go up like *Zabriskie Point*"), but it all works within the context of the film and injects *Dog Soldiers* with a great deal of humor and energy.

Sgt. Harry G. Wells (Sean Pertwee) orders his men to take cover during a training exercise. *20th Century Fox Home Entertainment / Photofest © 20th Century Fox Home Entertainment*

Meanwhile, the assured direction and masterful editing keep things feeling lively and propulsive even during quieter moments. Marshall uses the cramped quarters of the cabin to render the kinetic action sequences far more visceral and exhilarating, and he keeps the story moving at a brisk pace and allows the tension to build until it literally explodes during the nerve-wracking climax. *Dog Soldiers* constantly straddles the line between thievery and homage, but it feels fresh and exciting thanks to Marshall's deft direction, skillful editing, and witty dialogue.

Dog Soldiers also features spectacular gore effects and fantastic creature design. Marshall keeps the blood and guts flowing throughout the film, and he stages several nasty and inventive kills that horrify and delight in equal measure. Additionally, Marshall's decision to utilize practical effects throughout the film gives the werewolves a sense of heft and reality, which in turn ensures that they appear far more menacing than the weightless CGI lycanthropes found in films like *An American Werewolf in Paris* or *Twilight*. The monsters also benefit from the lower budget, because it forces Marshall to offer only fleeting glimpses of the creatures rather than let the camera linger on them and potentially reveal the seams in the costumes. Add in the excellent sound design, which features all sorts of bloodthirsty growls and eerie, otherworldly howls, and the werewolves become even more unsettling. In the end, *Dog Soldiers* boasts some excellent direction, but it succeeds as a horror film due to an effective combination of well-realized gore, top-notch practical effects, and stellar sound design.

Unfortunately, *Dog Soldiers* saddles Emma Cleasby's Megan with some terrible lines that sound somewhat forced (and more than a little misogynistic). Nevertheless, the film stands as an impressive debut and serves as a thrilling showcase for Marshall's considerable talents. He distills his various influences into an effective genre mash-up that features electrifying action, fun dialogue, and startling practical effects. These elements come together to make *Dog Soldiers* one of the all-time great werewolf movies, as well as a true cult classic.

See also *An American Werewolf in London* (1981), *The Howling* (1981), *Aliens* (1986), *Evil Dead II* (1987), *Ginger Snaps* (2000), *Blade II* (2002).

SPOTLIGHT: NEIL MARSHALL (1970–)

In 1995, Neil Marshall served as an editor and cowriter on Bharat Nalluri's debut film, *Killing Time*. At the same time, he continued developing his own projects, including his directorial debut *Dog Soldiers*. That film became a cult smash and opened the door for his second effort, *The Descent*, which earned over $57 million against a nearly $7 million budget. Marshall followed this up with *Doomsday*, a wildly frenetic genre mash-up that flopped with both critics and general audiences. Marshall took one last swing at the theatrical market with *Centurion*, an action-packed historical war film that follows members of the Ninth Roman Legion as they struggle to survive behind enemy lines. That film also failed at the box office, but Marshall found great success in the realm of television, directing episodes of shows like *Black Sails*, *Constantine*, *Game of Thrones*, *Hannibal*, and *Westworld*. He is currently developing a reboot of *Lost in Space* for Netflix and a new *Hellboy* film scheduled to hit theaters in 2019.

DONNIE DARKO (2001)

Director: Richard Kelly
Screenplay: Richard Kelly
Cast: Jake Gyllenhaal (Donnie Darko), Jena Malone (Gretchen Ross), Mary McDonnell (Rose Darko), Holmes Osborne (Eddie Darko), Maggie Gyllenhaal (Elizabeth Darko), Daveigh Chase (Samantha Darko), James Duval (Frank), Patrick Swayze (Jim Cunningham)
Specs: 113 minutes; color
Genre: drama, science fiction, thriller
Availability: DVD and Blu-ray (Arrow)

Plot

A brush with death sets a troubled teen on the path to unlocking the secrets of time and space, but along the way he becomes plagued by visions of a man in a creepy rabbit suit.

Background

   After graduating from film school in 1998, twenty-three-year-old Richard Kelly wrote a screenplay inspired by his childhood memories of a news story about a chunk of ice falling from the wing of a plane and crashing into the bedroom of a boy who miraculously managed to escape harm.[34] Kelly also drew on his own experiences growing up in Midlothian, Virginia, a small town just outside of Richmond.[35] He used these elements as the basis for a twisty time travel narrative that served as a poignant recollection of suburban America during the Reagan years. Kelly was determined to direct the film himself, thereby ensuring that his vision would make it to the screen intact,[36] but he failed to secure sufficient financing on his own. That changed when actress Drew Barrymore read the script. She offered to appear in the film and serve as an executive producer, and she helped Kelly raise a $4.5 million budget.[37] She also retained the services of several actors who might have otherwise refused to work with a first-time director, including 1980s hunk Patrick Swayze.[38]

   Donnie Darko commenced filming in 2000 and lasted only twenty-eight days.[39] The production proved quite stressful for Kelly: he lost twenty pounds during the shoot and clashed with producers who considered the film's extended musical sequences indulgent and unnecessary.[40] Shortly after completing the film, Kelly took it to the Sundance Film Festival and tried to secure a distribution deal, but all the major distributors turned him away because they had no idea how to market such a weird and difficult movie.[41] For a time, it seemed like *Donnie Darko* would go straight to video, but then director Christopher Nolan convinced Newmarket Films to pick it up.[42] Newmarket had recently scored a massive hit with Nolan's

Donnie (Jake Gyllenhaal, left), Gretchen (Jena Malone, center), and Frank (James Duval) take in a movie before the end of the world. *Pandora Cinema / Photofest © Pandora Cinema*

Memento, and they hoped to replicate that success with *Donnie Darko*.[43] Unfortunately, Newmarket released the film in the wake of the terrorist attacks of September 11, 2001,[44] apparently unaware that traumatized audiences might reject a film as downbeat and bizarre as *Donnie Darko*.[45]

Despite generally positive reviews, the film grossed less than $1 million during its theatrical run,[46] and it quietly disappeared from theaters soon after it opened. Newmarket released *Donnie Darko* to home video the following year, and it became a cult smash, first in Britain[47] and later in the United States, where it began to run as a midnight movie.[48] These days, *Donnie Darko* enjoys a reputation as one of the best science fiction films ever made, and it has spawned both a director's cut and a critically derided sequel that was made without Kelly's involvement.

Commentary

Donnie Darko is a fascinating and frustrating film that demands multiple viewings. The film features lithe direction and attractive cinematography, and it uses them to take viewers on a mind-bending journey through suburbia. In addition, *Donnie Darko* features exceptionally quotable dialogue (such as "Sometimes I doubt your commitment to Sparkle Motion!" and "Why are you wearing that stupid man suit?"), as well as a heady thematic undercurrent that will leave some viewers pondering the film for days (or years, if the ongoing online debates about the film's true meaning are any indication). The film also boasts a star-making performance from Jake Gyllenhaal as the title character and a terrific soundtrack that includes dozens of 1980s hits and Gary Jules's haunting cover of the Tears for Fears classic "Mad World." Finally, *Donnie Darko* includes two breathtaking musical interludes that make excellent use of long takes and smooth camera movement (like the one in which Donnie first arrives at school). An exuberant mishmash of sophisticated filmmaking, great music, and complex ideas make *Donnie Darko* a provocative and befuddling coming-of-age story that looks great and sounds even better.

Alas, the film takes itself way too seriously, and it suffers from some sluggish pacing and a wildly inconsistent tone. Kelly swings for the fences, but *Donnie Darko* ultimately proves too ambitious and is nowhere near as smart or funny as its young director seems to think. Kelly inundates the viewer with leaden humor and clumsy exposition, and he infuses everything on-screen with a sense of apocalyptic foreboding that becomes comical after a certain point. The stuff with Frank often feels silly while the weird bits of comedy (such as those involving the cartoonish Mrs. Farmer) only serve to undercut the tension. Furthermore, *Donnie Darko* becomes increasingly ponderous, and it collapses under its own weight as it builds to a somewhat unsatisfying conclusion. Furthermore, the title character comes across as thoroughly unlikable, making it difficult to care about anything that happens to him. Overall, *Donnie Darko* emerges as an overly ambitious head trip that never quite comes together, and the thrilling musical sequences suggest that Kelly's strengths lie with the fading music video format rather than feature-length motion pictures.

See also *Blue Velvet* (1986), *Fight Club* (1999), *The Sixth Sense* (1999), *Memento* (2000), *The Machinist* (2004), *Primer* (2004), *Shutter Island* (2010).

DRIVE (2011)

Director: Nicolas Winding Refn
Screenplay: Hossein Amini
Cast: Ryan Gosling (Driver), Carey Mulligan (Irene), Bryan Cranston (Shannon), Albert Brooks (Bernie Rose), Ron Perlman (Nino), Oscar Isaac (Standard), Christina Hendricks (Blanche)
Specs: 100 minutes; color
Genre: action, crime, drama
Availability: DVD and Blu-ray (Sony Pictures)

Plot

An enigmatic getaway driver falls for his attractive neighbor, but soon learns that her ex-con husband owes a large sum of money to some local gangsters. The driver decides to intervene but finds himself drawn into a vicious criminal underworld.

Background

First announced in 2008, the cinematic adaptation of James Sallis's 2005 novel *Drive* originally had Neil Marshall attached to direct for Universal Pictures.[49] Written by Oscar-nominated screenwriter Hossein Amini, the film languished in development hell until 2010. At that point, producers Marc Platt and Adam Siegel hired Ryan Gosling to play the lead character, and they allowed him to choose the director.[50] Gosling selected Danish filmmaker Nicolas Winding Refn,[51] who had made a name for himself directing gritty, visually stylish films like *Pusher* and *Bronson*. The film finally entered production in September 2010 for a six-and-one-half-week scheduled shoot with a budget of $15 million.[52]

Filming took place in Los Angeles, California, and during the shoot Refn and his family lived with Amini and members of the cast in a plush Los Angeles home.[53] Throughout production, Refn, Amini, and Gosling worked together to rewrite the script,[54] and they trimmed the lead character's dialogue down to less than 900 words total.[55] Meanwhile, Refn's other collaborators helped develop the film's distinctive atmospheric style. For instance, cinematographer Newton Thomas Sigel drew a great deal of inspiration from the crime films of Jean-Pierre Melville, while composer Cliff Martinez's ethereal electronic score imbued *Drive* with a retro 1980s feel.[56] Refn then worked with editor Thomas Newman to assemble the final cut of the film, and they eventually settled on a lean, propulsive version that runs one hour and forty minutes long.[57]

Drive opened on May 20 at the 2011 Cannes Film Festival, where it received ample praise and earned Refn a Best Director award. The film was even nominated for the prestigious Palme d'Or, but lost to Terrence Malick's *Tree of Life*. On September 16, 2011, *Drive* roared into US theaters to much critical acclaim and a modest amount of commercial success. The film went on to earn $76,175,166 worldwide, more than five times its $15 million budget.[58] In the years after its

The Driver (Ryan Gosling) prepares to make yet another a tense getaway. *FilmDistrict / Photofest* © *FilmDistrict*

release, *Drive* earned a devoted cult following due to its memorable characters and an abundance of style.

Commentary

Though clearly influenced by minimalist action classics like *Point Blank*, *Two-Lane Blacktop*, *The Driver*, and *Thief*, the languidly paced *Drive* immediately establishes its own identity thanks to Refn's signature stylistic excess. Awash in neon lights and high contrast colors that recall the action films of the 1980s, *Drive* is a visual treat that swaggers across the screen with an aggressively macho attitude. The script crackles with a sense of energy and vitality that draws the viewer deeper into the labyrinthine narrative. The cast consists of reliable character actors and young up-and-coming performers, all of whom deliver some of the best work of their careers, particularly Gosling and Albert Brooks (cast wonderfully against type as a small-time Jewish mobster with big-time ambitions). These elements come together to make *Drive* a taut, mesmerizing thriller with a powerful sense of forward momentum. The film represents the ultimate expression of Refn's brutal cinematic aesthetic, which draws on the work of directors like Sergio Leone, Martin Scorsese, and William Friedkin, among others.

Critics often dismiss Refn's films as hollow provocations that glorify violence and emphasize style over substance, but that is an altogether unfair assessment since Refn routinely uses his films to critique the violent male heroes that recur throughout popular culture. In *Drive*, the nameless protagonist recalls stoic movie tough guys played by the likes of Steve McQueen and Clint Eastwood, but he ultimately emerges as a tragic figure whose aggressive masculinity and rugged individualism doom him to remain separate from society. These qualities, along with his violent tendencies and explosive temper, also prevent the character from forging a relationship with his beautiful neighbor, Irene (played by the luminous Carey Mulligan), and their parting kiss remains the film's most beautiful and heartbreaking moment. In a lot of ways, the character serves to condemn the sort of solitary male heroes that tend to dominate mainstream cinema, particularly action movies, superhero films, and Westerns. Some viewers might find the relaxed pace and sleepy central performance tedious, but *Drive* features a surplus of style and a timely thematic undercurrent that combine to make it one of the best cult films of the early twenty-first century.

See also *Point Blank* (1967), *Two-Lane Blacktop* (1971), *The Driver* (1978), *Thief* (1981), *Baby Driver* (2017).

SPOTLIGHT: NICOLAS WINDING REFN (1970–)

Born in Copenhagen, Denmark, on September 29, 1970, writer/director Nicolas Winding Refn is the son of Danish director and editor Anders Refn and Danish photographer and cinematographer Vibeke Winding. In 1978, Refn's family relocated to New York City, where he attended the American Academy of Dramatic Arts but was expelled for throwing a table against a wall in a fit of anger. He moved back to Denmark and enrolled in the Danish Film School, though he dropped out almost immediately. In 1996, Refn's first feature film, *Pusher*, became a critically acclaimed international cult phenomenon. His next film, *Bleeder*, won numerous awards at film festivals around the world. Refn made his Hollywood debut in 2003 with *Fear X*, a critical and commercial flop that bankrupted him. He rebounded with *Pusher II* and *Pusher III*, both of which helped establish his signature fetishistic visual style, which he solidified with his next two films, the unconventional biopic *Bronson* and the psychedelic Viking epic *Valhalla Rising*. His greatest success came with *Drive*, a critical and commercial hit that was nominated for the Palme d'Or at the Cannes Film Festival. Since then, Refn has directed increasingly divisive films like *Only God Forgives* and *The Neon Demon*.

E

***EARTH GIRLS ARE EASY* (1988)**

Director: Julien Temple
Screenplay: Julie Brown, Charlie Coffey, Terrence E. McNally
Cast: Geena Davis (Valerie Gail), Jeff Goldblum (Mac), Jim Carrey (Wiploc), Damon
Wayans (Zeebo), Julie Brown (Candy Pink), Charles Rocket (Dr. Ted Gallagher),
Michael McKean (Woody)
Specs: 100 minutes; color
Genre: comedy, musical, romance, science fiction
Availability: DVD (Lionsgate Films)

Plot

When an alien spaceship crash lands in her pool, a young woman tries to help
the furry inhabitants assimilate, but things become complicated when she develops feelings for their sexy commander.

Background

Earth Girls Are Easy made a difficult transition from script to screen. It was originally set up at Warner Bros., with production set to begin in 1986 with a budget
of $14 million.[1] That all changed when director Julien Temple's previous film, *Ab-
solute Beginners*, bombed at the box office[2] and several big-name actresses turned
down the lead role of Valerie, including Molly Ringwald and Madonna.[3] Warner
Bros. decided to scrap the project entirely.[4] Other studios expressed interest in the
film itself, but none wanted Temple in the director's chair.[5] After exhausting all
his other options, Temple finally approached executives at French bank Crédit
Lyonnais, who agreed to put up $10 million and let Temple direct.[6] They then set
up a distribution deal with the De Laurentiis Entertainment Group,[7] and the film
commenced shooting in late 1987.[8]

The production remained rocky throughout, largely because Temple's perfectionism caused frequent delays.[9] More problems arose after principal photography wrapped; producers disliked Temple's cut of the film, and this led to nearly
five months' worth of postproduction tinkering, during which Temple removed
several scenes and one big production number.[10] Yet these changes also failed

Valerie Gail (Geena Davis) waits for her fiancé, Dr. Ted Gallagher (Charles Rocket, not pictured).
Vestron Pictures / Photofest © Vestron Pictures

to satisfy the producers, and they ordered reshoots late in the process.[11] As all this was happening, De Laurentiis Entertainment Group filed for bankruptcy.[12] Vestron Pictures purchased the distribution rights shortly after and planned to release the film in February of 1989,[13] but it remained in limbo until May of that year due to legal entanglements.[14]

Earth Girls Are Easy opened to generally positive reviews but flopped at the box office, earning less than a third of its production costs. The film disappeared from theaters a mere two weeks after it opened, having grossed less than $2 million,[15] but it became a cult hit on home video. While not quite as well-known as some other cult classics, *Earth Girls Are Easy* still left an imprint on popular culture due to frequent viewings at slumber parties across the United States.

Commentary

Earth Girls Are Easy offers up a kooky blast of sexy, silly fun, and it dazzles viewers with bright colors and an attractive cast, all of whom deliver delightfully comic performances. The film features Geena Davis and Jeff Goldblum at their absolute sexiest, and they demonstrate scorching chemistry that infuses the film with an erotic charge (which makes sense, considering they were dating at the time). Davis enchants as Valerie, a sweetly naive valley girl looking for Mr. Right. Meanwhile, Goldblum injects the film with an unbelievable amount of beefcake appeal as Mac, the leader of a group of furry, sex-starved extraterrestrials. Jim Carrey and Damon Wayans bring a manic energy to the film as Mac's intergalactic buddies, Wiploc and Zeebo, and Julie Brown steals the show as vibrant party girl,

Candy. She even contributes a couple of songs to the film's soundtrack (including the vivacious "Cause I'm a Blond").

The film also contains numerous in-jokes and silly gags that poke fun at the vapid Hollywood lifestyle. For instance, Michael McKean delivers a hilarious turn as Woody, a burned-out surfer dude of the sort found along the California coast (or at least in movies about the California coast). In addition, the film contains a cameo by Angelyne, a singer/actress/model who gained widespread notoriety after she plastered her own busty image on billboards throughout downtown Los Angeles. Angelyne embodied the hot pink and bleached hair aesthetic of 1980s Los Angeles, and her appearance in *Earth Girls Are Easy* suggests a satirical edge; Temple and his screenwriters clearly intended their film as an affectionate jab at Tinseltown and the wackos who live there. The film obviously adores these goofy yahoos, and therefore the satire feels more like gentle teasing rather than contempt. As such, *Earth Girls Are Easy* remains as endearingly silly as the day it came out, and it offers a fascinating peek into a bygone era and encourages viewers to laugh along with its cast of crazies.

See also *The Adventures of Buckaroo Banzai across the 8th Dimension* (1984), *Galaxy Quest* (1999).

ERASERHEAD (1977)

Director: David Lynch
Screenplay: David Lynch
Cast: Jack Nance (Henry Spencer), Charlotte Stewart (Mary X), Allen Joseph (Mr. X), Jeanne Bates (Mrs. X), Judith Roberts (Beautiful Girl across the Hall), Laurel Near (Lady in the Radiator), Jack Fisk (Man in the Planet), Jean Lange (Grandmother)
Specs: 89 minutes; black and white
Genre: fantasy, horror, science fiction
Availability: DVD and Blu-ray (The Criterion Collection)

Plot

Meek factory worker Henry Spencer learns that his girlfriend, Mary X, has given birth to a hideously deformed baby that wails day and night. The sound eventually drives Mary away, leaving Henry to care for the child on his own in a hellish industrial cityscape.

Background

Funded largely by donations from actress Sissy Spacek and her husband, Jack Fisk (a production designer, art director, and performer who plays the Man in the Planet in the film),[16] *Eraserhead* had a difficult transition from script to screen. After earning a scholarship to the American Film Institute's Center for Advanced Film Studies in 1970, David Lynch was given the opportunity to direct one of his own screenplays.[17] He originally chose *Gardenback*, a surreal

Eraserhead

Henry Spencer (Jack Nance) contemplates the existential horror of impending fatherhood. *Libra Films International / Photofest © Libra Films International*

tale about a man lusting after his next-door neighbor. However, Lynch became frustrated while developing it, so he instead suggested *Eraserhead*.[18] The board approved the project with a starting budget of $10,000, along with permission to film anywhere on the campus grounds.[19] Lynch began shooting on May 29, 1972, unaware of the long road ahead; production finally wrapped in 1976, over four years after it began.[20]

Eraserhead opened to small, disinterested audiences on March 19, 1977, at the Filmex film festival in Los Angeles[21] and seemed destined to languish in obscurity until Ben Barenholtz of Libra Films in New York City suggested running midnight screenings of the film.[22] Barenholtz pioneered the concept of the midnight movie, turning such unconventional films as *El Topo* and *Pink Flamingos* into massive cult hits.[23] Lynch agreed, and *Eraserhead* soon opened at the Cinema Village theater on Twelfth Street in Greenwich Village, where it played for an entire year to enthusiastic late-night audiences that included fellow cult auteur, John Waters.[24] The film soon became a cult classic, and its reputation has only grown in the years since its release. The United States Library of Congress added *Eraserhead* to the National Film Registry in 2004,[25] and in 2014 it was released on DVD and Blu-ray by the Criterion Collection. Despite its rather uncertain origins, *Eraserhead* has emerged as an enduring work of odd beauty that helped establish Lynch as a unique voice in the world of cinema.

Commentary

Shot in stunning black and white by cinematographers Herbert Cardwell and Frederick Elmes, *Eraserhead* immediately establishes a sense of oppressive despair as Henry navigates his way through an empty, crumbling, nearly postapocalyptic urban landscape. From there, the film piles on the misery, as Henry is forced to care for his sickly, mutant child. *Eraserhead* is not all doom and gloom, however, as it wisely balances out the misery with some darkly humorous moments, such as when Mary angrily struggles to retrieve her suitcase from under the bed before storming out of the rundown apartment she shares with Henry. Still, the film remains almost unbearably grim throughout, and therefore leaves the viewer feeling drained but also exhilarated by the exquisitely haunting images on display.

Over the years, *Eraserhead* has been viewed as a metaphor for all sorts of things, from the fear of fatherhood to the debilitating effects of industrialization to the crippling sense of loneliness that often accompanies urbanization. Given that the simple plot unfolds in an entirely stream-of-consciousness manner, the film lends itself to all these interpretations and more. Much like Terry Gilliam's *Brazil*, fantasy and dreams function as a recurring motif in *Eraserhead*. However, while dreams allow *Brazil*'s Sam Lowry to escape from the bureaucratic nightmare in which he lived, they fail to provide Henry with a similar outlet in *Eraserhead*; his dreams tend to descend into unsettling nightmares that mirror his increasingly dismal waking life. Thus, the film becomes a rather dreary experience, though one that offers viewers much to think about.

While some might find the extreme weirdness off-putting, those able to appreciate the film's bizarre tendencies will find themselves rewarded with a piece of nightmarish art. *Eraserhead* remains an important and provocative film nearly forty years on, largely because it evokes such strong reactions among viewers (it is a true "love it" or "hate it" affair). More than just a cult curiosity, *Eraserhead* stands as a classic of surrealist cinema.

See also *Night of the Living Dead* (1968), *Tetsuo: The Iron Man* (1989), *Pi* (1998).

SPOTLIGHT: DAVID LYNCH (1946–)

David Lynch burst onto the scene in 1977 with *Eraserhead*, which became a huge hit on the midnight movie circuit. Lynch next landed a gig directing *The Elephant Man* for executive producer Mel Brooks. That film earned Lynch his first mainstream success, and in 1984 De Laurentiis Entertainment Group hired him to direct a big-budget adaptation of Frank Herbert's epic science fiction novel *Dune* that flopped with both audiences and critics. However, Lynch rebounded with his next film, the crime thriller *Blue Velvet*, which received a great deal of critical acclaim in 1986. Lynch then turned his sights to television, creating the cult classic TV series *Twin Peaks*, which spawned a 1992 movie adaptation titled *Fire Walk with Me* and a reboot that debuted on Showtime in 2017. Lynch went on to direct such critically acclaimed cult films as *Wild at Heart*, *The Straight Story*, *Lost Highway*, *Mulholland Drive*, and *Inland Empire*. In addition to directing, Lynch is also an accomplished screenwriter, artist, musician, actor, and photographer.

EVIL DEAD II (1987)

Director: Sam Raimi
Screenplay: Sam Raimi, Scott Spiegel
Cast: Bruce Campbell (Ashley "Ash" J. Williams), Sarah Berry (Annie Knowby), Dan
    Hicks (Jake), Kassie Wesley DePaiva (Bobby Joe), Denise Bixler (Linda), Richard
    Domeier (Ed Getley), Jon Peakes (Professor Raymond Knowby), Lou Hancock
    (Henrietta Knowby)
Specs: 84 minutes; color
Genre: comedy, horror
Availability: DVD and Blu-ray (Lionsgate Films)

Plot

A group of strangers battle demonic forces in an isolated cabin in the woods.

Background

In 1983, writer/director Sam Raimi made a huge splash with *The Evil Dead*, an
ultra-low-budget horror film that became a critical and commercial smash. Unfortunately, Raimi's next film, *Crimewave*, bombed at the box office.[26] Desperate
for another hit, Raimi and his producing partner Rob Tapert set out to make *Evil
Dead II* in 1987.[27] They originally planned to send square-jawed hero Ash Williams

Ash Williams (Bruce Campbell, second from right) and the others prepare to battle the evil
Deadites. *Rosebud / Photofest © Rosebud*

back in time to the Middle Ages, in *Medieval Dead*, but they scrapped that idea (it eventually made its way into the second sequel, *Army of Darkness*).[28] Raimi wrote the script with longtime friend Scott Spiegel, and they needed a bigger budget for the ambitious sequel/remake.[29] Luckily, author and *Evil Dead* fan Stephen King convinced producer Dino De Laurentiis to finance the sequel with a nearly $4 million budget.[30] Raimi and Spiegel rewrote the script, and *Evil Dead II* entered production on May 10, 1986.[31]

Raimi shot most of the film on a set built in the gymnasium of the J. R. Faison Junior High School in Wadesboro, North Carolina.[32] Principal photography wrapped after five months, though Raimi conducted extensive reshoots in December 1986.[33] Raimi and his colleagues decided to release *Evil Dead II* unrated, so De Laurentiis set up a new distribution company called Rosebud Releasing Corporation rather than release the unrated film through his own company.[34] The film opened on March 13, 1987, in just a handful of theaters across the United States, but it still grossed nearly $6 million after just one month.[35] The film's reputation has grown steadily since then, and critics and fans alike now recognize it as one of the best horror films ever made. In 2015, Raimi resurrected the franchise with *Ash vs. Evil Dead*, a television series that debuted to critical acclaim and substantial media attention.

Commentary

The Evil Dead announced Raimi as a vital new talent, but *Evil Dead II* truly established his signature splatstick style, which he employed to great effect on subsequent films like *Darkman*, *Army of Darkness*, and *Drag Me to Hell*. In *Evil Dead II*, Raimi distills his myriad influences (which include H. P. Lovecraft's Cthulhu Mythos, the Z-grade monster movie *Equinox*, and the comedy stylings of the Three Stooges) into a delightfully demented gore fest that features loads of laughs and plenty of sick thrills. At the same time, he employs an array of inventive cinematic techniques that smooth over the film's low-budget shortcomings and render everything on-screen fresh and exciting. Meanwhile, star Bruce Campbell delivers a frantic performance as bumbling hero Ash Williams, a timid but romantic dweeb who emerges as a chainsaw-wielding badass over the course of the film. Overall,

SPOTLIGHT: SAM RAIMI (1959–)

As a child in Royal Oak, Michigan, Sam Raimi made his own short films using an 8 mm camera. In 1978, Raimi teamed with his friends Bruce Campbell and Rob Tapert to make *Within the Woods*, a short film they used to raise money for their first feature-length effort, *The Evil Dead*. That film became a critical and commercial hit that established Raimi's reputation as a director. Afterward, he directed several inventive genre films, including *Crimewave*, *Evil Dead II*, *Darkman*, *Army of Darkness*, and *The Quick and the Dead*. He also directed critically acclaimed mainstream movies like *A Simple Plan*, *For Love of the Game*, and *The Gift*, as well as box office juggernauts like *Spider-Man*, *Spider-Man 2*, and *Oz the Great and Powerful*. In addition, Raimi produced several successful television series and films through his production company, Renaissance Pictures.

SPOTLIGHT: BRUCE CAMPBELL (1958–)

Born in Royal Oak, Michigan, Bruce Campbell spent his teenage years acting in short films directed by his friend Sam Raimi. In 1979, Campbell and his buddies raised $350,000 to make *The Evil Dead*, a low-budget horror film that earned international attention and turned Campbell into a minor celebrity. Campbell then moved to Los Angeles and appeared in numerous genre flicks, including *Maniac Cop, Lunatics: A Love Story, Moontrap,* and *Mindwarp.* In 1987, Campbell returned to the role that made him famous when he played Ash Williams in *Evil Dead II,* and again in 1992 in *Army of Darkness.* Since then, Campbell has appeared in over 100 films and television shows, carving out a reputation as one of the most beloved performers in all of Hollywood. In 2015, Campbell once again assumed the role of Ash in the TV series *Ash vs. Evil Dead.*

Evil Dead II assaults viewers with a potent mixture of slapstick comedy, twisted imagery, and innovative filmmaking.

Of course, *Evil Dead II* tends to favor comedy over horror and is therefore more fun than scary. In addition, the seams sometimes show, and there are times when the low budget becomes abundantly clear. As such, viewers accustomed to the slick thrills of modern horror films like *Saw, The Conjuring,* or even the remake of *The Evil Dead* might find *Evil Dead II* quaint or corny. Nevertheless, it is impossible to overstate the film's impact on horror (and horror fans). Back in 1987, *Evil Dead II* felt like a revelation thanks to Raimi's boundless ingenuity, which ensured that the film looked and felt like nothing else at the time. Three decades on, *Evil Dead II* remains a groundbreaking and totally effective thrill ride, and its groovy legacy lives on in films like *Shaun of the Dead* (Edgar Wright cribbed a lot of his hyperactive visual style from Raimi) and *The Cabin in the Woods.*

See also *Night of the Living Dead* (1968), *The Evil Dead* (1981), *Re-Animator* (1985), *Army of Darkness* (1992), *The Cabin in the Woods* (2012).

F

FASTER, PUSSYCAT! KILL! KILL! (1965)

Director: Russ Meyer
Screenplay: Jackie Moran, Russ Meyer (story)
Cast: Tura Satana (Varla), Haji (Rosie), Lori Williams (Billie), Ray Barlow (Tommy), Sue Bernard (Linda), Dennis Busch (The Vegetable), Stuart Lancaster (Old Man), Paul Trinka (Kirk)
Specs: 83 minutes; black and white
Genre: action, comedy
Availability: Blu-ray (RM Films)

Plot

Three buxom, thrill-seeking go-go dancers kill a man in cold blood and take his young girlfriend hostage. While on the run, they hatch a plan to rob a rich old man who lives in the desert with his two sons, but soon discover he has his own sinister aims.

Background

Written by former child actor Jack "Jackie" Moran (*The Adventures of Tom Sawyer*; *Gone with the Wind*) and based on an original idea by director Russ Meyer,[1] *Faster, Pussycat! Kill! Kill!* is a low-budget sexploitation flick that bombed at the box office but nevertheless influenced popular culture for years afterward. Originally titled *The Leather Girls*[2] (and later *The Mankillers*[3]), Moran wrote the screenplay in just four days,[4] while sound editor Richard S. Brummer came up with the film's iconic final title during production.[5] Shooting in black and white to save money,[6] Meyer ran the production like a military operation, employing a small crew that consisted mostly of his old army buddies.[7] Yet his strict filmmaking style did not sit well with lead actress Tura Satana, and the two quarreled often.[8] Meyer also clashed with sixteen-year-old Susan Bernard and her overprotective mother, who remained on set throughout production to keep an eye on her underage daughter.[9] Additional conflicts arose between Bernard and her costars, particularly Satana, who reportedly frightened the girl.[10]

Varla (Tura Satana) uses her judo skills to dispatch a hapless man. *Eve Productions / Photofest ©
Eve Productions*

Faster, Pussycat! flopped during its initial release,[11] and critics either dismissed it
as sleazy trash or ignored it outright. Despite this poor reception, *Faster, Pussycat!*
still left a profound imprint on popular culture in the decades that followed, influ-
encing everything from music to television to film. For instance, 1980s hair metal
band Faster Pussycat took their name from the film's title,[12] while such musical superstars as Paul Oakenfold, White Zombie, and the B-52s have all included references to *Faster, Pussycat!* in their songs.[13] Popular TV shows like *The Simpsons* and
Buffy the Vampire Slayer also referenced the movie,[14] as did the direct-to-Netflix
movie *Pee-wee's Big Holiday.*[15] Meanwhile, fellow cult director John Waters regards
Faster, Pussycat! as one of the best films ever made[16] and has paid homage to it in
his own work.[17] Such pop cultural saturation reveals the film as more than just a
cheap skin flick, but rather a legitimate cult classic that continues to resonate with
a wide variety of audiences.

Commentary

While the lead actresses' rather generous talents serve as the main attraction,
Faster, Pussycat! Kill! Kill! offers more than just gratuitous sex and violence. It also
features snappy dialogue and provocative gender roles. Filmed on location in the
California desert, the film brings an extravagant rock-and-roll sensibility to the
screen, announcing its intentions right out of the gate with a lurid opening narration that establishes the tone for the next eighty-three minutes. The movie then

introduces the three leading ladies as they dance for a group of leering men. From there, the action cuts to Satana barreling down the highway in a Porsche 356 C and laughing maniacally as the film's theme song (performed by the Bostweeds) wails on the soundtrack. Thus, with incredible economy, *Faster, Pussycat!* announces itself as a hip showcase for fast cars, sexy women, and rock music.

The film also serves as a slyly satirical look at the battle of the sexes, and in that regard it offers plenty to chew on. For years, critics have debated whether *Faster, Pussycat!* is sexist rubbish or a feminist masterwork, but the truth lies somewhere in between. The film frequently sexualizes the lead actresses, particularly Satana, whose impressive cleavage remains on display throughout. However, *Faster, Pussycat!* never objectifies the women; instead, it depicts them as strong, complex individuals who take control of their own agency and sexuality. Granted, they use that sexuality for nefarious purposes, but the film complicates this portrayal by depicting most of the men in the film as equally reprehensible. More importantly, *Faster, Pussycat!* only punishes the women for their violent criminal behavior rather than their uninhibited natures. Thus, *Faster, Pussycat!* emerges as both feminist and sexist, offering cheesecake appeal while challenging stereotypical notions about gender and sexuality.

Faster, Pussycat! failed during its initial run, but its reputation has only grown in the years since. Critics now regard it as a masterpiece of cult cinema, as well as one of the best American films of the 1960s. In the long run, it does not matter if the film is empowering or exploitative (or both) because whichever view you take, *Faster, Pussycat!* remains a fun, sexy, influential romp.

See also *Lorna* (1964), *Motorpsycho!* (1965), *Mudhoney* (1965), *She-Devils on Wheels* (1968), *Death Proof* (2007).

SPOTLIGHT: RUSS MEYER (1922–2004)

After serving as a camera operator during World War II, Russ Meyer settled in Los Angeles and devoted his energies to documenting the female form in all its full-figured glory. He made his directorial debut in 1959 with *The Immoral Mr. Teas*, the first nudist comedy to earn over $1 million at the box office. Meyer earned a reputation as a connoisseur of large-breasted women after directing *Lorna*, *Mudhoney*, *Motorpsycho!* and *Faster, Pussycat! Kill! Kill!*—four outrageously titillating films that boast the talents of well-endowed starlets like Haji, Antoinette Cristiani, and, most memorably, Tura Satana. Meyer scored a surprise hit in 1968 with *Vixen!* and followed it with the hugely successful *Beyond the Valley of the Dolls* (written by the late film critic Roger Ebert) for 20th Century Fox. Unfortunately, his next studio film, *The Seven Minutes*, flopped, and Meyer returned to directing low-budget, independently produced sexploitation films. It is tempting to dismiss Meyer's films as little more than boob delivery systems, but even a cursory glance reveals them as much more. While his output declined during the 1970s, Meyer still produced an ample body of campy, satirical films that ensured his status as a cult icon.

FATEFUL FINDINGS (2013)

Director: Neil Breen
Screenplay: Neil Breen
Cast: Neil Breen (Dylan), Klara Landrat (Emily), Jennifer Autry (Leah), Victoria Vi-
    veiros (Amy), David Silva (Jim), John Henry Hoffman (Dr. Lee), Danielle Andrade
    (Aly), David Scott (Dr. Rosen)
Specs: 100 minutes; color
Genre: drama, fantasy, thriller
Availability: DVD (Panorama Entertainment)

Plot

A novelist who doubles as a computer scientist uses his amazing mystical powers to hack into government databases and expose state secrets.

Background

In 2005, Neil Breen decided to live out his childhood dreams of becoming a
filmmaker.[18] He used the money he made while working as a licensed architect to
make *Double Down*,[19] a bizarre, stream-of-consciousness psychological thriller that
became a minor cult hit after it was added to Netflix's streaming library.[20] Eight
years later, Breen attained widespread infamy among bad movie aficionados with
the release of his third self-financed film, *Fateful Findings*. In interviews, Breen
refuses to discuss details of the production but has stated that he handled most
of the behind-the-scenes duties himself. *Fateful Findings* premiered at the 2012
Butt-Numb-a-Thon, an invitation-only film festival organized by Harry Knowles,
founder of the website Ain't It Cool News.[21] The following year, *Fateful Findings*
played as part of the Midnight Adrenaline program at the Seattle International
Film Festival.[22] This exposure prompted Panorama Entertainment to purchase
the rights to distribute the film in the United States.[23] *Fateful Findings* has since
become a massive cult hit and is frequently compared to Tommy Wiseau's equally
demented debut feature, *The Room*.[24]

Commentary

A mixture of terrible dialogue, wooden performances, and endearingly awkward filmmaking turn *Fateful Findings* into one of the most entertaining bad
movies of all time. The disjointed narrative unfolds in a stream-of-consciousness
fashion, and the actors turn in some of the most unintentionally hilarious performances ever committed to film (starting with Breen himself as lead character
Dylan). *Fateful Findings* remains unpredictable from beginning to end, and important plot revelations frequently emerge from out of nowhere (such as the fact
that Dylan's wife harbors a crippling drug addiction, or that shady government
types have apparently been monitoring Dylan for some time). Such randomness
keeps things lively and ensures that no one can accuse the film of obviousness.

Dylan (Neil Breen) chastises corrupt government leaders and business executives. *Panorama Entertainment / Photofest © Panorama Entertainment*

Fateful Findings also features comically awful dialogue that consists of ham-fisted exposition and nonsensical outbursts ("I've been hacking into the most secret government and corporate secrets"). Meanwhile, the laughably incompetent film-making is sure to leave viewers scratching their heads as they try to make sense of the odd camera placements and weird editing choices. When combined with the stilted acting and the overly melodramatic music, *Fateful Findings* becomes a bad movie lover's dream.

Breen himself remains the main attraction in *Fateful Findings*, due to his robotic performance and complete lack of screen presence. Looking like the doughy, middle-aged love child of Don Henley and Keanu Reeves, Breen possesses all the raw sexuality of a melted crayon (the white one, not even one of the cool colors like Razzmatazz or Burnt Sienna). Nevertheless, attractive young women constantly throw themselves at him and rub their naked bodies against his pasty flesh. The film's supernatural elements and shocking (or, perhaps more accurately, "shocking") revelations make it clear that Breen fancies himself a visionary filmmaker on par with David Lynch or M. Night Shyamalan, but he lacks even a fraction of their talent. Nonetheless, he controlled nearly every aspect of the film; per the disclaimer that appears after the end credits, companies that contain "an 'N' or a 'B' in their name are fictitious. This work was actually done personally by 'Neil Breen.'" This applies to almost every single credit, from the sound editors (N J N Sound Assoc.) to the casting department (Casting N Entertainment, CNA), all the way down to craft services (Eats N' Eats Film Inc.). More than a triple threat, Breen is a one-man film crew (not unlike the far more talented Robert Rodriguez), and *Fateful Findings* is unquestionably a product of his insane imagination.

The film remains enjoyably absurd throughout, but at an hour and forty minutes, *Fateful Findings* fails to sustain its own delirious momentum, and it starts to drag during the somewhat interminable second act. Of course, the film picks up steam as it careens toward the completely bonkers finale, but some viewers will no doubt tire of *Fateful Findings* long before then. However, those who choose to stick things out until the end will find themselves rewarded with a captivatingly terrible film that builds to one of the most ridiculous and unbelievable climaxes in the history of cult cinema. In the end, *Fateful Findings* remains a masterpiece of trash cinema that gives *The Room* a run for its money, and therefore it absolutely deserves cult status.

See also *Manos: The Hands of Fate* (1966), *Dangerous Men* (2005), *Double Down* (2005), *The Room* (2005), *I Am Here...Now* (2009), *Birdemic: Shock and Terror* (2010), *Pass Thru* (2016).

SPOTLIGHT: NEIL BREEN (1958–)

Raised on the East Coast, director/writer/actor Neil Breen developed a love of cinema as a child and dreamed of someday making his own movies. Nevertheless, he opted to study architecture in college because he found the subject interesting. Upon graduating, Breen moved to California and became a licensed architect. He still harbored a passion for filmmaking, however, and in 2005 Breen used the money he made as an architect to finance his first film, *Double Down*, which played at film festivals across the United States and became a minor cult hit. Breen continued to work as an architect, and during this time he saved up more money, which he used to make his follow-up feature, *I Am Here... Now*. That film also gained a lot of attention on the festival circuit, and even earned a spot on *Paste* magazine's 2014 list of the 100 best B movies. In 2013, Breen released his third film, *Fateful Findings*, which introduced him to a wider audience and established his reputation as a cult auteur. He released his fourth film, *Pass-Thru*, in 2016.

FIGHT CLUB (1999)

Director: David Fincher
Screenplay: Jim Uhls
Cast: Brad Pitt (Tyler Durden), Edward Norton (the Narrator), Helena Bonham Carter (Marla Singer), Meat Loaf (Robert "Bob" Paulsen), Jared Leto (Angel Face)
Specs: 139 minutes; color
Genre: drama
Availability: DVD and Blu-ray (20th Century Fox)

Plot

An insomniac insurance investigator's life spirals out of control after he teams with a charismatic soap salesman to form an underground fight club. Things become even more complicated when an eccentric young woman enters the picture and ignites a ticking time bomb of primal male aggression.

Background

While working as a diesel fitter in Portland, Oregon, Chuck Pahalaniuk became involved in a physical altercation during a camping trip.[25] This incident served as the inspiration for Palahniuk's debut novel, *Fight Club*, which generated a lot of buzz in Hollywood, though most producers rejected it due to the excessive violence. The book eventually made its way to producers Ross Bell and Josh Donen, and they sent it to David Fincher, who loved it and wanted to direct the adaptation. Bell and Donen brought the project to Laura Ziskin at 20th Century Fox, and she optioned the rights to the novel for $10,000. She then hired Fincher to direct and asked Jim Uhls to write the screenplay.[26] While Uhls worked on the first draft, Fincher directed *The Game* for Polygram Filmed Entertainment, but afterward he returned to direct *Fight Club*.[27]

Fincher knew early on that he wanted Brad Pitt and Edward Norton as the leads,[28] but casting the female love interest proved difficult. At the time, Norton was dating Courtney Love, and she lobbied to play the part.[29] Meanwhile, the studio considered both Winona Ryder and Reese Witherspoon for the role.[30] Fincher objected to all these choices, largely because he wanted to cast against type and thought Helena Bonham Carter might be a good choice. The studio eventually relented, and *Fight Club* entered production in July of 1998.[31] Throughout the shoot, Fincher worked with stunt coordinators Mike Runyard, Damon Caro, and Jeff Imada to ensure the realism of the fight sequences.[32] Filming wrapped in December of 1998, and the studio announced plans to release *Fight Club* in July of 1999 but pushed the date back to August 6 after Fincher requested more time to conduct reshoots and complete postproduction.[33] Fox delayed the release yet again because they worried the film might get lost in the already overcrowded

Tyler Durden (Brad Pitt, center) and his followers watch a fight. *20th Century Fox / Photofest ©
20th Century Fox*

summer schedule[34] (though some speculated that the studio actually wanted to avoid associations with the Columbine High School massacre[35]).

Fight Club finally opened on October 15, 1999, and despite dismal reviews,[36] it reached the top spot at the box office during its opening weekend.[37] The film went on to earn just over $100 million worldwide,[38] but the studio still considered it a failure.[39] Over time, positive word of mouth caused *Fight Club*'s reputation to grow, and the film eventually emerged as a cult classic that routinely shows up on lists of the greatest films ever made. In 2004, *Fight Club* inspired a poorly received video game adaptation, and just over a decade later, Dark Horse Comics published the graphic novel *Fight Club 2*, which was written by Palahniuk and illustrated by Cameron Stewart.

Commentary

Fight Club assaults viewers with an exhilarating one-two punch of exquisite filmmaking and blistering social commentary. The film features slick direction, stunning cinematography, propulsive editing, convincing makeup, and pioneering visual effects. It also boasts a vibrant score by the Dust Brothers and knockout performances from Pitt, Norton, and Bonham-Carter. At the same time, *Fight Club* functions as a blistering takedown of American consumer culture and middle-class male ennui, and it serves up a scintillating deconstruction of violence and end-of-the-millennium anxieties (which have become even more pronounced during the first two decades of the twenty-first century). *Fight Club* struck a deep chord with Generation X audiences, and no wonder: even after nearly twenty years, the film is a visually inventive and endlessly entertaining thrill ride that offers a blunt (if somewhat ideologically muddled) exploration of existential aimlessness and male inadequacy.

Fincher's technical flair and visual wizardry injects everything on-screen with a visceral, kinetic intensity that reflects the lead characters' restless agitation. The film looks incredible and moves at a breathless clip thanks to Jeff Cronenweth's striking cinematography and James Haygood's dynamic editing. It also contains fantastic visual and makeup effects that remain impressive even now, and some brief but brutal fight sequences that are astonishing in their intensity. In addition, *Fight Club* benefits from Uhls's edgy screenplay, which features a startling climax that still holds the power to shock despite nearly two decades of pop cultural saturation. Of course, the film primarily serves as a showcase for the three leads, all of whom deliver unforgettable performances (particularly Pitt, who dominates the film). Overall, *Fight Club* stands as an engrossing, expertly directed film that features gorgeous visuals, tight writing, and engaging performances.

The film also includes a rich subtext regarding consumerism and masculinity. In some ways, *Fight Club* anticipated both the men's rights movement and the rise of Internet trolls, and Tyler Durden often feels like a reaction to the concept of the New Man. The film positions Tyler as the villain, but Pitt's magnetic, messianic performance makes it easy to see why so many young men misinterpret the film and consider the character a positive role model. Despite this confusion, *Fight Club* remains a darkly comic, deeply cynical cult classic that rewards multiple viewings.

See also *Pulp Fiction* (1994), *American Psycho* (2000), *Memento* (2000), *Donnie Darko* (2001).

FOXY BROWN (1974)

Director: Jack Hill
Screenplay: Jack Hill
Cast: Pam Grier (Foxy Brown), Antonio Fargas (Link Brown), Peter Brown (Steve Elias), Terry Carter (Michael Anderson), Kathryn Loder (Katherine Wall), Harry Holcombe (Judge Fenton), Sid Haig (Hays)
Specs: 92 minutes; color
Genre: action, crime, thriller
Availability: Blu-ray (Olive Films)

Plot

A sexy streetwise woman sets out to take down the mobsters who killed her boyfriend.

Background

In 1973, director Jack Hill scored a huge hit with *Coffy*, a blaxploitation film that made a star out of actress Pam Grier and generated a lot of money for American International Pictures (AIP).[40] The following year, AIP executive Larry Gordon asked Hill to develop a sequel titled *Burn, Coffy, Burn!*[41] However, tensions arose between Hill and the studio due to a misunderstanding: Hill attended a screening of a movie that AIP executives were keen to show, but he left midway through due to an illness.[42] The executives became offended and vowed never to work with the director again.[43] Nevertheless, AIP vice president Sam Arkoff invited Hill back to direct the sequel.[44] During the scriptwriting phase, the AIP sales department determined that sequels were not selling[45] and they decided to change the film's title to *Foxy Brown* late in the game, forcing Hill to rework the entire script in a short amount of time.[46]

The studio gave Hill a budget of $500,000,[47] the standard amount at the time for a "black" film. A large chunk of the money paid for Grier and Hill's salaries, which had increased due to their raised profiles, leaving little for the production itself.[48] Despite the limited time and resources, principal photography ran smoothly and *Foxy Brown* opened to mixed reviews in the spring of 1974. Some critics took issue with the hypersexualism, while others praised Grier's empowered performance.[49] The film grossed more than $2 million during its theatrical run,[50] making it less commercially successful than *Coffy*. However, *Foxy Brown* achieved greater cult status in the years after its release. Critics now recognize it as one of the most influential blaxploitation films ever made, and the title character continues to inspire strong female characters even today.

Commentary

Foxy Brown hinges almost entirely on Grier's iconic performance, which elevates the film from a sleazy but ultimately unremarkable exploitation curiosity

Foxy Brown (Pam Grier) seeks vengeance against the mobsters who killed her boyfriend. *American International Pictures (AIP) / Photofest © American International Pictures (AIP)*

to a genuine cult classic. As personified by Grier, Foxy becomes a force of nature, a bold and beautiful tornado that tears through both the film and the bad guys. In addition, Grier possesses more charisma and star power than most male action stars, particularly the bland hunks that routinely headline modern Hollywood blockbusters. Granted, Foxy endures several humiliations throughout the film (which features plenty of gratuitous nudity and an implied rape), but Grier makes sure the character remains dignified and capable no matter the situation. In her hands, Foxy emerges as the quintessential feminist ideal over the course of the film: equal parts smart, sexy, and tough. In the words of Antonio Fargas's Link, she is "a whole lotta woman."

Foxy Brown also benefits from Hill's decision to incorporate ideas about the black experience in the United States. By positioning Foxy and her friends as heroes battling a cartel of villainous white drug dealers and pimps, the film offers a harsh critique of American society and the power imbalances that maintain an unequal and altogether unfair status quo. As such, Foxy becomes a proud symbol of empowerment for women and other disenfranchised groups as she fights back against injustice and oppression. Of course, these inflammatory ideas often take a backseat to the violence and nudity, both of which remain the film's primary draws. Nonetheless, *Foxy Brown* still feels subversive even now because Hill managed to sneak some genuinely thoughtful ideological commentary into his trashy, exploitative potboiler.

While not necessarily a great film, *Foxy Brown* contains a fantastic lead performance, as well as some slyly provocative commentary on American society that still feels relevant today. As such, *Foxy Brown* remains every bit as sexy, brash, and competent as its leading lady.

See also *The Big Doll House* (1971), *Cleopatra Jones* (1973), *Coffy* (1973), *Friday Foster* (1975), *Sheba Baby* (1975), *Jackie Brown* (1997), *Proud Mary* (2018).

SPOTLIGHT: PAM GRIER (1949–)

In the late 1960s, Pam Grier moved to Los Angeles and took a job as a switchboard operator at American International Pictures. In 1971, she made her big screen debut in *The Big Doll House*. From there, Grier became the leading lady of the burgeoning blaxploitation movement by starring in films like *Coffy*, *Foxy Brown*, and *Sheba Baby*. While she worked steadily throughout the 1980s, Grier experienced a career resurgence in the late 1990s after she appeared in *Jackie Brown* for director Quentin Tarantino. This led to appearances in numerous films and television shows such as *The L Word* and *Smallville*. In 2010 she released a memoir titled *Foxy: My Life in Three Acts*.

SPOTLIGHT: JACK HILL (1933–)

While attending UCLA film school as a postgraduate student, Jack Hill befriended Francis Ford Coppola, and upon graduating they worked on several films together, including *The Terror* for producer Roger Corman. Hill made his directorial debut in 1966 with *Blood Bath* and followed this up with the films *Spider Baby or, The Maddest Story Ever Told* and *Pit Stop*. In the 1970s, Hill forged a professional partnership with actress Pam Grier, and together they made numerous exploitation films that went on to become cult classics, including *The Big Doll House*, *The Big Bird Cage*, *Coffy*, and *Foxy Brown*. His films have influenced numerous other directors, including Quentin Tarantino and Rob Zombie.

FREAKS (1932)

Director: Tod Browning
Screenplay: Willis Goldbeck, Leon Gordon
Cast: Wallace Ford (Phroso), Leila Hyams (Venua), Olga Baclanova (Cleopatra), Harry Earles (Hans), Daisy Earles (Frieda), Henry Victor (Hercules)
Specs: 64 minutes; black and white
Genre: drama, horror
Availability: DVD (Warner Bros.)

Plot

A trapeze artist and a circus strong man conspire to steal a sideshow performer's fortune, but they soon run afoul of his vengeful friends.

Background

In 1931, Universal Pictures scored a smash hit with its adaptation of *Franken-stein*, prompting other studios to produce their own horror movies.[51] Over at Metro-Goldwyn-Mayer (MGM), a young executive by the name of Irving Thalberg ordered scriptwriter Willis Goldbeck to come up with the most frightening horror film ever made.[52] Drawing inspiration from Clarence Aaron Robbins's short story "Spurs," Goldbeck teamed with Leon Gordon to write *Freaks*, a terrifying story set in a carnival sideshow.[53] Despite disliking the script, Thalberg decided to produce the picture, and he hired Browning to direct based on their previous collaboration on the acclaimed melodrama *The Unholy Three*.[54] Browning, who spent several years working with sideshow performers, leapt at the chance to direct *Freaks* for MGM.[55]

Prior to production, Thalberg ordered screenwriter Edgar Allan Woolf and comedian Al Boasberg to punch up the dialogue and add some comic relief to the script.[56] Thalberg then hired frequent Browning collaborator Merritt Gerstad to handle the film's cinematography. Meanwhile, Browning assembled his cast starting with Harry and Daisy Earles, a pair of siblings who performed in sideshows throughout the United States. Browning then looked at thousands of photographs of sideshow performers to choose the rest of the title characters.[57] From there, he turned his attention to casting the so-called normal characters. He initially wanted Myrna Loy as the wicked seductress Cleopatra, but Russian-born actress Olga Baclanova ultimately landed the role.[58] Similarly, he considered casting Jean Harlow

The sideshow performers celebrate the wedding of Hans (Harry Earles, not pictured) and Cleopatra (Olga Baclanova, not pictured). *MGM / Photofest © MGM*

as Venus, but instead went with Leila Hyams,[59] who had appeared in Browning's first sound film, *The Thirteenth Chair*. Henry Victor and Wallace Ford rounded out the ensemble as the villainous Hercules and heroic Phroso respectively. With the cast in place and rewrites complete, filming began on November 9, 1931.[60]

Freaks caused quite a stir on the MGM lot, and studio personnel overwhelmingly objected to the presence of the sideshow performers.[61] At one point, executive president Louis B. Mayer tried to shut down the production, but Thalberg convinced him to back off.[62] Despite all this, the production ran smoothly, and principal photography wrapped in late December of 1931. Two weeks later, Thalberg showed a ninety-minute cut of the film to a preview audience that fled the theater in disgust, prompting the producer to cut nearly thirty minutes from the film and tack on a newly shot happy and less violent ending.[63] This version of *Freaks* opened in Los Angeles on February 10, 1932, only to fail at the box office. It also received scathing reviews, and MGM pulled the film from release soon after. The United Kingdom banned the film outright.[64] *Freaks* effectively killed Browning's career,[65] but the film itself gained new life in the 1960s as the counterculture enthusiastically embraced *Freaks*, which later became a massive success on the midnight movie circuit.[66] These days, Browning's masterpiece enjoys a reputation as a cult classic, as well as one of the finest horror films ever made.

Commentary

More than eighty years on, *Freaks* retains its power to provoke and unsettle. The film contains lots of exploitative elements that feel icky and unnerving even now, particularly when the camera lingers on the sideshow performers solely to showcase their various deformities (which is appropriate given the setting, but still disturbing, especially when viewed from the comfort of the more "enlightened" twenty-first century). As such, sensitive viewers may find *Freaks* difficult to watch. Yet the film portrays the title characters with dignity, positioning them as tragically heroic figures while condemning those who cannot accept their differences. Thus, while the film repeatedly threatens to tip over into pure exploitation, *Freaks* nevertheless emerges as a complex and empathetic portrait of individuals who challenge societal standards of normality.

In addition, *Freaks* contains a great deal of humor (Phroso's reaction to the bearded lady's newborn baby is priceless), and viewers able to look past the film's more problematic elements will find an amusing film that sometimes feels more like a comedy than a straight-up horror film. Yet *Freaks* remains rather terrifying throughout, and it boasts several iconic moments guaranteed to leave the viewer's skin crawling long after the end credits role. These include the infamous wedding feast ("We accept you, one of us! Gooble gobble!"); the title characters slowly advancing on the villainous Cleopatra in the rain; and the shocking reveal of Cleopatra's fate. The film establishes a sense of dread early on by exposing the darkness that lies behind the colorful facade of the circus, first glimpsed when a visibly distraught Venus ends her relationship with Hercules. From there, Browning ratchets up the tension until it explodes during the highly unsettling climax. *Freaks* features lots of laughs, but it mainly takes audiences to some ugly places.

Along with the somewhat troubling elements already described, *Freaks* also suffers from some less-than-stellar performances (particularly from the title characters, none of whom were professional actors at the time), and the narrative often feels rushed, especially toward the end (likely due to studio meddling). Nevertheless, the film still holds the power to terrify and delight even after more than eight decades, and it accomplishes this while tackling difficult subject matter in a funny and sympathetic fashion.

See also *She Freak* (1967); *The Mutations*, also known as *The Freakmaker* (1974); *Freaked* (1993).

FRIDAY (1995)

Director: F. Gary Gray
Screenplay: Ice Cube, DJ Pooh
Cast: Ice Cube (Craig Jones), Chris Tucker (Smokey), Nia Long (Debbie), Tommy "Tiny" Lister (Deebo), John Witherspoon (Mr. Jones), Anna Maria Horsford (Mrs. Jones), Regina King (Dana Jones), DJ Pooh (Red)
Specs: 91 minutes; color
Genre: comedy
Availability: DVD and Blu-ray (Warner Bros.)

Plot

Two friends just want to hang out and smoke weed, but instead must deal with crackheads, sexual predators, psychopathic drug dealers, drive-by shootings, and the neighborhood bully.

Background

Ice Cube rose to prominence as a rapper during the late 1980s and early 1990s, first with Los Angeles gangsta rap outfit N.W.A. and then later as a solo artist. In 1991, Cube transitioned to acting when he landed a role in director John Singleton's groundbreaking movie *Boyz n the Hood*.[67] From there, Cube appeared in several other films that depicted the black experience as violent and depressing. Looking to counteract these negative depictions, Cube decided to make a semi-autobiographical movie that portrayed the lighter side of life in the ghetto.[68] He teamed with rapper/producer DJ Pooh to write the script,[69] and the duo planned to play the lead characters themselves.[70] Cube then enlisted director F. Gary Gray, who previously oversaw the videos for Cube's "It Was a Good Day" and "Natural Born Killaz."[71] From there, they set up a production deal with New Line Cinema, which offered to provide a budget of $3.5 million, but not with Pooh playing Smokey.[72] Cube and Pooh agreed that up-and-coming comic Chris Tucker should play Smokey,[73] and *Friday* entered production in August of 1994.

New Line gave Gray just twenty days to complete the film,[74] and the production moved at an exhausting pace. Like Cube, Gray also hailed from the South Central

Craig (Ice Cube, left) and Smokey (Chris Tucker) deal with increasingly bizarre shenanigans on their day off. *New Line Cinema / Photofest ©New Line Cinema*

area, and he chose to shoot the film in his old neighborhood (his childhood home and several of his friend's houses even appear on-screen).[75] Despite the rushed shooting schedule, the atmosphere on set remained loose throughout filming, and the actors improvised much of the dialogue. After completing principal photography, Gray worked with editor John Carter to complete the film. However, Cube and Tucker found the first cut too long,[76] so Gray trimmed it down to a more manageable ninety-one-minute run time. Test audiences loved this version of the film, and New Line believed they had a massive hit on their hands.[77] Unfortunately, the film failed to live up to the studio's lofty expectations.

Friday opened on April 28, 1995, and earned over $6 million during its opening weekend.[78] It received mostly positive reviews from critics and grossed over $27 million before ending its theatrical run,[79] but New Line still considered the film a flop.[80] The studio dumped the film on home video soon after it left theaters, at which point it emerged as a substantial cult hit that resonated with a wide audience due to its wacky characters, outrageous situations, and insanely quotable dialogue (for instance, the film introduced the term "Bye, Felisha!" into the cultural lexicon).[81] In the years after its release, *Friday* spawned two sequels and a short-lived animated series, and rumors of a fourth installment tentatively called *Last Friday* have swirled around Hollywood for years.[82] Regardless of whether that film ever materializes, the original *Friday* remains a cult classic that continues to impact popular culture long after its initial release.

Commentary

Infantile humor and a carefree attitude turn *Friday* into the hysterically funny peak of stoner comedy. The film features crude direction and a wildly inconsistent tone, but possesses a shaggy charm and an infectious energy that smooth over the occasional rough spots. *Friday* also contains plenty of dazzlingly funny dialogue ("If I catch him, I'm gonna beat him like I was his dad!"), not to mention some fantastic comedic performances, particularly from Tucker, who steals the show as impish drug dealer Smokey. The film offers up loads of inspired inanity (like Craig's comically nonsensical pot-induced hallucinations) and humorous running gags (such as the *Jaws*-like music that pops up whenever neighborhood bully Deebo rides by on his bike). It also boasts a great cast starting with Cube as Craig Jones, a hapless young man who finds himself in a variety of increasingly outrageous situations. John Witherspoon gets some of the film's biggest laughs as Craig's dad, while Anna Maria Horsford makes the most of her small role as Craig's mom. *Friday* also features memorable appearances from the likes of Bernie Mac, Tony Cox, and Tiny Lister Jr. However, Tucker owns the film, delivering a breakout performance that displays all the star power and charisma that would briefly turn him into one of the highest-paid actors in Hollywood.

At the same time, the film is aggressively offensive, and it includes a great deal of sexist jokes and vulgar humor. *Friday* mines a lot of its comedy from ethnic stereotypes (the Korean grocer who pops up briefly is particularly cringe-worthy) and takes a somewhat misogynistic attitude toward women, particularly those who fail to conform to conventional beauty standards (the scene in which Craig and his mom poke fun at an overweight woman is more than a bit uncomfortable). The film also suffers from somewhat flat direction and an uneven tone; *Friday* struggles to balance comedy with earnest drama, and it sometimes recalls cheesy television shows like *The Fresh Prince of Bel Air*. The last fifteen minutes in particular feel like a "very special episode" of any given UPN (United Paramount Network) sitcom as the film suddenly turns into a thoughtful meditation on gun violence and the dangers of life in the hood. Nonetheless, *Friday* succeeds thanks to a surplus of spirited hijinks and outrageously funny dialogue. It also offers an amusing but valuable peek into the street life of South Central, Los Angeles, that serves as a nice antidote to the seemingly endless parade of tragic crime stories and drug narratives set there.

See also *Half-Baked* (1998), *Pootie Tang* (2001), *Harold and Kumar Go to White Castle* (2004), *Pineapple Express* (2008).

G

GALAXY QUEST (1999)

Director: Dean Parisot
Screenplay: David Howard, Robert Gordon
Cast: Tim Allen (Jason Nesmith), Sigourney Weaver (Gwen DeMarco), Alan Rickman (Alexander Dane), Tony Shaloub (Fred Kwan), Sam Rockwell (Guy Fleegman), Daryl Mitchell (Tommy Webber), Enrico Colantoni (Mathesar), Patrick Breen (Quellek), Missi Pyle (Laliari), Jed Rees (Teb), Justin Long (Brandon)
Specs: 102 minutes; color
Genre: adventure, comedy, science fiction
Availability: DVD and Blu-ray (Warner Bros.)

Plot

The down-and-out cast members of a cheesy science fiction series inadvertently become embroiled in the conflict between a group of naive aliens and an evil intergalactic warlord.

Background

In 1999, producer Mark Johnson learned about David Howard's somewhat lackluster screenplay *Captain Starshine*, in which aliens mistakenly recruit a troupe of actors to battle a tyrannical interstellar warlord.[1] Johnson felt the central idea had merit, and he hired screenwriter Robert Gordon to rewrite the script from scratch.[2] Gordon channeled his love of the original *Star Trek* during the writing phase,[3] and after a few months he delivered a draft to Johnson, who took it to Walter Parkes at Dreamworks Pictures. Parkes greenlit the film based on the first draft and hired Harold Ramis to direct.[4] Ramis worked closely with Gordon to develop the script, but reportedly abandoned the project when he learned that the studio wanted Tim Allen to star.[5] At that point, Johnson convinced the studio to let Dean Parisot direct the film, now titled *Galaxy Quest*. Parisot had previously directed *Home Fries* for Johnson, and he was a huge *Star Trek* fan whose vision for the film aligned closely with Gordon's own ideas; rather than a satire of *Star Trek*, they wanted to make a great episode of the show.[6]

Jason Nesmith (Tim Allen, second from left) and the crew of the NSEA *Protector* prepare to jump into action. *Dreamworks / Photofest © DreamWorks*

Filming commenced on April 19, 1999, and throughout production, Allen repeatedly played jokes on his fellow actors.[7] Otherwise, the shoot ran smoothly, mostly because Dreamworks executives were preoccupied with making *Gladiator* and therefore left Parisot and his team to their own devices.[8] Principal photography wrapped on August 13, 1999, and *Galaxy Quest* opened in the United States on Christmas Day of that year. Despite being saddled with a feeble marketing campaign,[9] which included an early film marketing website and mockumentary,[10] *Galaxy Quest* emerged as a modest hit, grossing just over $90 million worldwide against an estimated $45 million budget.[11] It has since become recognized as a beloved cult favorite, and fans continue to clamor for an official sequel.[12] In 2013, during the annual Creation *Star Trek* convention in Las Vegas, fans voted *Galaxy Quest* the seventh best *Trek* movie, ahead of *Star Trek*: *The Motion Picture*, *Star Trek Into Darkness*, and three of the four *Next Generation* movies.[13]

Commentary

Galaxy Quest is a hilarious comedy that features impressive action, top-notch special effects, and legitimately touching dramatic moments. The film pokes fun at *Star Trek* and its fans, but even those unfamiliar with the show will find something to love in the delightfully silly humor and uproariously funny performances. *Galaxy Quest* contains several laugh-out-loud moments that require no direct knowledge of *Trek* or its many spin-offs (such as Guy Fleegman's disgusted reaction to Fred Kwan's make-out session with Thermian crewmember Laliari, a scene played to comic perfection by Sam Rockwell, Tony Shaloub, and Missy Pyle, respectively). Of course, *Galaxy Quest* also features plenty of outrageous gags designed to appeal to longtime *Trek* fans, and the whole thing becomes richer and funnier if viewers have at least a passing familiarity with the franchise.

The film also boasts superb special effects, and a handful of thrilling action sequences (the climactic battle is particularly exhilarating). Most importantly, though, *Galaxy Quest* contains great performances from the game cast, all of whom nail both the comedy and the drama with equal aplomb. Allen stands out as egotistical leading man Jason Nesmith, displaying a comedic range and remarkable sensitivity that extend far beyond the limits of his carefully crafted stand-up persona. He also brings a beefy sexuality to the character as he runs around shirtless while battling rock monsters. Meanwhile, Weaver draws on her history as a sci-fi icon and her reputation as a symbol of feminism to comment on the sexism and misogyny that afflict science fiction and its fandom today. The rest of the cast deliver stirring comedic performances (most notably Rickman as put-upon Shakespearean-trained actor Alexander Dane), and every single performer gets a moment to shine.

Galaxy Quest succeeds because the creators clearly have a lot of love for *Trek*, and they treat it and the subject of fandom with respect (as evidenced by the fact that Justin Long's nerdy fanboy character ultimately helps the crew of the NSEA *Protector* save the day). As such, *Galaxy Quest* feels like an affectionate roasting of *Trek* and its devotees rather than mean-spirited takedown, and the slick action, stellar effects, and outstanding comic performances ensure that the film will appeal to both fans and nonfans alike.

See also *Dark Star* (1974), *¡Three Amigos!* (1986), *Spaceballs* (1987), *Earth Girls Are Easy* (1988), *Killer Klowns from Outer Space* (1988), *Mars Attacks* (1996), *A Bug's Life* (1998).

GANJA & HESS (1973)

Director: Bill Gunn
Screenplay: Bill Gunn
Cast: Duane Jones (Dr. Hess Green), Marlene Clark (Ganja Meda), Bill Gunn (George Meda), Sam L. Waymon (Rev. Luther Williams), Leonard Jackson (Archie)
Specs: 110 minutes; color
Genre: drama, fantasy, horror
Availability: DVD and Blu-ray (Kino Lorber Films)

Plot

An ancient dagger turns two lovers into immortal vampires with an insatiable thirst for blood.

Background

In 1970, noted African American playwright and stage director Bill Gunn directed *Stop*, a film that offered an uncompromising look at homosexual and inter-

Dr. Hess Green (Duane Jones, left) teaches Ganja (Marlene Clark) how to survive following her transformation into an immortal vampire. *Kelly/Jordan Ent. / Photofest © Kelly/Jordan Enterprises*

racial relationships.[14] Unfortunately, Warner Bros. shelved *Stop* after it received an X rating from the Motion Picture Association of America.[15] Two years later executives at independent production company Kelly-Jordan Enterprises asked Gunn to direct a "black vampire" movie, and the director took the job despite some reservations.[16] He received a $350,000 budget and complete creative freedom from the studio, so he set off to make *Ganja & Hess*, a film in which vampirism functioned as an allegory for addiction.[17] Gunn cast Duane Jones (star of *Night of the Living Dead*) and Marlene Clark as the leads, and himself as a minor yet significant character.

Ganja & Hess opened on April 20, 1973, and earned favorable reviews.[18] Nevertheless, a poor showing at the box office prompted Kelly-Jordan to pull *Ganja & Hess* from theaters and sell it to Heritage Enterprises,[19] a distribution company that released a rescored and recut version of the film under the title *Blood Couple*.[20] In 1975, Goldstone Films released this cut as *Double Possession*.[21] Years later, this version of the film circulated on VHS under numerous different titles.[22] Meanwhile, Gunn's original cut of *Ganja & Hess* languished in relative obscurity until the Museum of Modern Art in Manhattan acquired a print and ran frequent screenings.[23] These days, *Ganja & Hess* is recognized as a landmark of independent black cinema and a classic of experimental horror, and in 2014 Spike Lee remade it as *Da Sweet Blood of Jesus*.

Commentary

Ganja & Hess offers viewers an intoxicating blend of raw but assured filmmaking, gripping performances, and a deep thematic undercurrent. The narrative unfolds in an elliptical fashion, turning an otherwise straightforward vampire story into something far more fascinating and engrossing. *Ganja & Hess* also deals with issues of African spirituality and black sexuality, providing valuable insight into the black experience in America, which has remained relatively unchanged since 1973. The film accomplishes this by equating vampirism to drug addiction and using both as allegories for slavery. These elements ensure that *Ganja & Hess* still feels fresh and vital even after more than four decades, particularly given the ongoing racial conflicts that continue to engulf the United States in the twenty-first century.

In addition to the metaphorical qualities already listed, Gunn directs *Ganja & Hess* with confidence, and he presents several breathtakingly beautiful compositions throughout (the shot of the Myrthian queen striding through a field while wearing a feathered headdress is particularly striking). The film also features hypnotic editing courtesy of Victor Kanefsky, whose clever cutting renders everything on-screen mesmerizing and dreamlike, and establishes a languorous pace that is occasionally punctuated with bursts of startling violence. Meanwhile, the unsettling soundtrack consists of a kaleidoscopic mix of asynchronous dialogue, rhythmic African chanting, and disconcerting noises. The seams sometimes show due to the extremely low budget, but the elegant filmmaking gives *Ganja & Hess* a sense of scope and significance that allow it to transcend its somewhat mercenary origins.

The lead actors both deliver daring performances that often feel improvisational and intimately confessional. As Ganja, Clark dominates the film with her commanding presence, and she turns her character into a strong, confident woman who nevertheless possesses a vulnerable side. Meanwhile, Jones brings a quiet intensity to his role as Dr. Hess Green, using his facial expressions and body language to instill the character with a sense of terse dignity and icy refinement. Clark and Jones also make for extremely attractive leads, and they infuse the film with a great deal of sex appeal. *Ganja & Hess* features great filmmaking and a rich subtext, but it also functions as a showcase for the talents of its two leads, who deliver powerful performances that elevate the material even further beyond its exploitative origins.

Sadly, *Ganja & Hess* drags a bit in the third act, and it could stand to lose about twenty minutes from the total run time. Yet these are minor complaints, especially when measured against the film's considerable strengths. *Ganja & Hess* offers viewers an enthralling, inventive tale of vampirism that centers on two intriguing characters brought to vivid life by talented, good-looking performers. At the same time, the film addresses thorny issues like drug addiction, slavery, race, gender, and spirituality, all of which means that *Ganja & Hess* still feels relevant and original even now.

See also *Blacula* (1972), *Vampire in Brooklyn* (1995), *Da Sweet Blood of Jesus* (2014).

GHOST WORLD (2001)

Director: Terry Zwigoff
Screenplay: Daniel Clowes, Terry Zwigoff
Cast: Thora Birch (Enid Coleslaw), Scarlett Johansson (Rebecca), Steve Buscemi (Seymour), Brad Renfro (Josh), Illeana Douglas (Roberta Allsworth), Bob Balaban (Enid's Dad), Teri Garr (Maxine)
Specs: 111 minutes; color
Genre: comedy, drama
Availability: DVD and Blu-ray (The Criterion Collection)

Plot

After graduating high school, two misfit teenage girls find their friendship tested when one of them sets out to help a lonely record collector find love.

Background

Director Terry Zwigoff made a name for himself in 1994 with the acclaimed documentary *Crumb*. For his follow-up film, he decided to heed his wife's advice and develop an adaptation of Daniel Clowes's graphic novel *Ghost World*.[24] Zwigoff identified with lead character Enid Coleslaw (an anagram of the creator's own name) because he also felt like an outsider during his high school years.[25] He approached Clowes about adapting the comic for the screen, and they wound up writing the screenplay together.[26] After consulting with an acting coach to learn how to direct actors, Zwigoff set about assembling his cast.

Producers initially wanted Christina Ricci as Enid, but Zwigoff cast former child star Thora Birch (who bore an uncanny resemblance to the character from the comic book) instead.[27] From there, Steve Buscemi agreed to play the pivotal role of Seymour, while sixteen-year-old Scarlett Johansson rounded out the central trio and delivered a breakout performance as Enid's best friend, Rebecca.[28] Throughout production, Zwigoff worked closely with Clowes to ensure that the film captured the essence of the source material.[29] For instance, he asked cinematographer Alfonso Beato to slightly oversaturate the image to replicate the distinct look and feel of the comic.[30] Nevertheless, Zwigoff managed to put his own stamp on the film using techniques he learned while directing documentaries, including long, leisurely shots that lingered on one image.[31]

Ghost World premiered at the Seattle International Film Festival on June 16, 2001,[32] and it entered wide release soon after on September 21, 2001. Critics praised the film for its thoughtful, believable portrayal of teen angst.[33] *Ghost World* also won several awards and became the first film based on a graphic novel or comic book to earn an Oscar nomination for Best Adapted Screenplay.[34] Sadly, the film failed to catch on with general audiences, and it grossed less than $9 million against a $7 million budget.[35] Nevertheless, *Ghost World* endures as a beloved cult classic and is now widely considered one of the finest comic book adaptations ever made.

Rebecca (Scarlett Johansson, left) and Enid (Thora Birch) spy on Seymour (Steve Buscemi, not pictured). *United Artists / Photofest © United Artists*

Commentary

Ghost World opens with a blast of infectious energy (the main character dances around her room to the energetic song "Jaan Pehechan Ho" from the Hindi film *Gumnaam*), and it spends the rest of its nearly two-hour run time balancing lots of laughs with a poignant story about growing up. It also presents an unconventional and bittersweet romance between two eccentric individuals and offers up a frank exploration of the anxiety that comes with facing an uncertain future. The film serves as a platform for the gifted performers, particularly Birch, who delivers a wonderfully deadpan performance as Enid and turns the character into a dryly sarcastic force of chaos who moves through the world making wry observations about everyone and everything with a perpetual smirk plastered on her face. *Ghost World* also functions as a showcase for Zwigoff's laidback but meticulous direction, which allows the film to unfold at a measured pace and features several charmingly colorful compositions throughout. In fact, despite a handful of troubling elements that have aged somewhat poorly, *Ghost World* remains an irreverent comedy that contains excellent performances, fine direction, and several genuinely affecting moments.

As mentioned, Birch emerges as the film's greatest strength, and she plays Enid as a complex young woman who longs to forge meaningful relationships but ends up alienating everyone as she struggles to stand out from the world around her. She seems profoundly lonely rather than mean-spirited, and Birch's nuanced performance ensures that Enid remains likable even when acting like a selfish and self-absorbed teenager. Meanwhile, Johansson displays a great deal of charisma and star power as Rebecca, while Buscemi turns in a delightfully cranky performance as Seymour, a dejected record collector who hates the world almost as much as he hates himself. In addition, Zwigoff's adroit direction keeps things light and fun throughout, and therefore *Ghost World* remains amusing and enjoyable even during the bleaker moments (such as Enid sobbing uncontrollably after she alienates her only friends and learns that she blew her best shot at getting in to art school). Of course, the film contains some potentially offensive elements, such as the subplot about the secret history of the Cook's Chicken restaurant chain or the liberal use of the word *retard*, but cult film fans who love sardonic humor, great acting, and clever direction will want to check out *Ghost World* as soon as possible.

See also *Crumb* (1994), *Romy and Michele's High School Reunion* (1997), *American Splendor* (2003).

SPOTLIGHT: TERRY ZWIGOFF (1949–)

Born in Appleton, Wisconsin, and raised in Chicago, Illinois, Terry Zwigoff relocated to San Francisco in the 1970s and joined a ragtime band fronted by unconventional underground artist Robert Crumb. Years later, Zwigoff transitioned into directing documentaries, starting in 1985 with *Louie Bluie*, an hour-long film about the little-known musician and artist Howard Armstrong. Zwigoff spent the next nine years working on *Crumb*, an offbeat documentary about Crumb and his brothers that won numerous awards and earned a great deal of critical acclaim. Zwigoff then transitioned into directing fiction films with *Ghost World*, a bittersweet comedy based on the comic book by Daniel Clowes (who also cowrote the film), which received extensive critical praise and an Academy Award nomination for Best Adapted Screenplay. Zwigoff followed this up with *Bad Santa*, a vulgar comedy that became his biggest commercial success when it grossed nearly $80 million worldwide. Unfortunately, his next film, *Art School Confidential*, fared less well, grossing just over $3 million worldwide and receiving mostly negative reviews from critics. While his cinematic career seems to have stalled, Zwigoff himself has developed a devoted cult audience and his films remain beloved to this day.

GREMLINS 2: THE NEW BATCH (1990)

Director: Joe Dante
Screenplay: Charles S. Haas
Cast: Zach Galligan (Billy Peltzer), Phoebe Cates (Kate Beringer), John Glover (Daniel Clamp), Robert Prosky (Grandpa Fred), Robert Picardo (Forster), Christopher Lee (Doctor Catheter), Haviland Morris (Marla Bloodstone), Dick Miller (Murray Futterman), Jackie Joseph (Sheila Futterman), Howie Mandel (Gizmo—voice), Tony Randall (Brain Gremlin—voice)
Specs: 106 minutes; color
Genre: comedy, fantasy, horror
Availability: DVD and Blu-ray (Warner Bros.)

Plot

The mischievous Gremlins return to run amok in a technologically advanced New York office building owned by an eccentric billionaire.

Background

In 1984, director Joe Dante scored a surprise hit with *Gremlins*, a Christmas-themed horror comedy produced by Steven Spielberg's Amblin Entertainment and released through Warner Bros. Pictures. The studio wanted to make a sequel, but Dante decided to move on to other projects.[36] Warner Bros. began developing the film without him, but when they failed to come up with any viable ideas, studio executives asked Dante to return to the property.[37] He said he would only come back if the studio granted him full creative freedom and gave him a bigger budget.[38] Warner Bros agreed to these conditions, and *Gremlins 2: The New Batch* entered production on May 26, 1989,[39] almost five years after the first film opened in theaters.

Dante shot *Gremlins 2* on location in and around New York City. Several actors from the first film returned to reprise their roles, including Zach Galligan, Phoebe Cates, Dick Miller, and Jackie Joseph. Dante also added several new cast members to the mix, including John Glover, Robert Picardo, and veteran character actor Christopher Lee. Dante also secured the services of Oscar-winning visual effects artist Rick Baker and tasked him with making a more diverse batch of creatures than those that appeared in the first film.[40] After roughly six months of shooting, the production wrapped in November of 1989,[41] and the finished film clawed its way into theaters on June 15, 1990.[42]

Gremlins 2 opened to mixed reviews and grossed just over $41 million at the box office, meaning that it failed to cover its $50 million budget.[43] Over the years, *Gremlins 2* developed a cult following, and some fans even prefer it to the original.[44] In 2015, Warner Bros. announced plans to reboot the *Gremlins* franchise,[45] potentially with another sequel.[46]

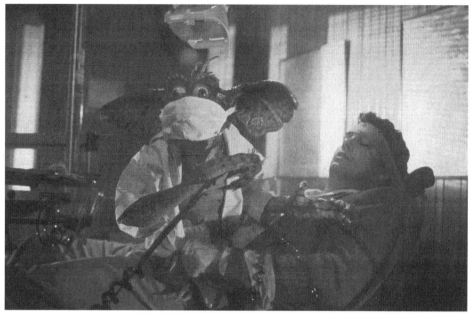

Billy Peltzer (Zach Galligan) struggles to escape the clutches of a crazed gremlin. *Warner Bros. / Photofest © Warner Bros.*

Commentary

Often referred to as a live-action cartoon (it even opens with a Chuck Jones–directed Looney Tunes short featuring Bugs Bunny and Daffy Duck), *Gremlins 2* doubles down on the first film's insanity and takes viewers on a madcap funhouse ride that contains lots of inventive silliness and absurdist comedy. This time out, Dante abandons the Capraesque sincerity of the original *Gremlins*, and instead unleashes a torrent of zany gags and sly references to the horror and sci-fi films he loved as a kid (as well as some contemporary films like Tim Burton's *Batman*). The jokes fly fast and furious, and while the deranged comedy occasionally proves overbearing, *Gremlins 2* nevertheless remains a gloriously silly riff on the original *Gremlins* and a jubilant celebration of pop culture.

The film also features fantastic effects, employing a combination of puppetry and animation to bring the mischievous monsters to life, and it offers up several imaginative takes on the title creatures, including a Bat Gremlin, a Spider Gremlin, and a somewhat horrifying Vegetable Gremlin. *Gremlins 2* has also gained a renewed relevance in recent years thanks to John Glover's performance as a gleefully clueless Donald Trump surrogate named Daniel Clamp, who comes off as overbearing and goofy. The character contains elements of Ted Turner (Daniel owns a cable network), but his marketing mind-set and ingratiating personality clearly align with Trump's public persona (the character becomes even more relevant given the numerous technical glitches that afflict Clamp Tower and reveal the owner as somewhat incompetent). Ultimately, *Gremlins 2* balances outrageously nonsensical humor with some truly gross imagery, and it stands as one of the most exhilaratingly demented cult films ever made.

See also *Ghoulies* (1984), *Gremlins* (1984), *Critters* (1986), *Munchies* (1987), *Hobgoblins* (1988).

SPOTLIGHT: JOE DANTE (1946–)

After graduating from the Philadelphia College of Art in the late 1960s, Joe Dante briefly worked as a film critic before landing a gig editing trailers for Roger Corman's New World Pictures. In 1976, Dante made his directorial debut with *Hollywood Boulevard*, an ultra-low-budget satire of the movie industry. Dante next directed *Piranha*, a *Jaws* rip-off that became a modest hit with critics and audiences. In 1980, Dante directed *The Howling*, a film that earned him a great deal of critical and commercial attention. Afterward, Steven Spielberg tapped Dante to direct *Gremlins*, which went on to become a surprise success. From there, Dante directed lively and inventive genre pictures like *Explorers*, *Innerspace*, *The Burbs*, *Gremlins 2: The New Batch*, and *Matinee*. He also worked in television, directing episodes of *Police Squad*, *Amazing Stories*, *The Twilight Zone*, *Tales from the Crypt*, and *CSI: NY*. In 2016, Dante unveiled *The Man with Kaleidoscope Eyes*, a long-gestating (and still unmade) biopic about the making of Corman's LSD movie *The Trip*.

GREY GARDENS (1976)

Director: Albert Maysles, David Maysles, Muffy Meyer, Ellen Hovde
Cast: Edith "Big Edie" Bouvier Beale, Edith "Little Edie" Bouvier Beale, Brooks Hyers, Norman Vincent Peale
Specs: 94 minutes; color
Genre: documentary, comedy, drama
Availability: DVD and Blu-ray (The Criterion Collection)

Plot

This compelling documentary focuses on Edith "Big Edie" Bouvier Beale and her daughter "Little Edie," two eccentric aging socialites who live together in a dilapidated East Hampton mansion.

Background

Throughout the late 1960s and early 1970s, brothers David and Albert Maysles directed trailblazing documentaries like *Salesman* and *Gimme Shelter*.[47] Their work eventually caught the attention of Jacqueline Kennedy Onassis and her sister Lee Radziwill, who asked the Maysleses to make a film about the Bouvier family.[48]

The brothers took the job, but they soon realized that Jackie and Lee's delightfully eccentric aunt, Edith "Big Edie" Bouvier Beale, and fifty-eight-year-old cousin, "Little Edie," were far more interesting subjects.[49] Therefore, the Maysleses scrapped the Bouvier documentary and offered the Beales $10,000 and 20 percent of the profits to appear on camera.[50] Desperate for money and hungry for attention, the two women agreed, and in September of 1973 the Maysles brothers brought nearly $50,000 worth of film and equipment into the Beales' collapsing East Hampton mansion known as Grey Gardens.[51]

With the help of their codirectors Ellen Hovde and Muffie Meyer, the Maysleses spent the next six weeks following Big Edie and Little Edie around the decrepit house cluttered with souvenirs of their past glories.[52] During the shoot, the Maysleses, Hovde, and Meyer took to wearing flea collars around their ankles to keep the bugs away.[53] By the time filming wrapped, the Maysleses had collected over sixty hours of footage, which Hovde, Meyer, and Susan Froemke spent six months editing into a coherent narrative.[54] On September 21, 1975, the Maysles brothers showed the finished film to the Beales at a private screening, and the two women loved what they saw.[55] The film later played at the 1975 New York Film Festival under the title *Grey Gardens*, and on February 20, 1976, it began its theatrical run at the Paris Theater in Manhattan.[56]

Grey Gardens received mixed reviews from critics, with some accusing the Maysleses of exploiting the Beales (though Little Edie publicly refuted such claims).[57] The film went on to become a minor box office hit at art house theaters around the country. Since that time, *Grey Gardens* has earned a reputation as a cult classic, particularly among gay men, who embraced the film due to Little Edie's campy attitude and outlandish fashion sense.[58]

Big Edie (left) and Little Edie relax during a quiet moment at Grey Gardens. *Portrait Releasing / Photofest © Portrait Releasing Inc.*

Commentary

Grey Gardens is a tragicomic but engrossing portrait of two deeply eccentric individuals with outsize personalities, and it offers an intimate look at a pair of slightly damaged women who seem to thrive on attention and conflict. At times the film threatens to tip over into voyeurism, but the Maysleses clearly care about their subjects and show the proper amount of respect toward the Beales throughout. As such, *Grey Gardens* feels lighthearted and fun (if somewhat bittersweet and melancholy) rather than exploitative or sleazy. This is largely due to the Beales themselves, two endlessly fascinating women who eagerly play to the camera in every scene. Little Edie especially enjoys being on camera, and she delights in showing off her unusual fashion sense while prancing around the crumbling mansion like a majorette and flirting with David (who remains entirely off-screen aside from one brief shot of him reflected in a mirror). Big Edie also takes advantage of her time in the spotlight, singing old songs and even flashing the camera. A combination of sensitive filmmaking and pleasantly weird subjects turns *Grey Gardens* into a whimsical and heartfelt peek into the lives of two captivating (though somewhat deranged) individuals.

A feeling of profound sorrow also permeates the film, most notably whenever Big Edie pines for her dead husband, or Little Edie admits that she longs to leave the Hamptons and relocate to the city. During these moments, it becomes evident that a deep-rooted sadness lies behind the wide smiles the two women flash to the camera. The Beales also erupt into brief but frightening bouts of anger, particularly Little Edie, who often rages about her treatment at the apparently stern hands of her father, whom she and Big Edie refer to as Mr. Beale. During one exceptionally tense moment, Little Edie threatens to push the filmmakers "under the goddamned bed" for insinuating that a man other than her father ever took care of Big Edie. The camera captures these moments from a concealed location, making it feel as though the viewer is stealing a look behind the thin and tattered curtain of civility the two women show to the world. These outbursts reinforce the idea that the decaying house serves as a physical manifestation of the Beales' dwindling fortunes and a depressing reflection of their deteriorating sanity. Thus, while *Grey Gardens* remains amusing throughout, the film sometimes feels more than a little heartrending.

Ultimately, *Grey Gardens* stands as a winsome and entertaining documentary that provides viewers with a touching (and occasionally gloomy) glimpse inside the lives of two proud and fiercely unconventional women who refuse to conform to societal standards. The film remains enjoyable even during the sad moments because it celebrates these two eccentric and iconoclastic women rather than approach their story with a sense of ghoulish curiosity.

See also *Portrait of Jason* (1967), *Gates of Heaven* (1978), *Crumb* (1994), *Fast, Cheap & Out of Control* (1997), *Ghost World* (2001), *Grizzly Man* (2005).

H

HAROLD AND MAUDE (1971)

Director: Hal Ashby
Screenplay: Colin Higgins
Cast: Ruth Gordon (Maude), Bud Cort (Harold), Vivian Pickles (Mrs. Chasen), Charles Tyner (Uncle Victor), Eric Christmas (Priest), Cyril Cusack (Glaucus), Ellen Geer (Sunshine Doré), Judy Engles (Candy Gulf), Shari Summers (Edith Phern), Tom Skerritt (Motorcycle Officer)
Specs: 91 minutes; color
Genre: comedy, drama, romance
Availability: DVD and Blu-ray (The Criterion Collection)

Plot

A ghoulish young man causes a scandal when he strikes up a romantic relationship with a free-spirited eighty-year-old woman.

Background

Colin Higgins wrote *Harold and Maude* while a grad student at UCLA film school in the late 1960s.[1] Higgins also worked as a pool boy for producer Edward Lewis, who took the script to producer Stanley Jaffe at Paramount Pictures.[2] Higgins wanted to direct the film, but the studio decided to hire Hal Ashby,[3] who had scored a modest hit in 1970 with his debut film *The Landlord*. Ashby appointed Higgins coproducer on *Harold and Maude* so the writer could remain on set and learn how to direct a film. Ashby then turned his attention to casting the title characters.[4]

Ashby and the studio tested several actors for the role of Harold before settling on Bud Cort.[5] Meanwhile, Ashby wanted an English or French actress to play Maude, but changed his mind when he met Ruth Gordon, who impressed him with her comedic chops.[6] Production commenced in December of 1970, and filming took place in and around the San Francisco Bay Area.[7] The shoot proved difficult as terrible weather caused Ashby to fall behind schedule, which angered the producers.[8] Additionally, Cort and Gordon shared a somewhat contentious

Maude (Ruth Gordon, right) introduces herself to Harold (Bud Cort) during a funeral. *Paramount Pictures / Photofest © Paramount Pictures*

relationship (though that changed following the death of Cort's father shortly after shooting wrapped).[9] During production, producer Charles B. Mulvehill asked Elton John to compose the film's soundtrack.[10] John declined but suggested Cat Stevens, who agreed to write two original songs for the film. Production wrapped in March of 1971.[11]

Harold and Maude opened on December 20, 1971, and received terrible reviews from critics.[12] It also alienated general audiences, who stayed away in droves.[13] Nevertheless, the film eventually developed a reputation as a darkly comic masterpiece, and it routinely shows up on lists of the greatest cult movies.[14] Moreover, it influenced an entire generation of filmmakers that includes Wes Anderson,[15] David O. Russell,[16] and Judd Apatow.[17]

Commentary

More than forty years after its initial release, *Harold and Maude* remains a delightfully unconventional romance that contains equal amounts of whimsical comedy and affecting drama. The film mines much of its humor from the lead characters' eccentric personalities (Harold attends funerals for fun, while Maude steals cars) and several wickedly funny sight gags (Harold's uncle was "General MacArthur's right-hand man" but is missing his own right arm). Some viewers might find the twee tomfoolery overwhelming, but those able to appreciate the film's idiosyncratic silliness will discover a witty comedy that features loads of memorable moments.

At the same time, *Harold and Maude* includes several touching and heartbreaking moments (such as Maude relating the tragic story of her umbrella and the film's bittersweet finale), all made more affecting by Cort and Gordon's excellent performances. In addition, Ashby puts the props, costumes, and makeup to good use throughout the film. For example, Maude attends a funeral while wearing a white dress and carrying a yellow umbrella, both of which set her apart from the rest of society and mark her as eccentric. Similarly, when the movie opens, Harold's skin appears nearly white, but he grows less pale as his relationship with Maude blossoms. These elements sometimes feel a bit heavy-handed, but they mostly add a richness and complexity to the film and its characters. Finally, *Harold and Maude* features a stellar soundtrack performed by Cat Stevens, and the songs all serve to supplement and comment on the action. These elements make *Harold and Maude* a peculiar and charmingly demented comedy, as well as one of the most heartwarming (if unconventional) love stories ever made.

See also *Brewster McCloud* (1970), *Rushmore* (1998), *There's Something about Mary* (1998).

SPOTLIGHT: HAL ASHBY (1929–1988)

Following a rough childhood, Hal Ashby hitchhiked to Los Angeles, where he landed a gig as a film editor. At the age of forty he made his directorial debut with *The Landlord*, a modest success that gained the attention of executives at Paramount Pictures, who hired Ashby to direct *Harold and Maude*. From there he built up a small but impressive body of work that includes acclaimed films like *The Last Detail, Shampoo, Bound for Glory, Coming Home,* and *Being There.*

SPOTLIGHT: BUD CORT (1948–)

Growing up in New York, Bud Cort harbored dreams of becoming an entertainer. He appeared in several school plays and community theater productions, eventually landing bit parts in commercials, soap operas, and Off-Broadway theater. From there, he formed acclaimed comedy partnerships with Jeannie Berlin and Judy Engles. Not long after, director Robert Altman cast Cort in a small role in *M*A*S*H* and then later as the lead in *Brewster McCloud.* Cort next appeared as the male lead in *Harold and Maude*, which became his signature role. In the nearly fifty years since, the singularly quirky Cort has appeared in numerous plays and films, including *Dogma* and *The Life Aquatic with Steve Zissou.* He has also popped up in television shows like *Criminal Minds* and *Eagleheart.*

HEATHERS (1988)

Director: Michael Lehmann
Screenplay: Daniel Waters
Cast: Winona Ryder (Veronica), Christian Slater (J.D.), Shannen Doherty (Heather Duke), Lisanne Falk (Heather McNamara), Kim Walker (Heather Chandler), Penelope Milford (Pauline Fleming), Glenn Shadix (Father Ripper), Lance Fenton (Kurt Kelly), Patrick Labyorteaux (Ram), Carrie Lynn (Martha "Dumptruck" Dunnstock)
Specs: 103 minutes; color
Genre: comedy, crime, drama
Availability: DVD and Blu-ray (Image Entertainment)

Plot

A popular but angst-ridden teenage girl meets a homicidal new kid, and together they murder their classmates and make the deaths look like suicides.

Background

In 1986, twenty-four-year-old video store clerk Daniel Waters (brother of future *Mean Girls* director Mark Waters) set out to write a novel about a young girl meeting the Antichrist.[18] Over time, the novel morphed into a screenplay about a pair of high school kids who kill their classmates and frame the deaths as suicides.[19] Titled *Heathers*, the script made its way to producer Denise Di Novi, who convinced executives at New World Pictures to produce the film with a $3 million budget.[20] Di Novi tapped recent film school graduate Michael Lehmann to direct.[21] She also sent the script to several up-and-coming young actresses, including Jennifer Connelly, Justine Bateman, and fifteen-year-old Winona Ryder, who ultimately landed the starring role of Veronica despite Waters's misgivings.[22] Meanwhile, nineteen-year-old Christian Slater won the role of murderous loner J.D., while his eighteen-year-old girlfriend Kim Walker accepted the part of lead antagonist Heather Chandler.[23] Sixteen-year-old television actress Shannen Doherty rounded out the principal cast as Chandler's scheming lieutenant, Heather Duke.[24] With the director in place and the cast locked in, filming commenced on July 5, 1988.[25]

Working on a tight thirty-three-day shooting schedule, Lehmann shot much of the film on location at a Los Angeles high school.[26] Sequences set in the characters' homes were shot on sets built inside the school gymnasium.[27] Much like a real high school, cliques soon formed among the teenage cast, though Slater remained aloof from everyone except Ryder, which caused some tension between him and Walker.[28] The shoot wrapped on August 17, 1988,[29] and *Heathers* hit theaters on March 31, 1989, just as New World filed for bankruptcy.[30] Despite some decent reviews, the film flopped at the box office, grossing just over $1 million during its entire theatrical run.[31] Later that same year, *Heathers* became a massive cult hit thanks to home video.[32] The Fox Television Network even considered producing a TV series based on the film, but went with *Beverly Hills 90210* instead,[33] though

Heather McNamara (Lisanne Frank, second from right) pressures Veronica (Winona Ryder, far right) into teasing other students. *New World Pictures / Photofest © New World Pictures*

TV Land later expressed interest in a series.[34] *Heathers* remains a cult favorite to this day, and it inspired other caustic teen-girl comedies like *Clueless*, *Jawbreaker*, and *Mean Girls*.[35] In 2010, Andy Fickman adapted *Heathers* as a tongue-in-cheek stage musical that ran Off-Broadway until August 4, 2014.[36]

Commentary

Heathers takes dead aim at the sort of saccharine after-school specials that featured attractive teenagers dealing with heavy issues like sex, drugs, and low self-esteem. The film drips with contempt for those melodramatic sob stories, and uses bitter sarcasm and a hipper-than-thou attitude to mock their self-righteous superiority. *Heathers* employs gallows humor to make a point about the high cost of popularity, mining lots of laughs from the otherwise thorny issue of teenage suicide. It also boasts memorable lines like "What is your damage, Heather?" and "This isn't just a spoke in my menstrual cycle." Waters possesses an uncanny understanding of how teenagers talk, and the film benefits from his keen insight into the ever-evolving lingo of youth culture. Granted, the humor takes on a much darker tone in the wake of the numerous school shootings that occurred after *Heathers* came out, but viewers who can get past that rather sizable hurdle will discover a devilishly funny black comedy that features loads of quotable dialogue.

Beyond the humor, the film offers viewers an uncompromising look at the high school experience of the 1980s, albeit one filtered through an outsider's perspective. *Heathers* pokes fun at tough topics like suicide and eating disorders, but it approaches teen angst in a thoughtful, heartfelt fashion. The film offers a touching and altogether sympathetic portrayal of luckless overweight outcast Martha Dunnstock's (a.k.a. Martha Dumptruck) struggle to fit in with her peers, and in doing so, it taps into widespread anxieties that continue to afflict teenagers around the world. *Heathers* also recognizes that teenagers often encounter a great deal of conflict and drama as they try to navigate a perilous social landscape consisting of cliques and high expectations. The film explores this idea through Veronica's efforts to become one of the popular kids, and via her tumultuous relationship with the attractive but abusive J.D., which serves as a dark reflection of the exhilarating craziness of young love. *Heathers* sets out to generate laughs, but it also realizes that high school is a scary place that often leaves people feeling emotionally traumatized for years afterward.

Heathers works even now because it uses acerbic wit and razor-sharp satire to parody other teen films and comment on American society. In addition, the film looks great thanks to some stylish visuals and attractive production design. Lehmann uses interesting shots to keep things lively, and the costumes remain totally very (to borrow some slang from the film) to this day. Of course, *Heathers* contains some rather insensitive homophobic humor, and the subject matter might leave contemporary viewers feeling uncomfortable, particularly given events that occurred after the film's release. Nonetheless, *Heathers* is a corrosively funny satire that understands teenagers far better than any film produced by the likes of John Hughes or Cameron Crowe.

See also *Clueless* (1995), *Jawbreaker* (1999), *Ghost World* (2001), *Mean Girls* (2004), *Jennifer's Body* (2009).

HEDWIG AND THE ANGRY INCH (2001)

Director: John Cameron Mitchell
Screenplay: John Cameron Mitchell
Cast: John Cameron Mitchell (Hedwig), Michael Pitt (Tommy Gnosis), Andrea Martin (Phyllis Stein), Miriam Shor (Yitzhak), Stephen Trask (Skszp), Theodore Liscinski (Jacek), Rob Campbell (Krzysztof), Maurice Dean Wint (Sgt. Luther Robinson)
Specs: 95 minutes; color
Genre: comedy, drama, musical
Availability: DVD (Warner Bros.)

Plot

A transgender punk-rock singer from East Berlin embarks on a concert tour that follows a former lover who stole her songs and used them to become a successful rock star.

Background

Hedwig and the Angry Inch began life as a character developed by actor John Cameron Mitchell and musician Stephen Trask. The two met on a flight during the early 1990s and forged an immediate connection.[37] They decided to collaborate on a project together and came up with a story about an East German rock-and-roll singer who survived a botched sex change operation.[38] After workshopping the character and several songs at the Squeezebox nightclub in New York City, they took their creation Off-Broadway in 1998 in a show written by Mitchell with music by Trask.[39] The production won several awards and soon gained the attention of Hollywood producers who wanted to adapt it as a film. The day after attending the show, Bob Shaye of New Line Cinema purchased the rights to the property and tapped Mitchell to both write and direct the film adaptation.[40]

In June of 1999, Mitchell attended the Sundance film labs so he could develop the script and learn how to direct.[41] After an intensive casting process, *Hedwig* entered production in July of 2000. Throughout filming, Mitchell worked closely with director of photography Frank DeMarco and editor/second unit director Andrew Marcus to ensure that the finished film looked as good as possible.[42] Mitchell also recorded most of his vocals on set to replicate the feeling of a live performance.[43] To generate interest in the film, Mitchell and Trask performed in character on *The Late Show with David Letterman* and *The Rosie O'Donnell Show*, and later received permission from Rosie O'Donnell to include a clip of their performance in the film.[44] Production wrapped in August 2000, and six months later the finished film premiered at the Sundance Film Festival,[45] where it won the Best Director and Audience Awards.[46]

Hedwig (John Cameron Mitchell) and the Angry Inch perform at a Bilgewater's restaurant. *New Line Cinema / Photofest © New Line Cinema*

Hedwig went on to win several more awards, including the award for Best Directorial Debut from the National Board of Review and the Performance of the Year Award from *Premiere* magazine.[47] Sadly, despite mostly positive reviews, *Hedwig* bombed at the box office, grossing less than $4 million against an estimated $6 million budget.[48] Over time, however, it fostered a devoted cult following, and these days the film enjoys a well-deserved reputation as one of the best and most daring musicals of the twenty-first century. On April 22, 2014, a new stage production of *Hedwig and the Angry Inch* opened on Broadway with actor Neil Patrick Harris in the lead role.[49]

Commentary

Hedwig's primary attraction lies with its fantastic soundtrack, which was ported over from the stage show and features catchy tunes that evoke the musical stylings of Lou Reed, Iggy Pop, and David Bowie (the holy trinity of "crypto-homo rockers" as Hedwig calls them). The film's story unfolds via songs that offer insight into the title character's tragicomic past and reveal her deep-seated loneliness and self-loathing. Trask's exquisite songwriting captures the spirit of the punk and glam rock icons already listed but also ensures that every tune has its own distinct identity. Viewers can bop along with upbeat ditties like "Sugar Daddy" and "Wig in a Box" (both of which still provide valuable information about the lead character's life), and then shed a tear while listening to the poignant refrains of "The Origin of Love" and "Wicked Little Town." Listening to these songs, it quickly becomes clear why *Hedwig* gained a reputation as one of the best movie musicals of the modern era in the years after its release.

In addition to great music, *Hedwig* offers plenty of bittersweet comedy and gorgeous filmmaking. The film is wickedly funny throughout and features several gut-busting moments, such as Hedwig and her bandmates performing on the tiny ninth stage at the Menses Fair (a celebration of women and music clearly patterned on the Lilith Fair). At the same time, *Hedwig* contains plenty of heartbreaking moments (like the devastated look on Hedwig's face after Luther leaves her, or Tommy mouthing "bye" to Hedwig before shuffling off into the darkness). The film also boasts some beautiful filmmaking, and Mitchell includes several stylish shots and interesting compositions throughout (see the shot of Tommy gazing into a mirror that covers part of Hedwig's face for just one example). *Hedwig* is both funny and moving, and Mitchell's assured direction keeps things lively as the film builds to a triumphant but ambiguous ending that recalls the finale of Bob Fosse's *All That Jazz*.

Hedwig failed to catch on with a wide audience, but it struck a chord with "misfits and losers" (to borrow a line from one of Hedwig's songs) who related to Hedwig's plight as an outsider. This cult audience helped the film live on long after it crashed and burned at the box office. In the end, *Hedwig* earns its place in the pantheon of cult films due to a winning combination of fantastic music, quotable dialogue, and gorgeous filmmaking.

See also *Phantom of the Paradise* (1974), *The Rocky Horror Picture Show* (1975), *The Adventures of Priscilla, Queen of the Desert* (1994), *Velvet Goldmine* (1998).

HOT ROD (2007)

Director: Akiva Schaffer
Screenplay: Pam Brady
Cast: Andy Samberg (Rod Kimble), Isla Fisher (Denise), Sissy Spacek (Marie Powell),
   Ian McShane (Frank Powell), Jorma Taccone (Kevin Powell), Bill Hader (Dave),
   Danny McBride (Rico), Will Arnett (Jonathan), Chris Parnell (Barry Pasternack)
Specs: 88 minutes; color
Genre: comedy
Availability: DVD and Blu-ray (Paramount Pictures)

Plot

To raise money for an operation that will save his abusive stepfather's life, an accident-prone wannabe stuntman devises his most outrageous stunt yet.

Background

Originally written by former *South Park* writer Pam Brady, *Hot Rod* was intended as a vehicle for breakout *Saturday Night Live* (*SNL*) star Will Ferrell.[50] Unfortunately, Paramount Pictures decided to shelve the project, and the script remained in limbo for several years. Meanwhile, the struggling comedy troupe the Lonely Island (consisting of Akiva Schaffer, Jorma Taccone, and Andy Samberg) landed gigs at *SNL* in 2005 and almost immediately scored a massive viral hit with "Lazy Sunday," a digital short that racked up millions of views on a new video-sharing website called YouTube. At that point, *SNL* creator Lorne Michaels convinced Paramount executives to not only resurrect *Hot Rod*, but also allow the members of the Lonely Island to direct and star in the film.[51] The studio also agreed to let the troupe rewrite the entire script, which became much more offbeat. Paramount gave them a budget of just over $25 million,[52] and filming commenced on July 24, 2006.

Shooting took place largely in Vancouver and British Columbia,[53] with Samberg performing many of his own stunts.[54] Principal photography wrapped on September 23, 2006, and *Hot Rod* opened on August 3, 2007.[55] It received mixed reviews from critics, though most skewed toward the negative.[56] The film also failed to catch on with general audiences, and it grossed less than $14 million during its entire theatrical run, which lasted just sixty-eight days.[57] For a time, it seemed like *Hot Rod* might stand as the Lonely Island's only shot at the big screen, but the film generated $24 million in DVD rentals in the United States alone.[58] At that point, positive word of mouth helped *Hot Rod* find a receptive audience among fans of anti-comedy and surreal humor. These days, fans recognize *Hot Rod* as a cult classic that was unfairly ignored upon release.

Commentary

Hot Rod is a loving send-up of 1980s teen movies and inspirational sports films that offers up loads of self-aware gags and savagely funny absurdist humor. The

Rod (Andy Samberg, second from right) and his friends prepare to perform the greatest stunt of all time. *Paramount Pictures / Photofest © Paramount Pictures*

film serves as the perfect platform for Samberg, who turns affable lunkhead Rod Kimble into a live-action cartoon character along the lines of Tom Cat or Wile E. Coyote. He spends the entire movie getting beaten up, blown up, and kicked around, and his personality alternates between smug blustering and overly dramatic histrionics. The film surrounds him with an incredible cast that includes comic geniuses like Bill Hader, Danny McBride, and Will Arnett, and wisely gives each one a moment to shine (Arnett's hysterical wailing of "Babe, wait!" is a thing of demented beauty). Even respected dramatic actors like Sissy Spacek and Ian McShane rise to the occasion and turn in sidesplitting performances as Rod's mother and stepfather, respectively (McShane in particular gets some of the film's biggest laughs with his constant needling of Rod's fragile masculinity). The riotously funny performances help turn *Hot Rod* into a masterpiece of comedic absurdity.

The film also indulges in bits of outrageous anti-comedy and self-reflexive genre deconstruction as it pokes fun at the tried-and-true tropes of both teen movies and sports films. For instance, following yet another fight with his stepfather, Rod retreats to his "quiet place" in the forest and performs an angry dance number/gymnastics routine that recalls both *Footloose* and *American Anthem*, and culminates with Rod tripping over a log and tumbling down a steep hill. The sequence lasts for a full two minutes and tests the audience's endurance as it goes from funny to exasperating and all the way back to funny again. The film also contains lots of inspired nonsense (like the uproarious but thoroughly weird "cool beans" sequence) and zany non sequiturs ("I'm freakin' pumped! I've been drinking green tea all goddamn day!") guaranteed to befuddle and amuse audiences

SPOTLIGHT: THE LONELY ISLAND

During the early 1990s, Andy Samberg, Akiva Shaffer, and Jorma Taccone met while attending Willard Junior High in Berkeley, California, and the trio remained fast friends throughout high school and college. In 2000, they moved to Los Angeles to make short films and music videos as the Lonely Island. Five years later, the troupe landed a gig writing for the MTV Movie Awards, and this earned them the attention of *Saturday Night Live* creator Lorne Michaels, who hired them to write for the show. Later that year, the Lonely Island gained national attention with the release of "Lazy Sunday," a digital short that became an online sensation. Other viral hits soon followed, including "Dick in a Box," "Jizz in My Pants," "I'm on a Boat," and "Like a Boss." In 2007, the three friends made the jump to the big screen with *Hot Rod*, a box office bomb that became a cult classic. They next worked behind the scenes on films like *MacGruber*, *The Watch*, and *Neighbors*. Since 2009, the Lonely Island has released three albums, and in 2016 they returned to the big screen with *Pop Star: Never Stop Never Stopping*, another hilarious comedy destined for cult status.

in equal measure. *Hot Rod* even smuggles some honest emotion in among all the wackiness, and the film clearly understands the pain of dealing with a sick parent. As such, *Hot Rod* emerges as an amusing, sweet-natured comedy that rewards multiple viewings.

See also *Tropic Thunder* (2008), *Land of the Lost* (2009), *MacGruber* (2010), *The Other Guys* (2010), *Popstar: Never Stop Never Stopping* (2016).

I

I'M GONNA GIT YOU SUCKA (1988)

Director: Keenen Ivory Wayans
Screenplay: Keenen Ivory Wayans
Cast: Keenen Ivory Wayans (Jack Spade), Bernie Casey (John Slade), Antonio Fargas (Flyguy), Steve James (Kung Fu Joe), Isaac Hayes (Hammer), Jim Brown (Slammer), Ja'net DuBois (Ma Bell), Dawnn Lewis (Cheryl), John Vernon (Mr. Big), Clu Gulager (Lt. Baker)
Specs: 88 minutes; color
Genre: action, comedy
Availability: Blu-ray (Kino Lorber Films)

Plot

A soldier returns home to find that his brother died in a gold chain–related overdose, so he teams up with a group of former black heroes from the 1970s to take down nefarious white crime boss, Mr. Big.

Background

Keenan Ivory Wayans spent much of the 1980s performing stand-up comedy in clubs throughout New York and appearing in minor television roles.[1] His big break finally arrived in 1987 when he teamed with Robert Townsend to cowrite and costar in *Hollywood Shuffle*, a wicked satire about the stereotypical portrayals of African Americans in film and television.[2] The film became a modest success,[3] and Wayans used his newfound cachet to make *I'm Gonna Git You Sucka*, a feature-length spoof of blaxploitation cinema that doubled as a loving homage.[4] Wayans credits Eddie Murphy with developing the idea for the film; while sitting around with friends and reminiscing about old blaxploitation movies, Murphy suggested making a parody of the genre, and even came up with the film's title.[5]

Soon after, Wayans set up a deal with United Artists, which gave him a $3 million budget and allowed him to both direct and star.[6] Wayans then cast several recognizable blaxploitation stars, including Antonio Fargas, Isaac Hayes, and Jim Brown. Filming wrapped after just forty-five days,[7] and *I'm Gonna Git You Sucka* opened to limited release in December of 1988 with a weak marketing campaign

Jack Spade (Keenan Ivory Wayans, center) teams with John Slade (Bernie Casey, left) and Hammer (Isaac Hayes) to take down Mr. Big (John Vernon, not pictured). *MGM/UA / Photofest © MCA/ Universal Pictures*

that ignored major markets.[8] However, positive audience response led to a wide release the following January.[9] *I'm Gonna Git You Sucka* received mixed reviews from film critics, but African American audiences enthusiastically embraced the film, which grossed $13 million at the box office and became a cult favorite in the years after its release.[10] Meanwhile, Wayans went on to create the highly successful sketch comedy series *In Living Color* for the Fox Network and direct the first two films in the *Scary Movie* franchise.

Commentary

Two years before Quentin Tarantino burst onto the scene, *I'm Gonna Git You Sucka* introduced an entire generation of impressionable suburban white kids to the world of blaxploitation cinema. The film is sidesplittingly funny (though modern audiences might find some of the humor offensive, particularly Fly Guy's poem during the "Pimp of the Year" sequence), and features plenty of self-reflexive humor and silly running gags (the repeated refrain of "You can either go out that window, or you can take the stairs" proves particularly funny and has a great payoff). Wayans and his collaborators are obviously well-versed in the clichés of blaxploitation cinema and 1970s-era martial arts movies, and they poke plenty of pointed but affectionate fun at both subgenres. The film's narrative riffs on obscure African American action flicks like *The Black 6*, *Gordon's War*, and *Mean Johnny Barrows*, and includes specific (not to mention funny) references to blaxploitation classics like *Blacula*, *Super Fly*, *Cleopatra Jones*, and *Three the Hard Way*, all of which makes *I'm Gonna Git You Sucka* a treat for fans of 1970s cult cinema.

The film features an incredible cast, and Fargas, Brown, and Hayes deliver fun performances that call back to their blaxploitation roots. In addition, *I'm Gonna Git You Sucka* includes amusing appearances from respected black actors like Clarence Williams III and future comedy stars like Chris Rock (who steals the show as a frustratingly cheap rib joint customer). The film also boasts a fantastic soundtrack that includes some great old-school hip-hop by groups like K-9 Posse and Boogie Down Productions. Of course, modern viewers might find some of the gags offensive (the brief parody of *The Exorcist* is rather misogynistic), and the film sometimes advances stereotypes and racist attitudes (most notably during the "First Annual Youth Gang Competition" sequence). Nevertheless, *I'm Gonna Git You Sucka* remains a pleasantly goofy comedy sure to delight fans of blaxploitation movies and action flicks. The film also serves up plenty of nonsensical silliness and wickedly funny comic performances, and it will therefore appeal to those who have never even heard of films like *Shaft* or *Foxy Brown*.

See also *Putney Swope* (1969), *Foxy Brown* (1974), *Pootie Tang* (2001), *Black Dynamite* (2009).

INVASION OF THE BODY SNATCHERS (1956)

Director: Don Siegel
Screenplay: Daniel Mainwaring
Cast: Kevin McCarthy (Dr. Miles J. Bennell), Dana Wynter (Becky Driscoll), Larry Gates (Dr. Dan "Danny" Kauffman), King Donovan (Jack Belicec), Carolyn Jones (Theodora "Teddy" Belicec), Jean Willes (Nurse Sally Withers), Ralph Dumke (Police Chief Nick Grivett), Virginia Christine (Wilma Lentz), Tom Fadden (Uncle Ira Lentz)
Specs: 80 minutes; black and white
Genre: horror, science fiction
Availability: Blu-ray (Olive Films)

Plot

Plantlike aliens invade a small town and replace the populace with emotionless duplicates, and only a small group of people stand in their way.

Background

In 1954, *Collier's* magazine published *The Body Snatchers*, a serialized science fiction story written by advertising executive Jack Finney.[11] Producer Walter Wanger saw great potential in the story, and he snatched up the movie rights after reading part one.[12] He then hired screenwriter Daniel Mainwaring and director Don Siegel to help him develop the adaptation. Wanger also changed the title to *Invasion of the Body Snatchers* to avoid confusion with Robert Louis Stevenson's short story

The Body Snatcher, which RKO had adapted for the screen in 1945.[13] From there, Wanger secured a budget of just over $450,000 from Allied Artists, but prior to production they asked him to cut it down to a more modest $380,000.[14] Wanger agreed, and the film entered production on March 23, 1955, with principal photography taking place in and around Sierra Madre, California.

Siegel originally envisioned the film as a comedy, because he found the central premise preposterous.[15] During production, Siegel shot several comedic scenes, but none made it into the final cut because executives at Allied Artists wanted a straight-up horror film.[16] Siegel also clashed with studio executives over the film's ending; originally, the lead character watches as trucks laden with hundreds of pods drive off to infect cities all over the United States. However, Allied Artists wanted a happier ending, and they ordered Siegel to shoot both a new intro and a new final scene.[17] Meanwhile, Wanger asked Orson Welles to narrate the film's opening and closing sequences, but scheduling conflicts prevented Welles from participating.[18] Wanger briefly considered sci-fi author Ray Bradbury as a replacement, but ultimately opted to eliminate the narration.[19] Filming lasted twenty-three days total, and *Body Snatchers* opened on February 5, 1956.

Despite a poor critical reception, the film became a hit with general audiences and grossed over $2 million during its initial theatrical run. Later, *Body Snatchers* became a staple of late-night television and developed a devoted cult following of

Dr. Miles J. Bennell (Kevin McCarthy, right) and his friends discover the alien pods. *Allied Artists Pictures Corporation / Photofest © Allied Artists Pictures Corporation*

viewers who appreciated its timely themes and low-budget charms. In 1994, the Library of Congress selected *Body Snatchers* for preservation in the United States National Film Registry.[20] These days, critics recognize *Body Snatchers* as one of the most influential science fiction films ever made, and it regularly pops up on "best of" lists, such as *Time* magazine's list of the top ten science fiction films from the 1950s.[21] The film spawned official remakes in 1978, 1993, and 2007, as well as numerous imitators like *Seedpeople* and *The Faculty*.

Commentary

Body Snatchers continues to feel both timely and terrifying more than sixty years after its initial release. The film establishes an oppressively claustrophobic atmosphere early on and maintains it throughout thanks to Siegel's exciting direction, which keeps things moving at a fast clip and allows the tension to simmer until it explodes during the chilling climax (which is somewhat deflated by the tacked-on bookending sequences). *Body Snatchers* also benefits from the gorgeous widescreen cinematography by Ellsworth Fredericks, who uses lighting, Dutch angles, and deep focus photography to render everything on-screen slightly off-kilter and unsettling. Add in Ralph Butler and Del Harris's creepy sound design and Carmen Dragon's bombastic but effectively eerie score, and *Body Snatchers* becomes a thoroughly tense experience that will leave viewers breathless with fear.

The film also lends itself to multiple interpretations, and over the years it has been viewed as everything from an allegory for McCarthyism to a metaphorical warning about the dangers of creeping Communism, and more. In *Body Snatchers*, the alien pod people seek to establish a world built on groupthink and subservience, and the proudly individualistic heroes struggle to halt this threat. The film clearly wants viewers to sympathize with the heroic Dr. Miles Bennell (Kevin McCarthy) and his small band of freedom fighters, and this likely explains why viewers continue to see the aliens as stand-ins for anyone who disagrees with them. Furthermore, *Body Snatchers* still resonates because the subtext fits a wide variety of situations (as evidenced by the remakes, all of which address different concerns). These days, the film could function as a commentary on the scourge of political correctness or a metaphor for the restrictive nature of conservatism, and both interpretations would hold merit.

An overwhelmingly creepy mood permeates *Body Snatchers*, and the filmmakers masterfully ratchet up the tension throughout. The reshot ending undercuts the terror somewhat, though not enough to sink the film. At the same time, *Body Snatchers* stands as a provocative film that supports numerous readings and taps into a wide variety of anxieties, and can therefore frighten viewers regardless of their political or ideological leanings. Of course, *Body Snatchers* works just fine as a straightforward horror movie about aliens trying to take over the world, but the thematic richness ensures that it continues to feel vital and terrifying even today.

See also *Invaders from Mars* (1953), *Invasion of the Body Snatchers* (1978), *Killer Klowns from Outer Space* (1988), *Seedpeople* (1992), *Body Snatchers* (1993), *The Faculty* (1998), *The Invasion* (2007).

THE IRON GIANT (1999)

Director: Brad Bird
Screenplay: Tim McCanlies (screenplay), Brad Bird (screen story)
Cast: Eli Marienthal (Hogarth Hughes), Harry Connick Jr. (Dean McCoppin), Jennifer Aniston (Annie Hughes), Vin Diesel (the Iron Giant), Christopher McDonald (Kent Mansley), John Mahoney (General Rogard), M. Emmet Walsh (Earl Stutz), James Gammon (Foreman Marv Loach/Floyd Turbeaux), Cloris Leachman (Mrs. Tensedge)
Specs: 86 minutes; color
Genre: action, adventure, comedy, drama, family, science fiction
Availability: DVD and Blu-ray (Warner Bros.)

Plot

After crash landing on Earth, a giant alien robot befriends a young boy and embarks on a heartwarming journey of self-discovery while trying to elude a paranoid government agent.

Background

Based on the children's novel *The Iron Man* by Ted Hughes, *The Iron Giant* took a circuitous route to the big screen. In 1989, Pete Townshend used the book as the basis for a concept album called *The Iron Man: A Musical*, which was later adapted as a stage musical in London.[22] Two years later, Richard Bazley pitched a film version of *The Iron Man* to legendary animator Don Bluth, who passed on the project.[23] Eventually, Des McAnuff, who adapted the Who's *Tommy* for the stage, convinced Warner Bros. Entertainment to produce an adaptation of *The Iron Man*,[24] and the studio tapped former *The Simpsons* animator Brad Bird to direct.

Although Bird wanted to write the script himself, the studio hired Tim McCanlies, writer of *Secondhand Lions*, to write the script;[25] together, they produced an adaptation Hughes applauded.[26] After production finally commenced on January 2, 1997,[27] Warner Bros. reduced the film's budget considerably due to the financial failure of their previous animated effort, *Quest for Camelot*.[28] Studio executives also implemented a tight shooting schedule and kept a watchful eye on the production throughout.[29] Nevertheless, Bird retained a great deal of creative freedom, and he fostered a collaborative environment during the animation phase.[30] He worked closely with his staff to develop the film and often changed scenes based on their input. In the end, he finished the film on time and under budget.

The Iron Giant opened in the United States on August 6, 1999, to widespread critical acclaim.[31] Unfortunately, it tanked at the box office, earning just over $22 million against a reported $55 million budget.[32] The film acquired a cult following in the years after its original release, thanks in part to television networks like TNT and Cartoon Network, both of which marketed *The Iron Giant* as an overlooked classic.[33] In the early 2000s, Cartoon Network routinely aired the film for twenty-four hours on both the Fourth of July and Thanksgiving, raising its profile even further.[34]

Hogarth introduces the Iron Giant to the townsfolk of Rockwell, Maine. *Warner Bros. / Photofest* © *Warner Bros.*

Commentary

The Iron Giant is a gorgeously animated film that balances a delightful sense of humor with some genuinely touching pathos. The film uses a combination of traditional hand-drawn animation and CGI (often made to look like conventional cel animation) to create lush visuals and thrilling action sequences. The warm, folksy look deliberately recalls old Norman Rockwell paintings, but like Rockwell's best paintings (such as *The Problem We All Live With*), *The Iron Giant* exposes the darkness that lies beneath the artificially wholesome facade of 1950s America. It accomplishes this primarily through the character of Kent Mansley, who resembles the clean-cut, square-jawed heroes that regularly popped up in sci-fi flicks produced throughout the Cold War era but ultimately reveals himself as a scheming, mistrustful coward. Furthermore, *The Iron Giant* contains bursts of exciting action that provide a nice contrast to the quaintness of life in sleepy small towns like the fictional Rockwell, Maine (yet another allusion to the famous painter). *The Iron Giant* uses these elements to critique the idea of nostalgia, even as the film offers up a wistful look at the past.

At the same time, the film provides plenty of laughs, and the gags benefit from some impeccable comic timing. *The Iron Giant* contains several humorous moments, like the one in which young protagonist Hogarth Hughes drinks espresso for the first time, or the hilarious exchange that occurs shortly after the titular character jumps into a lake and creates a massive tidal wave that deposits beatnik artist Dean in the middle of the road. It also includes several poignant and heartbreaking moments, such as Hogarth teaching the Iron Giant about death, or the climactic sequence that sees the Giant launch into space a la Superman to save Rockwell from nuclear destruction. Bird deftly balances the humor and sorrow, and ensures that neither overwhelms the other. As such, the film feels more true to life than most animated children's films, because it understands that life consists of highs and lows in equal measure.

The Iron Giant functions as a loving homage to superhero comic books and 1950s sci-fi flicks (not to mention *E.T. the Extra-Terrestrial*), but it also presents viewers with a thoughtful meditation on what it means to be a hero and how our choices define us, as well as a powerful antiviolence message. In addition, the film features excellent performances from every member of its talented voice cast, most notably Vin Diesel, who imbues the title character with a childlike sense of wonder and a deep internal conflict even though he barely speaks throughout the film (in a lot of ways, Diesel's work here feels like a dry run for his turn as Groot in the *Guardians of the Galaxy* franchise). These elements transform *The Iron Giant* into one of the all-time great animated movies, as well as the best Superman movie since Christopher Reeve first donned the tights back in 1978.

See also *The Rocketeer* (1991), *The Incredibles* (2004).

J

JOSIE AND THE PUSSYCATS (2001)
Director: Deborah Kaplan, Harry Elfont
Screenplay: Deborah Kaplan, Harry Elfont
Cast: Rachael Leigh Cook (Josie McCoy), Rosario Dawson (Valerie Brown), Tara Reid (Melody Valentine), Alan Cumming (Wyatt Frame), Parker Posey (Fiona), Gabriel Mann (Alan M.), Paulo Costanzo (Alexander Cabot), Missi Pyle (Alexandra Cabot), Donald Faison (D.J.), Seth Green (Travis), Breckin Meyer (Marco), Eugene Levy (Himself)
Specs: 98 minutes; color
Genre: comedy, musical
Availability: DVD (Universal Studios Home Entertainment)

Plot

The members of an up-and-coming teenage girl group stumble upon a corporate conspiracy to insert subliminal messages into popular music.

Background

Created by cartoonist Dan DeCarlo in the early 1960s, fictional girl band Josie and the Pussycats first appeared in comic books published by Archie Comics. In 1970, the group made the leap to television courtesy of prolific animation studio Hanna-Barbera Productions.[1] Just over thirty years later, Universal Pictures partnered with Metro-Goldwyn-Mayer to produce a live-action *Josie and the Pussycats* movie. They hired Deborah Kaplan and Harry Elfont, the duo behind surprise box office hit *Can't Hardly Wait*, to write and direct.[2] Rather than a frank adaptation of the cartoon band, Kaplan and Elfont decided to make the film a satire of corporate America and the advertising industry.[3] They cast Rachel Leigh Cook, Tara Reid, and Rosario Dawson as the title characters, and filled the supporting roles with a mix of comedy superstars and well-known character actors (including indie darling Parker Posey as the film's primary antagonist, Fiona). *Josie and the Pussycats* entered production on August 21, 2000, and shooting lasted until October 26, 2000.

The film opened wide on April 11, 2001,[4] and most critics dismissed it as insipid and dull[5] (an all-too-common occurrence when dealing with entertain-

Josie (Rachel Leigh Cook, center) and the Pussycats shoot a music video during their rapid rise to stardom. *Universal Pictures / Photofest © Universal Pictures*

ment aimed at teenage girls). They also lambasted the filmmakers for including dozens of corporate logos in the background of nearly every shot, indicating that they misunderstood the satirical intent behind the excessive product placement.[6] *Josie and the Pussycats* also failed to catch on with moviegoers, and it grossed less than $15 million worldwide against a reported $39 million budget.[7] The soundtrack fared somewhat better, selling 500,000 copies even as the movie sank at the box office.[8] Despite its reputation as a critical and commercial dud, the film eventually found an enthusiastic cult audience that embraced its ironic humor and grasped the filmmakers' message about subliminal advertising.[9] *Josie and the Pussycats* has since emerged as a cult classic, and the characters live on in a variety of media, including the popular television series *Riverdale*, which currently airs on the CW Television Network.

Commentary

Though certain aspects of the film now feel quaint (such as the portable CD players and the inexplicable popularity of Carson Daly), *Josie and the Pussycats* remains a delightfully silly reimagining of the source material that also functions as a sly send-up of corporatization, commercialization, and the homogenization of popular culture. *Josie and the Pussycats* includes an obscene amount of product placement, but uses it to lampoon the entire concept of advertising. The extreme amount of corporate branding serves as a wickedly funny commentary on the mercenary nature of the capitalist marketing machine that drives both blockbuster filmmaking and youth culture. At times, *Josie and the Pussycats* feels like a kid-friendly version of John Carpenter's *They Live*, particularly once the characters uncover the conspiracy to turn kids into mindless consumers, and the film ultimately reveals itself as much smarter and far more subversive than it initially appears.

In addition, *Josie and the Pussycats* features a superb soundtrack and some great performances. Cook plays Josie with a combination of wide-eyed innocence and adorable brashness (and just a hint of playful sexiness), while Reid proves adorably daffy as Pussycats drummer Melody. Sadly, Dawson's Valerie gets little more to do than stand around looking pensive, but she nevertheless remains luminous and tough throughout. Posey steals the show with her vampy performance as a mean girl haunted by her tragically unhip past, while Cumming shines as her slimy henchman. Missi Pyle and Paulo Costanzo make brief but memorable appearances as twins Alexandra and Alexander Cabot, the band's incompetent managers, while Seth Green, Breckin Meyer, and Donald Faison (and some other guy who remains unlisted on IMDb) delight as members of boy band Du Jour. In addition to the lively performances, *Josie and the Pussycats* features an infectious soundtrack made up of bouncy pop-punk scorchers like "3 Small Words," "Pretend to Be Nice," and "Spin Around," all sung by Letters to Cleo front woman Kay Hanley (who also provides Josie's singing voice in the film). Thus, while *Josie and the Pussycats* contains some deceptively smart satire, the acting and the music ensure that the film remains lively and lighthearted throughout.

Josie and the Pussycats stands as an endearingly goofy comedy that features great music and fun performances, but it also includes some clever commentary about consumerism, corporate greed, and the insidiousness of the advertising industry. More importantly, the film's central message about staying true to yourself still rings true and feels more vital than ever.

See also *Beyond the Valley of the Dolls* (1970), *The Brady Bunch Movie* (1995), *Jem and the Holograms* (2015).

K

KILLER KLOWNS FROM OUTER SPACE (1988)

Director: Stephen Chiodo
Screenplay: Charles Chiodo, Stephen Chiodo, Edward Chiodo (uncredited)
Cast: Grant Cramer (Mike Tobacco), Suzanne Snyder (Debbie Stone), John Allen Nelson (Dave Hansen), John Vernon (Curtis Mooney), Michael S. Siegel (Rich Terenzi), Peter Licassi (Paul Terenzi), Royal Dano (Farmer Gene Green)
Specs: 88 minutes; color
Genre: comedy, horror, science fiction
Availability: DVD and Blu-ray (MGM)

Plot

Two love-struck college students set out to save their sleepy California town from a horde of homicidal clowns that hail from the depths of space.

Background

The idea for *Killer Klowns from Outer Space* emerged when brothers Charles, Edward, and Stephen Chiodo determined that a clown peering out from another car was the scariest thing anyone could see while driving down a dark, lonely road.[1] They spent the next few years developing the story, which they originally called *Killer Klowns* but later changed to *Killer Klowns from Outer Space* to emphasize the humor and make it sound less like a slasher film.[2] Meanwhile, they based the characters on their childhood friends and even used many of their real names.[3] The Chiodos convinced executives at Trans World Entertainment to invest $2 million in the film,[4] and production began soon after on February 25, 1987.[5]

The Chiodos had done effects work on several other movies, but *Killer Klowns* marked their writing and directorial debut.[6] Therefore, they called in favors from many of their industry friends.[7] For instance, special effects artist Dwight Roberts designed and built the animatronic klown suits, while Gina Leslie of Fantasy II Film Effects oversaw many of the visual effects.[8] The Chiodos shot the film in and around the town of Watsonville, California, about twenty minutes outside of Santa Cruz.[9] Meanwhile, they filmed the climactic sequence on the Santa Cruz Beach Boardwalk, a location also featured in Joel Schumacher's *The Lost Boys*.[10]

The killer klowns from outer space terrorize the denizens of Crescent Cove. *MGM / Photofest* © *MGM*

The Chiodos instructed their performers to play the ridiculous events and dialogue completely straight, because they believed this would help sell the humor.[11] Production ran smoothly for the most part, though some tension arose when the executive producer insisted the klowns appear in the first reel rather than later in the film as the Chiodos originally intended.[12] Producers also demanded more klown mayhem, which meant the Chiodos had to gather more footage of the klowns terrorizing the town.[13]

Killer Klowns opened on May 27, 1988, and grossed over $15 million in just a few weeks.[14] Despite its success and cult longevity, the Chiodos have yet to realize their dreams of turning *Killer Klowns* into a franchise. They continue to try, however, and in 2011 they began developing a sequel/remake under the title *Return of the Killer Klowns from Outer Space in 3D*.[15] They are also reportedly producing a TV series based on the film.[16] Regardless of whether these projects ever come to fruition, the original *Killer Klowns* remains one of the best and most beloved cult films of all time.

Commentary

With *Killer Klowns*, the Chiodo brothers crafted a loving homage to the creature features of the 1950s and 1960s. The Chiodos clearly watched a lot of those movies, because they deftly send up all the major conventions and characters that routinely pop up in films such as *The Giant Gila Monster*, *The Creeping Terror*, and *It Came from Outer Space*. At the same time, they play with standard horror movie tropes—like the innocent young lovers who stumble upon the initial invasion and the square-jawed authority figure who steps up to face the threat—and subvert them in interesting ways. For instance, the female lead proves far more intelligent and capable than the somewhat clueless male heroes. Thus, while *Killer Klowns* both spoofs and pays tribute to Cold War–era monster movies and science fiction films, it also deconstructs them in a humorous fashion.

Yet, *Killer Klowns* has much more to offer than references to sixty-five-year-old alien invasion flicks. Even viewers unfamiliar with *X the Unknown* or *The Monolith Monsters* will find something to enjoy in *Killer Klowns*. The Chiodos incorporate all sorts of imaginative effects throughout the film, from stop-motion animation to incredibly detailed animatronic puppets. Furthermore, they pack every single frame full of wickedly funny clown-themed visual puns, including living balloon animals, popcorn guns, cotton candy cocoons, deadly shadow puppets, and more. The Chiodos' fertile imagination ensures that *Killer Klowns* remains lively and fun throughout, even during horrific sequences like the one in which a klown uses a character's corpse as a ventriloquist's dummy. As such, viewers remain engaged from beginning to end, even if they fail to recognize a specific reference to another film.

Killer Klowns' only real fault lies with the dull human characters, though even this seems intentional since the movies it parodies often suffered from a similar deficiency. While far from perfect, *Killer Klowns* still succeeds thanks to a great premise, creative effects, and the Chiodos' ability to effectively balance horror and comedy, all of which make it required viewing for cult movie fans even thirty years after its initial release.

See also *Invaders from Mars* (1953), *The Blob* (1958), *Plan 9 from Outer Space* (1959), *Night of the Living Dead* (1968).

L

THE LITTLE SHOP OF HORRORS (1960)

Director: Roger Corman, Charles B. Griffith (uncredited), Mel Welles (uncredited)
Screenplay: Charles B. Griffith, Roger Corman (uncredited)
Cast: Jonathan Haze (Seymour Krelboyne), Jackie Joseph (Audrey Fulquard), Mel Welles (Gravis Mushnick), Dick Miller (Burson Fouch), Myrtle Vail (Winifred Krelboyne), Jack Nicholson (Wilbur Force)
Specs: 72 minutes; black and white
Genre: comedy, horror
Availability: Blu-ray (Legend)

Plot

To save his job at a skid row flower shop, a timid young man named Seymour Krelboyne develops a new species of plant, but soon learns that it has an insatiable hunger for human flesh. Seymour embarks on a comical murder spree in his efforts to keep the plant alive and win the heart of his beautiful coworker, Audrey.

Background

Director Roger Corman developed *The Little Shop of Horrors* when he gained temporary access to a large office set built for another production that was about to wrap.[1] Though the set was scheduled for disassembly two days after principal production ended, Corman still asked the manager of the Producer's Studio if he could use it for his next film.[2] The manager agreed, and Corman immediately instructed screenwriter Charles B. Griffith to begin working on a script for a film about a private detective investigating a murder.[3] Instead, Griffith persuaded Corman to make another comedic horror film in the vein of their previous collaboration, *A Bucket of Blood*.[4] Corman then assembled a cast comprised mainly of stock actors who had appeared in his other films.[5] According to the director, production commenced after a three-day rehearsal period,[6] though other reports state that rehearsals lasted three weeks.[7]

For the interior sequences, Corman set up two cameras at different angles and rolled them simultaneously.[8] He shot quickly and often used the first take.[9] He

Seymour Krelboyne (Jonathan Haze, left) shows Audrey Jr. to Mr. Mushnik (Mel Welles, center) and Audrey (Jackie Joseph). *The Filmgroup / Photofest © The Filmgroup*

also spent little time on lighting, opting instead to just plug the lights in and roll cameras.[10] Meanwhile, Griffith spent two weekends shooting exterior scenes with the help of performer Mel Welles.[11] Upon completion, Corman found it difficult to secure a distribution deal, because some distributors—including Corman's longtime partners at American International Pictures—considered the film anti-Semitic.[12] Corman eventually released the film through his own production company, the Filmgroup Inc. *Little Shop* was met with mostly favorable reviews, and it generated a respectable profit during its theatrical run. Later, it became a fixture of late-night television. In 1982, composer Alan Menken and writer Howard Ashman produced a successful Off-Off-Broadway stage musical based on the film, which was itself adapted as a movie in 1986 and a short-lived animated series in 1991.

Commentary

Little Shop often seems somewhat shoddy, particularly in terms of the stiff camera setups and sloppy editing, but it benefits from a loose, almost improvisational feel that helps smooth over any rough spots. The talented cast deliver assured performances that help *Little Shop* transcend its low-budget origins and become something special. All the actors know exactly what kind of movie they are in and they give it their all to bring their one-dimensional characters to vivid life. Jack Nicholson is rightly praised for his brief but brilliant appearance as a masochistic dental patient, but everyone in the film deserves praise for turning in great comic performances that elevate the material.

Of course, the actors had strong material to work with, thanks to Griffith and Corman's amusing script, which features sick humor, ingenious wordplay, and totally over-the-top characters. Much of the humor is rooted in a specific time and place—jokes about *Dragnet* and the perils of cranberry farming will no doubt confuse modern audiences—but the film still works today because of the silly characters, outrageous situations, and witty dialogue. In addition, *Little Shop* pokes good-natured fun at horror's long-standing conventions, and genre fans will find a lot to love in the film's cheeky sense of humor. Comedic horror is often tough to pull off, but Corman and Griffith strike the exact right balance between big laughs and some genuinely haunting imagery (for instance, the moment when Audrey Jr.'s buds open to reveal the faces of its many victims proves quite disturbing).

With *Little Shop*, Corman delivered a low-budget, self-aware masterpiece that rises above its cheap origins thanks to an abundance of charm and cleverness. He would go on to make better, more technically polished films during his career, but none feel as fun or relaxed as this, his most beloved cult classic.

See also *The Old Dark House* (1932), *A Bucket of Blood* (1959), *Creature from the Haunted Sea* (1961), *Little Shop of Horrors* (1986).

SPOTLIGHT: ROGER CORMAN (1926–)

Known as the "King of the Cult Film," Roger Corman wrote, directed, and produced hundreds of movies during a storied career that spans over six decades, and nearly all his films turned a profit. His filmography contains numerous cult classics like *It Conquered the World*, *A Bucket of Blood*, *The Wasp Woman*, *The Little Shop of Horrors*, and *X: The Man with the X-Ray Eyes*. Between 1959 and 1964, Corman garnered great acclaim for directing a cycle of visually striking and playfully inventive films based on works by Edgar Allan Poe. These include *House of Usher*, *The Pit and the Pendulum*, *The Raven*, and *The Masque of the Red Death*. Over the years, Corman founded several production and distribution companies, such as the Filmgroup Inc., New World Pictures, Concorde Pictures, New Horizons, Millennium Pictures, and New Concorde. He also mentored several people who became major players in Hollywood, including Francis Ford Coppola, Martin Scorsese, Jack Nicholson, James Cameron, Robert De Niro, Peter Bogdanovich, Joe Dante, and Sandra Bullock. In 2009, Corman received an Academy Award for Lifetime Achievement, and he continues to produce cult movies like *Sharktopus* and *Death Race 2050*.

THE LOST SKELETON OF CADAVRA (2001)

Director: Larry Blamire
Screenplay: Larry Blamire
Cast: Larry Blamire (Dr. Paul Armstrong), Fay Masterson (Betty Armstrong), Brian
　　Howe (Dr. Roger Fleming), Andrew Parks (Kro-Bar), Susan McConnell (Lattis),
　　Jennifer Blaire (Animala), Dan Conroy (Ranger Brad), Robert Deveau (the Farmer),
　　Darren Reed (the Mutant)
Specs: 90 minutes; black and white
Genre: comedy, horror, science fiction
Availability: DVD (Sony—Mill Creek Entertainment)

Plot

In this loving send-up of Cold War–era horror and sci-fi films, a two-fisted scientist and his wife team up with a pair of aliens to battle an evil skeleton, a mad
scientist, and a rampaging mutant.

Background

After years spent writing and directing his own acclaimed stage plays, Larry
Blamire took a job developing web content for a new Internet start-up called Bali
Hai Interactive in 1997. The company shut down in the dotcom crash of 2000, leaving Blamire free to develop *The Lost Skeleton of Cadavra*, an affectionate spoof of
1950s sci-fi flicks. He wrote the script in five days, borrowing elements from a play
he wrote years earlier called *Bride of the Mutant's Tomb*.[13] He then raised a budget
of nearly $100,000[14] and set about assembling his cast. He first hired Brian Howe,
who convinced fellow actors Andrew Parks, Dan Conroy, and Faye Masterson to
appear in the film. Meanwhile, Blamire's wife, actress Jennifer Blaire, requested
the role of Animala.[15] From there, the rest of the cast quickly fell into place, and
production began shortly after.

Blamire shot *Lost Skeleton* in and around the Los Angeles area, with the bulk of
filming taking place in Bronson Canyon (a location used in many of the movies that
inspired Blamire's film).[16] The site permit turned out to be the production's larg-
est expense because Blamire purchased most of the props cheaply on eBay. This
includes the titular skeleton, which was a plastic classroom model that Blamire
picked up for around $100.[17] Other props were built from inexpensive household
items like cardboard tubes and caulk guns, while still others were found in the
cabin used in several sequences. Principal photography lasted roughly ten and a
half days, though Blamire and his team spent several more weeks on reshoots.[18]
Cinematographer Kevin F. Jones shot the entire film on a Canon XL1 MiniDV
camera, and he achieved the classic black-and-white look by filming in color and
then stripping out the color during postproduction.[19] Blamire and Bill Bryn Russell then spent several months editing the film on Final Cut Pro.[20]

Upon completion, Blamire screened twenty-five minutes of *Lost Skeleton* at
the IFC Center in Los Angeles, where it received an enthusiastic reaction.[21] He

The Skeleton flanked by his henchmen, Dr. Roger Fleming (Brian Howe, left) and Animala (Jennifer Blaire). *Sony Pictures Home Entertainment / © Sony Pictures Home Entertainment*

then took the finished film to several festivals, and it was eventually acquired by Sony Pictures after a screening at the American Cinematheque in Hollywood.[22] Sony released the film into theaters on February 6, 2004, and on DVD that June.[23] *Lost Skeleton* has since become a much-loved cult favorite that has spawned several sequels and spin-offs.

Commentary

Lost Skeleton is a pitch-perfect parody of the cheaply made Z movies that inundated drive-in theaters throughout the 1950s, and it expertly captures the look and feel of inept masterpieces like *Plan 9 from Outer Space, Robot Monster,* and *Queen of Outer Space.* Blamire's fondness for these films remains evident throughout, and he does an excellent job of re-creating their goofy charms. For instance, the script absolutely nails the redundant and altogether tone-deaf expositional dialogue that became a hallmark of films like *The Beast of Yucca Flats* and *Night of the Blood Beast.* More importantly, the gifted actors all rise to the occasion, delivering hilariously wooden performances that belie their actual skill and talent. In addition, Blamire flawlessly re-creates the visual aesthetic of low-budget Cold War flicks; from the gorgeous black-and-white cinematography to the awkward reaction shots to the miniatures that never quite match the real sets, *Lost Skeleton* looks like it could have played on a double bill with *King Dinosaur* in 1955. The film even features a gratuitous dance number!

While *Lost Skeleton* works fine on its own, it becomes even more effective if the viewer knows the films it parodies. Much of the humor arises from the silly characters, ridiculous dialogue, and ludicrous situations, but another layer reveals itself to viewers familiar with the tropes and conventions of the low-budget horror and sci-fi flicks produced during the 1950s. For example, *Lost Skeleton* features bargain basement effects, an extensive use of stock footage, and plenty of casual sexism and misogyny. Scenes frequently last just a beat too long, creating a sense of uncomfortable stiffness. The film even concludes with an earnest plea for understanding, as in *It Conquered the World* and *The Day the Earth Stood Still*. By employing such characteristics, *Lost Skeleton* establishes itself as a loving homage to the films of trash auteurs like Ed Wood, Coleman Francis, Edward Bernds, and Phil Tucker.

See also *Robot Monster* (1953), *It Conquered the World* (1956), *Plan 9 from Outer Space* (1959), *The Beast of Yucca Flats* (1961).

SPOTLIGHT: LARRY BLAMIRE (19??–)

In the 1970s, Larry Blamire studied illustration at the Art Institute of Boston, and eventually landed a gig illustrating science fiction magazines. He wrote and directed several acclaimed plays throughout the 1980s, including a science fiction thriller based on the Philadelphia Experiment. In 1997, Blamire developed the interactive animated web series *The Wise Eye Guys* for Bali Hai Interactive. After the company folded in 2000, Blamire wrote and directed *The Lost Skeleton of Cadavra*, an ultra-low-budget movie shot on digital video that became a cult hit in 2004. Afterward, Blamire made several other cult movies, including *Meet the Mobsters*, *Trail of the Screaming Forehead*, *The Lost Skeleton Returns Again*, and *Dark and Stormy Night*. He also developed the acclaimed web series *Tales from the Pub* and the album *The Audio AdventureBook of Big Dan Frater Vol. 1*. In 2012, Blamire announced production of *The Lost Skeleton Walks among Us*, but placed the film on hold while he worked on a book. Nevertheless, he launched a Kickstarter campaign in 2014 to raise funds for the production. He is currently working on the graphic novel series *Steam Wars* and a novel featuring the Paul Armstrong character from *Lost Skeleton*.

LOVE STREAMS (1984)

Director: John Cassavetes
Screenplay: Ted Allan, John Cassavetes
Cast: Gena Rowlands (Sarah Lawson), John Cassavetes (Robert Harmon), Diahnne Abbott (Susan), Seymour Cassel (Jack Lawson), Margaret Abbott (Margarita), Jakob Shaw (Albie Swanson)
Specs: 141 minutes; color
Genre: comedy, drama
Availability: DVD and Blu-ray (The Criterion Collection)

Plot

Following a messy divorce, a troubled woman reunites with her estranged brother, who became a moody, alcoholic writer during their years apart.

Background

In 1983, groundbreaking independent filmmaker John Cassavetes teamed with playwright Ted Allan to develop *Love Streams*, a film about two aging siblings who care for one another after everyone else abandons them. Based on Allan's play of the same name, which Cassavetes directed as part of a sequence called *Three Plays of Love and Hate*,[24] *Love Streams* entered production just as Cassavetes was diagnosed with cirrhosis of the liver and given only six months to live.[25] This might explain the chaotic production, which took place largely in Cassavetes's own home.[26] Abandoning his normal handheld aesthetic, Cassavetes shot *Love Streams* almost entirely in sequence, and he essentially discarded the original ending, which would have wrapped everything up in a straightforward fashion.[27]

By the time it hit screens in 1984, *Love Streams* bore little resemblance to the source material.[28] The film divided both critics and general audiences, though it did win the Golden Bear at the thirty-fourth Berlin International Film Festival in 1985.[29] Following its theatrical run, the film made its way to home video in the mid-1980s, albeit in a heavily edited form.[30] Thirty years later, the Criterion Collection finally released the full 141-minute cut of *Love Streams* on DVD and Blu-ray for the first time ever in the United States.[31] These days, critics and fans alike consider *Love Streams* a milestone of independent cinema, as well as one of the finest American films ever made.

Commentary

From the abrupt opening to the heartbreaking finale, *Love Streams* strikes an odd and slightly combative tone, but the shambolic narrative remains absorb-

Robert Harmon (John Cassavetes, kneeling) checks on his sister Sarah Lawson (Gena Rowlands) after she faints. *Cannon Film Distributors / Photofest © Cannon Film Distributors*

ing throughout due to the captivating performances from Cassavetes and his wife, Gena Rowlands, as a pair of damaged siblings. As the self-absorbed, self-destructive Robert, Cassavetes slithers through the film like a drunken, oily snake, turning his character into an aggressively boozy womanizer who nevertheless remains charming even when falling down a flight of stairs. Meanwhile, Rowlands turns in a frantic performance as Robert's sister, Sarah, an emotionally disturbed woman struggling to navigate her own life (a role not unlike the one she played in Cassavetes's *A Woman under the Influence*). The powerful performances and accomplished filmmaking turn *Love Streams* into an engrossing film that will leave audiences riveted from beginning to end.

The film becomes especially surreal during the third act, as Cassavetes offers glimpses into Sarah's psyche via a pair of bizarre dream sequences. At the same time, *Love Streams* builds toward a tense and bittersweet climax that proves especially heartbreaking due to the gritty realness of the performances. Upon recovering from an unidentified illness, Sarah decides to leave Robert's care and return home to her long-suffering family. Robert tries to convince her to stay, but to no avail. As she embraces him one final time, he mutters, "I don't want you to go." In return, she just smiles and walks out the door. The touching final shot of Robert waving good-bye through the rain-streaked window becomes even more poignant when considering Cassavetes was dying of cirrhosis at the time, transforming the film into a moving farewell to life itself (even though Cassavetes lived for five more years and made one more movie). The surreal touches and sense of unpredictability turn *Love Streams* into a difficult and occasionally frustrating film, but it stands as an emotionally rich and rewarding experience thanks to the affecting performances, masterful filmmaking, and spellbinding story.

See also *A Woman under the Influence* (1974), *Stranger Than Paradise* (1984), *Lost in Translation* (2003).

SPOTLIGHT: JOHN CASSAVETES (1929–1989)

Upon graduating from the American Academy of Dramatic Arts in 1950, John Cassavetes embarked on a career as an actor and appeared in several films and television dramas. In 1959, Cassavetes wrote and directed the groundbreaking low-budget independent film *Shadows*, which won the Critics Award at the Venice Film Festival in 1968. Cassavetes continued to act throughout the 1960s, appearing in films like *The Dirty Dozen* and *Rosemary's Baby*. Between 1968 and 1980, Cassavetes directed several independent films, including *Faces*, *Husbands*, *Minnie and Moskowitz*, *A Woman under the Influence*, *The Killing of a Chinese Bookie*, *Opening Night*, and *Gloria*. In 1983, he was diagnosed with cirrhosis of the liver prior to starting production on *Love Streams*, a film based on a play written by his friend Ted Allan. Though given just six months to live, Cassavetes survived to make one final film, the disastrous *Big Trouble*, which debuted in 1986. Cassavetes died in 1989, and is now remembered as a pioneer of American independent cinema.

M

MANOS: THE HANDS OF FATE (1966)

Director: Harold P. Warren
Screenplay: Harold P. Warren
Cast: Tom Neyman (the Master), John Reynolds (Torgo), Diane Adelson (Margaret), Harold P. Warren (Michael), Jackey Neyman Jones (Debbie), Stephanie Nielson (Master's Wife), Sherry Proctor (Master's Wife), Robin Redd (Master's Wife)
Specs: 70 minutes; color
Genre: horror
Availability: Blu-ray (Synapse Films)

Plot

During a fateful road trip, an unwitting family falls into the clutches of a sinister pagan cult.

Background

Manos: The Hands of Fate supposedly grew out of an encounter between screenwriter Stirling Silliphant and Harold P. Warren, an insurance and fertilizer salesman from El Paso, Texas.[1] According to legend, Warren met Silliphant while working as an extra on the TV series *Route 66*.[2] The two went out for coffee, and Warren boasted that anyone could produce a movie.[3] When Silliphant scoffed at this idea, Warren immediately outlined a script on some napkins.[4] In the days that followed, Warren raised $19,000 from local businessmen and dignitaries.[5] He then gathered a cast and crew comprised mainly of his community theater friends and aspiring models.[6] He cast John Reynolds as Torgo, and hired Tom Neyman, a local artist and community theater veteran, to serve as production designer and assume the role of the Master.[7] Warren decided to play the male lead himself,[8] and he cast Diane Adelson as the female lead despite her lack of experience.[9] Neyman's daughter, Jackie, played their daughter, Debbie. Finally, Warren gave lawyer and part-time actor William Bryan Jennings a supporting role, and appointed him president of Sun City Films.[10]

Filming took place mainly on an El Paso ranch owned by Judge Colbert Coldwell.[11] To save money, Warren shot without sound.[12] All dialogue was dubbed

Torgo (John Reynolds) spies on an unsuspecting Debbie (Diane, Adelson, not pictured) through the window. *Synapse Films/ © Ben Solovey*

during postproduction by Warren, Reynolds, Neyman, Jennings, and an unknown actress who voiced all the women in the film, including six-year-old Debbie.[13] Ernie Smith and James Sullivan edited *Manos* after hours at the local TV station, reportedly delivering the final cut in just four hours.[14] Tragically, Reynolds committed suicide a few months before the film's premiere, which took place at the Capri Theater in El Paso on November 5, 1966.[15] *Manos* was so poorly received that several members of the cast and crew snuck out after thirty minutes and went to a bar.[16] The film faded from memory in the years after its release but gained new life and a legion of rabid fans after it was featured in a 1993 episode of the cult television series *Mystery Science Theater 3000.*[17] Following a highly successful Kickstarter campaign launched by cinematographer Ben Solovey in 2015, *Manos* was painstakingly restored and rereleased to both DVD and Blu-ray.[18]

Commentary

Manos languished in obscurity for years, and with good reason: it is stilted and shoddily made, and the whole thing suffers from a sluggish pace and some truly dreadful performances. The cast's inexperience remains evident throughout, and the acting ranges from lifeless to histrionic. The clunky voice acting only makes things worse. Meanwhile, the sloppy editing results in several awkward pauses and scenes that last a beat or two longer than they should, and Warren's direction is lackluster and the camera rarely moves, rendering the film rather inert. Yet *Manos* occasionally evokes a weird, unsettling atmosphere, particularly in scenes involving the Master. Neyman clearly gives it his all, and his intense performance sometimes transcends the film's otherwise incompetent nature.

Unfortunately, *Manos* never approaches anything resembling conventional notions of good. In addition, it fails to work as camp because even at just seventy minutes long the dullness wears the viewer down long before the credits roll. Ultimately, the film only truly works as a curiosity. In some ways, *Manos* foreshadowed the independent film movement and therefore may appeal to hardcore fans of indie cinema and midnight movies, though it will no doubt test even their patience. Despite all this, the restored version of *Manos* is worth seeking out because the film looks better than ever; the colors pop, the sound is clear, and the improved picture quality reveals many little details that got lost in the murk of the original grindhouse version. Nonetheless, *Manos* remains a singularly terrible film.

See also *Plan 9 from Outer Space* (1959), *Eegah* (1962), *Santa Claus Conquers the Martians* (1964), *The Room* (2003), *Birdemic: Shock and Terror* (2010), *Fateful Findings* (2013).

SPOTLIGHT: *MYSTERY SCIENCE THEATER 3000*

Created by quirky stand-up comic Joel Hodgson, *Mystery Science Theater 3000* (a.k.a. *MST3K*) premiered on Minnesota's public access channel KTMA in 1988. The following year, the show made the jump to the burgeoning Comedy Channel (later Comedy Central), where it became a hit with lovers of trash cinema. In the show, two mad scientists send a hapless janitor into space aboard a satellite and force him to watch low-budget B movies alongside his homemade robot pals. To maintain their sanity, the crew of the *Satellite of Love* riff on each film, cracking hilarious jokes at a rapid-fire pace. Over the years, Hodgson and his dedicated riffers discovered or resurrected several films that seem ready-made for cult fandom, including *Manos: The Hands of Fate, Santa Claus Conquers the Martians,* and *Gamera.* In the years after the show's cancellation in 1999, former cast members created other movie riffing projects like The Film Crew, Rifftrax, and Cinematic Titanic. In 2016, Hodgson launched a highly successful Kickstarter campaign to revive *MST3K*, and a new version starring Jonah Ray, Patton Oswalt, Felicia Day, Hampton Yount, and Baron Vaughn debuted on Netflix on April 14, 2017.

MEAN GIRLS (2004)

Director: Mark Waters
Screenplay: Tina Fey
Cast: Lindsay Lohan (Cady Herron), Lizzy Caplan (Janis Ian), Rachel McAdams (Regina George), Lacey Chabert (Gretchen Wieners), Amanda Seyfried (Karen Smith), Jonathan Bennett (Aaron Samuels), Tina Fey (Ms. Norbury), Tim Meadows (Mr. Duvall), Amy Poehler (Mrs. George), Daniel Franzese (Damian), Ana Gasteyer (Cady's Mom), Neil Flynn (Cady's Dad)
Specs: 97 minutes; color
Genre: comedy
Availability: DVD and Blu-ray (Warner Bros.)

Plot

A worldly yet naive teenager moves to the Illinois suburbs and gets a lesson in the cruel laws of popularity when she befriends a clique of cool but shallow students known as the Plastics.

Background

While working on the NBC sketch comedy series *Saturday Night Live* in 2002, Tina Fey read Rosalind Wiseman's *Queen Bees & Wannabes*, a nonfiction book that offered an unflinching look at the behavior of teenage girls. Fey thought it might make a good movie, and she brought it to her boss, Lorne Michaels, who set up a production deal with Paramount Pictures.[19] Fey then wrote the screenplay for *Mean Girls*, which she based on her own high school experiences. To direct, the studio hired Mark Waters, who had recently helmed a successful remake of *Freaky Friday* starring Lindsay Lohan. Waters wanted to cast Lohan as lead antagonist Regina George, but Paramount chief Sherry Lansing thought Lohan should play main character Cady Heron, and she ordered Waters to make the switch.[20] Meanwhile, Rachel McAdams auditioned for the part of Cady, but she ultimately landed the role of Regina.[21] Amanda Seyfried also read for Regina, but was instead cast as dim bulb sidekick Karen based on a suggestion from Lorne Michaels.[22] Finally, Lacey Chabert won the part of insecure mean girl Gretchen Wieners. With the core cast assembled, *Mean Girls* entered production on September 27, 2003.

Waters shot the film in and around Toronto, Canada,[23] which stood in for Evanston, Illinois. The production ran smoothly, and principal photography wrapped on November 21, 2003. The Motion Picture Association of America slapped *Mean Girls* with an R rating due to several explicit gags and jokes, including one in which a girl explains that she uses jumbo tampons because she has a "wide-set vagina." The studio accused the ratings board of sexism, arguing that *Anchorman: The Legend of Ron Burgundy* earned a PG-13 rating even though main character Ron Burgundy parades around with a visible erection at one point. The ratings board eventually backed down and awarded *Mean Girls*

Cady (Lindsay Lohan, far left) tries to fit in with Regina George (Rachel McAdams, far right) and the other mean girls. *Paramount / Photofest © Paramount Pictures*

a PG-13, but only after Paramount agreed to cut some other objectionable material.[24] The film opened on April 30, 2004, and grossed $129 million in worldwide ticket sales during its entire theatrical run.[25] Since then, *Mean Girls* has become a bona fide pop culture phenomenon, spawning both a stand-alone straight-to-DVD sequel and a video game. *Mean Girls* remains a staple of slumber parties and quote-along screenings,[26] and a musical stage adaptation of the film premiered in Washington, DC in October of 2017.[27]

Commentary

Filled with smart comedy and genuine emotion, *Mean Girls* is a wickedly funny indictment of cliques and the desire for popularity. Like *Better Off Dead…* and *Heathers* before it, *Mean Girls* presents a fairly accurate depiction of the high school experience, and it features fully realized characters (most notably Lizzy Caplan as sarcastic Goth girl Janis Ian) and dozens of memorable lines (such as the immortal "Gretchen, stop trying to make 'fetch' happen!"). At the same time, *Mean Girls* occasionally gives itself over to some wonderfully silly digressions (particularly during the moments when Cady compares her classmates and their behavior to the animals she observed in Africa), and it features a handful of outrageously cartoonish gags that nevertheless work within the context of the film (like Regina's comically long scream, which lasts a full thirty seconds and recalls a similar bit from *The Simpsons*). The film balances the humor with plenty of heart and tackles some tough issues in a frank and altogether touching manner (though it remains acerbic throughout and never descends into schmaltz). As such, *Mean Girls* is sure to strike a chord with anyone who survived high school, regardless of whether they hung out with the burnouts, the desperate wannabes, or the Plastics.

In addition to the sardonic humor, *Mean Girls* also tackles still-relevant hot-button issues like bullying and slut-shaming (both of which have only increased in the age of social media). The film shines a harsh light on the behavior of teenage girls, and it offers an irreverent but irritated look at how society shames young women into believing they need to live up to an unattainable ideal of femininity, which in turn fuels the sort of petty jealousies that can lead to bullying and victimization. *Mean Girls* (rightly) suggests that girls and young women face a constant pressure to look and act a certain way, and those who fail to do so endure mockery and marginalization. In the film, such girls wind up in the pages of Regina's Burn Book, an intimidating pink tome that the Plastics use to collect rumors, stories, and gossip (like "Trang Pak made out with Coach Carr" or "Amber D'Alessio made out with a hot dog"). This pressure explains why Cady tries so hard to change herself (for instance, she pretends to be bad at math so Aaron will help her and find her more attractive), and why she puts up with Regina's backhanded barbs (as she explains, "The weird thing about hanging out with Regina is that I could hate her, but I still wanted her to like me"). The film understands teen girls and their behavior, but it also offers valuable insight into society itself, which explains why *Mean Girls* resonates more than ten years after its initial release.

Mean Girls offers up an endearingly funny and thoughtful look at growing up, and it features loads of crazy situations, wonderful characters, and unforgettable dialogue. It also grapples with some difficult topics and offers valuable life lessons. In the end, however, *Mean Girls* stands as a hilarious comedy that will have viewers laughing even as they nod their heads in recognition.

See also *Heathers* (1988), *Clueless* (1995), *Jawbreaker* (1999).

MEMENTO (2000)

Director: Christopher Nolan
Screenplay: Christopher Nolan
Cast: Guy Pearce (Leonard), Carrie-Anne Moss (Natalie), Joe Pantoliano (Teddy), Mark Boone Junior (Burt), Stephen Tobolowsky (Sammy Jankis), Jorja Fox (Leonard's Wife), Harriet Sansom Harris (Mrs. Jankis), Thomas Lennon (Doctor)
Specs: 113 minutes; color/black and white
Genre: mystery, thriller
Availability: DVD and Blu-ray (Lionsgate Films)

Plot

An ex-insurance investigator who suffers from anterograde amnesia searches for his wife's killer, but things become complicated when he meets a scheming bartender who wants to use his condition to her advantage.

Background

After discussing the idea during a road trip with his brother Jonathan in July of 1997, writer/director Christopher Nolan wrote the screenplay for *Memento*.[28] One year later, Newmarket Films read an early draft of Nolan's script,[29] and then optioned it with a $4.5 million budget to make the picture.[30] Nolan then set about casting the film. He initially wanted Brad Pitt in the lead role, but scheduling conflicts prevented that from happening.[31] Nolan met with several other actors, including Aaron Eckhart and Thomas Jane, but he eventually settled on Australian actor and musician Guy Pearce, star of *L.A. Confidential*.[32] Nolan filled the other roles soon after, and *Memento* entered production on September 7, 1999.[33]

Nolan shot the film mainly on location in various locales throughout Los Angeles, California.[34] The production moved swiftly, and principal photography wrapped on October 8, 1999, just twenty-five days after it began.[35] The finished film premiered at the Venice Film Festival on September 5, 2000, and received a standing ovation. From there, *Memento* toured the festival circuit and generated a great deal of positive buzz.[36] Nonetheless, finding an American distributor proved difficult because most studio heads worried that the film's unusual structure (the narrative plays out in reverse chronological fashion) would hurt its chances at the box office.[37]

Eventually, Newmarket decided to take a financial risk and distribute *Memento* themselves,[38] opening the film in 500 theaters across the United States on May 25, 2001.[39] Their gamble paid off, because *Memento* generated over $25 million in ticket sales before ending its theatrical run on September 16, 2001.[40] It also received glowing reviews and landed on numerous top ten lists that year.[41] *Memento* is now recognized as a bona fide cult classic, and it continues to inspire heated discussion and analysis even now thanks to its narrative complexity and tough themes.

Leonard Shelby (Guy Pearce) tries to find his wife's murderer. *IFC Films / Photofest © IFC Films*

Commentary

Memento opens with the main character shooting someone in the head, photographing the victim's corpse with a Polaroid camera, and then waiting for the image to slowly develop, all of which plays out in reverse. This startling introduction lets the audience know exactly what to expect from the rest of the film, which unfolds backward and places the viewer squarely in the shoes of lead character Leonard Shelby (Pearce). This unusual narrative gimmick turns an otherwise simple (and somewhat forgettable) crime story into something far more intriguing. Each new sequence leaves viewers feeling just as confused and disoriented as the protagonist, drawing them deeper into Leonard's predicament as they work to piece together the on-screen events along with him. Revealing the ending up front infuses *Memento* with an almost Hitchcockian feeling of suspense, and the film frequently recalls Alfred Hitchcock's *Rope*, which also opens with a murder and then generates tension as the audience waits for one of the characters to discover the victim's body. Viewers might think they know where *Memento* is headed, but the film still serves up plenty of twists as it races toward a tense finale that reveals the disturbing truth about Leonard and his activities.

The film also boasts expert filmmaking and fine acting. Pearce turns lead character Leonard Shelby into a compelling and tragic figure haunted by the death of his wife, but who also possesses a morbid sense of humor and an ironic wit. Meanwhile, Carrie Anne Moss gives a powerful and tough performance as Natalie, a classic femme fatale who manipulates Leonard into doing her bidding. Joe Pantoliano rounds out the central cast as Leonard's sidekick Teddy, an overbearing but charming undercover cop who harbors his own dark secret. Yet *Memento* truly belongs to Nolan, who directs the film with his usual meticulousness and transforms the whole thing into a mind-bending jigsaw puzzle that demands repeat viewings. The complex narrative structure ensures that *Memento* remains engrossing throughout, even during those moments when it threatens to run out of steam. Nolan receives a lot of help from director of photography Wally Pfister, whose crisp cinematography imbues the film with a cool intensity, and composer David Julyan, who underscores the action with a foreboding minimalist score. The assured filmmaking and powerful performances turn *Memento* into a superb neo-noir thriller guaranteed to linger in the viewer's mind for a long time.

See also *The Usual Suspects* (1995), *Fight Club* (1999), *Donnie Darko* (2001), *Mulholland Drive* (2001).

MIAMI CONNECTION (1987)

Director: Woo-sang Park, Y. K. Kim (uncredited)
Screenplay: Joseph Diamand, Woo-sang Park (story), Y. K. Kim (story)
Cast: Y. K. Kim (Mark), Vincent Hirsch (John), Joseph Diamand (Jack), Maurice Smith (Jim), Angelo Janotti (Tom), Kathy Collier (Jane), William Ergle (Jeff), Si Y Jo (Yashito), Woo-sang Park (Uncle Song)
Specs: 83 minutes; color
Genre: action, crime, thriller
Availability: DVD and Blu-ray (Drafthouse Films)

Plot

The members of multinational martial arts synth rock band Dragon Sound use their Tae Kwon Do skills to stop a gang of cocaine-dealing, motorcycle-riding ninjas from terrorizing Orlando, Florida.

Background

Miami Connection was a true labor of love for its creators, who wanted to use the film to promote the philosophy of Tae Kwon Do.[42] After seeing author, inspirational speaker, and ninth degree black belt Tae Kwon Do Grandmaster Y. K. Kim interviewed on a Korean talk show, director Woo-sang Park convinced the martial arts master that they should make a movie together.[43] Despite some initial reluctance, Kim agreed, and he raised $1 million to produce the film by borrowing money from friends, taking out loans, dipping into his savings, and mortgaging his martial arts school.[44] To cut costs, Kim recruited his friends and students as cast and crew.[45]

Mark (Grandmaster Y. K. Kim) leaps into battle against the deadly drug-dealing ninjas. *Image Entertainment / Photofest © Image Entertainment*

After a long, somewhat tumultuous production, Kim took *Miami Connection* to nearly every major distributor and several independents, but they all rejected it and advised Kim not to waste his time on such trash.[46] Eventually, a small distribution company called Manson International purchased *Miami Connection* for $100,000[47] (although Kim also recalls distributing it himself[48]) and released it into eight theaters throughout Florida in September of 1988.[49] Unfortunately, audiences of the time ignored the film, while critics trashed it.[50] At that point, Kim decided to forget about the movie and focus on his teaching and public speaking.[51] Years later, however, *Miami Connection* became something of a cult hit.[52] In 2009, Zach Carlson of the Alamo Drafthouse bought a 35 mm print of the film for fifty dollars on eBay and screened the film in 2010.[53] In 2012, boutique home video label Drafthouse Films rereleased *Miami Connection* to theaters and later on various home video formats, allowing cult movie fanatics to rediscover and embrace the film.[54]

Commentary

A genuine piece of outsider art, *Miami Connection* resembles professionally produced action films but feels nothing like them, and as such it becomes even more entertaining. Every aspect of *Miami Connection* reveals the inexperience of Kim and his collaborators: the story is a mess (plot threads are dropped without warning, and it often seems like the film wants to tell three different stories at once), the dialogue is laughable ("My mother was Korean, and my father was Black American"), and the performances are inept at best (the bad guy's three teenaged henchmen are particularly terrible). Yet these imperfections only add to the film's considerable charm. Everything on-screen is played completely straight, and Kim appears so sincere in his belief that friendship and Tae Kwon Do can solve all the world's problems that one cannot help but get swept up in the proceedings and cheer for Dragon Sound as they fight to save their adopted home from the vicious motorcycle ninjas.

Despite the incompetence of nearly all involved, *Miami Connection* features decent action sequences and legitimately catchy tunes (be prepared to have "Friends" stuck in your head for days after watching the movie). The action comes courtesy of director Park, who helmed several low-budget martial arts films before tackling *Miami Connection*. The songs, meanwhile, are primarily provided by Lloyd C. Sharp and the Lloyds Richards Band, though the two standout tracks ("Against the Ninja" and the aforementioned "Friends") were written by Angelo Janotti and Kathy Collier, who appear in the film as Tom and Jane respectively. Together, Janotti—who resembles a bargain basement version of John Oates—and Collier penned two painfully earnest and woefully dated synth rock anthems that establish Dragon Sound's cheesy 1980s aesthetic. At the same time, these insanely memorable earworms are guaranteed to set the viewer's toes to tapping.

Cynical viewers could easily write off *Miami Connection* as a terrible, poorly made movie that only becomes entertaining when viewed through a lens of ironic detachment, but that assessment is somewhat unfair. While the film offers plenty of opportunity for derision (for some of the worst acting ever put to film, check out the scene in which a rival band confronts the local club owner to demand Dragon Sound's spot), it also features exciting action, a sincere (albeit confusing) narrative, and a great soundtrack. The straightforward seriousness ensures that the movie transcends its badness and eventually warps all the way back around to being good (in a goofy, amateurish sort of way). Viewers in the mood for a "bad" movie they can laugh with rather than at could do a lot worse than *Miami Connection*.

See also *Manos: The Hand of Fate* (1966), *Hard Ticket to Hawaii* (1987), *Samurai Cop* (1991), *The Room* (2003), *Dangerous Men* (2005), *Fateful Findings* (2013).

SPOTLIGHT: DRAFTHOUSE FILMS

Per their mission statement, Drafthouse Films—the distribution arm of the Alamo Drafthouse theater chain—is dedicated to finding and releasing "provocative, visionary and artfully unusual films new and old from around the world." Founded by Tim League in 2010, the label has curated a diverse collection of films that includes powerful, award-winning documentaries (*The Act of Killing*, *The Overnighters*); weird, offbeat comedies (*Wrong*, *Cheap Thrills*); and critically acclaimed, Oscar-nominated dramas from around the world (*Bullhead*). More than anything, though, Drafthouse Films specializes in unearthing films that seem tailor-made for cult audiences. In addition to rescuing *Miami Connection* from obscurity, Drafthouse has rereleased forgotten or ignored flicks like *Wake in Fright*, *The Visitor*, *Ms .45*, *Roar*, and *Dangerous Men*. Best of all, the company restores each film to pristine perfection, and their Blu-ray and DVD releases come stacked with extra features. Essentially a Criterion Collection for cult cinema, Drafthouse Films is one of the best things to ever happen to cult film lovers.

MS .45 (1981)

Director: Abel Ferrara
Screenplay: Nicholas St. John
Cast: Zoë Lund (Thana), Bogey (Phil), Albert Sinkys (Albert), Darlene Stuto (Laurie), Helen McGara (Carol), Nike Zachmanoglou (Pamela), Abel Ferrara (First Rapist)
Specs: 80 minutes; color
Genre: crime, drama, thriller
Availability: DVD and Blu-ray (Drafthouse Films)

Plot

After falling victim to two vicious sexual assaults in one day, a mute seamstress embarks on a vengeful shooting rampage against the men of New York.

Background

Director Abel Ferrara grew up in Peekskill, New York, with his childhood friends Nicholas St. John and Jack McIntyre, and the three later formed a collaborative partnership that produced several films, including Ferrara's directorial debut, *The Driller Killer*.[55] In 1981, St. John wrote a screenplay for a lurid revenge thriller called *Ms .45*.[56] Ferrara loved it and agreed to direct.[57] He then embarked on a search for a woman to play the lead role of Thana, eventually settling on seventeen-year-old Zoë Lund (a.k.a. Zoë Tamerlis), a Columbia University student who impressed Ferrara with her worldliness and intelligence.[58] Ferrara cast her on the spot, and production commenced soon after.[59]

Ferrara shot the film for an estimated $62,000 and gathered much of the footage guerrilla style on the streets of New York City.[60] He hired musician Joe Delia to compose an atonal, pulsating score that used blaring saxophones to create a sense of unease and urgency.[61] Ferrara worked closely with Lund throughout the production, and she infused the film with a sense of feminist empowerment that was absent in the original script (this may explain why she later claimed she wrote and directed the film herself).[62] After production wrapped, Lund left for Italy and reportedly spent the next three years fighting with the Red Brigade, a violent left-wing paramilitary organization.[63] She returned to the United States in 1983 with a raging heroin habit and a sixty-year-old junkie boyfriend who claimed to be the brother of Gillo Pontecorvo, director of *The Battle of Algiers*.[64] The duo stole the print of *Ms .45*, reshot the ending, and screened the film at theaters throughout the United States to raise money for the Red Brigade.[65]

Prior to that, *Ms .45* opened in the United States on April 24, 1981. It became a mainstay of the rapidly declining grindhouse theaters, and nearly twenty years later Image Entertainment released it to DVD, albeit in a slightly edited form.[66] Over the years, *Ms .45* developed a reputation as a superior entry in the

Thana (Zoë Lund) prepares to attend a Halloween party, where she intends to continue her bloody rampage. *Rochelle Films / Photofest © Rochelle Films*

disreputable rape-revenge genre, which includes films like *I Spit on Your Grave* and *Savage Streets*. Furthermore, Lund's unique image of female liberation resonated with an entire generation of women, such as the members of Los Angeles punk outfit L7, who recorded a song called "Ms. 45."[67] In 2014, Drafthouse Films rereleased the uncut version of *Ms .45* to theaters and home video,[68] allowing a whole new generation of film fans to discover this masterpiece of cult cinema.

Commentary

Much like *Foxy Brown* benefits from Pam Grier's powerful turn as the title character, *Ms .45* revolves almost entirely around the performance of its lead actress. As mute seamstress Thana, Lund delivers a brave, intense, and altogether harrowing performance, displaying a world-weariness that belies her youth. This becomes even more impressive when considering that aside from a single whispered word, Lund remains silent throughout the film. Instead, she uses her body and extremely expressive face to imbue Thana with equal amounts of vulnerability and toughness. Lund's assured acting transforms Thana's muteness into a commentary on how women's voices often become silenced in society. Lund brings a great deal of nuance and ambiguity to the role, ensuring that Thana's violence appears excessive but also completely justified. Over the years, Lund's performance helped *Ms .45* earn a reputation as one of the most feminist films ever made, and nearly forty years on the film remains a raw, brutal, and uncompromising look at the subjective experience of women in a male-dominated world.

James Lemmo's camera work highlights the griminess of late 1970s/early 1980s New York, which reflects the filthy souls of the hardened and depraved men who live there. Meanwhile, Ferrara repeatedly positions the male characters as predators who stalk women in their endless search for sexual release (interestingly, Ferrara himself plays the masked man who first assaults Thana). He reinforces this idea by tossing in allusions to *Psycho* and *Taxi Driver*, two films that feature men preying on women in different ways. In the former, Norman Bates punishes a young woman who openly rejects sociocultural norms regarding feminine propriety, while in the latter Travis Bickle sets out to "save" an underage prostitute after another woman rejects his advances. In each film, the men use violence to suppress or control female sexuality and expression, and by referencing them Ferrara turns Thana's own violence into a natural (if self-destructive) response to such oppression.

Ms .45 shines a harsh light on the fear, hostility, and condescension that women routinely face throughout their lives. Lund's daring performance turns Thana into an avatar for women everywhere, and her violence becomes a blunt but effective metaphor for female liberation. The struggle for equality continues to rage well into the twenty-first century and shows no signs of stopping anytime soon, meaning that *Ms .45* still feels vital and important more than three decades after its initial release.

See also *Thriller: A Cruel Picture*, also known as *They Call Her One-Eye* (1973), *Foxy Brown* (1974), *I Spit on Your Grave* (1978), *Hard Candy* (2005).

N

NIGHT OF THE LIVING DEAD (1968)

Director: George A. Romero
Screenplay: John A. Russo, George A. Romero
Cast: Duane Jones (Ben), Judith O'Dea (Barbra), Karl Hardman (Harry), Marilyn
    Eastman (Helen), Keith Wayne (Tom), Judith Ridley (Judy), Kyra Schon (Karen
    Cooper)
Specs: 96 minutes; black and white
Genre: drama, horror, mystery
Availability: Blu-ray (Forgotten Films)

Plot

To escape a horde of flesh-eating zombies, a group of strangers barricade themselves inside an old farmhouse, but their chances of survival grow slimmer as the
night wears on.

Background

After a brief stint making commercials and industrial films, George Romero
decided to write and direct a horror film.[1] He raised a budget of $114,000 with the
help of his friends John Russo and Russell Streiner.[2] They then set about developing the story, which initially concerned aliens befriending a group of teenagers.[3]
This changed when Russo came up with an idea about undead ghouls rampaging
through the countryside and feasting on human flesh.[4] From there, the filmmakers
assembled their cast, starting with African American actor Duane Jones as the central protagonist. They then secured permission to shoot in a rundown farmhouse
in Evans City, Pennsylvania,[5] and *Night of the Living Dead* commenced filming in
June of 1967.

Production proved difficult, and Romero ran into several problems during the
shoot. For instance, the script included several scenes set in a basement, but the
crew deemed the farmhouse cellar unsuitable for filming, so Romero shot those
scenes later on a set built in the Latent Image offices in Pittsburgh.[6] Meanwhile,
the production only had enough time and film to get one take of each shot.[7] The
filmmakers also considered reshooting the entire film in color, but since they had
already gathered a week's worth of footage and would have to switch entirely

Zombies shamble toward the house in search of victims. *Continental Distributing Inc. / Photofest © Continental Distributing Inc.*

to 16 mm, they decided to stick with black and white.[8] The production wrapped in December of 1967, and Romero ran into further problems while editing the film because he shot on 35 mm but only had access to 16 mm editing equipment, meaning the crew had to transfer all the footage to 16 mm before Romero could assemble the final cut.[9]

Night of the Living Dead premiered on October 1, 1968, at the Fulton Theater in Pittsburgh[10] and sparked a great deal of controversy.[11] Yet it became extremely profitable, earning over $40 million at the box office.[12] Sadly, Romero failed to capitalize on the film's success because the theatrical distributor deleted the copyright notice from the final print.[13] As such, *Night of the Living Dead* entered the public domain upon release, and the distributor kept all the money.[14] Nevertheless, the film established Romero's reputation and spawned a lucrative franchise. It also kicked off the zombie genre that shambles on to this day,[15] and its DNA can be found in everything from *Shaun of the Dead* to *The Walking Dead* to the *Resident Evil* franchise.

Commentary

Night of the Living Dead looks and feels like a throwback to the low-budget horror and sci-fi flicks of the 1950s, but one that also points to the future of both genres. Drawing inspiration from Richard Matheson's classic novel *I Am Legend*, Romero crafts a simple but effective tale of survival horror, taking the core concept (a small group of survivors holed up in an isolated location and surrounded by monsters) and making it his own through a powerful blend of convincing gore effects, moody black-and-white cinematography, and sharp social commentary.

As mentioned, *Night of the Living Dead* caused a sensation when it first came out, and to this day it still holds the power to shock. The gore effects look disturbingly real even now thanks to some believable makeup and Romero's decision to use roasted ham and pig entrails as a stand-in for human innards. Meanwhile, the excellent sound design renders both the inhuman moans of the zombies and the bloodcurdling screams of their victims truly terrifying. In addition, Romero's direction and camerawork effectively build the tension until it explodes during the brutally violent climax. *Night of the Living Dead* also features solid performances throughout, though Jones stands out and his presence reinforces the film's (apparently unintentional) thematic undercurrent, which shines a harsh light on race relations in the United States.

A combination of shocking gore, skillful filmmaking, and timely social allegory allow *Night of the Living Dead* to transcend its low-budget origins and ensure that it remains a frightening and effective horror film, even as the zombie genre it spawned feels increasingly played out.

See also *Carnival of Souls* (1962), *Dawn of the Dead* (1978), *Day of the Dead* (1985), *Night of the Living Dead* (1990), *Shaun of the Dead* (2004).

SPOTLIGHT: GEORGE A. ROMERO (1940–2017)

After graduating from Carnegie Mellon University in the late 1960s, George Romero made several television commercials and industrial films for Image Ten Productions, a production company he cofounded with his friends John Russo and Russell Streiner. In 1968, Romero cowrote and directed the pioneering zombie film *Night of the Living Dead*. From there, he made several socially conscious horror films, including *The Crazies*, *Hungry Wives*, and *Martin*, all shot in and around his hometown of Pittsburgh, Pennsylvania. In 1978, Romero released *Dawn of the Dead*, an ambitious sequel that became a smash hit and opened many doors for Romero in Hollywood. From there, Romero helmed big-budget productions like *Knightriders*, *Creepshow*, and *Day of the Dead*. When those films all failed at the box office, Romero's career declined. After spending years directing duds like *Monkey Shines*, *The Dark Half*, and *Bruiser*, Romero mounted a comeback in 2005 with *Land of the Dead*, a zombie film that generated mostly positive reviews and decent box office. In the years after, Romero directed two more zombie films, wrote comic books, and lent his voice to video games like *Call of Duty: Black Ops* and *Zombie Squash*. He died on July 16, 2017.

> ## *THE NIGHTMARE BEFORE CHRISTMAS* (1993)
>
> *Director:* Henry Selick
> *Screenplay:* Caroline Thompson
> *Cast:* Chris Sarandon (Jack Skellington), Catherine O'Hara (Sally/Shock), William Hickey (Dr. Finkelstein), Glenn Shadix (Mayor), Paul Reubens (Lock), Danny Elfman (Jack Skellington—Singing Voice/Barrel/Clown with the Tear Away Face), Ken Page (Oogie Boogie)
> *Specs:* 76 minutes; color
> *Genre:* family, fantasy, musical
> *Availability:* DVD and Blu-ray (Disney/Buena Vista)

Plot

When he grows bored with his own annual holiday, the King of Halloween Town sets out to take over Christmas, but his efforts to spread joy and good cheer soon spin wildly out of control.

Background

The Nightmare before Christmas marks the directorial debut of animator Henry Selick, who stepped in at the request of his Disney Animation colleague Tim Burton. At the time, Burton was developing *Batman Returns* for Warner Bros., and he asked Selick to direct *Nightmare* in his place.[16] Featuring a screenplay by Caroline Thompson, the project was inspired by a poem Burton wrote while working on Disney films like *The Fox and the Hound* and *The Black Cauldron*.[17] Burton also designed the characters and developed the film's distinctive look.[18] He initially envisioned *Nightmare* as an animated television production in the vein of the old Rankin/Bass holiday specials, but the idea ultimately proved too weird for his bosses at Walt Disney Studios.[19] Years later, Disney underwent a regime change, and Jeffrey Katzenberg greenlit a theatrical version of the project with an $18 million budget.[20] *Nightmare* commenced filming on August 1, 1991, several weeks before Thompson finished writing the screenplay.[21]

Selick and his team spent nearly three years making *Nightmare*.[22] Selick opted to shoot the film at twenty-four frames per second, meaning it took roughly one full week to shoot a single minute of the film.[23] The animators needed to create unique motions for 110,000 total frames,[24] and they built 227 puppets, each with several different heads that allowed for the expression of every possible emotion.[25] The set included a network of secret passages that allowed the animators to move about freely while manipulating the characters.[26] Throughout production, Disney executives offered copious notes, but Burton and Selick managed to fend off most of these requests.[27] Nevertheless, studio executives worried that *Nightmare* might prove too dark and scary for children, and thus they decided to release the film through their Touchstone Pictures banner rather than the more kid-friendly Walt Disney Pictures.[28] The grueling production finally wrapped in June of 1993, and *Nightmare* opened in limited release on October 15, 1993.

Jack Skellington discovers Christmas Town. *Buena Vista Pictures / Photofest © Buena Vista Pictures*

Two weeks later it entered wide release on October 29, 1993, at which point it received mostly positive reviews and became a modest commercial hit, earning $50 million in the United States.[29]

In the years after its release, *Nightmare* developed an enthusiastic cult following and became a marketing juggernaut that spawned action figures, Halloween costumes, children's books, video games, and more. Disney has since embraced *Nightmare*, and in 2001 the studio proposed a CGI sequel, though Burton quickly nixed that idea.[30] Nevertheless, Disney rereleased a 3-D version of *Nightmare* into theaters in 2006. Since October of 2001, Disneyland theme park has also boasted a seasonal *Nightmare* theme for its Haunted Mansion attraction that features characters, decorations, and music from the film.[31]

Commentary

More than twenty years after it first stole the little black hearts of Goth kids everywhere, *Nightmare* endures as a lushly animated and darkly comic tour de force that contains enchanting visuals, catchy songs, and delightful characters. It also features a fun, inventive story and enthusiastic performances from the skilled voice cast. The film occasionally resembles Rankin/Bass holiday specials like *Rudolph the Red-Nosed Reindeer* and *Santa Claus Is Comin' to Town*, but Burton's idiosyncratic vision ensures that *Nightmare* stands on its own. Selick may have handled the directing duties, but the film feels like the culmination of Burton's signature fussy aesthetic.

From a purely visual standpoint, *Nightmare* recalls a German Expressionist pop-up book thanks to the whimsical set design and adorably bizarre characters.

The jagged buildings, twisted trees, and stark shadows imbue the film with a captivating weirdness that suggests Expressionist masterpieces like *The Cabinet of Dr. Caligari* (lead character Jack Skellington even vaguely resembles that film's Cesare the Somnambulist). Of course, Selick puts his own stamp on the film, which boasts graceful stop-motion animation that brings everything on-screen to vivid life and infuses each character with their own distinctive personality.

The film also features memorable songs written by Oingo Boingo front man and frequent Burton collaborator Danny Elfman, who also composed the haunting score and provided the lead character's singing voice. The soundtrack includes several lively tunes that are guaranteed to linger in the viewer's brain long after the film ends, including "This Is Halloween," "Kidnap the Sandy Claus," and the showstopping "What's This?" It also contains some moving ballads, like the melancholy "Jack's Lament" and the touching "Sally's Song." Meanwhile, the score alternates between jaunty and maudlin, but ensures that the film remains lighthearted even during the sad bits (such as a dejected Jack trudging through the forest on his way to discovering the doorway to Christmas Town).

In addition to the visuals and the music, the film also conveys a powerful message about remaining true to yourself and making the best of your situation, and in some ways Sally serves as a source of empowerment for young girls. These elements and more make *Nightmare* a charmingly weird stop-motion animated extravaganza that features great songs, iconic characters, and macabre humor.

See also *Mad Monster Party?* (1967), *James and the Giant Peach* (1996), *Monkeybone* (2001), *Coraline* (2009), *ParaNorman* (2012).

O

OFFICE SPACE (1999)

Director: Mike Judge
Screenplay: Mike Judge
Cast: Ron Livingston (Peter), Jennifer Aniston (Joanna), David Herman (Michael
  Bolton), Ajay Naidu (Samir), Diedrich Bader (Lawrence), Stephen Root (Milton),
  Gary Cole (Bill Lumbergh)
Specs: 89 minutes; color
Genre: comedy
Availability: DVD and Blu-ray (20th Century Fox)

Plot

Three dissatisfied office workers conspire to rob their employer, but a careless
mistake threatens to expose their shenanigans.

Background

In the early 1990s, aspiring animator Mike Judge created a series of four animated shorts based on his experiences working in San Diego.[1] Collectively known
as "Office Space," the shorts followed the plight of Milton Waddams, a luckless
office drone who suffers all sorts of indignities as he struggles to make it through
the workday.[2] The shorts premiered on MTV's animation showcase *Liquid Television* but gained wider exposure after they aired on *Saturday Night Live*.[3] By that
point, however, Judge had turned his attention to developing a new project
called *Beavis and Butt-Head*, which went on to capture the zeitgeist in a big way.[4]
Then, in 1998, 20th Century Fox scored a massive hit with *There's Something about
Mary*, and while searching for the next big comedy, the studio stumbled upon the
original "Office Space" shorts.[5] Fox executives convinced Judge to adapt them as
a feature-length film despite his initial hesitation.[6] He wrote a script, and *Office
Space* commenced filming soon after on May 4, 1998.

During the shoot, Judge worked with cinematographer Tim Suhrstedt, who
taught the novice director about lens and camera placement.[7] Unfortunately,
Fox executives disliked Judge's work and demanded he make several changes to
the film. Most notably, they wanted him to remove the gangsta rap used on the

Peter (Ron Livingston, center), Samir (Ajay Naidu, left), and Michael (David Herman, second from right) complain about their jobs with Tom (Richard Riehle). *20th Century Fox / Photofest © 20th Century Fox*

soundtrack[8] (they later changed their minds after the music tested positively with focus groups[9]). Filming wrapped on June 29, 1998, and *Office Space* opened on February 19, 1999,[10] only to fail at the box office.[11] Yet the film became a cult hit on home video, particularly among accountants and other office workers. It even inspired some fans to quit their jobs.[12] At that point, the studio asked Judge to make a sequel called *Office Space 2: Still Renting*, but Judge refused because he had suffered enough anguish while making the first film.[13] The original *Office Space* remains a cult favorite to this day, and in 2016 presidential candidate Senator Ted Cruz spoofed the film in a campaign commercial that featured a Hillary Clinton lookalike demolishing a personal email server.[14]

Commentary

Office Space expertly skewers the soul-crushing monotony of corporate life and the utter pointlessness of organizational culture. The film captures the infuriating obliviousness and petty cruelty of upper management, and serves as a sidesplitting send-up of the menial tasks and trivial nonsense that make the average office worker's life a living hell. Throughout *Office Space*, Judge's comedic sensibilities turn even the most mundane situations into fodder for amusing and engaging comedy (such as lead character Peter's growing exasperation over the TPS report covers, or the humorously heartbreaking saga of Milton's red Swingline stapler). The film also features instantly iconic dialogue ("Uh-oh! Sounds like somebody's got a case of the Mondays!") and boasts a phenomenal cast of extremely talented comedic performers, all of whom deliver amusing performances (especially Gary

Cole as unctuous middle manager Bill Lumbergh, and Stephen Root as put-upon ex-employee Milton). While the business landscape has changed dramatically since the film first came out, *Office Space* nevertheless stands as a rollicking satire of the corporate world.

In addition to the satirical elements, *Office Space* occasionally gives itself over to cartoonish nonsense, such as Peter's feverish nightmare involving his boss and new girlfriend, Joanna (played by Jennifer Aniston, who does her best in a slightly undercooked role), or the fate of his hapless older coworker, Tom (veteran character actor Richard Riehle). These outlandish asides make sense given Judge's background as an animator, and provide the film with a feeling of surreal weirdness that helps turn the somewhat conventional story into something far more outrageous and memorable. Judge backs the shenanigans with a soundtrack comprised primarily of hip-hop and gangsta rap tunes and uses them to convey the sense of anger, bitterness, and frustration that boils just beneath the surface of the central characters' buttoned-down, white-collar exteriors. Of course, certain aspects of *Office Space* have aged somewhat poorly (like the stuff about the Y2K virus and the mild gay panic humor), but not enough to sink the film itself. Overall, *Office Space* stands as a laid-back but viciously funny look at cubicle culture, as well as one of the weirdest studio comedies ever made.

See also *Being John Malkovich* (1999), *Fight Club* (1999), *Idiocracy* (2006).

SPOTLIGHT: MIKE JUDGE (1962–)

Mike Judge studied physics at the University of California, San Diego. Upon graduating in 1986, he took a job as a programmer at Support Systems Associates, Inc. The following year, he joined Parallax Graphics, a small start-up based in Silicon Valley. Judge soon tired of the corporate life, however, so he picked up his bass guitar and hit the road with a touring blues band. In 1989, Judge embarked on a career as an animator, using a Bolex 16 mm film camera to make his own animated shorts such as *Milton* and *Frog Baseball*. A few years later, Judge earned widespread fame when he created the smash hit television series *Beavis and Butt-Head*, which spawned both the feature-length film *Beavis and Butt-Head Do America* and the spinoff series *Daria*. In 1995, Judge teamed with former *The Simpsons* writer Greg Daniels to create the animated series *King of the Hill*, which became a hit with both audiences and critics. From there, Judge directed the live-action films *Office Space*, *Idiocracy*, and *Extract*, and created the TV shows *The Goode Family* and *Silicon Valley*.

P

PEE-WEE'S BIG ADVENTURE (1985)

Director: Tim Burton
Screenplay: Phil Hartman, Paul Reubens, Michael Varhol
Cast: Paul Reubens (Pee-wee Herman), Elizabeth Daily (Dottie), Mark Holton (Francis Buxton), Diane Salinger (Simone), Judd Omen (Mickey)
Specs: 91 minutes; color
Genre: adventure, comedy, family
Availability: DVD and Blu-ray (Warner Bros.)

Plot

An eccentric man-child embarks on a wild cross-country adventure in search of his stolen bicycle.

Background

In 1981, comedians Paul Reubens and Phil Hartman developed *The Pee-wee Herman Show* while performing together as part of the Los Angeles–based improvisational comedy troupe the Groundlings.[1] Based on a character created by Reubens in the late 1970s, the stage show ostensibly functioned as a parody of low-budget children's TV shows like *The Howdy Doody Show* and *Captain Kangaroo*.[2] The show became a hit and eventually landed on HBO,[3] prompting Warner Bros. to hire Reubens and Hartman to develop a Pee-wee Herman film. Drawing inspiration from Vittorio De Sica's Neo-realist masterpiece *Bicycle Thieves*, Reubens and Hartman wrote a script that saw Pee-wee searching for his stolen bicycle.[4] Meanwhile, Reubens demanded the services of novice director Tim Burton, who had generated positive buzz with his short films *Vincent* and *Frankenweenie*.[5] Reubens and Hartman worked with Michael Varhol to complete the script,[6] and *Pee-wee's Big Adventure* commenced filming on January 8, 1985.[7]

Burton shot most of the film in various locations throughout California and San Antonio, Texas.[8] During production, Burton and Reubens clashed with Warner Bros. executives, particularly over the shooting schedule.[9] Filming wrapped on April 1, 1985,[10] at which point Burton asked Oingo Boingo front man Danny Elfman to compose the film's score.[11] Executives at Warner Bros. found *Pee-wee's*

Pee-wee (Paul Reubens) dreams of riding his beloved bike in the Tour de France. *Warner Bros. / Photofest © Warner Bros.*

Big Adventure quite bizarre and decided to dump it in theaters with a low-profile limited release on August 9, 1985.[12] The film nevertheless became a minor hit with both critics and audiences,[13] grossing just under $41 million at the box office.[14] The film turned Pee-wee Herman into a household name and became a massive cult hit on home video, spawning two inferior follow-ups and the beloved children's television show *Pee-wee's Playhouse*.

Commentary

Filled with boundless imagination and a playfully anarchic spirit, *Pee-wee's Big Adventure* sends up Hollywood clichés and pays homage to the power of cinema. The film feels unlike anything else thanks to Burton's distinctly weird vision and Reubens's chaotic humor. *Pee-wee's Big Adventure* features a wealth of hilarious gags and gut-busting performances, and mines quite a few laughs from the title character's childlike exuberance and charming eccentricities. Burton descended into self-parody long ago, but *Pee-wee's Big Adventure* still feels fresh and inventive (not to mention hysterically funny) more than thirty years after its initial release.

At the same time, it soon becomes apparent that Pee-wee's sweetly innocent exterior hides a great deal of selfishness and anger. In many ways, the character anticipates the emotionally stunted man-child that has become a staple of Hollywood comedies produced by the likes of Judd Apatow and Adam Sandler. Pee-wee fills his house with relics of his youth, but he lashes out at anyone who stands in the way of his desires. The character elicits laughs when he attacks his chubby neighbor or hisses at a mugger in a dark alley, but these sequences also reveal the rage and violence that lurk just beneath the surface of his childish simplicity. Thus, while the bright colors and silly humor may appeal to the kiddie crowd, the film reveals that lovable characters like Pee-wee sometimes harbor a darkness that drives them to extremes.

Pee-wee's Big Adventure is a delightful romp that contains loads of manic weirdness. The title character's subsequent cinematic outings offered diminishing returns, but his first big-screen adventure remains amusing long after it first debuted.

See also *Better Off Dead...* (1985), *One Crazy Summer* (1986), *Ernest Goes to Camp* (1987), *Beetlejuice* (1988), *The Nightmare before Christmas* (1993).

SPOTLIGHT: TIM BURTON (1958–)

While working as an animator at Walt Disney Animation, Tim Burton made the live-action short film *Frankenweenie*, in which a boy brings his pet dog back from the dead. That project gained the attention of executives at Warner Bros., and in 1985 they hired Burton to direct *Pee-wee's Big Adventure*, which became a surprise hit for the studio. Three years later, Burton scored another success with *Beetlejuice*, starring Michael Keaton as the titular bio-exorcist. Warner Bros. next hired Burton to direct *Batman*, with Keaton stepping into the role of the Caped Crusader. That film became a massive hit in the summer of 1989 and rocketed Burton to the A-list. From there, Burton directed several quirky genre films, including *Edward Scissorhands*, *Batman Returns*, *Ed Wood*, and *Mars Attacks*. In addition, he has directed high-profile remakes and adaptations like *Planet of the Apes*, *Big Fish*, *Charlie and the Chocolate Factory*, *Dark Shadows*, and *Miss Peregrine's Home for Peculiar Children*. He also produced numerous films, including cult favorite *The Nightmare before Christmas*.

PHANTASM (1979)

Director: Don Coscarelli
Screenplay: Don Coscarelli
Cast: A. Michael Baldwin (Mike), Bill Thornbury (Jody), Reggie Bannister (Reggie), Angus Scrimm (the Tall Man), Lynn Eastman-Rossi (Sally), David Arntzen (Toby), Bill Cone (Tommy)
Specs: 88 minutes; color
Genre: fantasy, horror, science fiction
Availability: Blu-ray (Well Go USA)

Plot

A group of teenagers battle a mysterious grave robber who commands an army of misshapen zombies.

Background

After striking out with his first two feature films, writer/director Don Coscarelli decided to make a horror movie, because they often proved successful at the box office.[15] Drawing inspiration from a variety of sources like *Something Wicked This Way Comes*, *Invaders from Mars*, and *Suspiria*,[16] Coscarelli developed a dreamlike story about a young boy confronting an unfathomable evil. He received $300,000 from private investors, including his own father,[17] and his mother designed costumes, makeup, and some special effects[18]—a true family affair. He assembled a cast and crew comprised of friends and aspiring professionals like A. Michael Baldwin and Reggie Bannister, who had appeared in Coscarelli's previous film, *Kenny & Company*.[19] With all the pieces in place, *Phantasm* entered production on November 17, 1977.[20]

Principal photography lasted over a year,[21] and Coscarelli shot most of the film in the San Fernando Valley in Chatsworth, California. Filming took place primarily on the weekends,[22] with grueling workdays that sometimes lasted up to twenty hours.[23] Coscarelli rewrote the script several times throughout the production, which caused some frustration among the actors.[24] Coscarelli spent another eight months on postproduction.[25] The first cut ran over three hours long, but after a calamitous test screening Coscarelli edited the film down to just eighty-eight minutes.[26] That version of the film premiered in theaters on March 28, 1979, and while it received mostly dismissive reviews, it still grossed nearly $12 million at the box office.[27] The film later became a fixture of late-night television, at which point it developed an enthusiastic cult audience thanks to its iconic villain and

The Tall Man (Angus Scrimm, right) catches Jody (Bill Thornbury) snooping around the mortuary. *MGM / Photofest © MGM*

bizarre nonlinear plot. Now recognized as one of the best horror films ever made, *Phantasm* spawned four sequels, the most recent of which hit theaters in 2016.

Commentary

Even now, *Phantasm* retains its power to unsettle viewers and leave them wondering what they just watched. Coscarelli's merciless but meticulous editing ensures that events unfold in a disjointed and confusing manner. The film refuses to follow conventional logic and often feels like a terrifying fever dream projected on the screen. Meanwhile the actors remain committed to the horror throughout, making it easier for the viewer to buy into the film's reality. Everyone involved delivers top-notch performances, though Baldwin stands out due to his understated but effective turn as Mike, an ordinary kid facing extraordinary circumstances. Angus Scrimm delivers an instantly iconic performance as the Tall Man, and it becomes easy to see why he became a fan favorite in the years after the film's release.

Of course, *Phantasm* shares little in common with modern mainstream horror films that tend to generate scares via overbearing soundtracks and obnoxious jump scares. As such, modern audiences might find the film a bit dull, because it spends more time on building suspense than on trying to make viewers leap out of their seats. At the same time, however, *Phantasm* features some genuinely frightening shocks, most notably during the sequence in which the flying silver sphere first bursts onto the screen. Yet *Phantasm* is more of a slow burn, and Coscarelli uses weirdness and unpredictability to unsettle viewers. In fact, those who watch the film will most likely feel confusion as opposed to outright terror. While modern audiences may find the film tedious, *Phantasm* nevertheless remains a profoundly strange and disturbing flick.

See also *Phantasm II* (1988), *Phantasm III: Lord of the Dead* (1994), *Phantasm IV: Oblivion* (1998), *Bubba Ho-Tep* (2002), *John Dies at the End* (2012), *Phantasm: Ravager* (2016).

SPOTLIGHT: DON COSCARELLI (1954–)

At just nineteen years old, Don Coscarelli wrote and directed *Jim, the World's Greatest*, an independently produced feature-length film distributed by Universal Pictures. He followed this up with the comedic drama *Kenny & Company*, which proved quite popular in Japan but failed everywhere else. Three years later Coscarelli scored an international hit with *Phantasm*, a surreal horror film that became a beloved cult classic followed by four sequels. From there, Coscarelli specialized in writing and directing quirky genre films like *The Beastmaster*, *Survival Quest*, *Bubba Ho-Tep*, and *John Dies at the End*. Coscarelli also directed an episode of the Showtime series *Masters of Horror*, and wrote the screenplays for *Phantasm: Ravager* and *Bubba Nosferatu: Curse of the She-Vampires*.

PHANTOM OF THE PARADISE (1974)

Director: Brian De Palma
Screenplay: Brian De Palma
Cast: Paul Williams (Swan), William Finley (Winslow/the Phantom), Jessica Harper
   (Phoenix), Gerrit Graham (Beef), George Memmoli (Philbin)
Specs: 92 minutes; color
Genre: comedy, drama, fantasy, musical, romance, thriller
Availability: Blu-ray (Shout! Factory)

Plot

After mysterious record tycoon Swan betrays him and steals his music, idealis-tic composer Winslow Leach is disfigured in an accident and disappears. He re-surfaces weeks later as the masked Phantom and sets out to sabotage the opening of Swan's new club, the Paradise. However, Winslow falls under Swan's seduc-tive spell once more and sells his soul to write music for a beautiful singer named Phoenix. When the duplicitous producer betrays him yet again, the Phantom embarks on a bloody crusade to punish Swan and anyone else who wronged him.

Background

One year after making a name for himself with the taut psychological thriller *Sisters*, maverick director Brian De Palma unleashed the overblown rock opera *Phantom of the Paradise* on unsuspecting (and largely uninterested) audiences. Af-ter raising a $750,000 budget, De Palma and producer Edward R. Pressman began the long and difficult process of bringing *Phantom of the Paradise* to the screen.[28] Shooting occurred during the winter of 1973, with the abandoned theater, the Majestic, in Dallas serving as the set for the Paradise.[29]

Phantom had a rocky production. The film was originally called *Phantom of the Fillmore* after the famous San Francisco music venue.[30] However, when promoter Bill Graham refused to let De Palma use the name,[31] the director changed the title, first to *Phantom*, and finally to *Phantom of the Paradise*.[32] In addition, Swan's record label went from Swan Song Records to Death Records after Led Zeppelin's manager, Peter Grant, established a real label called Swan Song Records and threatened to block the film's release. De Palma and editor Paul Hirsch scrambled to remove all references to Swan Song, either by optically printing over them or removing them entirely.[33] The scheduled seven-week shoot turned into ten weeks, and the budget blossomed to $1.1 million.[34]

After all that, the film died at the box office upon its release on October 31, 1974,[35] though its soundtrack received Golden Globe and Academy Award nomi-nations.[36] Meanwhile, audiences in Winnipeg embraced the film; *Phantom of the Paradise* opened there on December 26, 1974, and remained in theaters for four and a half months.[37] No one knows why it caught on there,[38] but this small success likely served as the genesis for the film's devoted (not to mention ever-growing) cult following, which includes directors Edgar Wright and Guillermo Del Toro and the band Daft Punk.

The Phantom (William Finley) plays a tune for the devilish Swann (Paul Williams, not pictured). *Twentieth Century Fox Film Corporation / Photofest © Twentieth Century Fox Film Corporation*

Commentary

Though occasionally messy due to some last-minute tinkering by the studio, *Phantom of the Paradise* stands as De Palma's most visually arresting film. It resembles a deranged live-action comic book and inundates the viewer with excessive style and exaggerated acting, particularly during the chaotic third act. Yet it also offers up an intelligent and deeply cynical satire of the music industry. Arriving on screens nearly a year before the aesthetically similar *The Rocky Horror Picture Show*, De Palma's film melded music and horror to poke fun at fame, nostalgia, and the mercenary nature of television. Despite these heavy themes, *Phantom of the Paradise* remains brash and funny throughout, and it is buoyed by excellent performances and some truly hilarious black comedy.

The soundtrack remains the film's greatest strength, as it features fantastic songs that span several different genres and styles. Written by multitalented composer Paul Williams (who plays Swan in the film), the music riffs on everything from 1950s doo-wop to glam metal. As such, the soundtrack highlights the tensions that exist between nostalgia and innovation. Williams found success writing songs for bands like Three Dog Night, the Carpenters, and other easy listening acts. *Phantom of the Paradise* allowed him to stretch his creative wings a bit, and his enthusiasm shines through in every song, all of which are integral to the plot but also stand on their own as great tunes.

Ultimately, *Phantom of the Paradise* stands head and shoulders above other more popular rock operas of the 1970s because it dares to shine a light on the issues that defined that tumultuous period. The film wears its influences on its sleeve, referencing everything from *Faust* to *Frankenstein* to *The Phantom of the Opera* (with just a dash of *The Picture of Dorian Gray* and "The Cask of Amontillado"). De Palma also doubles down on his signature stylistic excesses, employing numerous split-diopter shots, mirrors, and layered foregrounds/backgrounds. While the film is not for everyone, viewers who can tune into *Phantom of the Paradise*'s darkly humorous wavelength will reap great rewards.

See also *The Rocky Horror Picture Show* (1975), *Hedwig and the Angry Inch* (2001).

SPOTLIGHT: BRIAN DE PALMA (1940–)

Brian De Palma studied physics at New York City's Columbia University, but his love of film soon sent him down a different path. After watching *Citizen Kane* and *Vertigo* in the early 1960s, De Palma withdrew from Columbia to study theater at Sarah Lawrence College. During this time he discovered the work of directors like Michelangelo Antonioni, Jean-Luc Godard, and Alfred Hitchcock, all of whom eventually influenced his own work. After directing seven independent films throughout the 1960s, De Palma hit the big time in 1973 with *Sisters*, the film that established his signature voyeuristic style and announced him as an important member of the emergent New Hollywood movement. He then wrote and directed *Phantom of the Paradise*, which flopped, and *Obsession*, which became an unexpected financial success. He followed these with a smash hit adaptation of Stephen King's novel, *Carrie*. In the more than three decades that followed, De Palma earned a reputation as a director of stylish and often sleazy films, including *Dressed to Kill*, *Blow Out*, *The Untouchables*, *Mission: Impossible*, and *Femme Fatale*.

PI (1998)

Director: Darren Aronofsky
Screenplay: Darren Aronofsky, Sean Gullette (story), Eric Watson (story)
Cast: Sean Gullette (Max Cohen), Mark Margolis (Sol Robeson), Ben Shenkman (Lenny Meyer), Pamela Hart (Marcy Dawson), Stephen Pearlman (Rabbi Cohen), Samia Shoaib (Devi), Ajay Naidu (Farrouhk)
Specs: 84 minutes; black and white
Genre: drama, thriller
Availability: DVD (Lionsgate)

Plot

A paranoid mathematician who suffers from debilitating headaches becomes the target of powerful forces after he stumbles upon a number that unlocks the secrets of the universe.

Background

In 1995, aspiring filmmakers Darren Aronofsky and Eric Watson attended the Independent Feature Film Market in New York.[39] Afterward, they decided to make *Pi*, a movie inspired by the ultralow-budget aesthetic of Japanese director Shin'ya Tsukamoto, the man responsible for such visually inventive films as *Tokyo Fist* and *Tetsuo, the Iron Man*.[40] Aronofsky and Watson teamed with actor Sean Gullette to develop the story, which grew out of one of Aronofsky's old script ideas about a man using a knife to remove a microchip from his brain.[41] The trio also drew inspiration from Rod Serling's classic television series *The Twilight Zone*.[42] They spent eight months writing the screenplay,[43] and then secured a budget of $60,000 raised via contributions from Aronofsky's family and friends.[44] Shooting commenced on October 14, 1996, and wrapped just over one month later.[45]

The production moved at an exhausting pace, and the filmmakers pushed themselves to the limits of their endurance throughout the shoot. Aronofsky tasked cinematographer Matthew Libatique with developing a stark black-and-white visual palette that recalled Frank Miller's *Sin City* comics.[46] Scenes in the main character's apartment were shot on a cramped set built inside a lighting warehouse owned by Gullette's father and located in the rough neighborhood of Bushwick.[47] Meanwhile, Aronofsky shot several scenes on the streets of New York City but was unable to secure location permits, meaning the crew had to keep an eye out for police.[48] By the time principal photography wrapped on November 15, 1996, the filmmakers had shot 53,000 feet of 16 mm film, resulting in twenty-three hours' worth of footage.[49] Aronofsky and editor Oren Sarch then spent ten months assembling the final cut of the film.[50]

Lenny Meyer (Ben Shenkman, right) confronts Max Cohen (Sean Gullette) about the number that could unlock the secrets of the universe. *Live Entertainment / Photofest © Live Entertainment*

Pi debuted at the 1998 Sundance Film Festival, where it caused a sensation and earned Aronofsky the prestigious Directing Award.[51] Artisan Entertainment purchased *Pi* for $1 million[52] and gave it a limited theatrical release, at which point it became a critical darling that grossed over $3 million in the United States alone.[53] From there, the film won several more awards, and it made headlines when it became the first film available for download via the Internet.[54] These days, *Pi* remains a cult favorite and critics consider it a milestone of independent cinema.

Commentary

Aronofsy's keen eye for detail and unique approach to storytelling ensure that *Pi* remains riveting from beginning to end. He loads *Pi* with surrealistic touches that frequently recall Luis Buñuel and Salvador Dali's 1929 silent masterpiece *Un Chien Andalou*, and uses repetitive imagery and dialogue to generate a feeling of oppressive tension. Meanwhile, the cramped set design and Libatique's gritty black-and-white cinematography create a brutal visual aesthetic, while the gripping narrative offers up a heady mixture of psychological terror and Kabbalistic mysticism, all set to an eerie, propulsive score by Clint Mansell. Sound designer Brian Emrich punctuates everything with a cacophony of dissonant, atonal noises designed to leave some viewers feeling disoriented and abused. Nevertheless, *Pi* stands as a rewarding film that features an engrossing story and plenty of visual inventiveness.

Pi also serves as a showcase for Gullette, who delivers a powerful performance, instilling Max with a quiet intensity that hides an explosive anger. At the same time, he ensures that the character remains sympathetic throughout the film, particularly during scenes when he falls prey to devastating headaches that leave him writhing in pain on the floor. The rest of the cast all turn in fine supporting performances, particularly Mark Margolis as Max's mentor, Sol, but the acting takes a back seat to the visceral filmmaking and highly stylized production

SPOTLIGHT: DARREN ARONOFSKY (1969–)

Born in Brooklyn, New York, Darren Aronofsky studied film at Harvard University. In 1991, his senior thesis film became a finalist for the National Student Academy Award. Five years later, Aronofsky set out to make his first feature film, *Pi*, which became a hit at the 1998 Sundance Film Festival and thrust Aronofsky into the spotlight. He followed it up with *Requiem for a Dream*, a harrowing drama about addiction based on a novel by Hubert Selby Jr., that opened to great acclaim in October of 2000. Aronofsky spent the next six years developing his third film, *The Fountain*, which debuted to mixed reviews and disastrous box office on November 22, 2006. Aronofsky rebounded with *The Wrestler* and *Black Swan*, two critically acclaimed hits that earned numerous award nominations. In 2011, Aronofsky embarked on his biggest production yet with *Noah*, an unconventional retelling of Noah's Ark that grossed over $362 million worldwide. He followed this up with *Mother!*, a claustrophobic and darkly comic retelling of the Old Testament released in 2017. Aronofsky also wrote the screenplay for director David Twohy's horror film *Below* and served as executive producer on director David O. Russell's Oscar-winning drama *The Fighter*. Aronofsky's own films remain cult favorites beloved by his legion of devoted fans.

design, which generates a feeling of claustrophobia even during the sequences when Max ventures outside his apartment. Overall, *Pi* remains an audacious exercise in style that features exhilarating filmmaking and strong performances, not to mention one of the most thrilling debut films ever made.

See also *Fight Club* (1999), *Memento* (2000), *Requiem for a Dream* (2000), *Donnie Darko* (2001), *Primer* (2004).

PINK FLAMINGOS (1972)

Director: John Waters
Screenplay: John Waters
Cast: Divine (Divine/Babs Johnson), Mary Vivian Pearce (Cotton), David Lochary
   (Raymond Marble), Mink Stole (Connie Marble), Danny Mills (Crackers), Edith
   Massey (Edie), Channing Wilroy (Channing), Cookie Mueller (Cookie), Paul Swift
   (the Egg Man)
Specs: 93 minutes; color
Genre: comedy, crime
Availability: DVD (New Line Home Entertainment)

Plot

A group of depraved misfits compete with a sleazy Baltimore couple for the title of "Filthiest Person Alive."

Background

After bursting onto the indie scene with *Multiple Maniacs*, writer/director John Waters found worldwide success with *Pink Flamingos*, an ultralow-budget "exercise in poor taste" that became a massive hit on the midnight movie circuit in 1973. Shot for just $10,000–$12,000 and starring legendary drag queen Divine (a.k.a. Harris Glenn Milstead),[55] *Pink Flamingos* caused a sensation when it first came out because it included explicit depictions of perverse sexuality and depraved behavior. Waters shot the film primarily on weekends and spent his weekdays raising money to keep the production going.[56] He gathered much of the footage on location at a rundown farmhouse in Phoenix, Maryland.[57] Meanwhile, the actors often endured pitiful conditions on set,[58] and Waters even asked Divine to eat a pile of dog feces for the film's notorious final scene.

Pink Flamingos premiered at the Baltimore Film Festival in 1972 and immediately became a hit with fans of underground cinema.[59] New Line Cinema purchased the film[60] and sent a copy to Ben Barenholtz, owner of the Elgin theater in New York City and the man credited with originating the concept of the midnight movie.[61] Barenholtz ran midnight screenings of *Pink Flamingos*, and it became a huge cult hit, particularly among hipsters and members of the gay community.[62] From there, *Pink Flamingos* garnered international attention, and it played in

Babs Johnson (Divine) receives a gift from her adoring family. *Fine Line Features / Photofest © Fine Line Features*

theaters around the world, though Australia,[63] Norway, and some provinces in Canada banned the film due to its shocking content.[64] Nonetheless, the film rocketed both Waters and Divine to international stardom, and the Museum of Modern Art added it to its permanent collection in 1975.[65] These days, *Pink Flamingos* enjoys a reputation as a landmark of cult cinema, and it remains an enduring favorite among gay viewers due to its camp appeal.

Commentary

Guaranteed to turn the stomach and test the gag reflex of even the most hardened viewer, *Pink Flamingos* is a gleeful assault on good taste that features loads of filthy fun and an iconic performance from Divine. The film still feels radical and shocking even after more than forty years, and it continues to challenge mainstream sensibilities and push the boundaries of tastefulness. Yet Waters never exploits the characters in his films. Rather, he shoves viewers' faces in filth and exploits their disgust. Waters clearly loves the extravagant weirdos that populate his films, and in *Pink Flamingos* his sympathies lie firmly with Divine and her disgustingly demented family. As such, the film emerges as a subversive thumb to the eye of conventional taste, but one that contains plenty of heart and lots of laughs (at least for those capable of appreciating the unrestrained weirdness).

Divine is the main attraction in *Pink Flamingos*, delivering the performance of a lifetime as a defiantly gaudy woman who takes great pride in being the "Filthiest Person Alive." She delights in tormenting squares and pushing the limits of bad taste, and lives by a simple motto: "Kill everyone now! Condone first degree murder! Advocate cannibalism! Eat shit! Filth is my politics! Filth is my life!" At the same time, she loves her family, and dotes on her egg-obsessed mother, Miss Edie (played by Waters regular Edith Massey), and her chicken-loving son, Crackers (Danny Mills). Of course, some might say she dotes on Crackers too much, particularly during one of the film's most scandalous scenes. Nonetheless, Divine remains oddly likable even as she engages in incest or violently executes her bitter rivals Connie and Raymond Marbles (who earn their living by kidnapping young women, impregnating them, and then selling the babies to lesbian couples). *Pink Flamingos* inundates viewers with vile imagery throughout, but Divine's lusty performance and Waters's deft touch ensure that the film remains amusing rather than excruciating (although the infamous final shot will leave even the toughest viewer feeling a little bit queasy).

Pink Flamingos proved highly influential on both cinema and American culture, because it helped make trash mainstream and even rendered it somewhat acceptable. The film basically turned depravity into a cottage industry. Nevertheless, *Pink Flamingos* retains its power to shock over four decades later, and it stands as a thoroughly transgressive experience that continues to delight and disgust cult film fans long after its release.

See also *Multiple Maniacs* (1970).

SPOTLIGHT: JOHN WATERS (1946–)

In 1969, John Waters wrote and directed *Mondo Trasho*, his first feature-length film. The following year, Waters released *Multiple Maniacs*, which found underground success in places like New York, Philadelphia, and San Francisco. In 1972, Waters earned international acclaim with *Pink Flamingos*, a transgressive black comedy that became a massive cult hit. From there, Waters specialized in making outrageous films that featured a regular group of likeminded performers collectively known as the Dreamlanders, including *Female Trouble*, *Desperate Living*, and *Polyester*. In 1989, Waters scored a crossover hit with *Hairspray*, which was later adapted as a popular stage musical. He followed this up with *Cry-Baby* and *Serial Mom*, both of which earned mainstream attention. Waters then produced a series of films that straddled the line between his conventional sensibilities and his anarchic past, including *Pecker*, *Cecil B. Demented*, and *A Dirty Shame*. In the years since his debut, Waters has written two successful memoirs and become something of an American cultural icon.

PLAN 9 FROM OUTER SPACE (1959)

Director: Edward D. Wood Jr.
Screenplay: Edward D. Wood Jr.
Cast: Gregory Walcott (Jeff Trent), Mona McKinnon (Paula Trent), Duke Moore
   (Lieutenant Harper), Tom Keene (Colonel Edwards), Carl Anthony (Patrolman
   Larry), Paul Marco (Patrolman Kelton), Tor Johnson (Inspector Clay), Dudley
   Manlove (Eros), Joanna Lee (Tanna), John "Bunny" Breckinridge (Ruler)
Specs: 79 minutes, black and white
Genre: horror, science fiction
Availability: Blu-ray (Legend)

Plot

Aliens invade Earth and reanimate the corpses of the recently deceased in a bid to
prevent humanity from creating a doomsday weapon known as a Solaranite bomb.

Background

Edward D. Wood Jr. made his feature directorial debut in 1953 with the low-
budget exploitation film *Glen or Glenda*. Three years later, he began developing an
epic science fiction film he hoped would establish him as a major Hollywood talent. Wood received funding for the film from the Baptist Church,[66] though church
officials reportedly objected to the film's original title of "Grave Robbers from
Outer Space" on moral grounds and urged Wood to change it to the less offensive
Plan 9 from Outer Space.[67] In addition, the cast and crew agreed to be baptized prior
to the start of production in November of 1956.[68]

Filming took place mainly at Quality Studios,[69] an independent soundstage in
Hollywood, on sets built from balsa wood and cardboard. Wood secured several
police cars and uniforms from Tor Johnson's son, Karl, a uniformed officer serving
with the San Fernando Police Department who also appears in the film.[70] Wood
used genuine military stock footage to supplement his own shots of the United
States Army fending off an armada of flying saucers, and he also incorporated
footage of Bela Lugosi he shot prior to the actor's death in August of 1956.[71] Wood
hired his wife's chiropractor, Tom Mason, to double for Lugosi even though the
two looked nothing alike.[72] Mason, who was much taller than Lugosi, simply
covered his face with a cape for the role.[73] Production wrapped in early 1957, but
the film remained in limbo until July of 1959, when Valiant Pictures released it on
a double bill with *Time Lock*, a British thriller featuring a young Sean Connery.[74]

Starting in 1961, *Plan 9* aired frequently on late-night television, but remained
relatively obscure until 1980, when Harry and Michael Medved dubbed it the
"worst film of all time" in their satirical book *The Golden Turkey Awards: The Worst
Achievements in Hollywood History*.[75] At that point, *Plan 9* became a beloved cult
classic, and in 1994, director Tim Burton offered up a fictionalized account of the
film's production in his award-winning biopic *Ed Wood*.

The reanimated corpse of Inspector Clay (Tor Johnson, center) attacks the alien ruler (John Breckinridge, far left). *Photofest ©WRITER_EDITOR: JG*

Commentary

Plan 9 lives up to its reputation as the worst movie ever made thanks to writer/ director/producer/editor Ed Wood's famed incompetence. The film contains several gaffes: boom mics appear in multiple shots, actors bump into unstable sets and props, and plumbing hardware remains noticeable in scenes set aboard the flying saucer. In addition, the actors struggle to deliver their overly complicated lines, which only vaguely resemble actual human speech. Meanwhile, the flying saucers are unmistakably cheap model kits suspended from fishing wire and therefore come across as silly rather than threatening. All of this renders *Plan 9* charmingly inept and explains why the film continues to captivate bad movie lovers more than fifty years after its initial release.

Beyond the mistakes and low-budget tackiness, however, *Plan 9* is mostly dull, and even at just seventy-nine minutes long, it drags quite a bit. The film offers some delightful camp value early on but wears out its welcome during the almost interminable second act, which brings the proceedings to a screeching halt. *Plan 9* regains some momentum toward the end, but many viewers will have understandably tapped out by that point. Ultimately, the idea of *Plan 9* remains funnier and more enjoyable than the actual film, which is tedious and inert. This is a shame because at the core of Wood's campy but clumsy film lies an interesting story about aliens unleashing a horde of zombies upon the world.

See also *Robot Monster* (1953), *Bride of the Monster* (1955), *The Little Shop of Horrors* (1960), *The Beast of Yucca Flats* (1961).

SPOTLIGHT: EDWARD D. WOOD JR. (1924–1978)

Following a stint in the military, Ed Wood spent years trying to break into the film industry. He finally got his chance in 1952 when he was hired to write and direct a film based on the life of Christine Jorgensen, the first person in the United States to undergo sex reassignment surgery. The resultant film, *Glen or Glenda*, bore little resemblance to Jorgensen's actual story, but it provided much insight into Wood's own psyche; though heterosexual, Wood dabbled in transvestism and harbored a fetish for Angora sweaters. The film also revealed his lack of talent, which became a hallmark of subsequent cinematic efforts like *Bride of the Monster*, *Jail Bait*, and *Plan 9 from Outer Space*. Despite his incompetence behind the camera, Wood still made several relentlessly campy movies with the help of his devoted friends, including Bela Lugosi, Vampira, and Tor Johnson. When his film career dried up, Wood made a living writing trashy novels and short stories under various pseudonyms. He suffered an alcohol-related heart attack in 1978 and died in relative obscurity. Nearly twenty years later, his life received the biopic treatment in Tim Burton's *Ed Wood*.

POINT BREAK (1991)

Director: Kathryn Bigelow
Screenplay: W. Peter Iliff, Rick King (story)
Cast: Patrick Swayze (Bodhi), Keanu Reeves (Johnny Utah), Gary Busey (Pappas),
    Lori Petty (Tyler), John C. McGinley (Ben Harp), James Le Gros (Roach), John
    Philbin (Nathaniel), Bojesse Christopher (Grommet)
Specs: 122 minutes; color
Genre: action, crime, drama, thriller
Availability: DVD and Blu-ray (Warner Bros.)

Plot

An undercover FBI agent infiltrates a gang of thrill-seeking bank robbers, only to fall under the spell of their charismatic leader.

Background

Coproducer Rick King dreamed up the story for *Point Break* while lounging on a beach reading an *LA Weekly* article about Los Angeles being the bank-robbery capital of the United States.[76] He paid screenwriter W. Peter Iliff $6,000 to write the script,[77] which languished in development hell until up-and-coming director Kathryn Bigelow decided to make the film.[78] She rewrote the screenplay with her then-husband James Cameron, who went uncredited due to an issue with the Writers Guild of America.[79]

When casting the film, producers considered Johnny Depp, Charlie Sheen, and Matthew Broderick for the lead role, but Bigelow insisted on Keanu Reeves.[80] Meanwhile, Patrick Swayze, who had recently scored a huge hit with *Ghost*, lobbied hard to play main antagonist Bodhi.[81] Producers agreed because he brought some much-needed star power to the project. Bigelow then cast unconventional actress Lori Petty as female love interest Tyler.[82] Prior to production, Reeves, Swayze, and Petty traveled to the Hawaiian island of Kauai and spent two months training with former professional surfer Dennis Jarvis.[83] Principal photography commenced on July 9, 1990, and wrapped on October 24, 1990. The finished film opened on July 12, 1991.[84]

Point Break became a modest box office success, grossing over $83 million worldwide against a reported $24 million budget,[85] despite critical dismissal.[86] In the years after its release, *Point Break* became a beloved cult favorite that paved the way for other adrenaline-fueled action flicks like *The Fast and the Furious* and *Torque*, as well as Edgar Wright's thrilling genre mash-up *Hot Fuzz*. It also begat an interactive stage show called *Point Break Live!* which premiered in 2003,[87] and a forgettable remake that hit theaters in December of 2015 and receded from memory soon after that.

Bodhi (Patrick Swayze, right) tells Johnny Utah (Keanu Reeves) all about the tao of surfing. *Twentieth Century Fox / Photofest © Twentieth Century Fox*

Commentary

Point Break takes viewers on an exhilarating thrill ride that boasts dynamic direction and energetic camerawork. Throughout the film, Bigelow employs a restless camera that drops viewers into the middle of the action and instills everything on-screen with a feeling of perpetual forward momentum. She also serves up several stylish and energetic action sequences, such as the frantic foot chase through the gardens and back alleys of a sleepy residential neighborhood. In addition, *Point Break* features gorgeous cinematography and presents viewers with dozens breathtaking images. Add in the evocative score by Mark Isham and the humorous dialogue ("You're sayin' the FBI's gonna pay me to learn to surf?"), and *Point Break* emerges as an immensely enjoyable action flick that features stunning visuals and some of the most thrilling chase sequences ever put to film.

Point Break also features excellent performances from the stellar cast, particularly Reeves and Swayze, both of whom instill the film with lots of thoughtful toughness and beefcake appeal. Reeves plays Johnny Utah with a combination of stiff superiority and easygoing charm, and he proves adept at both the action beats and the more dramatic moments, balancing Utah's toughness with a great deal of vulnerability and enthusiasm. Meanwhile, Swayze is mesmerizing as Bodhi, a spiritual adrenaline junkie who gets off on robbing banks. His natural charisma and dreamy looks transform the character into a sensitive but manipulative tough guy who understands the power he holds over others and uses it to his advantage at every turn. Thankfully, Petty balances out all the machismo as Tyler, the feisty, sexy young woman who steals Johnny's heart and repeatedly calls Bodhi out on his nonsense (though she becomes a bit of a damsel in distress by the end). *Point Break* suffers from some occasional sluggish bits and half-baked moments, but the slick filmmaking and fun performances ensure that the film remains a blast of "100 percent pure adrenaline" from beginning to end.

See also *Road House* (1989), *The Fast and the Furious* (2001), *Dhoom* (2004), *Torque* (2004), *Hot Fuzz* (2007).

SPOTLIGHT: KATHRYN BIGELOW (1951–)

Upon graduating from Columbia University with a master's degree in film in 1979, Kathryn Bigelow embarked on a career as a filmmaker. In 1982 she teamed with Monty Kathryn Montgomery to codirect *The Loveless*, a feature-length biker film that starred a then-unknown Willem Dafoe. She then set off on her own, and between 1987 and 1995 she directed stylish and exhilarating genre films like *Near Dark*, *Blue Steel*, *Point Break*, and *Strange Days*, as well as an episode of the TV miniseries *Wild Palms*. Bigelow spent the next few years working in television, directing episodes of *Homicide: Life on the Street*. She returned to the big screen with the commercial and critical flops *The Weight of Water* and *K-19: The Widowmaker*. She then directed an episode of the short-lived TV series *Karen Sisco* before scoring a high-profile success with *The Hurt Locker*, which won the Oscar for Best Picture in 2010 (Bigelow also became the first woman to ever win an Academy Award for Best Director). Since then, Bigelow has specialized in directing critically acclaimed films based on true events, including the controversial thriller *Zero Dark Thirty* and the period drama *Detroit*.

POOTIE TANG (2001)

Director: Louis C.K.
Screenplay: Louis C.K.
Cast: Lance Crouther (Pootie Tang), J. B. Smoove (Trucky), Jennifer Coolidge (Ireenie), Reg E. Cathey (Dirty Dee), Robert Vaughn (Dick Lecter), Wanda Sykes (Biggie Shorty), Chris Rock (JB/Radio DJ/Pootie's Father), Mario Joyner (Lacey)
Specs: 81 minutes; color
Genre: action, adventure, comedy, musical
Availability: DVD (Paramount)

Plot

Streetwise recording artist Pootie Tang battles the evil CEO of Lecter Corp, who wants to use Pootie's image to market addictive products like cigarettes and fast food to unsuspecting kids.

Background

As a child, comedian Louis C.K. loved talking gibberish, and this obsession later served as the inspiration for a sketch that appeared on *The Chris Rock Show* in 1997.[88] In it, writer/performer Lance Crouther plays Pootie Tang, a laid-back dude who speaks garbled nonsense but gets away with it because he exudes coolness and confidence. The audience loved the bit, and Pootie soon became a recurring character on the show.[89] Eventually, host Chris Rock encouraged C.K. to make a Pootie Tang movie, and C.K. set off to write *Pootie Tang in Sine Your Pitty on the Runny Kine*.[90] Upon completing the screenplay, C.K. set it aside and forgot about it until years later when he and Rock were hired to write a movie for Paramount.[91] The producers liked C.K.'s work and asked if he had any other projects lying around.[92] The comedian dug up the script for *Pootie Tang* and sent it to them along with some tapes from *The Chris Rock Show*.[93] Impressed, Paramount executives offered to produce the film with a $2 million budget and release it through their Paramount Classics division.[94] In addition, they wanted C.K. to direct the film himself.[95] C.K. agreed, and production commenced in July of 2000.

During filming, studio executives came to believe that *Pootie Tang* could become a substantial hit along the lines of *Austin Powers: International Man of Mystery*.[96] Thus, they transferred the project to the main Paramount Pictures division and increased the budget to $4 million.[97] They also ordered C.K. to rewrite the script, because they wanted it to receive a PG-13 rating from the Motion Picture Association of America's ratings board.[98] At first, C.K. bristled at this suggestion, but he soon came to see it as an interesting challenge and made significant changes to the screenplay.[99] Filming wrapped in August of 2000, and during the editing process Paramount reportedly fired C.K. and hired editor Ali LeRoi to recut the film.[100] *Pootie Tang* opened on July 1, 2001, to scathing reviews and dismal box office. C.K. disowned the film, declaring that it strayed from his original vision.[101] Nevertheless, *Pootie Tang* gained an enthusiastic cult following, most

Pootie Tang (Lance Crouther, second from right) and his crew. *Paramount Pictures / Photofest* ©
Paramount Pictures

notably among comedians and hip-hop artists.[102] C.K. went on to create and star
in the acclaimed television series *Louie*.

Commentary

Pootie Tang opens and closes with a humorous framing device that calls back to
the character's sketch show origins and serves as a perfect introduction to Pootie
and his world. The film begins with television broadcaster Bob Costas interview-
ing Pootie (Crouther, in a highly amusing performance) about his new movie, *Sine
Your Pitty on the Runny Kine*. Costas then shows a clip from the film, which plays
out in its entirety before finally coming back to the interview segment, at which
point Costas deadpans, "You know, that is the longest damn movie clip I have
ever seen." This bit of nonsense perfectly encapsulates the comedic sensibilities
of *Pootie Tang*, an outrageously zany send-up of blaxploitation films and action-
oriented blockbusters. The film contains an abundance of hilarious dialogue
("Man, that car's so big, it's got its own sky") and crazy characters (such as Bad
Bitty, Dirty Dee, Biggie Shorty, and Pootie himself), and it inundates viewers with
plenty of absurdist nonsense (like the sequence in which Pootie hallucinates his
dead parents as a cow and a cornstalk). The foolishness all unfolds with brilliant
comic timing, and at just eighty-one minutes, *Pootie Tang* moves quickly and
never overstays its welcome.

The film also features excellent comic performances, starting with Crouther,
who generates lots of laughs with his relaxed physicality and brilliant delivery

of C.K.'s inventive gibberish ("Dirty Dee, you're a baddy daddy lamatai tebby chai!"). Meanwhile, Robert Vaughan delivers a scenery-chewing turn as dastardly villain Dick Lecter, a character not unlike the one he played in *BASEketball* (another cult favorite starring *South Park* and *Cannibal! The Musical* creators Trey Parker and Matt Stone). Jennifer Coolidge steals the show as Ireenie, Lecter's beautiful but abusive girlfriend/henchwoman, while Wanda Sykes turns Pootie's love interest Biggie Shorty into the film's funniest character via her low-key performance and wickedly funny line deliveries ("You think that just cuz a girl likes to dress fancy and stand on the corner next to some whores, that she's hookin'?"). The film also boasts amusing cameos from some of the top names in comedy (including Laura Kightlinger, Todd Barry, Jon Glaser, and David Cross), as well as a brief appearance by musical superstar Missy Elliot. When combined with C.K.'s outrageous script and the dynamic editing (credited to Doug Abel), the performances help turn *Pootie Tang* into a lively and thoroughly wacky comedy that will definitely sine your pitty on the runny kine. Sa da tay!

See also *Putney Swope* (1969), *I'm Gonna Git You Sucka* (1988), *Black Dynamite* (2009).

PULP FICTION (1994)

Director: Quentin Tarantino
Screenplay: Quentin Tarantino, Roger Avary (story)
Cast: John Travolta (Vincent Vega), Samuel L. Jackson (Jules Winnfield), Uma Thurman (Mia Wallace), Eric Stoltz (Lance), Rosanna Arquette (Jody), Bruce Willis (Butch Coolidge), Ving Rhames (Marsellus Wallace), Tim Roth (Pumpkin), Amanda Plummer (Honey Bunny), Christopher Walken (Captain Koons)
Specs: 154 minutes; color
Genre: comedy, crime, drama
Availability: DVD and Blu-ray (Lionsgate Films)

Plot

The lives of several disreputable people intersect across four exhilarating stories of violence and redemption.

Background

In 1990, young video store clerk Quentin Tarantino teamed with his friend and coworker, Roger Avary, to develop a short film they could use as a calling card, but the idea evolved into something bigger.[103] Instead of a single short, they decided to make *Pulp Fiction*, a feature-length anthology comprised of three different shorts.[104] Tarantino began writing the script in the fall of 1990, but by early 1991 it remained incomplete.[105] That summer, he met producer Stacey Sher at the premiere of *Terminator 2: Judgment Day* and told her about *Pulp Fiction*.[106] Sher took the idea to her producing partner, Danny DeVito, who convinced executives at TriStar Pictures to pay Tarantino $900,000 to write and direct the film.[107]

Vincent (John Travolta, left) and Jules (Samuel L. Jackson) unleash great vengeance and furious anger on Brett (Frank Whaley, not pictured) and his pals. *Miramax Films / Photofest © Miramax*

In early 1992, Tarantino and Avary moved to Amsterdam to write the screenplay for *Pulp Fiction*.[108] The first draft came in at 500 handwritten pages,[109] but Tarantino trimmed it down to 200 pages before delivering it to TriStar.[110] Sadly, studio head Mike Medavoy disliked the script and shelved the project.[111] Undaunted by this setback, Tarantino's production partner, Lawrence Bender, sent the script to Miramax chief Harvey Weinstein, who offered to produce the film for $8.5 million.[112] Tarantino insisted on final cut and a percentage of the film's gross, and he also wanted to cast John Travolta and give him top billing.[113] Weinstein agreed to these terms, and *Pulp Fiction* entered production on September 20, 1993, after nearly two weeks of rehearsals.[114]

The shoot ran smoothly and wrapped on November 30, 1993. *Pulp Fiction* premiered on March 21, 1994, at the Cannes Film Festival, where it caused a sensation and won the Palme d'Or.[115] The film entered wide release later that year and became a massive hit. It also met with controversy largely due to the graphic violence and language,[116] as well as the depictions of drug use.[117] In addition, Tarantino and Avary engaged in a highly publicized dispute regarding the film's screenplay.[118] Despite all this, *Pulp Fiction* captured the zeitgeist of the 1990s, and it endures as a beloved cult film due to its quotable dialogue, outrageous characters, and rapid-fire pop culture references.

Commentary

Over the years, *Pulp Fiction* has become duly recognized as a game-changing film that irrevocably altered the cinematic landscape and cast a long shadow over popular culture. In the more than two decades since its debut, the film kicked off numerous debates, with fans and critics alike offering up hundreds of different interpretations of Tarantino's seminal masterpiece. Even today, *Pulp Fiction* encourages discussion and analysis due to its themes of violence, loyalty, redemption, and more. Additionally, it includes several iconic moments (far too many to list here) and pays homage to cinema's past by referencing everything from *Kiss Me Deadly* to *Saturday Night Fever* to *The Deer Hunter*. As mentioned earlier, *Pulp Fiction* captured the essence of the 1990s, a decade that defies easy categorization but that nevertheless experienced a series of startling challenges to the status quo. Tarantino's film embodies that disruptive spirit, and it sent shockwaves throughout the world of cinema that continue to be felt today.

In addition to its thematic richness, *Pulp Fiction* also boasts assured direction, unique dialogue, excellent performances, and a terrific soundtrack. Tarantino's direction demonstrates a laid-back confidence, and he infuses the film with a sense of style and originality even as he draws inspiration from the long-take classicism of 1970s cinema. Meanwhile, the dialogue crackles with energy and vitality, and it emerges as the true star of the film. Debate continues to rage over just how much Avary contributed to the script, but the dialogue clearly belongs to Tarantino, who injected his own distinctive rhythm into every single line. Tarantino's dialogue often sounds unnatural, but it makes even the most mundane events feel majestic and always serves a purpose (for instance, an early conversation about Quarter Pounders resurfaces when Jules and Vincent try to retrieve Marsellus Wallace's briefcase from Brad and his pals). Of course, the dialogue only works because the cast members make it sound authentic, particularly Samuel L. Jackson, whose performance outshines even that of comeback kid John Travolta. Finally, the film features an incredible soundtrack, which includes an eclectic mix of cool 1970s hits and hip 1990s tunes and thereby reinforces the film's patchwork identity.

Tarantino's deft direction and singular dialogue turned *Pulp Fiction* into one of the defining films of the 1990s. An effective combination of thematic depth and sheer entertainment value ensures that it will remain a cult classic for years to come.

See also *Kiss Me Deadly* (1955), *Black Sabbath* (1963), *Stranger Than Paradise* (1984), *Reservoir Dogs* (1992), *Jackie Brown* (1997).

SPOTLIGHT: QUENTIN TARANTINO (1963–)

In 1987, twenty-five-year-old video store clerk Quentin Tarantino cowrote and directed *My Best Friend's Birthday*. He spent the next few years trying to break into the movie business and finally got his chance in 1992 when he wrote and directed the independent crime thriller *Reservoir Dogs*. That film was an immediate hit and opened the door for Tarantino's follow-up feature, *Pulp Fiction*, which became a bona fide sensation in 1994. Three years later, Tarantino made *Jackie Brown*, a blaxploitation-themed adaptation of Elmore Leonard's novel *Rum Punch*. Since then, Tarantino has directed several stylized cult films that pay homage to cinema's past, including *Kill Bill*, *Death Proof* (one half of the *Grindhouse* double feature), *Inglourious Basterds*, *Django Unchained*, and *The Hateful Eight*. He also has an impressive list of writing credits that includes films like *True Romance*, *Natural Born Killers*, *Four Rooms*, and *From Dusk till Dawn*.

PUNISHER: WAR ZONE (2008)

Director: Lexi Alexander
Screenplay: Nick Santora, Art Marcum, Matt Holloway
Cast: Ray Stevenson (Frank Castle/The Punisher), Dominic West (Billy/Jigsaw),
  Julie Benz (Angela), Doug Hutchison (Loony Bin Jim), Colin Salmon (Paul Budi-
  ansky), Wayne Knight (Micro), Dash Mihok (Martin Soap)
Specs: 103 minutes; color
Genre: action, crime, drama, thriller
Availability: DVD and Blu-ray (Lionsgate Films)

Plot

The streets of New York become a literal war zone when violent vigilante the
Punisher battles the disfigured criminal Jigsaw and his demented brother, Loony
Bin Jim.

Background

Marvel Comics' popular vigilante character the Punisher first exploded into
live action in a low-budget 1989 adaptation directed by Mark Goldblatt and
featuring Dolph Lundgren as the title character. That film went straight to video
in the United States,[119] but became a minor cult hit with Punisher fans. Nevertheless, the character retreated to the realm of comic books and remained there
until Lionsgate released *The Punisher* in 2004. Directed by Jonathan Hensleigh
and starring Thomas Jane, this new adaptation became a box office hit, and the
studio immediately set about developing a sequel.[120] However, Jane dropped out
of the project because he disliked the script, so Lionsgate decided to just reboot
the property instead.[121] The script was rewritten and sent to Lexi Alexander, director of *Green Street Hooligans*, who initially passed but changed her mind when
Lionsgate agreed to let her make the film as violent as she wanted.[122] The studio
then searched for a new Punisher, eventually settling on Ray Stevenson,[123] who
prepared for the role by training with the United States Marine Corps.[124]

Punisher: War Zone entered production on October 22, 2007, and the shoot proved
extremely difficult. Alexander clashed with studio executives throughout production. For instance, she wanted to cast Freddie Prinze Jr. as the villainous Jigsaw,[125]
but Lionsgate executives gave the role to Dominic West, star of HBO's *The Wire*.
Alexander also battled with the studio over the film's music; she worked with a
composer to create an original score for the film, but Lionsgate tossed it out and
hired Michael Wandmacher to compose new music that recalled Hans Zimmer's
score for *The Dark Knight*.[126] Alexander also earned the ire of Punisher fans when she
announced that she planned to discard the character's iconic skull logo (as a com-
promise, she eventually added a faded skull emblem to Stevenson's costume).[127]
The troubled production wrapped on December 14, 2007, and *Punisher: War Zone*
opened on December 5, 2008,[128] nearly three months after its originally scheduled
release date of September 12, 2008.[129] Critics savaged the film, which bombed at the
box office, grossing just over $8 million against a reported $35 million budget.[130]

The Punisher (Ray Stevenson) doles out some punishment. *Lions Gate / Photofest © Lions Gate*

Despite its critical and commercial failure, *Punisher: War Zone* found some vocal supporters, most notably comedian Patton Oswalt.[131] However, Marvel seems content to pretend the film never happened. In 2011, the rights to the character reverted to Marvel Studios, and four years later the Punisher appeared on season 2 of Netflix's *Daredevil*, this time played by Jon Bernthal (formerly of *The Walking Dead*). Fans hailed this interpretation of the character, prompting the streaming giant to develop *The Punisher*, a thirteen-episode live-action series that debuted in 2017. Meanwhile, Stevenson assumed the role of Volstagg in *Thor* and *Thor: The Dark World*, though he got one final shot at playing the Punisher when he voiced the character in a 2009 episode of Marvel's animated *The Super Hero Squad Show*.

Commentary

Boasting a fierce combination of slick filmmaking, visceral action, and brutal fight sequences, *Punisher: War Zone* feels like a violent and crass comic book come to vivid life. The film features an exaggerated, neon-tinged visual palette that evokes the four-color funny books that first unleashed the character. *Punisher: War Zone* is awash in bright primary colors (though it suffers from a bit of orange-and-teal syndrome, a problem that afflicts most modern Hollywood blockbusters), and the crisp cinematography captures the sweaty griminess of New York (though the film was shot mainly in Montréal). In addition, Alexander incorporates several visually interesting framing techniques that recall comic book panels, most notably during the sequence when the Punisher descends into his subterranean lair (the stark shadows turn the frame into a square, and the resulting image looks like it was torn right out of a *Punisher* comic). She also serves up audacious action and vicious fight sequences sure to leave the audience cheering and cringing at the same time. Altogether, *Punisher: War Zone* features intense filmmaking that reflects the lead character's own extreme attitude.

As the Punisher, Stevenson delivers an appropriately forceful and monosyllabic performance, and thus far he remains the best on-screen incarnation of the character (though Bernthal gives him a run for his money). He sells the action while also conveying the Punisher's inner turmoil with his soulful eyes, which seem to be constantly on the verge of shedding tears. Furthermore, Stevenson looks eerily like a Timothy Bradstreet drawing, making him a perfect fit for the character from a purely visual standpoint. Meanwhile, West is clearly having a blast as Jigsaw, and he tears through the film, chewing the scenery and growling his lines in a ridiculously exaggerated accent (the way he draws out the word *cops* is incredible). Meanwhile, the fantastic makeup perfectly reflects the character's twisted soul. As Jigsaw's demented brother, Looney Bin Jim, Doug Hutchison matches West's intensity, delivering an incredibly physical performance that involves him throwing himself about the set while acting completely deranged. The actors all elevate the material, and committed performances ensure that *Punisher: War Zone* remains gritty but fun throughout.

In addition to the exhilarating action, *Punisher: War Zone* includes some knowing humor and laugh-out-loud moments (the Punisher's encounter with the parkour gang remains a hilarious highlight of the film), and it even features some genuinely touching moments, particularly between the Punisher and Grace, the young daughter of an FBI agent accidentally killed by the tortured vigilante. *Punisher: War Zone* earns its R rating thanks to some delirious violence and ridiculous gore (most notably during the film's bloody finale), but it also provides viewers with plenty of cheesy fun. Cult movie fans will want to give it a shot as soon as possible.

See also *Crank* (2006), *Kick-Ass* (2010), *Super* (2010).

PUTNEY SWOPE (1969)

Director: Robert Downey Sr.
Screenplay: Robert Downey Sr.
Cast: Arnold Johnson (Putney Swope), Stan Gottlieb (Nathan), Allen Garfield (Elias Jr.), Archie Russell (Joker), Ramon Gordon (Bissinger), Bert Lawrence (Hawker), Joe Madden (Mr. Syllables), David Kirk (Elias Sr.), Don George (Mr. Cards)
Specs: 84 minutes; black and white/color
Genre: comedy
Availability: DVD (The Criterion Collection)

Plot

After the chairman of an advertising agency dies, the executive board inadvertently elects the token African American employee as his successor. Hilarity ensues when the new boss replaces all the employees with militant black activists and refuses to advertise harmful products.

Background

In the late 1960s, writer/director Robert Downey Sr. aligned himself with a group of New York underground filmmakers who caught the attention of influential film critic Jonas Mekas of the *Village Voice*.[132] Mekas championed Downey's work after seeing *Chafed Elbows*, an experimental short film that takes a comedic look at incest.[133] Using his newfound notoriety, Downey raised $250,000 to make *Putney Swope*, a scathing satire of the advertising industry that also took aim at corporate corruption and race relations in the United States.[134] Downey hired actor Arnold Johnson to play the title character (though Johnson supposedly kept flubbing his lines, so Downey himself dubbed the character's dialogue during postproduction).[135] Upon completing the film, Downey showed it to Donald Rugoff, a film distributor who also owned several theaters throughout New York City.[136] Rugoff agreed to screen *Putney Swope* in one of his theaters, and much to his surprise the film became quite popular.[137] Not long after, actress Jane Fonda mentioned *Putney Swope* during an appearance on *The Tonight Show*, and ticket sales spiked the very next day.[138]

Putney Swope caused a sensation during its initial release, but eventually faded from the popular consciousness to the point that only hard-core film fanatics even remembered the film existed.[139] That changed in recent years as people like come-

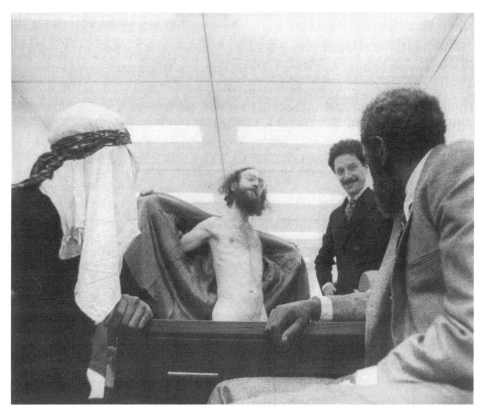

Mr. Bad News (Allan Arbus, center) auditions for Putney Swope (Arnold Johnson, far right) and the rest of the Truth and Soul, Inc. executive board. *Cinema V / Photofest © Cinema V*

dian Louis C.K. and director Jim Jarmusch have cited *Putney Swope* as an influence on their own work.[140] Meanwhile, director Paul Thomas Anderson inserted several references to *Putney Swope* in his breakthrough film *Boogie Nights*.[141] In 2008, director Martin Scorsese embarked on a project to restore *Putney Swope* along with two of Downey's other films as part of his work with the Film Foundation, an organization dedicated to the preservation and restoration of cinema.[142] Scorsese was joined in this endeavor by New York's Anthology Film Archives and the folks at the Criterion Collection, a prestigious boutique label that released five of Downey's films on DVD in 2012.[143] *Putney Swope* has since earned a much-deserved reputation as a cult classic, and many fans consider it Downey's best film.

Commentary

Infused with righteous anger and an anarchic spirit, *Putney Swope* is a hilarious send-up of the advertising industry, as well as a biting satire of consumerism, politics, race relations, and capitalist ideology. The film features outrageously comical dialogue and humorous situations, and it delivers several scathing ad parodies that still feel fresh and funny even after nearly fifty years. The film often feels like a series of cartoonish sketches rather than a coherent narrative, and the gags fly fast and furious as the movie unfolds in an almost surrealistic fashion, moving from one situation to the next with little regard for what came before. It also features uproarious commercial parodies that capture the mercenary nature of actual advertisements (like the one for a swinging airline, which recalls comedian Bill Hicks's classic routine about the link between sex and advertising). Meanwhile, characters spout humorously nonsensical lines (such as Mrs. Swope's precoital declaration of "I'm gonna bend your johnson, Swope!" or Mr. Syllables's repeated refrain of "How many syllables, Mario?" during the fateful boardroom meeting that opens *Putney Swope*), and the film becomes increasingly chaotic as it barrels toward a literally explosive climax.

At the same time, *Putney Swope* confronts racism head on, and it tackles some extremely prickly gender issues, particularly regarding masculinity and male privilege. In the film, the "token black" becomes the new chairman of the board, and after he assumes power, he changes the name of the agency to Truth and Soul, Inc. and replaces the entire staff with black nationalists except for one token white employee. Thus, the film becomes a savagely funny inversion of American society. *Putney Swope* also gleefully mocks politicians, depicting the president of the United States as an incompetent, thickly accented little person who takes orders from a bald Nazi (a characterization that feels oddly relevant in the era of the Trump administration). The satire even takes aim at the title character, a virtuous man who eventually abandons his principles in the name of the almighty dollar. Over the course of the film, Putney goes from benevolent overlord to petty dictator, firing people left and right and engaging in blatant sexism (at one point, he catches two employees canoodling in an office and fires the woman but allows the man to keep his job). As such, *Putney Swope* suggests that absolute power corrupts absolutely, and even the most noble individual can succumb to its allure.

Unfortunately, *Putney Swope* fails to sustain its own momentum, and at a certain point the film simply runs out of steam. It also drags in the second act, and several sequences go on way too long, such as the one where Putney solicits ideas from his staff, or the interminable scene in which the president's bodyguard is repeatedly interrupted while trying to tell jokes. Despite these flaws, *Putney Swope* stands as a pointed satire that ridicules everything from consumer culture and racial discrimination to political corruption and its own lead character, and it still resonates almost five decades after its initial release.

See also *Watermelon Man* (1970), *Greaser's Palace* (1972), *Stranger Than Paradise* (1984), *The Hudsucker Proxy* (1994).

R

RE-ANIMATOR (1985)

Director: Stuart Gordon
Screenplay: Dennis Paoli, William Norris, Stuart Gordon
Cast: Jeffrey Combs (Herbert West), Bruce Abbott (Dan Cain), Barbara Crampton (Megan Halsey), David Gale (Dr. Carl Hill), Robert Sampson (Dean Halsey), Gerry Black (Mace), Carolyn Purdy-Gordon (Dr. Harrod)
Specs: 104 minutes; color
Genre: comedy, horror, science fiction
Availability: DVD and Blu-ray (Image Entertainment)

Plot

A young medical student becomes an unwitting accomplice in his new housemate's attempts to resurrect the dead.

Background

In the early 1980s, after spending years directing and producing plays for Chicago's Organic Theater,[1] Stuart Gordon decided to direct a movie based on H. P. Lovecraft's "Herbert West—Re-Animator," a macabre tale about a young man who brings the dead back to life.[2] Gordon originally considered developing the story for stage and television,[3] but special effects artist Bob Greenberg convinced him it would work better as a film.[4] Heeding his friend's advice, Gordon wrote the screenplay with Dennis Paoli and William Norris. Greenberg then introduced Gordon to producer Brian Yuzna, who put up a $900,000 budget[5] and worked out a distribution deal with Empire Pictures, a company founded by B-movie stalwart Charles Band.[6]

Re-Animator entered production in early 1985. Gordon initially wanted to shoot on 16 mm black-and-white film at the Organic Theater, but Yuzna convinced him to move the production to Hollywood and shoot in color.[7] Filming lasted eighteen days,[8] and as soon as principal photography wrapped, Gordon returned to Chicago to resume his duties at the Organic Theater, leaving Yuzna to oversee postproduction.[9] *Re-Animator* opened in theaters on October 18, 1985, and grossed over $2 million in North America.[10] It also received raves from respected critics

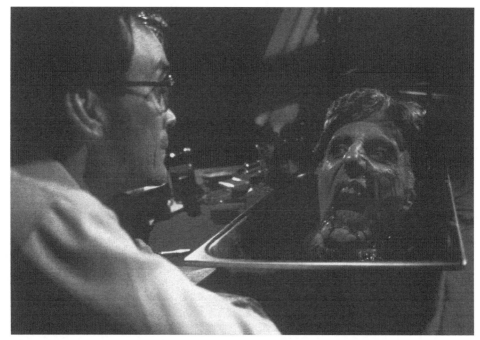

Herbert West (Jeffrey Combs, left) reanimates the severed head of his nemesis, Dr. Carl Hill (David Gale). *Empire Pictures / Photofest © Empire Pictures*

like Roger Ebert,[11] Pauline Kale,[12] and Janet Maslin.[13] When the film hit home video in 1986, it developed a cult following among horror fans and became popular enough to spawn two sequels, *Bride of Re-Animator* and *Beyond Re-Animator*.[14] In 2006, Gordon announced a third sequel titled *House of Re-Animator*, but it currently remains unproduced.[15] In 2011, Gordon translated the original film to the stage as *Re-Animator: The Musical*.[16]

Commentary

Re-Animator is an excessively gory and deliriously gonzo exercise in Grand Guignol horror that still works like gangbusters more than thirty years after its original release. The film boasts a gruesome sense of humor and offers up loads of spectacular gore effects as it builds to the apocalyptic, blood-soaked finale. The carnage remains startling throughout and will likely leave some viewers feeling nauseous as they watch the film through their fingers, but the macabre humor serves to lighten the tension somewhat. *Re-Animator* offers up laughs and scares in equal measure thanks to a bloody good combination of ghoulish comedy and astonishing gore.

The film also features an incredible cast led by Jeffrey Combs, who delivers a standout performance as brilliant but cocky medical student Herbert West. Watching *Re-Animator*, it becomes easy to see why Combs became such a beloved character actor (second only to Bruce Campbell) in the years after the film's release. Meanwhile, David Gale matches Combs's intensity as the villainous Dr.

Hill, playing the character with an abundance of mustache-twirling glee. Not to be outdone, legendary scream queen Barbara Crampton lights up the screen as the hero's girlfriend, Megan, while Bruce Abbot grounds the film as handsome and heroic leading man Dan Cain. The talented cast injects *Re-Animator* with a great deal of lively energy that transforms the film from a low-budget gore fest into a legitimate cult classic.

See also *From Beyond* (1986), *The Pit and the Pendulum* (1991), *Castle Freak* (1995), *Dagon* (2001).

SPOTLIGHT: STUART GORDON (1947–)

In the late 1960s, Stuart Gordon studied theater at the University of Wisconsin–Madison, but he dropped out in the 1970s to move to Chicago and launch the Organic Theater with his wife, Carolyn. After producing and directing several hit plays, Gordon decided to try his hand at filmmaking with *Re-Animator*, a grisly adaptation of an H. P. Lovecraft story that found great success with both critics and audiences. He followed this with *From Beyond*, another Lovecraft adaptation that built up a cult following in the years after its release. From there, Gordon specialized in writing and directing innovative genre fare like *Dolls*, *Robot Jox*, *The Pit and the Pendulum*, *Fortress*, *Castle Freak*, *Dagon*, and *Stuck*. In addition to his film work, he also directed episodes of the television show *Masters of Horror*.

SPOTLIGHT: JEFFREY COMBS (1954–)

Jeffrey Combs studied acting at both the Pacific Conservatory of the Performing Arts and the University of Washington in Seattle. Upon graduating in the late 1970s, he toured various regional theaters before moving to Los Angeles in 1980. Over the next four years, Combs landed small roles in several films, but his big break came in 1985 when he played Herbert West in *Re-Animator*. Afterward, Combs appeared in genre films like *From Beyond*, *The Pit and the Pendulum*, *The Guyver*, *Fortress*, *Castle Freak*, *The Frighteners*, *House on Haunted Hill*, and *I Still Know What You Did Last Summer*. He returned to his signature role twice more in *Bride of Re-Animator* and *Beyond Re-Animator*. In addition to his film work, Combs has appeared on television shows such as *Beauty and the Beast*, *Babylon 5*, *Star Trek: Deep Space Nine*, and *Star Trek: Enterprise*.

REEFER MADNESS (1936)

Director: Louis J. Gasnier
Screenplay: Arthur Hoerl, Lawrence Meade (original story), Paul Franklin (additional dialogue)
Cast: Dorothy Short (Mary), Kenneth Craig (Bill), Lillian Miles (Blanche), Dave O'Brien (Ralph), Thelma White (Mae), Carleton Young (Jack), Warren McCollum (Jimmy), Patricia Royale (Agnes), Joseph Forte (Dr. Carroll), Harry Harvey Jr. (Junior)
Specs: 66 minutes; black and white
Genre: drama
Availability: DVD (20th Century Fox)

Plot

A group of restless teenagers find their lives spiraling out of control after they succumb to the allure of marijuana.

Background

In the late 1930s, a church group set out to warn unsuspecting parents about the dangers of marijuana.[17] They teamed with producer George Hirliman to make *Tell Your Children*, a melodramatic film that purportedly portrayed the harrowing effects of cannabis use. However, in 1939 producer Dwain Esper purchased *Tell Your Children* and recut it for distribution on the exploitation circuit.[18] Over the next few years, the film played in various territories under such salacious titles as *The Burning Question, Dope Addict, Doped Youth, Love Madness,* and, most famously, *Reefer Madness*. The film carried an improper copyright notice and soon fell into the public domain, allowing a man named Albert Dezel to use it in roadshow screenings starting in 1951.[19] At that point, *Reefer Madness* became something of a cult item, particularly among counterculture types.

In the early 1970s, Keith Stroup, founder of the National Organization for the Reform of Marijuana Laws (a.k.a. NORML), acquired a print of *Reefer Madness* from the Library of Congress, and he screened it on college campuses throughout California to raise funds for his organization.[20] The film soon emerged as an underground hit and gained the attention of Robert Shaye, an executive at New Line Cinema who snatched up the distribution rights. *Reefer Madness* then became a sensation on the midnight movie circuit, generating healthy profits for New Line.[21] These days, *Reefer Madness* continues to find new fans thanks to its unintentional campiness and overwrought moralizing. In 1992, Sean Abley adapted the film for the stage. Six years later, Dan Studney and Kevin Murphy (not the one from *Mystery Science Theater 3000*) produced a stage musical based on the film, which was later adapted as a made-for-TV movie in 2005.

Cops bust a den of dope smokers. *George A. Hirliman Productions Inc. / Photofest © George A. Hirliman Productions Inc. / 20th Century Fox*

Commentary

With its combination of earnest self-righteousness and cornball sincerity, *Reefer Madness* inspires lots of unintended laughs as it strives to warn viewers about the "violent narcotic" marijuana (or, as the filmmakers spell it, "marihuana"). The film strikes a histrionic tone throughout and features plenty of over-the-top situations (like a stoned young man driving recklessly through town and running down an unsuspecting pedestrian) and melodramatic dialogue (discussing a "most tragic" case with an FBI agent, high school principal Dr. Alfred Carroll sadly intones, "Just a young boy . . . under the influence of drugs . . . who killed his entire family with an ax").

Reefer Madness often addresses viewers directly and uses archival footage of drug busts to "inform" viewers about the dangers of marijuana. As such, the film feels more like a somber instructional or educational film, not unlike the ones that routinely popped up on the brilliant television series *Mystery Science Theater 3000* (and in fact, former *MST3K* alums Michael J. Nelson, Kevin Murphy, and Bill Corbett mocked *Reefer Madness* for their movie riffing service, Rifftrax). Yet *Reefer Madness* also offers up lurid thrills intended solely to titillate (such as the long, lingering shots of Mae dressing, or the sequences of half-dressed young people partying in Mae's swanky uptown apartment). These elements explain why *Reefer Madness* continues to fascinate and delight audiences more than eighty years after its initial release.

Reefer Madness builds to a comically tragic climax in which one character leaps to her death rather than testify against a reefer-smoking friend who winds up committed to an asylum for "the rest of his natural life" anyway. Nevertheless, *Reefer Madness* cannot sustain its manic momentum, and it soon runs out of steam and descends into tedium despite its brisk sixty-six-minute run time. In addition, the film's sanctimonious sermonizing grows tiresome at a certain point. Ultimately, the idea of *Reefer Madness* proves much funnier than the film itself, and its legions of ironic fans have clearly overstated the allure of its camp appeal. Despite all that, cult film fans will want to fire up *Reefer Madness* as soon as possible (provided they temper their expectations beforehand).

See also *Up in Smoke* (1978), *Dazed and Confused* (1993), *The Stoned Age* (1994), *Half Baked* (1998).

REPO MAN (1984)

Director: Alex Cox
Screenplay: Alex Cox
Cast: Emilio Estevez (Otto), Harry Dean Stanton (Bud), Tracey Walter (Miller), Olivia Barash (Leila), Sy Richardson (Lite), Susan Barnes (Agent Rogersz), Fox Harris (J. Frank Parnell)
Specs: 92 minutes; color
Genre: comedy, crime, science fiction, thriller
Availability: DVD and Blu-ray (The Criterion Collection)

Plot

After stealing a car, a young suburban punk stumbles into the exciting, intense, and altogether weird world of repo men.

Background

In the early 1980s, recent UCLA film school grad Alex Cox wrote a screenplay based on his experiences driving around with a repo man, and this served as the basis for his debut feature film, *Repo Man*.[22] Cox spent the next two years trying to sell the film with the help of his production partners, Peter McCarthy and Jonathan Wacks.[23] Eventually, video coordinator Abbe Wool introduced the trio to producer Harry Gittes, who put them in contact with Mike Nesmith, a former member of the Monkees turned film producer.[24] After reading a few pages of the script, Nesmith agreed to executive produce the film, and he managed to secure a $1.8 million budget from Universal Pictures.[25]

Cox originally wanted his friend Dick Rude to play lead character Otto,[26] but Wacks and McCarthy nixed that idea because they wanted Emilio Estevez instead.[27] Estevez's manager refused to show him the script,[28] but casting director Victoria Thomas managed to slip a copy of the script to the actor, who agreed to appear in the film soon after.[29] Meanwhile, Cox wanted veteran performer

Otto (Emilio Estevez) settles into his new life as a repo man. *Universal / Photofest © Universal*

Harry Dean Stanton as Otto's mentor, Bud, but Stanton's agent suggested they hire Mick Jagger instead.[30] Cox stuck to his guns, however, and eventually landed his first choice. Shooting commenced in July of 1983,[31] and throughout production Cox clashed with Stanton, who refused to learn his lines or take direction until the director pointed out that his actions violated his Screen Actors Guild contract.[32] Cox also fought with the film's producers over cinematographer Robby Müller's aesthetic choices, and this culminated in a physical confrontation between Cox and Wacks.[33]

The tumultuous production wrapped in August of 1983,[34] and *Repo Man* premiered at the Berlin Film Festival in February of 1984,[35] followed by an extremely limited release in the United States a month later.[36] Despite some critical acclaim, *Repo Man* disappeared from theaters after just a few short weeks.[37] The accompanying soundtrack album sold well and generated renewed interest in the film, which developed a cult audience after it hit home video and entered heavy rotation on cable television. These days, *Repo Man* enjoys a well-deserved reputation as a cult classic beloved by punks and outsiders the world over.

Commentary

Even now, *Repo Man* remains a low-budget, high-concept masterpiece that boasts memorable dialogue, outrageous characters, and a cutting-edge soundtrack comprised of early 1980s punk classics. It also functions as a savage send-up of such disparate topics as religion, consumerism, nuclear fears, Reagan-era ideology, 1960s radicalism, and the white suburban punk lifestyle. The film contains dozens of iconic lines (including "A repo man spends his life getting into tense situations," "Let's go get sushi and not pay," and the famous "plate o' shrimp" monologue) and several witty running gags (such as the car air fresheners that randomly pop up throughout the film, the generic products that line the shelves at every store, and Otto's loser friends robbing every store that he and Bud visit). It also features an excellent soundtrack that includes energetic tunes from Black Flag, Suicidal Tendencies, Circle Jerks, Iggy Pop, and more.

Repo Man also offers up some incisive commentary on the destructive effects of conformity, consumer culture, and the conservative ideology espoused by President Ronald Reagan and his political descendants. The numerous shots of downtown Los Angeles reveal a decaying city that is slowly being swallowed by the detritus of a consumerist society, which includes people crushed under the weight of the American Dream. The film also lampoons religion while simultaneously mocking Baby Boomers who abandoned their radical ideals to blindly follow hucksters like L. Ron Hubbard and Jimmy Swaggart. *Repo Man* accomplishes all this while mixing elements of Westerns, sci-films, road movies, and 1970s paranoid thrillers into a funny and defiant postmodern stew. *Repo Man* is a crude, unconventional comedy that unleashes a righteous fury on every aspect of a crumbling society. More than thirty years on, *Repo Man* remains a bizarre, rebellious, and hilarious cult film.

See also *The Adventures of Buckaroo Banzai across the 8th Dimension* (1984), *Sid and Nancy* (1986), *Walker* (1987), *Repo Chick* (2009).

SPOTLIGHT: ALEX COX (1954–)

After graduating from Bristol University, Alex Cox moved to Los Angeles to attend the UCLA School of Theater, Film, and Television. While there, he wrote and directed the surreal short film, *Sleep Is for Sissies*. Cox later formed Edge City Productions with his friends Peter McCarthy and Johnathan Wacks, and together they raised funds for Cox's directorial debut, *Repo Man*, which bombed at the box office but became a cult hit on home video. Cox followed it with *Sid and Nancy*, an independently produced biopic about the relationship between Sex Pistols bassist Sid Vicious and his girlfriend, Nancy Spungen. The film received some critical acclaim but earned the ire of Pistols front man John Lydon due to its inaccuracies. From there, Cox directed other uncompromising films like *Straight to Hell*, *Walker*, *Highway Patrolman*, and *Three Businessmen*. Between 2011 and 2015, Cox taught production and screenwriting at the University of Colorado–Boulder, and while there he teamed with students and recent graduates to produce a crowdfunded adaptation of Harry Harrison's science fiction novel, *Bill the Galactic Hero*. In 2016, he set up an Indiegogo campaign to raise funds for an unconventional Western called *Tombstone Rashomon*.

ROAD HOUSE (1989)

Director: Rowdy Herrington
Screenplay: R. Lance Hill, Hilary Henkin
Cast: Patrick Swayze (Dalton), Kelly Lynch (Doc), Sam Elliott (Wade Garrett), Ben
   Gazzara (Brad Wesley), Marshall R. Teague (Jimmy), Julie Michaels (Denise), Red
   West (Red Webster), Sunshine Parker (Emmet), Jeff Healey (Cody), Kevin Tighe
   (Tilghman)
Specs: 114 minutes; color
Genre: action, thriller
Availability: DVD and Blu-ray (MGM)

Plot

A tough, philosophical bouncer sets out to clean up the rowdiest bar in Missouri, but his efforts upset a cutthroat business tycoon.

Background

Following a string of massive hits that included _Predator_ and _Die Hard_, prolific producer Joel Silver turned his attention to developing _Road House,_ an action flick about a bouncer who liberates a small Missouri town from the clutches of a corrupt businessman. Silver hired newcomer Rowdy Herrington to direct and cast Patrick Swayze and Annette Bening in the lead roles.[38] Noted tough guy Ben Gazzara agreed to play the main villain while Sam Elliot stepped in as the wizened mentor figure.[39] Filming commenced in April of 1988, and though set in Missouri, principal photography took place almost entirely in Santa Clarita, California.[40] Like the director, the production remained rowdy throughout. It became obvious early on that Swayze and Bening lacked chemistry, so Silver replaced Bening with Kelly Lynch.[41] The actors performed their own stunts under the watchful eye of kickboxing champion and action star Benny "The Jet" Urquidez.[42] Yet accidents happened, such as when Marshall Teague accidentally clobbered Swayze with a log during one of their fight scenes.[43] The wild production wrapped after a few weeks, and _Road House_ hit theaters on May 19, 1989.[44]

The film opened to negative reviews and middling box office, and it quickly disappeared from theaters.[45] _Road House_ later became a substantial hit on home video,[46] and it soon garnered a legion of devoted fans who embraced its silly dialogue and over-the-top action. In 2003, theater director Timothy Haskell adapted the film for the stage in an Off-Broadway musical production titled _Road House: The Stage Version of the Cinema Classic That Starred Patrick Swayze, Except This One Stars Taimak from the 80s' Cult Classic "The Last Dragon" Wearing a Blonde Mullet Wig._[47] Three years later, director Scott Ziehl helmed a direct-to-DVD sequel called _Road House 2: The Last Call._[48] In 2015, Metro-Goldwyn-Mayer announced a remake of the film directed by Nick Cassavetes and starring former UFC Bantamweight champion Ronda Rousey,[49] but the project seemingly fell apart after Rousey's loss to Holly Holm at UFC 193.[50] Regardless of whether the remake ever sees the

Dalton (Patrick Swayze) performs tai chi. *United Artists / Photofest © United Artists*

light of day, the original *Road House* remains a much-loved cult classic that left a profound imprint on the pop culture landscape.

Commentary

An abundance of cheesy dialogue, one-dimensional performances, and rampant homoeroticism help make *Road House* a campy cult classic. The film takes a dusty Western narrative and gives it a neon-inflected 1980s makeover complete with brilliantly stupid tough-guy one-liners like "Nobody ever wins a fight," "I'll get all the sleep I need when I'm dead," and the immortal "Pain don't hurt." Best of all, the actors deliver these lines with total sincerity, which makes the dialogue even funnier than if it had been played for laughs. Of course, the film's primary draw lies in the charismatic lead performance of quintessential 1980s heartthrob Swayze, who uses his ropy musculature and dancer's grace to turn Dalton into a convincing badass who also functions as a believable romantic lead. He also provides *Road House* with plenty of beefcake appeal; throughout the film, the camera lingers on Swayze's lean, often shirtless body as he wrestles with bad guys, woos Lynch's Doc, or performs tai chi on a riverbank. Meanwhile, Gazzara delivers a scenery-chewing turn as main antagonist Brad Wesley, while Elliot puts his trademark laconic charm to good use in his role as veteran bouncer Wade Garrett.

Herrington's direction keeps things lively throughout, particularly during the numerous fight sequences, which are wild and over the top but nevertheless display a gritty intensity. *Road House* also features some startling violence, most notably the moment when Dalton rips out a bad guy's throat with his bare hands. While the film never reaches the spectacularly bloody heights of many twenty-first-century action or horror films, the violence in *Road House* is shocking in its intensity, especially when compared to the otherwise laid-back comic attitude that permeates the film's first two acts. Nevertheless, *Road House* remains enjoyable throughout, even though the violence occasionally feels more than a bit excessive. Indeed, while watching *Road House*, it becomes easy to see why it earned a reputation as a cult classic; it is a gleefully mindless masculine melodrama that offers sexy thrills and fist-pumping action.

See also *Tango & Cash* (1989), *The Last Boy Scout* (1991), *Point Break* (1991), *Tombstone* (1993).

THE ROCKETEER (1991)

Director: Joe Johnston
Screenplay: Danny Bilson, Paul De Meo, William Dear (story)
Cast: Bill Campbell (Cliff Secord a.k.a. the Rocketeer), Jennifer Connelly (Jenny), Alan Arkin (Peevy), Timothy Dalton (Neville Sinclair), Paul Sorvino (Eddie Valentine), Terry O'Quinn (Howard Hughes)
Specs: 108 minutes; color
Genre: action, adventure, comedy, family, science fiction
Availability: DVD and Blu-ray (Disney/Buena Vista)

Plot

A handsome young pilot uses a prototype jetpack to foil a sinister plot hatched by Nazi spies during World War II.

Background

Created in 1982 by writer/artist Dave Stevens,[51] who drew inspiration from the Commando Cody serials of the 1950s,[52] *The Rocketeer* took nearly ten years to fly from comic books to the silver screen. After several false starts, Stevens gave the rights to Danny Bilson and Paul De Meo in 1985, and the trio worked with writer/director William Dear to adapt the property.[53] Eventually, Walt Disney Studios purchased the rights and planned to release a trilogy of Rocketeer films through their Touchstone Pictures label.[54] However, studio chairman Jeffrey Katzenberg decided to release a more kid-friendly version of the film under the Walt Disney Pictures banner so that the studio could promote a line of Rocketeer toys.[55] Bilson and De Meo spent the next few years fine-tuning the screenplay, which underwent numerous revisions prior to shooting.[56] Dear dropped out prior to the start of production,[57] and Disney replaced him with director Joe Johnston.[58] Filming commenced on September 19, 1990.[59]

The Rocketeer (Bill Campbell) prepares to launch into action. *Buena Vista Pictures / Photofest © Buena Vista Pictures*

Poor weather and numerous other issues plagued the production throughout.[60] Stevens provided input into character and set design during filming, which caused tension between him and Disney executives, but support from Johnston forced Disney to acquiesce.[61] The budget increased from $25 million to $40 million,[62] and the troubled production was fifty days behind schedule by the time filming wrapped on January 22, 1991.[63] Disney released *The Rocketeer* on June 21, 1991, and advertised it heavily,[64] spending $19 million on television commercials alone.[65] The studio also set up tie-in endorsements with Pizza Hut and Mars candies,[66] and slapped the character's likeness on everything from computer games to children's clothing.[67] Despite all this, *The Rocketeer* grossed less than $10 million during its opening weekend.[68] Throughout its entire theatrical run, it grossed just over $46 million dollars, and the studio considered it a failure.[69] Nevertheless, *The Rocketeer* soon developed a fervent cult following,[70] and in 2016 Disney announced plans to reboot *The Rocketeer* franchise.[71]

Commentary

Even after nearly thirty years and dozens of other superhero movies, *The Rocketeer* stands as a soaring adventure yarn that offers a mix of lighthearted fun, rousing action, and gorgeous Art Deco style. The film presents an old-fashioned adventure in the vein of *Raiders of the Lost Ark*, but it quickly establishes its own identity via a combination of playful visuals and exciting, high-flying spectacle. In addition, *The Rocketeer* nails the period details (particularly in terms of the superb costumes and sumptuous production design) and contains several charming allusions to Hollywood's past (for instance, the film's villain is clearly inspired by Errol Flynn while his hulking henchman Lothar resembles B-movie star Rondo Hatton).

The film also benefits from some excellent casting and energetic performances, starting with Bill Campbell as the title character. Campbell makes for a convincing (if somewhat bland) leading man, and he evokes the sort of broad-shouldered, square-jawed, two-fisted heroes found in old movie serials (like those that inspired *The Rocketeer* and its source material). Meanwhile, Jennifer Connelly is breathtaking as Jenny, the hero's spunky gal who unfortunately becomes a bit of a damsel in distress near the end of the film (though Connelly displays a great deal of presence throughout). Allan Arkin puts his dryly comic sensibilities to good use as Peevy, the Rocketeer's faithful sidekick, while Timothy Dalton clearly relishes his role as the handsome-but-dastardly Neville Sinclair, a conceited actor who specializes in swashbuckling roles and secretly works for the Nazis.

The Rocketeer emerged in the wake of Tim Burton's massively successful *Batman* and around the same time as other early comic book extravaganzas like *Darkman* and *Dick Tracy*, but it distinguishes itself from these other films through a combination of thrilling heroics, delightful performances, and sincere reverence for the Golden Age of Hollywood. In some ways, the film feels like a trial run for Johnston's later work on *Captain America: The First Avenger*, which similarly balanced World War II–era nostalgia with slick superhero pageantry. Yet *The Rocketeer* stands entirely on its own, and even now it remains a fun and fresh successor to the legacy of Indiana Jones that unfortunately failed to launch.

See also *Dick Tracy* (1990), *The Shadow* (1994), *The Phantom* (1996), *Sky Captain and the World of Tomorrow* (2004), *Captain America: The First Avenger* (2011).

ROCK 'N' ROLL HIGH SCHOOL (1979)

Director: Allan Arkush, Joe Dante (uncredited)
Screenplay: Richard Whitley, Russ Dvonch, Joseph McBride, Allan Arkush (story), Joe Dante (story)
Cast: P. J. Soles (Riff Randall), Dey Young (Kate Rambeau), Vincent Van Patten (Tom Roberts), Clint Howard (Eaglebauer), Mary Woronov (Ms. Evelyn Togar), Paul Bartel (Mr. McGree), Lynn Farrell (Angel Dust), Joey Ramone (Himself), Johnny Ramone (Himself), Dee Dee Ramone (Himself), Marky Ramone (Himself)
Specs: 93 minutes; color
Genre: comedy, musical
Availability: Blu-ray (Shout! Factory)

Plot

Punk legends the Ramones team up with a group of rebellious teenagers to thwart a tyrannical principal's efforts to outlaw rock-and-roll music.

Background

A few years after cofounding New World Pictures with his brother Gene, prolific independent film producer Roger Corman asked Allan Arkush to direct *Disco High*, a film about disco-loving students rebelling against their teachers.[72] Arkush previously worked as an editor and second-unit director on several Corman films, and he leapt at the chance to direct his own picture.[73] He also convinced Corman to change the title to *Rock 'n' Roll High School*.[74] Arkush then developed a story inspired by a scenario he came up with as a teenager, in which his favorite rock band performed at his high school.[75] He combined this idea with his teenage daydreams of racing motorcycles through the hallways and punishing the lunch ladies, and this became the basis for *Rock 'n' Roll High School*.[76] Arkush brought this idea to the notoriously frugal Corman, who put up a $185,000 budget,[77] though that amount eventually increased to $300,000.[78]

With financing secured, Arkush approached Todd Rundgren about appearing in the film, but the two parties failed to reach an agreement.[79] Arkush then contacted Cheap Trick, but that deal similarly fell through.[80] A friend at Warner Bros. suggested Devo, but their aesthetic clashed with Arkush's vision for the film.[81] Arkush eventually settled on the Ramones because he found the idea of lead singer Joey Ramone as a rock idol funny.[82] The director then turned his attention to casting central character Riff Randel. Darryl Hannah auditioned, but the role ultimately went to P. J. Soles because she offered to supply her own wardrobe (not to mention Arkush thought she was brilliant).[83] Principal photography commenced soon after on the campus of South Central Los Angeles's Mount Carmel High School,[84] which had closed in 1976.[85]

Riff Randell (P. J. Soles, center) and the Ramones take over Vince Lombardi High. *New World Pictures / Photofest © New World Pictures*

As with most Corman films, production moved at a rapid pace.[86] The hurried schedule took a physical toll on Arkush, who collapsed from exhaustion on the penultimate day of shooting and had to be rushed to the hospital.[87] During his recovery, Joe Dante stepped in for a day to shoot the film's central musical number.[88] Otherwise, principal photography ran smoothly, particularly once Arkush learned that directing the Ramones consisted mainly of teaching them their lines and shooting their scenes as quickly as possible.[89] Despite a noticeable lack of acting ability, the band proved good sports, and even contributed several ideas to the film (such as the fantasy sequence in Riff's bathroom).[90] *Rock 'n' Roll High School* found some success upon release, but its reputation truly grew in the years afterward thanks to frequent midnight screenings and heavy rotation on MTV.[91] In 1991, the film spawned a forgettable sequel starring Corey Feldman.

Commentary

Like the Ramones' music, *Rock 'n' Roll High School* captures the anarchic spirit of rock and roll, but reveals the goofy underbelly that lies beneath the genre's hip exterior. The film skewers the clichés that normally plague high school movies, and it balances clever jokes with broadly silly humor (the "ear mail" sequence is especially hilarious). Of course, younger viewers may find the film corny and off-putting, and they might be tempted to write off *Rock 'n' Roll High School* as little more than a stuffy collection of dad jokes. Yet those who can appreciate the film's wackiness will discover a fun musical that rocks hard even as it pokes fun at itself.

Rock 'n' Roll High School includes numerous great performances (particularly Paul Bartel and Mary Woronov), but the film absolutely belongs to Soles, who delivers an iconic turn as lead character Riff Randell. Soles puts an adorable pixieish spin on teenage rebellion, and she imbues the entire film with a sense of boundless energy and charming impulsiveness. In addition, the film boasts a killer soundtrack (which also features Paul McCartney and Chuck Berry) and gorgeous widescreen cinematography by Dean Cundey (who lensed many of John Carpenter's movies, including *The Thing*).

Rock 'n' Roll High School rises above its budgetary limitations thanks to the endearingly silly humor and delightful performances. More importantly, though, the film shuns standard high school movie clichés and flips the script on the archetypes usually found in such films (for instance, Tom Roberts would normally fill the role of the handsome, well-liked jock, but here he comes off as awkward and unpopular). For these reasons and more, cult movie fans should enroll in *Rock 'n' Roll High School* as soon as possible.

See also *Death Race 2000* (1975), *This Is Spinal Tap* (1984), *Detroit Rock City* (1999), *Walk Hard: The Dewey Cox Story* (2007).

THE ROCKY HORROR PICTURE SHOW (1975)

Director: Jim Sharman
Screenplay: Jim Sharman, Richard O'Brien
Cast: Tim Curry (Dr. Frank-N-Furter), Susan Sarandon (Janet Weiss), Barry Bostwick (Brad Majors), Richard O'Brien (Riff Raff), Patricia Quinn (Magenta), Nell Campbell (Columbia), Jonathan Adams (Dr. Everett V. Scott), Peter Hinwood (Rocky Horror), Meat Loaf (Eddie), Charles Gray (the Criminologist)
Specs: 100 minutes; color
Genre: comedy, horror, musical, science fiction
Availability: Blu-ray (20th Century Fox)

Plot

After their car breaks down on a cold rainy night, two American sweethearts fall into the clutches of a pansexual transvestite from outer space.

Background

While living in London during the early 1970s, struggling actor Richard O'Brien developed *They Came from Denton High*, a musical inspired by his love of science fiction, B movies, and glam rock.[92] Titled *The Rocky Horror Show*, the musical premiered in 1973 at the small Royal Court Theatre,[93] but it eventually made its way to the much larger Kings Road Theatre, where it ran for six years.[94] The show debuted in Los Angeles in 1974, and 20th Century Fox decided to produce a film adaptation soon after.[95] For the film version, Fox agreed to retain the original cast and crew in exchange for a reduced budget and tighter shooting schedule,[96] as well as the inclusion of at least some American actors.[97] O'Brien and Sharman hired real-life lovers Barry Bostwick and Susan Sarandon to play the clean-cut Brad Majors and his naive fiancée Janet Weiss,[98] and the film entered production on October 21, 1974, under the new title *The Rocky Horror Picture Show*.[99]

Just before shooting commenced, Fox underwent a regime change, and the new head of the studio nearly pulled the plug on the whole project.[100] Luckily, he changed his mind and basically left the inexperienced filmmakers to their own devices during the six-week-long production.[101] Sharman shot much of the film at Bray Studios and Oakley Court, an old country house located near the Hammer studios in Maidenhead, Berkshire, England.[102] Principal photography wrapped on December 19, 1974,[103] at which point Sharman and editor Graeme Clifford retreated to Elstree Studios to wrap up postproduction.[104]

Rocky Horror premiered at London's Rialto Theater on August 14, 1975,[105] only to alienate both audiences and critics. The film disappeared from theaters soon after, but it later became a huge hit on the midnight movie circuit, developing an enthusiastic cult following that turned it into the longest continuously running film to date.[106] It also inspired audience participation, with devoted fans dressing as their favorite characters and performing scenes as the film plays on the screen behind them. Over time, *Rocky Horror* became a cultural phenomenon, and it remains one of the most popular and beloved cult films ever made.

Dr. Frank-N-Furter (Tim Curry, center) and his minions welcome some new guests to the party. Twentieth Century Fox Film Corporation / Photofest © Twentieth Century Fox Film Corporation

Commentary

For a lot of folks, *Rocky Horror* stands as the epitome of cult cinema, and more than forty years on, the film endures as a silly and sexy musical romp that features fantastic songs, witty dialogue, and outrageous characters. It also boasts an iconic performance by Tim Curry as Dr. Frank-N-Furter, the self-proclaimed sweet transvestite from the planet Transsexual in the galaxy of Transylvania. He is clearly having a ton of fun as he prances around looking like the love child of Freddie Mercury and Divine, and his performance infuses the film with a great deal of sex appeal and snarky humor. *Rocky Horror* wraps these elements in an appealing, relatively inoffensive package that remains lively and amusing throughout. In addition, the film openly celebrates difference and contains numerous nods to the trashy, low-budget films that lurk at the margins of Hollywood's past. Thus, it becomes easy to see why *Rocky Horror* remains the glammed-up grand dame of all cult films, and why it inspired such devotion from an audience of misfits who love nothing more than to perform along with the movie.

Rocky Horror also includes several rockin' tunes that tap into the flashy spirit of glam rock and pay loving homage to the cheap sci-fi flicks and tacky B-movies of yore. "The Time Warp" is perhaps the film's most famous song, but it shares the spotlight with equally buoyant tracks like "Sweet Transvestite," "Dammit Janet," and "Hot Patootie—Bless My Soul." The soundtrack also features genuinely moving numbers like "Over at the Frankenstein Place" and "I'm Going Home." In addition, *Rocky Horror* contains delightfully inane lines like "Do you think I made a mistake splitting his brain between the two of them?" or "If only we were amongst friends . . . or sane persons!"—all of which are delivered in a winking fashion and are guaranteed to elicit at least a few chuckles from the audience. The songs, performances, and dialogue all ensure that *Rocky Horror* remains a light-hearted and sensual experience.

Of course, the weirdness sometimes feels a bit too calculated, and one could easily dismiss *Rocky Horror* as "baby's first cult movie," a quaint gateway film that can potentially lead to harder (and some might say better) stuff like *Faster, Pussycat! Kill! Kill!* or *Pink Flamingos*. Nonetheless, *Rocky Horror* stands on its own as a devilishly fun cult film that offers plenty of great music, memorable lines, and delightfully bizarre characters.

See also *Pink Flamingos* (1972), *Phantom of the Paradise* (1974), *Shock Treatment* (1981), *Hedwig and the Angry Inch* (2001).

ROMY AND MICHELE'S HIGH SCHOOL REUNION (1997)

Director: David Mirkin
Screenplay: Robin Schiff
Cast: Mira Sorvino (Romy White), Lisa Kudrow (Michele Weinberger), Janeane Garofalo (Heather Mooney), Alan Cumming (Sandy Frink), Julia Campbell (Christy Masters), Vincent Ventresca (Billy Christianson), Elaine Hendrix (Lisa Luder), Justin Theroux (Cowboy), Camryn Manheim (Toby Walters)
Specs: 92 minutes; color
Genre: comedy
Availability: DVD and Blu-ray (Disney/Buena Vista)

Plot

Despite a series of personal and professional failures, two lifelong friends set out to impress their former classmates at their ten-year high school reunion.

Background

In 1988, legendary producer Aaron Spelling financed *Ladies' Room*, a stage play set entirely in a Mexican restaurant bathroom during happy hour.[107] Written by Robin Schiff, the show included two dim-witted supporting characters named Romy and Michele that Schiff developed after overhearing a conversation between two women in a Los Angeles nightclub bathroom.[108] She originally intended to make them the leads in a sitcom, but thought audiences might tire of these characters quickly so she inserted them into *Ladies' Room* instead.[109] Alex Schwartz and Gaye Hirsch of Touchstone Pictures saw the play and convinced Schiff to develop a screenplay about the two airheads attending their ten-year high school reunion.[110] Touchstone hired Emmy-winning TV writer David Mirkin (of *The Simpsons* and *The Larry Sanders Show*) to direct even though he lacked experience behind the camera.[111] Lisa Kudrow originated the role of Michele in *Ladies' Room* and she returned to play the character in the film,[112] while Mira Sorvino stepped into the role of Romy, against the recommendations of her rep-

Romy (Mira Sorvino, right) and Michele (Lisa Kudrow) prepare to attend their high school reunion. *Touchstone Pictures / Photofest © Touchstone Pictures*

resentatives.[113] Filming commenced on April 27, 1996, and principal photography wrapped on June 22 of that year.[114]

Romy and Michele opened in theaters on April 25, 1997, and received generally positive reviews from critics.[115] The film fared less well with audiences, but positive word of mouth propelled *Romy and Michele* to a $29 million box office haul in North America alone.[116] Over time, the film achieved cult status thanks to its extremely quotable script and unexpectedly silly humor, and fans routinely quote the film and dress up as the characters for Halloween. In 2005, Schiff attempted to resurrect the property when she wrote and directed *Romy and Michele: In the Beginning*, a TV movie starring Katherine Heigl as Romy and Alexandra Breckenridge as Michele.[117] Unfortunately, it failed to generate much interest and was quickly forgotten. Meanwhile, a musical stage adaptation of *Romy and Michele* premiered at the 5th Avenue Theatre in Seattle, Washington, in June, 2017.[118] Regardless of whether this new version succeeds or fails, the original film remains a beloved cult classic among fans who strive to make every day a Romy and Michele day.

Commentary

More than twenty years after its initial release, *Romy and Michele* remains a delightfully goofy celebration of female friendship and empowerment. On the surface, the film seems like little more than a charming comic confection that offers viewers a simplistic look at tough issues like friendship, failure, and perseverance. Yet a closer inspection reveals *Romy and Michele* as a fiercely feminist film because it celebrates female achievement and possesses a keen awareness of the barriers presented by sexism and classism. The characters of Romy and Michele persist despite encountering both chauvinism and economic discrimination (such as when Michele applies for a job at a Versace outlet), and they manage to succeed without compromising their ideals or identities. The viewer feels compelled to root for Romy and Michele, because the movie treats them with compassion and respect from the start.

Beyond the subtext, the film succeeds as a straight-up comedy because it features plenty of daffy humor and funny performances. *Romy and Michele* benefits from Mirkin's solid direction, and the gags succeed thanks to his comic sensibilities. Of course, Mirkin receives a lot of help from the talented cast, particularly Sorvino and Kudrow, both of whom bring warmth and knowing humor to their performances, making the title characters feel instantly iconic and authentic. Meanwhile, Janeane Garofalo, Alan Cumming, Julia Campbell, Justin Theroux, and the rest of the supporting cast all get opportunities to show off their considerable chops (Camryn Manheim conveys her character's deep-seated pain in a single line). The hilarious performances ensure that *Romy and Michele* provides lots of laughs, and even viewers who fail to pick up on the feminist themes will find something to love in the film.

In a lot of ways, *Romy and Michele* presaged the Judd Apatow brand of comedy that currently dominates film and television. Rather than emotionally stunted man-children clinging to their pasts, however, the film features two stalled-out young women haunted by the youth they tried to leave behind. As such, it paved the way for female-centric comedies like *Bridesmaids* and *Trainwreck* but works much better than either of those films. Some of the jokes fall flat and the film occasionally leans too hard on nostalgia, but *Romy and Michele* still succeeds because it treats its title characters with respect and therefore sends a message to girls and young women about remaining true to themselves despite what others may think.

See also *Ghost World* (2001), *Bridesmaids* (2011), *Sisters* (2015), *Trainwreck* (2015).

THE ROOM (2003)

Director: Tommy Wiseau
Screenplay: Tommy Wiseau
Cast: Tommy Wiseau (Johnny), Juliette Danielle (Lisa), Greg Sestero (Mark), Philip Haldiman (Denny), Carolyn Minnott (Claudette), Robyn Paris (Michelle), Mike Holmes (Mike), Dan Janjigian (Chris-R), Kyle Vogt (Peter), Greg Ellery (Steven)
Specs: 99 minutes; color
Genre: drama
Availability: DVD and Blu-ray (Wiseau-Films)

Plot

A successful banker shares an intense intimate relationship with his beautiful fiancée, but things turn sour after she sleeps with his best friend.

Background

In 2002, aspiring actor Tommy Wiseau decided to write, produce, direct, and star in his own movie, based on a 600-page book he wrote, despite a lack of experience behind the camera.[119] Using funds drawn from his own seemingly endless fortune, Wiseau made *The Room*, a semiautobiographical romantic melodrama inspired by the work of Tennessee Williams, Orson Welles, and Alfred Hitchcock.[120] Friend and fellow actor Greg Sestero agreed to work as part of the production crew,[121] though he eventually graduated to playing one of the lead characters. Throughout the production, Wiseau made several odd decisions that inflated the film's budget to about $6 million.[122] For instance, he shot on 35 mm film and high-definition video at the same time,[123] but rather than rent cameras, he purchased them at a high cost.[124] In addition, he ordered expensive sets built and shot several scenes multiple times. He also drove away many members of the cast and crew, including two cinematographers and three actors.[125] The turbulent production wrapped after six months, and *The Room* premiered on June 27, 2003, at the Laemmle Fairfax and Fallbrook theaters in Los Angeles.[126] To promote the film, Wiseau purchased a billboard near Highland Avenue in Hollywood and plastered it with an unsettling image of his own face.[127]

Despite Wiseau's efforts, *The Room* failed at the box office, grossing less than $2,000 during its initial theatrical run.[128] Critics savaged the film, but *The Room* still found some fans,[129] many of whom reached out to Wiseau to let him know how much they enjoyed his movie.[130] Encouraged by this response, Wiseau arranged a midnight screening of *The Room* in June of 2004, and it proved so successful that he booked several more showings over the next few months.[131] At that point, the film developed a cult audience that included celebrities like Paul Rudd, David Cross, Patton Oswalt, Seth Rogan, and Kristen Bell.[132] Word of mouth eventually propelled *The Room* to international cult status. The film hit DVD in 2005,[133] at which

Johnny (Tommy Wiseau, left) and Mark (Greg Sestero) have a heart-to-heart talk on the rooftop of their building. *Chloe Productions/TPW Films / Photofest © Chloe Productions/TPW Films / Photofest*

point even more people discovered Wiseau's daft masterwork. Sestero chronicled the making of *The Room* in his popular 2013 nonfiction book *The Disaster Artist*, which actor/writer/director James Franco later adapted as a film.[134] These days, *The Room* enjoys a well-deserved reputation as a campy cult classic, and its audience continues to grow as more people become ensnared by its dopey allure.

Commentary

A combination of enjoyably amateurish acting and comically overwrought melodrama helped turn *The Room* into a modern-day camp classic and a masterpiece of incompetence that takes ironic appreciation to an entirely new level. The film announces its ineptness before the opening credits roll, as the whole thing kicks off with two different Wiseau-Films production logos. This sort of clumsiness continues throughout *The Room*, which boasts stilted performances, an incomprehensible narrative, and nonsensical dialogue that only barely resembles human speech. It often feels like someone fed the entire screenplay into an off-brand translation software, translated it into a random language, and then back into English. Characters enter and exit completely at random (like the guy who pops up during the climactic birthday party to chastise Lisa for cheating on Johnny), and the film drops plot threads left and right (such as Claudette's mid-film revelation that she definitely has cancer). Add in the excessively maudlin score and thoroughly unattractive sex scenes that go on way too long (and feature obscenely loud moans and grunts clearly added during postproduction), and *The Room* becomes one of the best bad movies of the twenty-first century.

Wiseau himself is the main reason to watch *The Room*, largely due to his weird looks, strange accent, and peculiar mannerisms (not to mention his complete misunderstanding of how a chicken sounds), which often make him seem like an alien trying to mimic human behavior. He delivers an intensely bizarre performance as lead character Johnny, and he spends the entire movie stumbling around like a drunken sleepwalker and mumbling his lines in a thick Eastern European accent that renders nearly every word unintelligible (this becomes even funnier when considering that most of the dialogue was dubbed in post). Like Edward D. Wood Jr., Wiseau clearly possesses an infectious enthusiasm for filmmaking but harbors precious little actual talent. *The Room* defies conventional notions of good and bad, but it remains endlessly entertaining from beginning to end. It also offers a fascinating peek inside the mind of its profoundly odd creator and stands as an amusingly awful flick even after more than fifteen years. Cult movie fans should pay a visit to *The Room* as soon as possible.

See also *Manos*: *The Hands of Fate* (1966), *Miami Connection* (1987), *Troll 2* (1990), *Dangerous Men* (2005), *Birdemic*: *Shock and Terror* (2010), *Fateful Findings* (2013).

SPOTLIGHT: TOMMY WISEAU (19??–)

Little is known about enigmatic weirdo Tommy Wiseau, because he remains tight-lipped about his early life in interviews. Supposedly born in Poznań, Poland, in the 1950s, Wiseau claims he grew up in New Orleans, Louisiana. As a young man, Wiseau reportedly moved to Strasbourg, France, and worked as a dishwasher under the alias "Pierre," but fled the country after a wrongful arrest during a drug raid at a youth hostel. From there, Wiseau settled in San Francisco, California, and sold toys to tourists visiting Fisherman's Wharf. After spending a few years working odd jobs, Wiseau founded Street Fashions USA, a company that sold irregular blue jeans at discounted prices. He later made a fortune purchasing and renting out large retail spaces throughout San Francisco and Los Angeles. After surviving a near-fatal car crash, Wiseau decided to pursue his dreams of becoming a filmmaker and actor. He wrote, directed, and starred in *The Room*, which soon developed a devoted following and turned Wiseau into a beloved cult figure. Despite making only one film, Wiseau served as the vanguard for a new wave of trash auteurs that includes Neil Breen, James Nguyen, and Josh Rad.

RUSHMORE (1998)

Director: Wes Anderson
Screenplay: Wes Anderson, Owen Wilson
Cast: Jason Schwartzman (Max Fischer), Bill Murray (Herman Blume), Olivia Williams (Rosemary Cross), Seymour Cassel (Bert Fischer), Brian Cox (Dr. Nelson Guggenheim)
Specs: 93 minutes; color
Genre: comedy, drama
Availability: DVD and Blu-ray (The Criterion Collection)

Plot

A precocious fifteen-year-old prep school student befriends a misanthropic fifty-year-old millionaire, but their budding camaraderie turns into a bitter rivalry when they both fall for the same woman.

Background

In 1996, director Wes Anderson and actor Owen Wilson made their feature film debut with *Bottle Rocket*, a comedic crime flick that delighted critics but flopped with general audiences.[135] For their follow-up, they dusted off a screenplay called *Rushmore*, which they wrote a few years earlier and was inspired by their own childhood experiences.[136] In the early part of 1997, the duo brought the project to New Line Cinema, but the two parties failed to agree on the budget.[137] Soon after, producer Barry Mendel helped Anderson and Wilson set up a deal with Joe Roth of Walt Disney Studios, who offered to produce *Rushmore* for $10 million.[138]

With their budget secured, Anderson and Wilson searched for someone to play lead character Max Fischer. They eventually settled on seventeen-year-old actor Jason Schwartzman, nephew of Francis Ford Coppola.[139] The duo then turned their attention to casting Herman Blume, the millionaire who befriends Max. Anderson and Wilson had written the part for Bill Murray but assumed that casting him was a long shot at best. Luckily, Murray's agent was a fan of *Bottle Rocket*, and he convinced the actor to read *Rushmore*.[140] Murray liked it so much he agreed to appear in the film for $9,000, far less than his normal salary.[141] Production commenced in November of 1997, and Anderson shot the film in and around Houston, Texas, with his old high school doubling as Rushmore Academy.[142]

Shooting wrapped in February of 1998, and *Rushmore* premiered at the Telluride Film Festival on September 8 of that year.[143] It then spent the next few weeks touring the festival circuit before opening in limited release in New York City and Los Angeles on December 11, 1998.[144] The film finally entered wide release on February 5, 1999,[145] and it grossed just over $17 million during its theatrical run.[146] It also revitalized Bill Murray's career, and his performance earned him several awards.[147] *Rushmore* has since become a beloved cult film, and it helped establish Anderson's signature style, which can be seen in subsequent films like *The Royal Tenenbaums, The Life Aquatic with Steve Zissou, The Darjeeling Limited, Fantastic Mr. Fox, Moonrise Kingdom,* and *The Grand Budapest Hotel.*

Max Fischer (Jason Schwarztman, right) and Herman Blume (Bill Murray) strike up an unlikely friendship that soon turns into a rivalry. *Buena Vista Pictures / Photofest © Buena Vista Pictures*

Commentary

Rushmore strikes a perfect balance between whimsy and melancholy, and presents viewers with a delightfully bittersweet fable about love, loss, and the pain of growing up. As mentioned, *Rushmore* marks the genesis of Anderson's trademark "dollhouse" aesthetic, which is marked by flat, perfectly centered compositions. It also serves up a hip soundtrack consisting of British Invasion–era hits and a lilting score by Devo front man Mark Mothersbaugh, and boasts fun performances from the entire cast. As such, *Rushmore* emerges as a funny, heartfelt, and utterly enjoyable comedy with a style all its own.

Anderson's direction remains the film's primary draw, and his unique framings and arrangements give the film a one-of-a-kind look and render everything on-screen quaint and slightly cartoonish (which makes sense when considering that he drew inspiration from Charles Schultz's classic newspaper comic strip, *Peanuts*). While watching *Rushmore*, it soon becomes clear why so many other filmmakers tried (and failed) to replicate Anderson's singular style, and why films like *Garden State*, *Napoleon Dynamite*, *Little Miss Sunshine*, and *The Book of Henry* all feel like hollow, lifeless knockoffs in comparison.

Rushmore also features excellent performances from the spirited cast. Murray stands out as Blume, delivering a funny yet touching performance as a lonely middle-aged man searching for meaningful companionship. Schwartzman imbues lead character Max with a sense of prideful ambition that belies his deep-seated insecurities. Olivia Williams breathes life into her slight role as Rosemary Cross, a kind elementary school teacher who becomes an unwitting object of affection for both Max and Blume. The character mainly serves to set the plot in motion, but Williams transforms her into a lovely and exuberant woman plagued by an immense sadness brought on by the death of a loved one.

While the quirkiness might prove overwhelming for some, *Rushmore* still has plenty to offer thanks to the lively performances and spirited direction. The film possesses an abundance of peculiar charm and features loads of memorable characters and unforgettable dialogue. As such, discerning cult movie fans will want to enroll in *Rushmore* as soon as possible.

See also *The 400 Blows* (1959), *If....* (1968), *Brewster McCloud* (1970), *Harold and Maude* (1971), *Submarine* (2010).

S

SCOTT PILGRIM VS. THE WORLD (2010)

Director: Edgar Wright
Screenplay: Michael Bacall, Edgar Wright
Cast: Michael Cera (Scott Pilgrim), Mary Elizabeth Winstead (Ramona Flowers), Kieran Culkin (Wallace Wells), Ellen Wong (Knives Chau), Allison Pill (Kim Pine), Mark Webber (Stephen Stills), Johnny Simmons (Young Neil), Anna Kendrick (Stacey Pilgrim), Aubrey Plaza (Julie Powers), Chris Evans (Lucas Lee), Brandon Routh (Todd Ingram), Jason Schwartzman (Gideon Graves)
Specs: 112 minutes; color
Genre: action, comedy, fantasy, romance
Availability: DVD and Blu-ray (Universal Studios Home Entertainment)

Plot

A young rock musician meets the woman of his dreams, but to win her heart he must first contend with her seven evil exes and his own spurned teenage ex-girlfriend.

Background

Director Edgar Wright first learned about Bryan Lee O'Malley's graphic novel series *Scott Pilgrim* in 2004, when producers Jared LeBoff and Adam Siegel asked him to direct the adaptation.[1] Wright agreed, and he worked with screenwriter Michael Bacall to develop the script.[2] Wright also worked closely with O'Malley to ensure that the film reflected both of their sensibilities.[3] Casting began in June of 2008, about two years before the start of production, and Wright consulted with O'Malley throughout the process. Wright and producer Nira Park wanted Michael Cera for the title character, but worried that he was too young for the part. However, it took several years to develop the film, and Cera eventually aged into the role.[4] They also cast Mary Elizabeth Winstead as female lead Ramona Flowers and Ellen Wong as Scott's ex-girlfriend Knives Chau. Wright then rounded out the rest of the cast with a mix of hot young stars and talented up-and-comers.[5]

Following an eight-week rehearsal period, *Scott Pilgrim vs. the World* finally entered production on March 30, 2009.[6] Shooting took place mainly in Toronto,

Scott Pilgrim (Michael Cera, left) introduces himself to Ramona Flowers (Mary Elizabeth Winstead). *Universal Pictures / Photofest © Universal Pictures*

Canada, and Wright featured several local landmarks in the film, including Sonic Boom, the Toronto Public Library, and a Pizza Pizza.[7] Throughout production, Wright and veteran cinematographer Bill Pope worked diligently to replicate the look and feel of the source material.[8] The finished film premiered on February 26, 2011, at the Yubari International Fantastic Film Festival in Japan. The film entered wide release in North America on August 13, 2010, and while it received generally favorable reviews from critics, it nevertheless flopped with general audiences. Yet *Scott Pilgrim* quickly developed a devoted cult audience that appreciated its flashy visual style and offbeat humor. It also spawned a popular soundtrack album and a video game adaptation, and it launched the careers of several performers who went on to become huge stars in the years after the film's release.

Commentary

With *Scott Pilgrim*, Wright delivers one of the most visually inventive films of his career, which is quite a feat considering he also directed *Shaun of the Dead, Hot Fuzz*, and *The World's End*. In seeking to replicate the look and feel of the source material, Wright managed to develop a film grammar that evokes video games and anime, both of which influenced O'Malley's graphic novel series. Wright makes extensive use of imaginative effects and imagery throughout the film and puts them in service of several hilarious visual gags (such as when Scott realizes that Ramona went through a "sexy phase," or when he and his bandmates face off against twin DJs in a raucous battle of the bands). All of this ensures that *Scott Pilgrim* remains kinetic and exciting even during the most mundane sequences, such as the scene in which Scott sits in his cramped apartment and waits for a package to arrive.

While the visuals alone make *Scott Pilgrim* worth watching, the film also features a great story that contains a rich thematic undercurrent. As in the comics, Scott's battle against Ramona's seven evil ex-lovers serves as an allegory for his attempts to come to terms with his new romantic partner's sexual past and his own feelings of self-doubt. Throughout the film, the expertly shot fight sequences function as visual representations of Scott's own inner conflict over whether he belongs with Ramona; Scott suffers from lingering insecurities resulting from a bad breakup a few years earlier, and they have greatly affected his subsequent relationships. At the same time, he struggles to deal with the fact that he lied to Knives and broke her heart. Ultimately, Scott must learn to love and respect himself before he can hope to win Ramona's love and respect in return. Thus, *Scott Pilgrim* is more than just an action-packed and comedic love story; it also functions as a lesson in how to build and maintain healthy relationships.

While some viewers will no doubt find the quick cuts and relentless pace exhausting, *Scott Pilgrim* nevertheless remains a sweet, funny, and visually creative film that rewards multiple viewings thanks to its groundbreaking visual effects, sly humor, and touching love story.

See also *Hot Fuzz* (2007), *Speed Racer* (2008), *Detention* (2011), *The World's End* (2013).

SPOTLIGHT: EDGAR WRIGHT (1974–)

Edgar Wright spent his teenage years making short films with an 8 mm camera. At the age of twenty, he directed *A Fistful of Fingers*, a low-budget British western that landed him a gig directing TV shows for the Paramount Comedy Channel. A few years later, Wright worked with actors Simon Pegg and Jessica Hynes to develop *Spaced*, a highly cinematic sitcom that became an international cult hit. In 2005, Wright made his feature film directorial debut with *Shaun of the Dead*, a romantic zombie comedy that starred Pegg (who cowrote the screenplay with Wright) and *Spaced* alum Nick Frost. The film became a surprise box office hit and earned several award nominations. From there, Wright directed a handful of visually inventive genre-bending films like the action comedy *Hot Fuzz*, the action-packed romantic comedy *Scott Pilgrim vs. the World*, the comic science fiction film *The World's End*, and the dazzling heist flick/sort-of-musical *Baby Driver*. In addition to his feature film work, Wright also contributed a fake trailer to Quentin Tarantino and Robert Rodriguez's *Grindhouse*. In 2011, he cowrote the screenplay for director Steven Spielberg's animated adaptation of *The Adventures of Tintin* and served as executive producer on cult sensation *Attack the Block*.

THE SHAWSHANK REDEMPTION (1994)

Director: Frank Darabont
Screenplay: Frank Darabont, based on the novella *Rita Hayworth and Shawshank Redemption* by Stephen King
Cast: Tim Robbins (Andy Dufresne), Morgan Freeman (Ellis Boyd "Red" Redding), Bob Gunton (Warden Norton), William Sadler (Heywood), Clancy Brown (Captain Hadley), Gil Bellows (Tommy), Mark Rolston (Bogs Diamond), James Whitmore (Brooks Hatlen)
Specs: 142 minutes; color
Genre: crime, drama
Availability: DVD and Blu-ray (Warner Bros.)

Plot

A man struggles to keep hope alive after he is falsely convicted of a double murder and sentenced to lifelong incarceration in Maine's Shawshank State Prison.

Background

After spending several years toiling in the trenches of the film industry, screenwriter Frank Darabont turned his attention to adapting Stephen King's novella *Rita Hayworth and Shawshank Redemption* for the screen.[9] King expressed doubt that the story could lend itself to a film, but Darabont had a plan and in 1992 he set about writing a screenplay that honored the source material but also took several liberties with it.[10] Eight weeks later, Darabont sent the completed script to various studios around Hollywood. It eventually made its way to producer Liz Glotzer at Castle Rock Entertainment, and she liked it so much she threatened to quit unless her colleagues agreed to make the picture.[11] From there, Castle Rock founder Rob Reiner offered Darabont a rumored $3 million to direct *Shawshank* himself.[12] After much soul searching, Darabont agreed,[13] and principal photography commenced on June 16, 1993.[14]

Darabont shot the film on location inside the former Ohio State Reformatory,[15] though he staged some scenes on nearby sets.[16] Principal photography took place during the particularly humid summer of 1993, and both cast and crew faced a punishing work schedule as they filmed between fifteen and eighteen hours a day, six days a week.[17] They spent much of that time inside the prison, which proved a bleak experience for all involved.[18] Shooting wrapped on September 10, 1993,[19] and Darabont worked with Richard Francis-Bruce to edit the footage. The film's first cut ran quite long, and Glotzer ordered a shorter version.[20] Darabont and Francis-Bruce came back with a leisurely paced film that ran nearly two and a half hours, and after a successful round of test screenings, this version opened in theaters on September 23, 1994.[21] The film received mostly favorable reviews but bombed at the box office. After ten weeks, *Shawshank* had grossed just $16 million[22] and would end up earning just over $28 million against a $25 million budget.[23]

Red (Morgan Freeman, second from left) and Andy (Tim Robbins, center) try to keep hope alive despite their unfortunate situation. *Photofest Inc.*

Shawshank hit home video in the early part of 1995 and quickly became one of the most rented films of that year.[24] Its audience grew even larger thanks to repeat showings on the cable network TNT.[25] In the years since, *Shawshank* has developed a reputation as one of the most beloved films of all time, and it routinely winds up on "best of" lists. In 2008, *Shawshank* surpassed *The Godfather* to become the number one film on the Internet Movie Database's Top 250,[26] a user-generated list of the greatest movies of all time, and it remains in that spot as of this writing.

Commentary

Featuring impeccable acting and first-rate direction, *Shawshank* is a profoundly moving celebration of the human spirit that offers a harrowing but spiritually uplifting look at life in prison. One could easily dismiss the film as sentimental and manipulative, but it earns every bit of emotion as it provides viewers with a poignant message about keeping hope alive. *Shawshank* takes great pains to remind viewers that "hope is a good thing, maybe the best of things, and no good thing ever dies," and that everyone must make the choice to either "get busy living, or get busy dying." In lesser hands, these sentiments could easily come across as simplistic, heavy-handed moralizing, but Darabont turns them into an encouraging mission statement designed to inspire viewers to strive for something better. In *Shawshank*, hope emerges as the most important thing in the world, and the film goes out of its way to convince viewers to embrace that idea (which has only become more resonant during the second decade of the twenty-first century, when nearly every single news headline and political outcome seems to herald the end of liberal democracy). Of course, *Shawshank* hammers that theme into the ground, and the whole thing goes on a bit too long (it should end with the bus carrying Red driving off into the distance). Yet the film remains a rousing story of hope that ambles toward a triumphant conclusion.

In addition to Darabont's graceful direction and Roger Deakins's exquisite cinematography, *Shawshank* boasts captivating performances by Tim Robbins and Morgan Freeman as lead characters Andy and Red, respectively, two men determined to remain positive and hopeful in the face of overwhelming adversity. It also features stereotypical characters (especially Warden Norton, who becomes little more than a sneering villain as the film wears on) and a simplistic but compelling narrative that contains plenty of stirring moments (like the one in which Andy broadcasts an opera record to his fellow inmates even though he knows it will land him in solitary confinement) and heartbreaking interludes (such as the devastating story of what happens to elderly convict Brooks Hatlen after he wins parole). Altogether, *Shawshank* is a touching if somewhat hard-edged film that looks great and contains some truly affecting performances, as well as a straightforward but powerful narrative guaranteed to leave audiences riveted.

See also *Cool Hand Luke* (1967), *The Green Mile* (1999), *The Majestic* (2001), *The Mist* (2007).

SHOCK CORRIDOR (1963)

Director: Samuel Fuller
Screenplay: Samuel Fuller
Cast: Peter Breck (Johnny Barrett), Constance Towers (Cathy), Gene Evans (Boden),
    James Best (Stuart), Hari Rhodes (Trent), Larry Tucker (Pagliacci), Paul Dubov (Dr.
    J. L. Menken), Chuck Roberson (Wilkes)
Specs: 101 minutes; black and white
Genre: drama, mystery
Availability: DVD and Blu-ray (The Criterion Collection)

Plot

A journalist out to win a Pulitzer Prize commits himself to an insane asylum so that he can investigate a murder that occurred there, but he soon succumbs to madness himself.

Background

In the late 1940s, Samuel Fuller wrote a script called "Straightjacket" for director Fritz Lang.[27] The screenplay followed a reporter investigating a murder committed in an insane asylum, and Fuller wanted to use it to shine a light on the appalling living conditions that existed in psychiatric institutions throughout the United States.[28] Unfortunately, the project fell apart because Lang changed the lead character to a woman so that he could cast Joan Bennett in the role.[29] Years later, Fuller rewrote the story as *The Long Corridor*, only this time he set out to tackle contemporary issues like McCarthyism and Jim Crow laws.[30] Over time, the asylum became a metaphor for the United States itself,[31] and the story addressed anxieties surrounding racism, nuclear warfare, and sexual perversion.[32] At that point, Fuller changed the title to *Shock Corridor* to better reflect the madness of the era.[33]

Producer Bill Shiffrin helped Fuller set up a two-picture deal with Samuel Firks, a real estate tycoon who agreed to give Fuller a share of the profits and final cut on the film.[34] Production commenced shortly after, and Fuller worked at a frantic pace, shooting the entire film in about ten days on the same soundstage where John Ford filmed *The Informer*.[35] Throughout the production, Fuller collaborated with cinematographer Stanley Cortez, who previously worked on such classic films as *The Magnificent Ambersons* and *The Night of the Hunter*.[36] Upon release in September 1963, *Shock Corridor* became a hit with audiences and critics alike, though Fuller failed to reap the full rewards of the film's success because Firks supposedly kept all the profits for himself.[37] In the decades after its release, *Shock Corridor* developed a reputation as a cult classic, and in 1996 the United States National Film Registry selected the film for preservation in the Library of Congress.[38]

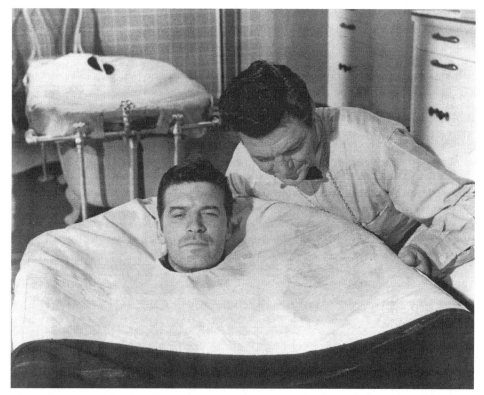

Johnny Barrett (Peter Breck, left) undergoes water therapy. *Allied Artists / Photofest* © *Allied Artists*

Commentary

With *Shock Corridor*, Fuller delivers an outrageously exploitative flick that also functions as a thoughtful and engaging parable about the degradation of the American psyche. The film portrays taboo topics like incest and nymphomania in a trashy, provocative fashion, and Fuller forgoes artfulness in favor of a down-and-dirty approach that exposes the thin line between sanity and madness. At the same time, *Shock Corridor* explicitly addresses heavy issues like racism and nuclear war, turning it into a sly social commentary on the Cold War culture of the 1960s. The film features plenty of lurid thrills, but it also takes a hard look at the negative effects of the reactionary, often violent response to the sociopolitical upheavals occurring at the time. Given that many of the issues explored in the film continue to plague the United States today (e.g., racial intolerance, institutionalized corruption, nuclear proliferation), *Shock Corridor* still resonates over fifty years later.

Shock Corridor also features excellent performances from the entire cast, though Peter Breck anchors the film with his unhinged turn as journalist Johnny Barrett. He delivers a fearless, exaggerated performance, and remains completely committed (no pun intended) throughout the film. Meanwhile, Constance Towers brings strength and dignity to her role as Cathy, Barrett's long-suffering girlfriend who reluctantly agrees to pose as his sister. James Best (perhaps best known as Sherriff Roscoe P. Coltrane in the 1980s television series *The Dukes of Hazzard*) gives a powerful performance as emotionally scarred soldier Stuart, and his monologue remains a highlight of the film. Similarly, Hari Rhodes stuns as Trent, an African American college student who believes himself the Grand Wizard of the KKK (this character preceded Dave Chappelle's black white supremacist Clayton Bigsby by about fifty years). Finally, Larry Tucker injects some much-needed comedy into the film as Pagliacci, a hefty inmate who befriends Barrett.

Over fifty years after its initial release, *Shock Corridor* remains an engrossing and entertaining film that offers cheap thrills and deep thoughts in equal measure.

SPOTLIGHT: SAMUEL FULLER (1912–1997)

At age seventeen, Samuel Fuller worked as a crime reporter and political cartoonist at the *New York Evening Graphic*. During this time, he wrote pulp novels like *Make Up and Kiss* and *The Dark Page*. Fuller later joined the United States Army as an infantryman and fought battles in Africa, Sicily, Normandy, Belgium, and Czechoslovakia. Afterward he transitioned into screenwriting, penning scripts for films like *Hats Off*, *Gangs on the Waterfront*, *Shockproof*, and more. From there he directed such uncompromising films as *I Shot Jesse James*, *The Baron of Arizona*, and the highly successful *The Steel Helmet*. Between 1948 and 1989 Fuller made twenty-three films, many of which have become cult classics, including *Shock Corridor*, *The Naked Kiss*, and *White Dog*. In 1981 he moved to Paris, France, where his films enjoyed a great deal of popularity. He also wrote several novels, including *Brainquake*, a so-called lost novel posthumously published by Titan Books in 2014. New York publishing house Alfred A. Knopf released Fuller's autobiography, *A Third Face*, through their theater and cinema arm in 2002.

Moreover, it still feels relevant because it addresses a variety of sociocultural issues that continue to impact the United States well into the twenty-first century.

See also *The Naked Kiss* (1964), *One Flew Over the Cuckoo's Nest* (1975).

SLACKER (1991)

Director: Richard Linklater
Screenplay: Richard Linklater
Cast: Richard Linklater (Should Have Stayed at Bus Station), Rudy Basquez (Taxi Driver), Jean Caffeine (Roadkill), Jan Hockey (Jogger), Stephan Hockey (Running Late), Mark James (Hit-and-Run Son), Samuel Dietert (Grocery Grabber of Death's Bounty)
Specs: 97 minutes; color
Genre: comedy, drama
Availability: DVD and Blu-ray (The Criterion Collection)

Plot

This sprawling existential film follows a loose-knit group of eccentric oddballs and overeducated young people living in Austin, Texas.

Background

In the late 1980s, aspiring filmmaker Richard Linklater lived in a 120-year-old house nestled in the West Campus area of Austin, Texas, and it was there that he conceived the idea for *Slacker*,[39] an ambling, virtually plotless film that defined an entire generation. Linklater wrote a treatment and purchased a 16 mm Arriflex camera and fifty rolls of film.[40] He then assembled his cast by handing out stickers that said, "If you want to be in an interesting movie, show up at this audition" to people he found fascinating.[41] After raising a budget of about $23,000,[42] Linklater shot *Slacker* on location in Austin during one of the hottest summers in decades (the cast and crew often endured temperatures of 100 degrees or more).[43] Principal photography ran throughout July of 1989 and wrapped after a few weeks.[44] In May of 1990, the finished film became a smash hit at the Seattle International Film Festival, prompting Orion Pictures to acquire the distribution rights.[45]

Orion released *Slacker* on July 5, 1991,[46] and the film grossed an impressive $1.2 million domestically.[47] Unfortunately, Orion Home Video bungled the home video release, and for years afterward *Slacker* remained hard to find.[48] Nonetheless, the film became a cult classic beloved by misfits and disaffected kids everywhere, and it inspired an entire generation of independent filmmakers that included Kevin Smith, who cites *Slacker* as the film that motivated him to make *Clerks*.[49] Linklater's film also captured the zeitgeist of the 1990s,[50] and the term *slacker* soon gained widespread popularity as cultural critics used it to describe an entire generation of aimless young people.[51]

Three aimless souls discuss Madonna's Pap smear. *Orion Pictures / Photofest © Orion Pictures*

Commentary

Slacker opens with a nameless character (played by Linklater himself) telling a disinterested cab driver about his dreams, including one that saw him "just traveling around, you know, staring out the windows of buses, and trains, and cars." This wordy opening monologue serves as a perfect introduction to the film itself, in which nothing much happens and the free-roaming camera follows the loonies and loafers who prowl the streets of Austin bloviating about anything and everything. *Slacker* presents a crude but compelling portrait of the disillusioned suburban Gen Xers who wander in and out of the film. The rambling, episodic narrative jumps from one situation to the next, and, like Jim Jarmusch's *Stranger Than Paradise*, the whole thing feels more like a series of interconnected short stories than a straightforward storyline. The film contains amateurish acting (which makes sense given that the cast consists primarily of nonactors from the Austin area) and unpolished filmmaking (boom mics occasionally pop into shots, and minor continuity errors abound), but Linklater's enthusiastic direction helps smooth over some of these rough spots.

At the same time, the film fails to sustain its own momentum, and soon becomes little more than a meandering, scatterbrained bore. *Slacker* favors dialogue over story, but the dialogue quickly proves tiresome as the characters ramble on about conspiracy theories and trivial matters. The whole thing occasionally feels like an exceptionally dull freshmen philosophy seminar. Furthermore, *Slacker* overstays its welcome by about twenty minutes, and some sequences prove more compelling than others, but even then, none are as interesting or engrossing as Linklater seems to think. Linklater would put the shambolic narrative techniques he developed here to better use on subsequent features like *Dazed and Confused*, *Boyhood*, and the *Before* trilogy, all of which benefit from absorbing narratives and interesting characters. *Slacker* deserves its reputation as a cult classic and a milestone of independent cinema due to Linklater's direction and innovative approach to narrative structure, but the nonchalant pointlessness and self-absorbed characters leave the film feeling more like an endurance test than anything else.

See also *Stranger Than Paradise* (1984), *Clerks* (1994), *Waking Life* (2001).

SPOTLIGHT: RICHARD LINKLATER (1960–)

In 1987, Richard Linklater used his savings to make his first feature-length film, *It's Impossible to Learn to Plow by Reading Books*. Three years after that, he founded his own production company and made *Slacker*, an unconventional film that earned raves on the festival circuit and established Linklater's reputation as a filmmaker. He then made *Dazed and Confused*, a cult smash that launched the careers of Matthew McConaughey and Ben Affleck. Linklater found similar success in 1995 with the minimalist romantic drama *Before Sunrise*, which grossed over $5 million theatrically and won the Silver Bear for Best Director at the forty-fifth Berlin International Film Festival. Unfortunately, his next film, *subUrbia*, received mixed reviews and bombed at the box office, as did his first Hollywood feature, *The Newton Boys*. Over time, Linklater earned a reputation as one of the most daring and eclectic filmmakers in American cinema thanks to his work on films like *Waking Life, School of Rock, Before Sunset, A Scanner Darkly, Before Midnight, Boyhood*, and *Everybody Wants Some!!*

SORCERER (1977)

Director: William Friedkin
Screenplay: Walon Green
Cast: Roy Scheider (Jackie Scanlon a.k.a. Juan Dominguez), Bruno Cremer (Victor Manzon a.k.a. Serrano), Francisco Rabal (Nilo), Amidou (Kassem a.k.a. Martinez), Ramon Bieri (Corlette), Peter Capell (Lartigue)
Specs: 121 minutes; color
Genre: adventure, drama, thriller
Availability: Blu-ray (Warner Bros.)

Plot

To earn enough money to return to their home countries, four desperate men agree to transport unstable nitroglycerine over 200 miles of rough jungle terrain so that oil workers can cap a well that exploded and caught fire.

Background

After finding great success with *The Exorcist*, writer/director William Friedkin turned his attention to developing a modestly budgeted adaptation of Georges Arnaud's novel *Le salaire de la peur*, previously adapted by Henri-Georges Clouzot in 1953 as *The Wages of Fear*.[52] Friedkin wanted to direct a grittier version of the story that followed the same basic outline.[53] He appointed Walon Green to write the script,[54] and then focused on assembling his cast.[55] Friedkin originally wanted Steve McQueen to star, but the actor demanded that his then-wife, Ali McGraw, costar in the film. Friedkin refused this request, so McQueen dropped out.[56] Friedkin then approached other tough-guy stars like Clint Eastwood and Jack Nicholson, but none accepted the offer.[57] The director finally settled on Roy Scheider as the lead, and the rest of the cast fell into place from there.

Sorcerer eventually ballooned into a much larger production; the budget initially jumped from $2.5 million to $15 million,[58] and later escalated to $22 million.[59] This was partly due to delays caused by the location shooting, which proved so costly that Universal Pictures partnered with Paramount Pictures.[60] Filming was scheduled to occur in Ecuador, but quickly moved to the Dominican Republic due to safety concerns.[61] Problems occurred throughout filming; some cast and crew members suffered from gangrene while others were busted for drug use, and Friedkin came down with malaria.[62] While filming the bridge-crossing scene, the truck fell into the river several times, with actors and stuntmen onboard.[63] The troubled production finally wrapped after ten grueling months.[64]

Sorcerer opened at Mann's Chinese Theater on June 24, 1977,[65] and audiences flocked to see the latest effort from the director of *The Exorcist*. Unfortunately,

Two desperate men navigate a treacherous crossing. *Paramount Pictures / Universal Pictures / Photofest © Paramount Pictures / Universal Pictures*

poor word of mouth rapidly doomed the film's reputation. To make matters worse, *Star Wars* had opened just a month earlier, and Friedkin's film could not compete with that juggernaut.[66] Thus, *Sorcerer* pulled in only $9 million worldwide,[67] less than half of its total production budget. Following the film's poor performance at the U.S. box office, producers reedited it and changed the title to *The Wages of Fear* for release in the United Kingdom, where it played on a double bill with *The Last Dinosaur*. In the years since, *Sorcerer's* reputation has grown steadily, and it received a restoration in 2013 and a limited theatrical rerelease in 2014.[68] It is now considered one of Friedkin's best films, as well as one of the finest movies of the 1970s.

Commentary

For years, *Sorcerer* remained largely forgotten due to its reputation as a commercial and critical flop, which is a shame since it is a gripping film that boasts stunning visuals, intense performances, and thrilling set pieces. The cinematography by Dick Bush and John M. Stephens highlights the breathtaking jungle locales, and emphasizes the grime and sweat that seem to cover everyone and everything on-screen. The editing and camera angles create a sense of immediacy that draws the viewer deeper into the main characters' plight. In addition, the pulsating synth score by Tangerine Dream heightens the tension and mirrors the desperation felt by the four men as they risk their lives for a chance to return home. Meanwhile, all four leads deliver intense performances, though Scheider and Bruno Cremer are the standouts. These elements all turn *Sorcerer* into a harrowing film that fails to eclipse *The Wages of Fear* but undoubtedly deserves to stand alongside Clouzot's take on the material.

Like *The Thing*, Friedkin's film reveals how madness and masculinity often become intertwined. With films like *The French Connection*, *Sorcerer*, *Cruising*, and *To Live and Die in L.A.*, Friedkin offered up powerful tales of physically rugged men undergoing their own personal crises of masculine identity. In *Sorcerer*, the four leads are pushed to the limits of their manliness and none comes away unscathed. They all agree to risk their lives to escape the sweltering village and the surrounding jungle that imprisons them. Yet the film makes it clear that even if they succeed they will remain trapped by their own stoicism and toughness. This thematic undercurrent turns *Sorcerer* into a rich and expertly crafted film that still resonates nearly forty years after its original release. With *Sorcerer*, Friedkin drags viewers through a hellish jungle landscape and takes them on an intense, nerve-wracking thrill ride that will leave them feeling every bit as exhausted and pummeled as the characters.

See also *The Wages of Fear* (1953), *Aguirre, the Wrath of God* (1972), *The Thing* (1982).

SPEED RACER (2008)

Director: Lana Wachowski, Lilly Wachowski
Screenplay: Lana Wachowski, Lilly Wachowski
Cast: Emile Hirsch (Speed Racer), Matthew Fox (Racer X), Christina Ricci (Trixie), Susan Sarandon (Mom Racer), John Goodman (Pops Racer), Roger Allam (Royalton), Rain (Taejo Togokahn), Paulie Litt (Spritle Racer), Kick Gurry (Sparky)
Specs: 135 minutes; color
Genre: action, family, sport
Availability: DVD and Blu-ray (Warner Bros.)

Plot

A young racecar driver sets out to become grand champion of the World Racing League, but first he and his family must thwart the machinations of an evil corporate tycoon.

Background

First announced in September of 1992,[69] the live-action adaptation of the Japanese cartoon series *Speed Racer* took a long and circuitous road to the big screen. In 2006, Warner Bros. hired Lana and Lilly Wachowski to write and direct the film.[70] After making a string of R-rated action films, the Wachowskis jumped at the chance to helm a family film that might allow them to reach an even wider audience. Moreover, they loved the cartoon as kids, and it inspired much of their own work.[71] Their version would maintain the essence of the original while updating it for the new millennium. Joel Silver produced, while John Gaeta, who previously won an Academy Award for his work on the Wachowskis' breakthrough film, *The Matrix*, was brought on board to oversee the visual effects.[72]

Principal production took place at Babelsberg Studios in Potsdam, Germany.[73] As with *The Matrix*, the Wachowskis advanced the art and technique of filmmaking on *Speed Racer*; they shot the film almost entirely against green screen,[74] though several real locations were photographed with a revolutionary 360-degree camera and composited in later.[75] The film also marks the first time the Wachowskis shot on high-definition video rather than film;[76] this allowed them to layer the image so that the foreground and background both remained completely in focus, thereby creating the appearance of a live-action anime. The Wachowskis brought in video game designers to model the racetracks (which look like something straight out of Nintendo's *F-Zero* or *Mario Kart* video games).[77]

Production lasted from June 5, 2007, until August 25, 2007, and *Speed Racer* premiered at the Nokia Theater in Los Angeles on April 26, 2008. The film entered general release a few weeks later,[78] grossing just over $18.5 million in its opening weekend. Unfortunately, response was mixed, and most reviews tended toward the unfavorable. The film's box office plunged over 50 percent during its second weekend, and it left theaters on August 1, 2008, after grossing nearly $94 million worldwide, far less than its reported $120 million production budget.[79] Despite its

Speed Racer (Emile Hirsch) races to win the Casa Cristo 5000. *Warner Bros. / Photofest © Warner Bros.*

rather high-profile failure, *Speed Racer* later emerged as a well-regarded cult film, with many critics offering reappraisals of the film that praised its energy, ambition, and visual style.[80] Though it faltered a bit on its way to the finish line, *Speed Racer* eventually earned some well-deserved accolades.

Commentary

Despite its reputation as a box office failure, *Speed Racer* is perhaps the Wachowskis' most visually accomplished and purely enjoyable film to date. The film immediately announces itself as a candy-colored assault on the senses that recalls 1960s animation as filtered through thoroughly modern cinematic storytelling techniques. *Speed Racer* expertly captures the look and feel of anime, which often concerns itself with establishing a specific tone or feeling rather than creating a sense of reality. In that regard, the film succeeds spectacularly, because it strikes the exact right balance between serious and silly; the family drama draws the viewer in, but it never becomes so overwhelming that it drags the film down. Plus, the Wachowskis are not above tossing the occasional poop joke into the middle of a particularly tense sequence. Overall, *Speed Racer* establishes itself as a visually stylish, painfully earnest, and wholly enjoyable romp that is equal parts thrilling, touching, and funny.

The characters remain the film's greatest strength, and Speed and his family all prove extremely likable and inspiring (and yes, this includes Spritle and Chim Chim). The characters often seem shackled to their pasts, but they nevertheless manage to change both themselves and the future by the time the credits roll. From *The Matrix* to *Jupiter Ascending*, the Wachowskis routinely populate their films with fiercely unconventional characters who transform the world by transforming themselves. Like Neo and Jupiter Jones, Speed also leads by example, demonstrating the liberating power that comes from a willingness to challenge the status quo. In the end, *Speed Racer* deserves a much better reputation, because it delivers jaw-dropping, visually stunning action while serving up a colorful parable for staying true to one's convictions.

See also *Sky Captain and the World of Tomorrow* (2004), *Scott Pilgrim vs. the World* (2010), *Ghost in the Shell* (2017).

SPOTLIGHT: THE WACHOWSKIS

Maverick filmmakers Lilly and Lana Wachowski burst onto the scene in 1996 with *Bound*, a neo-noir thriller that became a cult hit in the years after its release. They hit the big time with their next film, *The Matrix*, which captured the zeitgeist in a way that few films have before or since. The Wachowskis returned to the realm of cult cinema a few years later when they released two high-profile sequels to their signature hit back-to-back; both *The Matrix Reloaded* and *The Matrix Revolutions* were eagerly anticipated by mainstream audiences, but wound up alienating all but the first film's most devoted fans. Afterward, the Wachowskis worked mainly on innovative and offbeat films that appealed to an increasingly small but fervent fan base. Films like *Speed Racer*, *Cloud Atlas*, and *Jupiter Ascending* all failed at the box office, but still developed enthusiastic and vocal followings comprised of viewers who delight in the films' unconventional sensibilities. From the start, the Wachowskis have used their various projects to champion a variety of queer issues, and they continued this tendency with the short-lived but much-loved cult Netflix series *Sense8*.

STARSHIP TROOPERS (1997)

Director: Paul Verhoeven
Screenplay: Edward Neumeier
Cast: Casper Van Dien (Johnny Rico), Denise Richards (Lt. Carmen Ibanez), Dina Meyer (Dizzy Flores), Jake Busey (Ace Levy), Neil Patrick Harris (Carl Jenkins), Clancy Brown (Sgt. Zim), Michael Ironside (Jean Rasczak)
Specs: 129 minutes; color
Genre: action, science fiction
Availability: DVD and Blu-ray (Sony Pictures)

Plot

In the distant future, a group of conventionally attractive young people set out to protect humanity from a race of giant intergalactic insects.

Background

In the mid-1990s, Sony Pictures embarked on a science fiction project called *Bug Hunt at Outpost Nine*, in which a future military battles space insects.[81] Screenwriter Edward Neumeier penned the script, which he then brought to *Robocop* director Paul Verhoeven.[82] However, producers soon recognized the similarities to Robert A. Heinlein's controversial science fiction novel *Starship Troopers*, and Sony sought to secure the film rights,[83] though failed to do so until after shooting commenced.[84] Verhoeven disliked the book, and he tasked Neumeier with rewriting the screenplay so that it satirized the authoritarian attitudes celebrated in Heinlein's novel.[85] Verhoeven then assembled a cast of impossibly gorgeous actors who called to mind the Aryan soldiers in Leni Riefenstahl's Nazi propaganda piece *Triumph of the Will*.[86]

The film commenced shooting on April 29, 1997, and during production, the studio underwent several shake-ups, leaving Verhoeven to work in relative freedom.[87] Nevertheless, minor problems arose throughout. For instance, Verhoeven shot several sequences in Hell's Half Acre in Natrona County, Wyoming, where temperatures often exceed 100 degrees Fahrenheit, and filming halted for an entire week after actor Jake Busey succumbed to heat stroke.[88] In addition, some of the cast refused to appear nude on camera unless Verhoeven and cinematographer Jost Vacano agreed to disrobe as well (they did).[89] Verhoeven also grew dissatisfied with the graphics work partway through production, so he asked visual effects company Banned from the Ranch Entertainment to create or redesign nearly every graphic seen in the film.[90] Finally, early test screenings led the director to change minor points to the romantic subplot.[91]

Starship Troopers opened on November 4, 1997, and received overwhelmingly negative reviews from American critics who apparently misinterpreted the film's satire.[92] Nevertheless, the film grossed over $120 million worldwide against a $105 million budget,[93] spawning two direct-to-DVD sequels and a computer-animated television series. It also garnered an enthusiastic cult audience that eagerly embraced the over-the-top gore and sly wit.[94] Critics have since reappraised *Starship Troopers*, and many now consider it one of the most misunderstood films of all time.[95]

Johnny Rico (Casper Van Dien) battles a tanker bug. *TriStar / Photofest © TriStar*

Commentary

Starship Troopers takes viewers on a rip-roaring thrill ride through a war-torn future filled with exhilarating action sequences and remarkable gore. The film features top-notch effects that hold up to this day, and uses them to create dazzling space vistas and stirring intergalactic battle sequences. It also employs an astounding blend of CGI and animatronics to bring the giant alien bugs to horrifying life. *Starship Troopers* also contains some spot-on satire that lampoons right-wing militarism and the nationalist ideologies that often underlie American foreign policy. Though released four years before the terror attacks of September 11, 2001, the film appears to take dead aim at the sort of xenophobic and jingoistic attitudes that fueled the costly War on Terror, and it continues to resonate well into the twenty-first century. Over twenty years on, *Starship Troopers* stands as a violent, bloody spoof of big-budget sci-fi action flicks that boasts superb effects and exciting action sequences.

Unfortunately, the film does such a great job of aping big, brainless blockbusters that it kind of becomes one itself in the process. *Starship Troopers* fails to strike the right balance between satire and spectacle, and the bombastic action repeatedly overwhelms the more ironic elements (so much so that the viewer could easily miss them). Furthermore, the satire often feels inelegant and heavy-handed (especially when compared to the vastly superior *Robocop*), and much of the humor lands with a thud. In addition, aside from Busey and Neil Patrick Harris, the beautiful but bland actors deliver somewhat vapid performances, though one could argue that they fit the film's tone and therefore function as an intentional parody of the weak acting often found in bloated blockbusters. *Starship Troopers* also proves mostly boring, especially since it prevents viewers from becoming emotionally invested in anything that happens on-screen. In the end, *Starship Troopers* features some intelligent satire of warmongering and propaganda, but it bungles the execution and fails to stick the landing.

See also *Aliens* (1986), *Robocop* (1987), *Total Recall* (1990).

SPOTLIGHT: PAUL VERHOEVEN (1938–)

After graduating from the University of Leiden, Paul Verhoeven directed the award-winning documentary *The Royal Dutch Marine Corps* while serving as a conscript in the Dutch Navy. Upon leaving the navy in 1969, Verhoeven directed the popular Dutch television series *Floris*. From there, Verhoeven made *Business Is Business* (a.k.a. *Diary of a Hooker*), followed by *Turkish Delight*, which earned an Academy Award nomination for Best Foreign Language Film in 1974. Verhoeven gained international fame with *Soldier of Orange*, a harrowing true story about the Dutch resistance in World War II that won the 1979 LA Film Critics Award for best foreign language film. A few years later, Verhoeven directed *Flesh and Blood*, his first American film. He then moved to Hollywood and spent more than a decade making violent and provocative blockbusters like *Robocop*, *Total Recall*, *Basic Instinct*, *Showgirls*, *Starship Troopers*, and *Hollow Man*. After his last few films flopped, Verhoeven returned to Europe to cowrite and direct the well-received war film *Black Book*, and in 2016, he directed the incendiary French psychological thriller *Elle*.

STRANGE BREW (1983)

Director: Rick Moranis, Dave Thomas
Screenplay: Rick Moranis, Dave Thomas, Steve De Jarnatt
Cast: Rick Moranis (Bob McKenzie), Dave Thomas (Doug McKenzie), Max von Sydow (Brewmeister Smith), Paul Dooley (Claude Elsinore), Lynne Griffin (Pam Elsinore), Angus MacInnes (Jean LaRose)
Specs: 90 minutes; color
Genre: comedy
Availability: Blu-ray (Warner Bros.)

Plot

Two bumbling Canadian brothers land jobs at a local brewery and become embroiled in a sinister plot to take over the world using beer laced with mind-controlling substances.

Background

In 1980, comedians Rick Moranis and Dave Thomas debuted their new characters Bob and Doug McKenzie—two extremely Canadian brothers who gab about distinctly Canadian topics like beer, bacon, and hockey—during the third season of Canadian sketch comedy show *SCTV*.[96] The characters became incredibly popular, and in 1981 Moranis and Thomas released *The Great White North*, an album of sketches and comedic songs featuring the McKenzies.[97] The record sold more than one million copies, cracked the *Billboard* top ten, and earned a Grammy nomination for Best Comedy Album.[98] Moranis and Thomas then quit *SCTV* to work on a McKenzie brothers movie called *Strange Brew*.[99]

Moranis and Thomas wrote the script with screenwriter Steve De Jarnatt.[100] The duo originally wanted someone else to direct the film, but they ultimately agreed to do it themselves under the tutelage of producer Jack Grossberg.[101] *Strange Brew* entered production on October 12, 1982, with a $4 million budget.[102] Filming took place throughout Ontario,[103] though Moranis and Thomas shot several scenes in an old brewery located in Prince George, British Columbia.[104] Principal photography wrapped on December 17, 1982;[105] *Strange Brew* opened in Canada on August 19, 1983, and premiered in the United States the following weekend.[106]

Strange Brew received mixed reviews[107] and grossed less than $9 million at the box office during its entire theatrical run.[108] Luckily, the film found a more receptive cult audience when it landed on home video and cable television. The McKenzie brothers have remained popular for more than three decades, and in the late 1990s Moranis and Thomas announced a sequel to *Strange Brew* called *Home Brew*. Unfortunately, the funding dried up almost immediately and the project fell apart soon after.[109] In 2009, a ten-episode cartoon series titled *The Animated Adventures of Bob & Doug McKenzie* debuted on Canada's Global Television Network, and four years later Canadian brewery Phillips Brewing Company introduced Elsinore Beer, named after the brewery that appears in *Strange Brew*.[110]

Bob (Rick Moranis, left) and Doug McKenzie (Dave Thomas) on the set of their television show, *Strange Brew*. *MGM / Photofest © MGM*

Commentary

Strange Brew packs an almost overwhelming amount of absurdist humor, knowing satire, and cartoonish sight gags into its brisk ninety-minute run time. The film's greatest strength lies in the interplay between Thomas and Moranis. The duo spent years honing their characters on *SCTV* before bringing them to the big screen, and it shows as they effortlessly play off one another and make even the dopiest gags come alive solely through their body language and facial expressions. Of course, they surrounded themselves with a great supporting cast, nearly all of whom deliver excellent comic performances. Paul Dooley stands out as Claude Elsinore, a spineless and conniving character who generates some of the film's biggest laughs. Meanwhile, Von Sydow is appropriately menacing as Brewmeister Smith, but even he brings the funny with his amusingly exasperated reactions to the nonsense happening around him (his seething delivery of the line "What the stink are they doing in there?" remains one of the film's funniest moments).

Strange Brew also contains some shrewd satirical humor and sneakily sophisticated gags. The film features several charming metajokes and a cheerful awareness of cinematic conventions (for instance, a spinning newspaper must be flipped over to reveal the pertinent headline, while a ghostly apparition uses fancy special effects to flash the words "Nice effects, eh?" on the wall of the brewery's cafeteria). In addition, the film will delight English lit fans, because it includes numerous allusions to Shakespeare's *Hamlet*, with Bob and Doug as incompetent (and perpetually drunk) stand-ins for Rosencrantz and Guildenstern (though the

McKenzie Brothers take a much more active role in their story than their literary forebears do in *Hamlet*). *Strange Brew* even sneaks some subversive material in among the ridiculousness. For instance, the film comments on Canada's status as a British colony when a picture of Queen Elizabeth falls off a courtroom wall after the judge bangs his gavel. Thus, *Strange Brew* proves much smarter than it initially appears.

Granted, the foolishness takes center stage, and *Strange Brew* features a wealth of ridiculous sight gags (many involving Bob and Doug's dog, Hosehead) and humorously idiotic dialogue ("I am your father, Luke. Give in to the dark side of the force, you knob"). As such, *Strange Brew* emerges as a hilarious and deceptively smart comedy that will leave audiences howling with laughter.

See also *The Blues Brothers* (1980), *Pee-wee's Big Adventure* (1985), *Wayne's World* (1992), *Beerfest* (2006).

STRANGER THAN PARADISE (1984)

Director: Jim Jarmusch
Screenplay: Jim Jarmusch
Cast: John Lurie (Willie), Eszter Balint (Eva), Richard Edson (Eddie), Cecillia Stark (Aunt Lotte), Danny Rosen (Billy)
Specs: 89 minutes; black and white
Genre: comedy, drama
Availability: DVD (The Criterion Collection)

Plot

Three inveterate slackers embark on a road trip that takes them from New York to Cleveland, and finally to a Florida suburb where they stumble upon a fortune.

Background

In 1980, Jim Jarmusch made a name for himself with his debut feature, *Permanent Vacation*. He then spent the next four years developing his follow-up film, *Stranger Than Paradise*.[111] It began life as a thirty-minute short shot on leftover film stock donated by director Wim Wenders,[112] simply called *The New World*,[113] that appeared in the 1983 International Film Festival Rotterdam.[114] Jarmusch later expanded it to feature length after raising $120,000, which he used to shoot additional footage.[115] This new extended version of *Stranger Than Paradise* premiered at the Cannes Film Festival in 1984[116] and won the Caméra d'Or award for debut films.[117] It became a critical smash throughout Europe and the United States after it was released on October 1, 1984, and went on to gross more than $2 million.[118] Over time, the film developed a reputation as a landmark of independent cinema, and it frequently shows up on lists of the all-time greatest cult movies.

Eva (Ester Balint, top left), Eddie (Richard Edson, bottom left), and Willie (Rod Lurie) stop for a rest before continuing their road trip. *Samuel Goldwyn Company / Photofest © Samuel Goldwyn Company*

Commentary

More than thirty years after changing the face of independent cinema, *Stranger Than Paradise* stands as an engrossing cinematic experience. The film features stark black-and-white cinematography, and Jarmusch's simple direction keeps things lively throughout. *Stranger Than Paradise* consists of several single-take long shots, and the somewhat episodic narrative unfolds with a sense of laid-back aimlessness that reflects the characters and their negligible ambitions. The film often feels like a sequence of interconnected short stories or a series of brief one-act plays strung together rather than a linear, coherent storyline. Meanwhile, the spare, low-budget filmmaking instills everything on-screen with a gritty realness that draws the viewer deeper into the narrative. The European influence becomes evident early on; *Stranger Than Paradise* often resembles films like *Breathless* or *L'Avventura*, both in terms of how it looks and in the way it balances sardonic playfulness with an apparent lack of forward momentum. While not for everyone, *Stranger Than Paradise* possesses a peculiar charm that will resonate with those who can appreciate a leisurely tale that goes nowhere and refuses to offer any sort of real resolution.

Little happens during the brisk eighty-nine-minute run time, but *Stranger Than Paradise* remains captivating from beginning to end thanks in large part to the actors. John Lurie, Eszter Balint, and Richard Edson all deliver relaxed but engaging performances that feel completely honest, and they make their characters come alive even during scenes in which they do little more than sit around and stare at the television set. In *Stranger Than Paradise* the characters drift from one situation to the next, motivated more by boredom and pitiful economic circumstances than a desire to change themselves or explore the world around them. The central characters refuse to evolve, a fact reinforced by their rather drab surroundings, which look the same no matter where they go. Nevertheless, they all appear to care for one another and remain likable throughout, making it easier for the viewer to care for them even when they engage in shady activities or make poor decisions. Some viewers will understandably find *Stranger Than Paradise* tedious, but others will find themselves swept up by the relaxed pace and compelling characters.

See also *Permanent Vacation* (1980), *Down by Law* (1986), *Slacker* (1991), *Clerks* (1994).

SPOTLIGHT: JIM JARMUSCH (1953–)

In the late 1970s, Jim Jarmusch attended New York University's Tisch School of the Arts, where he studied under renowned director Nicholas Ray. While Jarmusch ultimately failed to earn his degree from the university, he still made a splash with his low-budget debut feature film *Permanent Vacation*, which won the Josef von Sternberg Award at the International Filmfestival Mannheim-Heidelberg in Germany. Four years later, Jarmusch released his second film, *Stranger Than Paradise*, which established both his reputation and his idiosyncratic style. From there, Jarmusch wrote and directed several acclaimed minimalist features that span a variety of genres, including *Down by Law, Mystery Train, Night on Earth, Dead Man, Ghost Dog: The Way of the Samurai, Coffee and Cigarettes, Broken Flowers, The Limits of Control, Only Lovers Left Alive,* and *Paterson*. In addition to his film work, Jarmusch also directed music videos for artists like Talking Heads, Big Audio Dynamite, Tom Waits, Neil Young, and the Raconteurs. He also racked up several acting credits and served as executive producer on smaller independent films like *Explicit Ills, Uncle Howard,* and *Porto*.

SWEET SWEETBACK'S BAADASSSSS SONG (1971)

Director: Melvin Van Peebles
Screenplay: Melvin Van Peebles
Cast: Melvin Van Peebles (Sweetback), Simon Chuckster (Beetle), Hubert Scales (Mu-Mu), John Dullaghan (Commissioner), Rhetta Hughes (Old Girlfriend), John Amos (Biker), Mario Van Peebles (Young Sweetback/Kid)
Specs: 97 minutes; color
Genre: crime, drama, thriller
Availability: Blu-ray (Vinegar Syndrome)

Plot

A black male prostitute kills two racist white cops and becomes the target of a massive manhunt.

Background

The groundbreaking *Sweet Sweetback's Baadasssss Song* forever altered the cinematic landscape after it almost singlehandedly put independent black filmmaking on the map.[119] Writer, director, editor, and star Melvin Van Peebles (who also composed the film's score[120]) shot *Sweet Sweetback* independently for somewhere between $150,000 and $500,000.[121] Van Peebles's first film, *The Watermelon Man*, became a box office hit for Columbia Pictures, and the studio offered Van Peebles a three-picture deal.[122] However, he turned down the offer because he found working for big Hollywood studios far too restrictive.[123] Instead, Van Peebles struck out on his own to make *Sweet Sweetback*, which he funded entirely himself (largely because the studios overwhelmingly refused to give him any money).[124]

Van Peebles shot *Sweet Sweetback* in just nineteen days, during which time he performed all his own stunts and appeared in several explicit sex scenes[125] (he claims that he contracted gonorrhea while shooting one of them[126]). The funding dried up during production, but a $50,000 donation from comedian Bill Cosby allowed Van Peebles to finish the film.[127] Principal photography wrapped in June of 1970, and *Sweet Sweetback* premiered on April 23, 1971. The Motion Picture Association of America slapped the film with an X rating, and Van Peebles responded by marketing *Sweet Sweetback* with the provocative tagline, "Rated X by an all-white jury!"[128]

Initially, the film played in just two theaters in Detroit and Atlanta, but it quickly expanded to other markets and eventually grossed more than $15 million at the box office.[129] The film divided critics, with some dismissing it as misogynistic and

Sweetback (Melvin Van Peebles) tries to avoid the cops. *Cinemation Industries / Photofest* © *Cinemation Industries*

stereotypical while others hailed it as revolutionary and vital.[130] *Sweet Sweetback* gave rise to blaxploitation cinema as other studios scrambled to replicate its success,[131] and the film is now considered a cult classic as well as an important milestone in the history of African American cinema.

Commentary

Sweet Sweetback is a crude, hallucinatory, and highly confrontational film that establishes a rebellious attitude right from the start. The film opens with a prostitute seducing an underage boy (played by Van Peebles's own son Mario, who would himself go on to become an actor and filmmaker of some renown). Meanwhile, the credits proclaim that the film stars "the Black Community" and is "dedicated to all the Brothers and Sisters who had enough of the Man." Thus, *Sweet Sweetback* immediately establishes that it refuses to play by Hollywood's rules, and it remains angry and defiant throughout. Van Peebles takes an almost cinema verité approach to the material, using handheld cameras to capture the plight of African Americans in the United States. As such, the film becomes a howl of anger directed squarely at the Man, which *Sweet Sweetback* makes abundantly clear during an early funeral sequence in which a preacher states that the deceased succumbed to "an overdose of black misery." The film offers up a violent revenge fantasy infused with righteous fury and plenty of gallows humor, and it leaves no question about its ultimate meaning as it tries to alert the world to the oppression happening in cities throughout America.

At the same time, the film advances some racist stereotypes, particularly that of the hypersexual, hyperviolent, barely verbal black male who communicates primarily with his fists or his penis. *Sweet Sweetback* also features some stunningly sexist attitudes, and the women in the film mainly serve as sexual conquests for the hero. Likewise, the film contains quite a bit of homophobic humor, most notably during an early sequence in which a gay man appears dressed as a fairy complete with a sparkler wand. In addition, *Sweet Sweetback* makes its point early on and then descends into tedium, and the numerous shots of the lead character running from the law eventually become boring and repetitive. The film also leans too heavily on experimentation and gradually turns into little more than a collection of random images strung together with only the barest hint of a coherent narrative. The whole thing builds to an abrupt ending that fails to offer a sense of resolution and feels more like a shrug than a fist raised in triumph (despite the message that pops up just before the end credits and angrily warns viewers that "a baad asssss nigger is coming to collect some dues"). Thus, while *Sweet Sweetback* lives up to its reputation as a pioneering film, it ultimately reveals itself as an abstract and amateurish effort that falls apart long before the end.

Sweet Sweetback presents viewers with one long, psychedelic chase sequence that unfortunately lapses into incoherence at a certain point and includes more than a few troubling elements. Nevertheless, the film helped African American cinema cross over into the mainstream and therefore deserves recognition as one of the all-time great cult movies.

See also *Putney Swope* (1969), *Pink Flamingos* (1972), *Ganja & Hess* (1973), *Foxy Brown* (1974), *I'm Gonna Git You Sucka* (1988).

T

THE TEXAS CHAINSAW MASSACRE (1974)

Director: Tobe Hooper
Screenplay: Kim Henkel, Tobe Hooper
Cast: Marilyn Burns (Sally), Paul A. Partain (Franklin), William Vail (Kirk), Teri Mc-
    Minn (Pam), Allen Danziger (Jerry), Gunnar Hansen (Leatherface), Edwin Neal
    (Hitchhiker)
Genre: horror
Availability: Blu-ray and DVD (Dark Sky Films)

Plot

A group of unsuspecting teens encounter a family of cannibalistic killers during a trip through the backwoods of Texas.

Background

While working as an assistant film director at the University of Texas at Austin,[1] Tobe Hooper came up with an idea for an excessively gory film about a family of cannibals living in isolation in the backwoods of Texas. Drawing inspiration from current events like Watergate, Vietnam, and the crimes of Ed Gein, Hooper collaborated with Kim Henkel to craft a brutally violent narrative that also featured a great deal of dark humor.[2] The pair titled their story *Leatherface*, and upon finishing the screenplay they convinced Hooper's friend Bill Parsley to finance the film for $60,000 in return for 50 percent of the profits.[3] Hooper then assembled a cast of mostly unknown actors who had appeared in television commercials and stage shows.[4] Hulking Icelandic-American performer Gunnar Hansen landed the pivotal role of Leatherface.[5] The film entered production in July of 1973, and shooting took place in and around central Texas.[6]

The four-week shoot proved excruciating for both cast and crew, mainly because temperatures often reached 100 degrees or more.[7] The humidity took a toll on Hansen as he routinely spent twelve to sixteen hours a day in costume.[8] Meanwhile, the actors suffered several injuries due to their inexperience. For instance, while shooting the film's climactic chase sequence, Hansen tripped while carrying a chainsaw and almost sliced his own arm off.[9] During production, the film's

Leatherface (Gunnar Hansen) pursues Sally (Marilyn Burns, not pictured). *Bryanston Distributing Company / Photofest © Bryanston Distributing Company*

budget increased exponentially, and different sources put the final cost at anywhere between $93,000 and $240,000.[10] The difficult shoot wrapped on August 14, 1973,[11] and Hooper spent eight months working with editors J. Larry Carroll and Sallye Richardson to assemble the footage.[12]

While editing the film, Hooper made sure to limit the on-screen gore to ensure *Texas Chainsaw* secured a PG rating.[13] Nevertheless, the Motion Picture Association of America slapped the film with an X and only agreed to change it to an R after Hooper cut out several more minutes of disturbing footage.[14] The finished film opened in Austin, Texas, on October 1, 1974,[15] and received mixed reviews.[16] Nevertheless, audiences flocked to *Texas Chainsaw*, and the film grossed over $30 million in the United States and Canada alone.[17] It also proved highly controversial, and several countries banned it outright.[18] These days *Texas Chainsaw* is widely considered a cult classic, as well as one of the all-time great horror movies. It also generated a long-lasting franchise, inspired numerous copycats, and essentially kicked off the slasher subgenre that dominated horror throughout the 1980s.[19]

Commentary

Texas Chainsaw offers viewers a punishing yet rewarding experience, and it absolutely lives up to its reputation as one of the most frightening horror movies ever made. Hooper imbues the film with a terrifying sense of verisimilitude, shooting everything with a gritty authenticity that renders *Texas Chainsaw* far scarier than more polished productions (such as the slick but inert 2003 remake, for example). Throughout the film, the violence explodes in swift and brutal bursts that catch the audience by surprise but never feel like cheap jump scares. Furthermore, the stunningly realistic gore effects remain shocking, especially when compared to the glossy CGI blood used in a lot of modern horror films. Hooper also makes excellent use of asynchronous sound, punctuating the horrific events with guttural growls, weird noises, and (most famously) the eerie sound of a flashbulb popping and then recharging. All these elements combine to create an atmosphere of unrelenting terror that will leave the viewer feeling uncomfortable long after *Texas Chainsaw* ends.

Hooper also uses cinematography and mise-en-scène to generate an oppressive feeling of dread that permeates everything on-screen. Daniel Pearl's camerawork highlights the wide-open spaces of central Texas and juxtaposes them with shots of the cramped interiors of the kids' van and the creepy house owned by Leatherface and his relatives. In doing so, Pearl infuses the film with an overwhelming sense of isolation and hopelessness. In addition, the actors all deliver solid performances, particularly Marilyn Burns, whose histrionic turn as Sally guarantees her place in the scream queen hall of fame. Likewise, Hansen is a suitably imposing presence as Leatherface, and he brings the character to terrifying life almost entirely via body language and high-pitched squeals. While watching *Texas Chainsaw*, it soon becomes clear why so many other films copied its formula.

Texas Chainsaw remains one of the scariest and most influential horror films of all time. It altered the trajectory of horror for more than a decade and stands as an exhilarating, visceral experience that remains utterly terrifying even after several years and dozens of inferior sequels, knockoffs, and remakes.

See also *Three on a Meathook* (1972), *Deranged: Confessions of a Necrophile* (1974), *The Texas Chainsaw Massacre 2* (1986), *Leatherface: Texas Chainsaw Massacre III* (1990).

THE THING (1982)

Director: John Carpenter
Screenplay: Bill Lancaster
Cast: Kurt Russell (R. J. MacReady), Wilford Brimley (Dr. Blair), Keith David (Childs), T. K. Carter (Nauls), David Clennon (Palmer), Richard Dysart (Dr. Copper), Charles Hallahan (Vance Norris), Richard Masur (Clark), Donald Moffat (Garry), Peter Maloney (George Bennings), Joel Polis (Fuchs), Thomas G. Waites (Windows)
Specs: 109 minutes; color
Genre: horror, science fiction
Availability: Blu-ray (Shout! Factory)

Plot

A shapeshifting alien terrorizes a group of increasingly paranoid men stationed at an isolated Antarctic research facility.

Background

In 1975, producers Stuart Cohen and David Foster decided to develop a new adaptation of John W. Campbell's short story "Who Goes There," previously adapted by Howard Hawks and Christian Nyby in 1951 as *The Thing from Another World*.[20] Cohen and Foster negotiated a deal with executives at Universal Pictures, who agreed to produce the film under the title *The Thing*.[21] From there, Foster searched for a director while Cohen met with several screenwriters, including Tobe Hooper, Kim Henkel, John Landis, and David Wiltse.[22] Unfortunately, Cohen failed to reach an agreement with any of them. Studio executives suggested science fiction author William F. Nolan, but Cohen disliked his take on the material.[23] At that point, the studio decided to shelve the project indefinitely.[24]

The Thing lay dormant until 1979, when the success of *Alien* prompted Universal to resurrect the project.[25] John Carpenter, who had recently scored a massive hit of his own with *Halloween*, agreed to direct but opted not to write the screenplay.[26] Cohen considered several other writers before settling on Bill Lancaster, who delivered his first draft in the fall of 1980.[27] The studio greenlit the film soon after.[28] Carpenter assembled his cast, which included frequent collaborator Kurt Russell, and in December of 1981 he traveled to the frigid town of Stewart, British Columbia, to shoot *The Thing*.[29]

Principal photography wrapped in early 1982, and *The Thing* slithered into theaters on June 25, the same day as Ridley Scott's *Blade Runner*.[30] Carpenter's film received negative reviews and sank at the box office, earning less than $20 million against a $15 million budget.[31] However, it became a cult hit on home video, and these days *The Thing* enjoys a reputation as one of the finest horror films ever

MacReady (Kurt Russell, second from left) and the desperate crew of the research station hatch a plan to deal with their unwelcome alien visitor. *Universal Pictures / Photofest © Universal Pictures*

made. In 2011 it spawned a lackluster prequel/remake, and it has since spread to other media, generating comic books, a video game, and even a board game.

Commentary

With its story of an unknowable horror that hails from the depths of space and causes madness in those it encounters, *The Thing* captures the spirit of H. P. Lovecraft better than any existing adaptation of the author's work (including *Re-Animator* and *From Beyond*). Carpenter fills the entire film with a palpable sense of dread, and he uses the isolated setting to create an oppressive atmosphere of paranoia and hopelessness. He also strikes the exact right balance between blockbuster entertainment and thoughtful social commentary. *The Thing* functions as a terrifying monster movie that offers viewers a nerve-racking thrill ride built on relentless terror, gruesome imagery, and an overwhelming sense of nihilism. At the same time, the film reflects the lingering Cold War anxieties of the Reagan years and serves as a sly rebuke against the macho attitudes that defined the era.

In addition, the film looks and sounds great. Dean Cundey's stunning widescreen cinematography helps ratchet up the terror and reinforce the themes of isolation and mistrust, because it emphasizes the stark contrast between the vast emptiness of the cold, unforgiving landscape and the cramped, claustrophobic spaces of the research outpost. Meanwhile, Rob Bottin's groundbreaking special effects assault the viewer with one horrific image after another, all of which retain their power to shock even after more than thirty years. Furthermore, legendary composer Ennio Morricone provides a pulsing score that remains unobtrusive throughout but still infests everything on-screen and makes the film completely unsettling. Finally, the masterful sound design features inhuman roars and otherworldly noises that will leave the viewer feeling uncomfortable long after the credits roll. In terms of filmmaking, *The Thing* stands as an unparalleled masterpiece of craft and technique.

SPOTLIGHT: JOHN CARPENTER (1948–)

In the early 1970s, John Carpenter studied film at the University of Southern California. While there, he made *Dark Star*, a short film that was expanded to feature length and released theatrically in 1975. He followed this with *Assault on Precinct 13*, a gritty crime thriller inspired by Howard Hawks's *Rio Bravo*. In 1978, Carpenter wrote and directed *Halloween*, a low-budget independent horror film that became a smash hit and spawned a long-running franchise. Carpenter next directed the TV movie *Someone's Watching Me!* and the miniseries *Elvis*. He returned to the world of theatrical features in 1980 with *The Fog*, a moody ghost story that received mixed reviews but nevertheless became a modest commercial hit. From there, Carpenter directed such acclaimed genre classics as *Escape from New York*, *The Thing*, *Starman*, *Big Trouble in Little China*, *Prince of Darkness*, *They Live*, and *In the Mouth of Madness*. In addition to his film work, Carpenter cowrote the video game *Fear 3* and cocreated the comic books *Asylum* and *Tales for a HalloweeNight*. In 2014, Carpenter released his debut album *Lost Themes* and followed it up two years later with *Lost Themes II*.

The Thing is justifiably regarded as an effective and influential horror film that profoundly impacted popular culture. Its influence lingers on in things like the *Resident Evil* franchise, Quentin Tarantino's snowbound Western *The Hateful Eight*, the Netflix series *Stranger Things*, and more.

See also *The Thing from Another World* (1951), *The Fly* (1986), *Leviathan* (1989), *In the Mouth of Madness* (1994), *The Faculty* (1998), *The Hateful Eight* (2015), *Life* (2017).

THIS IS SPINAL TAP (1984)

Director: Rob Reiner
Screenplay: Christopher Guest, Michael McKean, Harry Shearer, Rob Reiner
Cast: Christopher Guest (Nigel Tufnel), Michael McKean (David St. Hubbins), Harry Shearer (Derek Smalls), Rob Reiner (Marty DiBergi), Tony Hendra (Ian Faith), June Chadwick (Jeanine Pettibone), R. J. Parnell (Mick Shrimpton), David Kaff (Viv Savage)
Specs: 82 minutes; color
Genre: comedy
Availability: DVD and Blu-Ray (Metro-Goldwyn-Mayer)

Plot

A filmmaker follows an aging British heavy metal band on their ill-fated comeback tour across the United States.

Background

In 1978, Rob Reiner directed a pilot for *The TV Show*, an hour-long comedy show that featured a sketch about a goofy English rock band written by Reiner, Christopher Guest, Michael McKean, and Harry Shearer.[32] Six years later, the skit served as the inspiration for Reiner's feature-length directorial debut, *This Is Spinal Tap*. Norman Lear supported the film with his production company, Embassy Pictures, giving the group a $2 million budget.[33] Rather than write a full script, Reiner and his three buddies decided to improvise most of the film and allow the actors to ad-lib nearly every scene.[34] Reiner simply provided the performers with an idea of what he wanted and left the rest up to them.

Principal photography on *Spinal Tap* commenced in late 1982,[35] and Reiner shot more than 100 hours of footage over nearly thirty days.[36] He then spent the next nine months editing it down to eighty-two minutes for the film's theatrical release.[37] *Spinal Tap* opened on March 2, 1984,[38] and while it received generally positive reviews from critics, it failed to find an audience during its initial theatrical run.[39] Nevertheless, the film became a massive cult hit on home video, and it quickly earned a reputation as one of the best comedies ever made. It also spawned two successful albums and a made-for-television sequel called *The Return of Spinal Tap*.[40]

The members of Spinal Tap kick off their latest world tour. *Embassy Pictures / Photofest © Embassy Pictures*

Commentary

Filled with iconic lines (such as "These go to 11" and "It's like, how much more black could this be, and the answer is none . . . none more black") and unforgettable moments (which include the band getting lost under the stage in Cleveland, and the little people dancing around a tiny Styrofoam monument during the performance of "Stonehenge"), *Spinal Tap* captures the look and feel of music documentaries while offering up plenty of laughs. The film features a wealth of great running gags (particularly the one about the band's endless roster of deceased drummers) and excellent comedic performances. The core actors play off each other exceedingly well thanks to their impressive improv skills, but they receive a lot of help from the incredible supporting cast, which includes Fran Drescher, Paul Schaeffer, Bruno Kirby, Fred Willard, and Reiner himself. The funny dialogue, lively performances, and outrageous situations guarantee *Spinal Tap*'s reputation as one of the funniest movies ever made.

The film also features fantastic music that evokes the spirit of heavy metal, but also deconstructs and pokes fun at the genre. Songs like "Stonehenge," "Hell Hole," and "Tonight I'm Gonna Rock You Tonight" all display excellent musicianship (particularly from Guest, who delivers blistering guitar solos on nearly every song), and function as hard-rocking tunes that stack up against the output of real metal bands like AC/DC or Metallica. At the same time, the nonsensical lyrics mock the metal genre's aura of self-importance (consider the opening lines of "Heavy Duty": "No light fantastic ever crosses my mind/That meditation stuff can make you go blind/Just crank that volume to the point of pain/Why waste good music on a brain?"). Meanwhile, songs like "Big Bottom" and "Sex Farm" openly lampoon the sexism and misogyny found in metal tunes like "It's So Easy" by Guns N' Roses or "Girls, Girls, Girls" by Mötley Crüe.

In many ways, *Spinal Tap* anticipates (and perhaps inspired) actual rock documentaries like *The Decline of Western Civilization Part II: The Metal Years*, *Metallica: Some Kind of Monster*, *Anvil: The Story of Anvil*, and *I Am Thor*. The film offers a pitch-perfect send-up of the 1980s metal scene, which consisted of equal parts arrogance, sexism, and cluelessness. It also captures the inherent sadness of a "forty-five-year-old rock 'n' roller farting around in front of people less than half their age," as Shearer's Derek Smalls laments late in the film. Yet *Spinal Tap* clearly cares for its title characters, and it understands the appeal of the rock star dream. Thus, while the film mines a lot of humor from the band's foibles, it also roots for them, making *Spinal Tap* a warm and winsome comedy that also contains a satirical edge.

See also *The Decline of Western Civilization II: The Metal Years* (1988), *A Mighty Wind* (2003), *Metallica: Some Kind of Monster* (2004), *Anvil: The Story of Anvil* (2008), *I Am Thor* (2015), *Popstar: Never Stop Never Stopping* (2016).

THE TOXIC AVENGER (1984)

Director: Michael Herz, Lloyd Kaufman
Screenplay: Joe Ritter, Lloyd Kaufman (story)
Cast: Andree Maranda (Sara), Mitch Cohen (the Toxic Avenger), Jennifer Babtist (Wanda), Cindy Manion (Julie), Robert Prichard (Slug), Gary Schneider (Bozo), Pat Ryan (Mayor Peter Belgoody), Mark Torgl (Melvin Ferd)
Specs: 82 minutes; color
Genre: action, comedy, horror, science fiction
Availability: DVD and Blu-ray (Troma)

Plot

Nerdy mop boy Melvin Ferd falls into a vat of toxic waste and mutates into the Toxic Avenger, a hideously deformed creature of superhuman size and strength who uses his powers to battle evil in Tromaville, New Jersey.

Background

Following a string of raunchy sex comedies like *The First Turn-On!* and *Squeeze Play!* Troma Entertainment cofounders Lloyd Kaufman and Michael Herz set out to make a horror film called *Health Club Horror*, but the story proved difficult.[41] During a business trip to the Cannes Film Festival in 1983, Kaufman decided to add comedy and make the monster the hero, and suddenly everything clicked.[42] To develop the story, Kaufman drew inspiration from several different sources, including Mary Shelley's *Frankenstein*, the Preston Sturges film *Hail the Conquering Hero*, and news stories about environmental degradation.[43] Kaufman and Herz

The Toxic Avenger (Mitchell Cohen) uses his superhuman size and strength to stop some bad guys from getting away. *Troma Entertainment / Photofest © Troma Entertainment*

then raised a $500,000 budget, and they hired screenwriter Joe Ritter to write the script and artist Jennifer Aspinall to design the creature.[44] From there, Kaufman and Herz assembled their cast, and filming commenced in the summer of 1983.

During production, Kaufman changed the title from *Health Club Horror* to *The Toxic Avenger* after a business associate convinced him that doing so would help the film perform better in the foreign market.[45] Eight months after production wrapped, Kaufman attempted to set up a distribution deal but failed to find anyone interested in the film.[46] Just when all hope seemed lost, the manager at the Bleecker Street Cinema in New York booked *The Toxic Avenger* for a series of midnight screenings that turned the film into a massive cult hit.[47] In the years afterward, *The Toxic Avenger* spawned three sequels, an animated series called *The Toxic Crusaders*, and a line of comic books published by Marvel.[48] The title character (known affectionately by fans as "Toxie") now serves as the mascot for Troma Entertainment.

Commentary

Filled with gross-out humor and low-budget charm, *The Toxic Avenger* is a gleefully manic blast of superhero fun inspired by comic books and slasher flicks. The film assaults viewers with dozens of outrageously funny lines ("All right everybody, drop your tacos or I'll blow your brains out!") and cartoonish sight gags (such as the title character urinating a torrent of thick, green toxic waste). *The Toxic Avenger* also established the anarchic Troma style, which can be seen in subsequent efforts like *Class of Nuke 'Em High; Sgt. Kabukiman, NYPD;*

Tromeo and Juliet; and *Terror Firmer*—all cult classics in their own right. While the shameless stupidity, extreme gore, and tasteless humor will likely leave some viewers cold, *The Toxic Avenger* nevertheless remains an enjoyably absurdist romp that delivers a timely message about environmental pollution that resonates well into the twenty-first century.

Kaufman's direction keeps things lively as the film unfolds in a chaotic fashion that often recalls a hyperactive child trying to tell a story. The amateurish performances and inept acting align with the overall slapdash tone. In addition, *The Toxic Avenger* features charmingly cheap effects and amusing fight scenes. Of course, the film also contains loads of culturally insensitive jokes (after killing a woman inside a laundromat, Toxie quips "No ticky, no washy" in a stereotypically Chinese accent) and politically incorrect humor (the flamboyantly gay hairdressers immediately leap to mind). Yet the cleverly satirical jabs at both corporate America and the police ensure that the film still feels relevant long after its initial release. Thus, despite some woefully out-of-date gags, *The Toxic Avenger* is an agreeably dopey gore fest that actually has something to say.

See also *Class of Nuke 'Em High* (1986); *The Toxic Avenger Part II* (1989); *The Toxic Avenger Part III: The Last Temptation of Toxie* (1989); *Sgt. Kabukiman, NYPD* (1990); *Cannibal! The Musical* (1993); *Terror Firmer* (1999); *Citizen Toxie: The Toxic Avenger IV* (2000).

SPOTLIGHT: TROMA ENTERTAINMENT

In the mid-1970s, Yale University graduates Lloyd Kaufman and Michael Herz formed Troma Entertainment, a company dedicated to making and distributing a wide variety of films. In 1984, Troma scored a surprise hit with *The Toxic Avenger*, an outrageous superhero film that kicked off a lucrative franchise. From there, Troma unleashed several low-budget independent films that mix low-brow humor with high-brow social commentary, including *Class of Nuke 'Em High, Surf Nazis Must Die, Troma's War,* and *Chopper Chicks in Zombie Town.* Troma also launched the careers of numerous performers and creative types who went on to find great success in Hollywood, such as Kevin Costner, Samuel L. Jackson, Marissa Tomei, Vincent D'Onofrio, Billy Bob Thornton, Trey Parker, Matt Stone, James Gunn, and more. In 1999, Kaufman founded the Tromadance Film Festival as an alternative to the more mainstream Sundance Film Festival. Troma Entertainment remains the longest-running independent movie studio in North America, and they continue to produce off-the-wall cult flicks like *Poultrygeist: Night of the Chicken Dead, Return to Nuke 'Em High: Vol. 1,* and *B.C. Butcher.*

TRICK 'R TREAT (2007)

Director: Michael Dougherty
Screenplay: Michael Dougherty
Cast: Anna Paquin (Laurie), Brian Cox (Mr. Kreeg), Dylan Baker (Steven), Rochelle
    Aytes (Maria), Leslie Bibb (Emma), Monica Delain (Janet), Lauren Lee Smith
    (Danielle), Quinn Lord (Sam/Peeping Tommy)
Specs: 82 minutes; color
Genre: fantasy, horror, thriller
Availability: DVD and Blu-ray (Warner Bros.)

Plot

This anthology horror film features five tales of terror connected by a mysterious trick-or-treater dressed in tattered orange pajamas and a mask made from a burlap sack.

Background

While studying film at New York University in 1996, Michael Dougherty wrote and directed *Season's Greetings*, an animated short film in which a shadowy figure stalks a young boy named Sam on Halloween night.[49] This short served as a precursor for *Trick 'r Treat*, a feature-length anthology horror film that also features the character of Sam. After shopping around the script for years, Dougherty took it to Bryan Singer, for whom he had written *X-Men 2* and *Superman Returns*, and he agreed to produce the film with a $12 million budget.[50] Singer then set up a distribution deal with Warner Bros., and *Trick 'r Treat* entered production soon after in November 2006.[51] To save money, Dougherty decided to shoot the film entirely on location in Vancouver, British Columbia. Principal photography wrapped in January of 2007,[52] and Dougherty worked with editor Robert Ivison to prepare a final cut of the film in time for the proposed October 2007 release date.

Sadly, Warner Bros. dropped *Trick 'r Treat* from the schedule without explanation. Perhaps studio executives realized that *Saw IV* was slated for release around the same time and did not want *Trick 'r Treat* siphoning off any business from their juggernaut horror franchise.[53] Or maybe they were upset over the box office failure of *Superman Returns*. Whatever the case, Warner Bros. decided to shelve *Trick 'r Treat* indefinitely.[54] Despite this setback, the film played various film festivals between 2007 and 2009, including the Fantastia International Film Festival,[55] and during this time it racked up several awards, such as the Best Horror Movie, Best Director and Best Supporting Actor awards at the 2009 Fright Meter Awards.[56]

Trick 'r Treat became something of a cult hit among festival attendees, many of whom took to the Internet to implore Warner Bros. to release the film in theaters so that it could find an even bigger audience. Unfortunately, the studio ignored these pleas and dumped *Trick 'r Treat* on DVD in October of 2009.[57] Luckily, the film found a receptive audience and its cult grew exponentially. *Trick 'r Treat* has since spawned action figures and comic books, and in 2009 Dougherty announced a sequel that has yet to materialize.[58]

Sam (Quinn Lord) prepares to terrorize some unsuspecting trick-or-treaters. *Warner Bros. Entertainment / Photofest © Warner Bros. Entertainment*

Commentary

With its postmodern sensibilities and jokey attitude, *Trick 'r Treat* is an amusing throwback to the horror anthologies of old that boasts sumptuous visuals, nasty humor, and an intensely creepy atmosphere. The film begins with an inventive title sequence that evokes old EC horror comics like *Tales from the Crypt* and *The Vault of Horror*. This introduction gives viewers a pretty good preview of the film itself, which recalls movies like *Trilogy of Terror* and *Creepshow* as it cheerfully subverts and celebrates the well-trod clichés of the horror genre. In addition, *Trick 'r Treat* features an immensely talented cast, nice practical effects, spectacular gore, and a brisk eighty-two-minute run time that prevents it from overstaying its welcome. From the unnerving opening sequence to the deeply eerie final shot, *Trick 'r Treat* remains an exuberant holiday horror flick that offers up plenty of frightening fun and darkly comic humor.

The different segments work well on their own, but Dougherty expertly weaves them all together as characters from one tale drift through the background of another or become directly involved in the action. The opening segment functions as a loving homage to John Carpenter's *Halloween*, and it perfectly sets the stage for the other tales of terror. In "The Principal," Dylan Baker stars as a murderous middle school principal who torments a disobedient student played by Brett Kelly (better known as Thurman Merman in *Bad Santa* and its sequel). Next up is "The School Bus Massacre Revisited," a chilling tale that feels like Carpenter's *The Fog*. "Surprise Party," meanwhile, presents a darkly droll spin on "Little Red Riding Hood" that references *The Company of Wolves*, director Neil Jordan's own excessively stylish take on the fable. Finally, "Meet Sam" offers a nice twist on the standard slasher formula, and while watching, one can easily see why Sam became such a hit with horror fans and almost instantly achieved iconic status (even if the reveal of his true face proves more silly than scary).

Trick 'r Treat opens with a bang and builds to a satisfying ending, and overall it remains an enjoyably scary treat that will have viewers smiling with delight even as they peek at the screen through their fingers.

See also *Tales of Terror* (1962), *Trilogy of Terror* (1975), *Creepshow* (1982), *Grim Prairie Tales* (1990), *Tales from the Darkside: The Movie* (1990), *The ABCs of Death* (2012), *V/H/S* (2012).

U

UHF (1989)

Director: Jay Levey
Screenplay: "Weird Al" Yankovic, Jay Levey
Cast: "Weird Al" Yankovic (George Newman), Victoria Jackson (Teri Campbell), Kevin McCarthy (R. J. Fletcher), Michael Richards (Stanley Spadowski), David Bowe (Bob Steckler), Stanley Brock (Harvey Bilchik), Anthony Geary (Philo), Trinidad Silva (Raul Hernandez), Gedde Watanabe (Kuni), Billy Barty (Noodles MacIntosh), Fran Drescher (Pamela Finkelstein)
Specs: 97 minutes; color
Genre: comedy
Availability: DVD and Blu-ray (Shout! Factory)

Plot

Incurable dreamer George Newman uses his wacky imagination to turn a small UHF TV station into the most popular network in town. In the process, he draws the ire of a rival station's CEO, who sets out to destroy George and his unique brand of programming.

Background

By 1985, "Weird Al" Yankovic enjoyed a great deal of popularity thanks to song parodies such as "Eat It." Prompted by this success, Yankovic and his manager, Jay Levey, decided to make a Weird Al movie.[1] They approached executives at New Line Cinema, who told them to come back with a script.[2] Yankovic and Levey spent the next eight months writing the first draft of the screenplay.[3] Given Yankovic's reputation as a song parodist, they thought the movie should include parodies of movies, television shows, and commercials.[4] Unfortunately, New Line rejected the script, and the project remained in limbo until producers Gene Kirkwood and John Hyde of Cinecorp brought it to executives at Orion Pictures, who agreed to finance the film for just under $5 million.[5] Gray Frederickson, producer of *The Godfather* and *The Godfather: Part II*, came on as executive producer, and filming commenced in Tulsa, Oklahoma, a month later.[6]

Producers initially failed to find anyone willing to direct, so Levey decided to handle directing duties himself even though he had never directed a film before

Inveterate dreamer George Newman ("Weird Al" Yankovic) imagines himself as an adventurer. *Orion / Photofest © Orion*

(he had directed some of Yankovic's music videos).[7] Despite Levey's inexperience, the production ran smoothly, and both cast and crew greatly enjoyed the shoot.[8] Once production wrapped, *UHF* seemed like it might emerge as the breakout hit of 1989; the film reportedly received the highest test screening numbers since the original *RoboCop*.[9] Orion viewed *UHF* as the solution to their financial woes and thought Yankovic could become the next Woody Allen.[10] Unfortunately, neither prediction proved correct. *UHF* opened on July 21, 1989, just one month after box office juggernauts like *Indiana Jones and the Last Crusade*, *Lethal Weapon* 2, and *Batman*.[11] Critics hated *UHF*, and audiences stayed away in droves,[12] but the film became quite popular in the years after its release and now enjoys a well-deserved reputation as a cult classic.

Commentary

Unlike many of the films included in this book, *UHF* contains no deep intellectual meaning, nor does it function as a metaphor for any sort of prevailing ideological or sociocultural issues. It is simply an absurdist comedy that features loads of perfectly timed and executed gags, and it never aspires to be anything more. As such, *UHF* emerges as one of the funniest movies ever made. Yankovic spent years honing his comic sensibilities as a song parodist, and his humor successfully translates to the screen in the form of pitch-perfect pop culture parodies that fly by at a rapid pace. In addition, Yankovic and Levey filled their cast with extremely talented performers, including a pre-*Seinfeld* (and pre-controversy) Michael Richards, who takes physical humor to new heights as fan-favorite character

Stanley Spadowski. Thus, while it might not have much to say, *UHF* is guaranteed to leave the viewer howling with laughter.

At the same time, the film sort of unwittingly lays bare the inherent silliness of popular culture, because it punctures the bubble of self-importance that often surrounds mass media (particularly music, film, and television). Much like Yankovic's song parodies, *UHF* satirizes a wide array of popular culture, and it pokes fun at everything from trashy daytime talk shows to high-profile prestige films like *Ghandi*. Yet the parodies never feel malicious, and it quickly becomes clear that the creators hold a great deal of affection for the things they mock. The film spoofs and celebrates pop culture in equal measure, and unlike many modern parodies, the comedy in *UHF* emerges from a positive place. While the film may prove too hackneyed or bizarre for some viewers, those who can appreciate its endearingly goofy charms will discover a hilarious comedy that rewards multiple viewings.

See also *Pee-wee's Big Adventure* (1985), *Amazon Women on the Moon* (1987), *Ernest Goes to Camp* (1987), *Stay Tuned* (1992), *Wayne's World* (1992), *The Cable Guy* (1996).

SPOTLIGHT: "WEIRD AL" YANKOVIC (1959–)

In the late 1970s, the man now known as "Weird Al" Yankovic achieved a great deal of success writing and performing parodies of popular songs, many of which aired on the radio show hosted by Barry Hansen (a.k.a. Dr. Demento). Yankovic released his first self-titled album in 1983 but achieved widespread fame the following year with his second album, *"Weird Al" Yankovic in 3-D*, which contained the hit single "Eat It," a parody of Michael Jackson's "Beat It." From there, Yankovic earned a well-deserved reputation as the world's premiere song parodist, releasing fourteen albums during a nearly forty-year career. Over the years, Yankovic frequently ventured into other media like film and television, most notably as the star and cowriter of the cult classic *UHF*. In 2016, Yankovic served as the bandleader on the IFC series *Comedy Bang! Bang!* and he currently enjoys a second career as an author of quirky children's books.

V

V FOR VENDETTA (2005)

Director: James McTeigue
Screenplay: Lilly Wachowski, Lana Wachowski
Cast: Hugo Weaving (V), Natalie Portman (Evey), Stephen Rea (Finch), Stephen Fry (Deitrich), John Hurt (Adam Sutler), Tim Pigott-Smith (Creedy), Rupert Graves (Dominic), Roger Allam (Lewis Prothero)
Specs: 132 minutes; color
Genre: action, drama, thriller
Availability: DVD and Blu-ray (Warner Bros.)

Plot

In the London of the near future, a masked freedom fighter enlists the aid of a young woman in his crusade to topple a fascist regime.

Background

A few years before they changed the cinematic landscape with *The Matrix*, Lana and Lilly Wachowski considered adapting Alan Moore and David Lloyd's acclaimed graphic novel *V for Vendetta*.[1] They wrote a draft of the screenplay in the mid-1990s—around the same time their debut film *Bound* hit theaters—but decided to put the project on hold to direct the *Matrix* trilogy. During postproduction on *The Matrix Revolutions*, they gave assistant director James McTeigue a copy of the book and asked him to helm the adaptation.[2] McTeigue agreed, and the trio set about developing the film for Warner Bros. While the book was set in the 1990s and functioned as a thinly veiled critique of life in Thatcherite Britain, McTeigue and the Wachowskis updated the story to address contemporary events like the War on Terror.[3]

V for Vendetta entered production on March 7, 2005, and faced immediate criticism from author Alan Moore, who had suffered negative experiences with previous adaptations of his work. Moore openly denounced the filmmakers' decision to change V's cause from anarchy to freedom, and he asked the studio to remove his name from the film.[4] Meanwhile, lead actor James Purefoy abandoned the production six weeks into filming, leaving producers scrambling to replace him.[5]

V (Hugo Weaving) makes his grand entrance. *Warner Bros. / Photofest © Warner Bros.*

Hugo Weaving eventually stepped into the role and dubbed over Purefoy's remaining scenes.[6] The film also generated controversy when rumors emerged that former prime minister Tony Blair's son Euan, who worked as a runner on *V for Vendetta*, helped the production gain unprecedented access to British Parliament and the Clock Tower.[7] The difficult production finally wrapped on June 9, 2005, and the finished film opened on March 17, 2006, debuting at number one at the box office in the United States.

V for Vendetta went on to become a minor hit, grossing over $130 million worldwide over the course of nine months.[8] The film received mixed reviews, with some critics hailing it as interesting and engaging, while others dismissed it as a depressing dud filled with ugly visuals and adolescent political allegory.[9] At the same time, members of the LGBTQ community praised the film for its positive and nuanced depiction of homosexual characters.[10] In the years since its release, *V for Vendetta* has inspired political activists around the world, and the Guy Fawkes mask worn by the lead character has emerged as a popular symbol for protest groups like Anonymous.[11] The film remains a cult favorite, and some fans make a point to watch it every November 5.

Commentary

While far from perfect, *V for Vendetta* succeeds thanks to its extreme earnestness and overabundance of visual flair. Granted, some of the criticisms regarding the film's simplistic approach to complex political issues hold merit, and it often feels as though a better title might have been *Activism for Dummies* or *Baby's First Revolution*. The film's one-dimensional exploration of intricate ideological matters becomes even more glaring when compared to the source material, which has far more room to explore topics like fascism, anarchy, and the loss of freedom and individuality. Yet *V for Vendetta* is pitched to a mainstream audience and therefore cannot help but lose some of the nuances regarding the central themes. Despite all this, the film finds the exact right balance between stylistic action and thought-provoking ideas. As such, *V for Vendetta* emerges as an exciting cinematic spectacle that contains crude but vital musings about totalitarianism and the cost of liberty, and it broadcasts these ideas to an audience that might otherwise miss them.

By dropping elements from the book, McTiegue and the Wachowskis streamlined the narrative and trimmed a great deal of fat from the story (for instance, they completely excise a pointless and rather silly subplot about a character falling in love with a computer). Of course, some alterations are more successful than others; for instance, the love story between V and Evey feels a bit cliché at times, and some of the character motivations lose their authenticity when making the leap from page to screen. For the most part, though, the changes allow the film to carve out its own identity. At the same time, the creative team wisely translated several sequences directly from the source material, including a powerful one in which a jailed Evey discovers a letter written by a deceased political prisoner named Valerie. This entire sequence becomes even more effective than it was in the book, largely due to actress Natasha Wightman's incredibly moving voiceover narration. Thus, the film captures the spirit of the book, but succeeds in distinguishing itself from its inspiration.

V for Vendetta benefits from a blunt but effective approach to some tough concepts, and the kinetic action sequences and winning performances allow the film to rise above its faults. Thus, while some might be tempted to dismiss it as a bombastic bore that features a juvenile understanding of complicated matters, *V for Vendetta* nevertheless remains a provocative and altogether thrilling exploration of fascism and rebellion that has only become more relevant with each passing year.

See also *The Matrix* (1999), *Speed Racer* (2008), *Watchmen* (2009).

W

WAITING FOR GUFFMAN (1996)

Director: Christopher Guest
Screenplay: Christopher Guest, Eugene Levy
Cast: Christopher Guest (Corky St. Clair), Fred Willard (Ron Albertson), Catherine
   O'Hara (Sheila Albertson), Eugene Levy (Dr. Allan Pearl), Parker Posey (Libby
   Mae Brown), Bob Balaban (Lloyd Miller), Lewis Arquette (Clifford Wooley), Don
   Lake (Phil Burgess)
Specs: 84 minutes; color
Genre: comedy
Availability: DVD (Warner Archive Collection)

Plot

A group of amateur performers with big showbiz dreams stage an original musical to celebrate their small Midwestern town's 150th anniversary, but the director raises the stakes when he invites a Broadway theater critic to attend the show.

Background

Roughly twelve years after delivering a breakout performance in Rob Reiner's directorial debut *This Is Spinal Tap*, Christopher Guest helmed his own faux documentary with *Waiting for Guffman*, a loving send-up of community theater and small-town America. In place of a script, Guest worked with *SCTV* alum Eugene Levy to outline the story and come up with broad character sketches.[1] Guest then enlisted his *Spinal Tap* costars Michael McKean and Harry Shearer to help compose songs for *Red, White, and Blaine*, the musical staged in the film.[2] From there, Guest assembled a cast of talented actors who he felt could handle the improvised nature of the film.[3]

Guffman entered production in the early part of 1995, and principal photography lasted twenty-nine days, with the city of Lockhart, Texas, standing in for the fictional town of Blaine, Missouri.[4] Guest shot fifty-eight hours of footage, and then spent the next eighteen months working with editor Andy Blumenthal to assemble the final eighty-four-minute-long cut of the film.[5] *Guffman* premiered at the Boston Film Festival on August 21, 1996,[6] and then opened wide in the United

Corky St. Clair (Christopher Guest, center) and the rest of the theater troupe perform a number from *Red, White, and Blaine. Castle Rock Entertainment / Photofest © Castle Rock Entertainment*

States on January 31, 1997.[7] Unfortunately, the film failed to catch on with general audiences and grossed just under $3 million during its entire theatrical run, meaning it failed to recoup its estimated $4 million budget.[8] Yet *Guffman* almost instantly became a cult favorite, and it helped build anticipation for Guest's subsequent mockumentaries, *Best in Show*, *A Mighty Wind*, and *Mascots*.

Commentary

Guffman offers up plenty of laughs and lots of genuinely touching moments thanks to its colorful characters, hilarious dialogue, and silly situations. The film primarily serves as a vehicle for the immensely talented actors, all of whom deliver wonderfully comic performances. Like *This Is Spinal Tap*, *Guffman* mines humor from the characters and their eccentricities but refrains from mocking them outright. As such, the audience laughs with the characters rather than at them, and *Guffman* remains a delightfully humorous and pleasantly good-natured film that elicits lots of laughs even after more than two decades.

The adorably amateurish production of *Red, White, and Blaine* remains a highlight of the film due to its terrible acting, awkward choreography, and awful (yet catchy) music. It helps that Guest and his fellow actors are skilled enough to convincingly portray the lousy acting and tone-deaf singing, and they stumble and stutter their way through the show, belting out the laughable songs with an earnest enthusiasm that compels viewers to cheer them on. Furthermore, the characters' joyfulness while performing onstage renders the bittersweet finale even more touching, and guarantees that viewers will feel every bit as disappointed as Corky and his cast of marginally talented misfits when things fail to go exactly as planned.

Alas, after more than twenty years, some aspects of the film have aged rather poorly, particularly the characterization of Corky as a closeted but stereotypically flamboyant gay man (complete with a pronounced lisp), which now feels a bit insensitive but is somewhat smoothed over by the fondness that the film and the other characters hold for him. Regardless, *Guffman* remains a fun, lighthearted mockumentary that possesses a lot of heart, and cult film fans will want to book a trip to Blaine at their earliest convenience.

See also *This Is Spinal Tap* (1984), *Man Bites Dog* (1992), *Best in Show* (2000), *A Mighty Wind* (2003), *What We Do in the Shadows* (2014), *Mascots* (2016).

SPOTLIGHT: CHRISTOPHER GUEST (1948–)

Upon graduating from Bard College, Christopher Guest embarked on a career as an actor, appearing in several theatrical productions during the early 1970s. From there, he scored bit parts in several films, including *The Hot Rock, Death Wish, Lemmings,* and *The Long Riders*. Guest met Rob Reiner while working on the 1982 film *Million Dollar Infield,* and they decided to collaborate on a project along with Michael McKean and Harry Shearer. This resulted in the surprise hit film *This Is Spinal Tap*. Guest then joined the cast of *Saturday Night Live,* during which time he directed a handful of prefilmed sketches and short films. He returned to films the following year with roles in *The Princess Bride* and *Little Shop of Horrors*. After a few years spent kicking around Hollywood as a character actor, Guest directed the mockumentaries *Waiting for Guffman, Best in Show,* and *A Mighty Wind*. Since then Guest has directed films like *For Your Consideration* and *Mascots,* and created the short-lived television series *Family Tree* for HBO.

WALK HARD: THE DEWEY COX STORY (2007)

Director: Jake Kasdan
Screenplay: Judd Apatow, Jake Kasdan
Cast: John C. Reilly (Dewey Cox), Jenna Fischer (Darlene Madison), Tim Meadows (Sam), Matt Besser (Dave), Chris Parnell (Theo), Kristen Wiig (Edith), Harold Ramis (L'Chaim), David Krumholtz (Schwartzberg), Raymond J. Barry (Pa Cox), Margo Martindale (Ma Cox), Jonah Hill (Older Nate), Craig Robinson (Bobby Shad)
Specs: 96 minutes; color
Genre: comedy, musical
Availability: DVD and Blu-ray (Mill Creek Entertainment)

Plot

After his brother dies tragically during an innocent childhood machete fight, aspiring singer Dewey Cox embarks on the road to superstardom. Along the way, he struggles to overcome all sorts of adversity and win the love of his beautiful backup vocalist, Darlene.

Background

Writer/director Jack Kasdan hatched the idea for *Walk Hard: The Dewey Cox Story* in 2005 after watching several music biopics like *Ray* and *Walk the Line*. Kasdan noticed that these films tended to hit the same familiar beats no matter whose lives they chronicled, and he decided to make a movie that satirized the entire genre.[9] He took his idea to fellow director Judd Apatow, who offered to help write the screenplay. Before they could do that, however, they needed to develop the soundtrack, because the film hinged almost entirely on the music. They tasked music producer Mike Andrews with creating an entire catalog of songs that encompassed over fifty years' worth of music.[10] Andrews rose to the task, compiling a list of historically accurate tunes that parodied several different artists and musical styles from the 1950s onward. Meanwhile, Kasdan and Apatow concentrated on completing the script, which eventually landed on the 2006 Blacklist, a list of the best unmade scripts for that year. They then cast actor John C. Reilly as lead character Dewey Cox because he could sing and play guitar.[11] *Walk Hard* entered production in February of 2007.

Kasdan and Apatow set out to make a comedic film that still looked and felt like a prestigious Oscar-winning biopic. They used outrageous humor to poke fun at the clichés that often plague biopics, most notably via the purposeful miscasting of the various celebrity cameos (for instance, musician Jack White plays Elvis, while Jack Black, Paul Rudd, Justin Long, and Jason Schwartzman play the Beatles).[12] Prior to the film's release date, Reilly embarked on a short promotional tour during which he performed as Dewey Cox in cities throughout the United States.[13] *Walk Hard* opened in theaters on December 21, 2007, and received generally positive reviews from critics. Unfortunately, the film left gen-

Dewey Cox (John C. Reilly, right) and Darlene Madison (Jenna Fischer) perform a duet. *Columbia Pictures / Photofest © Columbia Pictures*

eral audiences confused,[14] and it grossed just $18 million at the U.S. box office, far less than its $35 million budget.[15] Nevertheless, *Walk Hard* earned a handful of Golden Globe nominations, and the title song even received a Grammy nomination for Best Song Written for Motion Picture, Television or Other Visual Media. Columbia Pictures released *Walk Hard* on DVD and Blu-ray on April 8, 2008, at which point the film attracted a small but fervent cult following that continues to grow to with each passing year.

Commentary

Walk Hard features an incredible cast, a terrific soundtrack, and lots of inspired silliness, all of which turn the film into a masterpiece of nonsensical humor that brilliantly skewers the tired tropes of the entire music biopic genre. *Walk Hard* inundates viewers with gleefully unhinged comedy and hysterically funny self-referential gags, and it boasts legitimately great songs that lampoon a wide variety of musical styles. Reilly anchors the film with his riotously funny performance as Dewey, imbuing the character with a volatile mix of sweet naïveté and barely suppressed rage. The film surrounds him with a stellar supporting cast made up of some of the funniest and most talented comic performers around. *Walk Hard* also features fun cameos from a bevy of comedians and musicians, many of whom are deliberately miscast as famous celebrities like Buddy Holly (Frankie Muniz), the Big Bopper (John Ennis), and Elvis Presley (Jack White of the White Stripes). The actors repeatedly declare who they are supposed to be ("And as Ringo Starr, I'm not so interested in meditation; I just like to have fun") and deliver blatantly obvious exposition ("Did you hear that? I'm Dewey's twelve-year-old girlfriend!") in a screamingly funny send-up of the formulaic conventions that routinely pop up in music biopics like *Great Balls of Fire!* or *The Doors*. At the same time, *Walk Hard* features plenty of playful wackiness that requires no direct knowledge of movies like *Ray* or *Walk the Line*, meaning it will also appeal to viewers who have never watched a music biopic in their lives (but those familiar with the genre will find the film even funnier).

Walk Hard offers up loads of self-aware comedy and metajokes (such as when grunge rocker Eddie Vedder ushers a seventy-one-year-old Dewey to the stage to perform "his final masterpiece that will sum up his entire life"), and it frequently winks at the audience to assure them that the filmmakers are also in on the joke (at one point, Paul Rudd's John Lennon declares, "There's no limit to what we can . . . imagine" while staring directly into the camera). *Walk Hard* also features a side-splittingly funny use of full-frontal male nudity, and presents viewers with some raucous drug humor (most notably during the zany animated LSD trip that pays homage to *Yellow Submarine* and Dewey's riotous PCP freak out, during which he makes like the Incredible Hulk and tosses a car). In addition, the film contains some gorgeous filmmaking, and Uta Briesewitz's stunningly elegant cinematography masterfully mimics the look and feel of the expensive prestige films that *Walk Hard* mocks. It also perfectly captures the period details and uses them to generate lots of big laughs (as in the sequence involving Dewey's ill-fated 1970s variety show). Toss in the outstanding soundtrack, which features catchy tunes like "Let's Duet" and the titular track, and *Walk Hard* emerges as an irreverently silly cult classic that doubles as one of the most enjoyable musicals ever made.

See also *Beyond the Valley of the Dolls* (1970), *The Rutles* (1978), *The Blues Brothers* (1980), *This Is Spinal Tap* (1984), *A Mighty Wind* (2003), *Frank* (2014), *Pop Star: Never Stop Never Stopping* (2016).

THE WARRIORS (1979)

Director: Walter Hill
Screenplay: David Shaber, Walter Hill
Cast: Michael Beck (Swan), James Remar (Ajax), Dorsey Wright (Cleon), Brian Tyler (Snow), David Harris (Cochise), Tom McKitterick (Cowboy), Marcelino Sánchez (Rembrandt), Terry Michos (Vermin), Deborah Van Valkenburgh (Mercy), Roger Hill (Cyrus), David Patrick Kelly (Luther)
Specs: 92 minutes; color
Genre: action, thriller
Availability: Blu-ray (Paramount Pictures)

Plot

New York street gang the Warriors are framed for the murder of a charismatic gang leader, and they must now race back to their own turf while staying one step ahead of every other gang in town.

Background

Following the commercial and critical failure of *The Driver*, writer/director Walter Hill and producer Larry Gordon embarked on an adaptation of Sol Yurick's novel *The Warriors*.[16] Paramount Pictures offered to produce the film with a reported $4 million budget.[17] Gordon and Hill accepted the studio's offer and then traveled to New York to scout locations and assemble a cast of mostly unknown theater actors.[18] *The Warriors* entered production on June 26, 1978,[19] and the film quickly ran over budget and fell behind schedule.[20] Aside from some interiors filmed at Astoria Studios, Hill shot the movie on location throughout the streets of New York City.[21] The low budget prevented Hill from hiring professionally trained Hollywood stuntmen, but he nevertheless managed to secure the services of stunt coordinator Craig R. Baxley, who worked closely with the cast to ensure that the fight sequences looked realistic.[22] After four grueling months, the production wrapped in September of 1978.[23]

The Warriors opened on February 9, 1979, and became a surprise box office hit despite mostly negative reviews (though renowned film critic Pauline Kael raved about *The Warriors* in her review for the *New Yorker*).[24] Sadly, the film's momentum screeched to a halt when the press linked it to a series of violent gang deaths. At that point Paramount pulled the advertising,[25] and *The Warriors* disappeared from theaters soon after. The film later became a hit on the midnight movie circuit, and heavy rotation on basic cable helped it achieve cult classic status.[26] In 2005 Rockstar Games released a video game based on *The Warriors*, and rumors of a remake have swirled around Hollywood for years.[27]

Swan (Michael Beck, center) and the rest of the Warriors work out how to get home after they are framed for the murder of Cyrus (Roger Hill). *Paramount Pictures / Photofest © Paramount Pictures*

Commentary

The Warriors taps into the same myths and legends that inspired superhero comic books, and it incorporates both these influences into its narrative and visual palette. Hill sends his heroes on a Homeric odyssey through a colorful and highly stylized version of New York City. The film also features a Greek chorus of sorts in the form of a nameless, mostly faceless DJ played by Lynne Thigpen, who broadcasts frequent updates on the gang's progress and uses her musical selections to comment on the action. Additionally, the gang uniforms frequently resemble the brightly colored costumes worn by the heroes and villains of the Marvel and DC universes. Hill made the connection to comic books even more explicit in the 2005 director's cut, which relies on comic book–style panels to transition between sequences (a choice that proved mostly unsuccessful as it disrupts the flow of the film and ruins some crucial reveals).

In addition, *The Warriors* features breathtaking action and moves at a relentless pace as it follows the title characters' desperate flight to Coney Island. Hill stages the action sequences in a straightforward and blunt fashion that offers a clear view of every single punch and kick. Though somewhat sluggish by the standards of modern action films, *The Warriors* remains exciting throughout as the title characters fight for their lives in a variety of interesting settings (including a subway bathroom and a dilapidated boardwalk). Meanwhile the story unfolds at breakneck speed, and the film introduces characters and situations with an economy rarely found in twenty-first-century action flicks. Rather than waste time on unnecessary backstory or pointless exposition, *The Warriors* just barrels ahead and expects the audience to keep up. In other words, characterization takes a back seat to the action, which feels vital and energetic despite a lack of camera movement and rapid-fire editing.

The Warriors draws on folkloric tradition and comic book tropes to turn a simple tale of urban warfare into something far more ambitious. Though it tells a rather intimate story, the film feels epic thanks to Hill's skillful direction, which offers low-budget thrills and rousing action in equal measure. No wonder discerning action fans still love to "come out and play-ay" with *The Warriors*.

See also *A Clockwork Orange* (1971), *Escape from New York* (1981), *Streets of Fire* (1984).

SPOTLIGHT: WALTER HILL (1942–)

Following a brief stint in the mailroom at Universal Pictures, Walter Hill entered the Directors Guild of America training program. From there, he landed a gig as an apprentice on television shows like *Gunsmoke, Wild Wild West,* and *Bonanza.* Eventually, Hill transitioned into film, working as assistant director on both *The Thomas Crown Affair* and *Bullitt,* and writing screenplays such as *Hickey and Boggs* and *The Getaway.* Hill made his directorial debut in 1975 with *Hard Times,* which became a huge commercial success. His next film, *The Driver,* fared less well, but Hill rebounded with *The Warriors* in 1979. Since then he has written and directed numerous films, including *Southern Comfort, 48 Hrs.,* and *Streets of Fire.* He also served as a producer on the *Alien* franchise and directed several episodes of television shows like *Tales from the Crypt* and *Deadwood.*

WET HOT AMERICAN SUMMER (2001)

Director: David Wain
Screenplay: Michael Showalter, David Wain
Cast: Janeane Garofalo (Beth), David Hyde Pierce (Henry), Michael Showalter (Coop), Marguerite Moreau (Katie), Michael Ian Black (McKinley), Zak Orth (J. J.), A. D. Miles (Gary), Paul Rudd (Andy), Elizabeth Banks (Lindsay), Christopher Meloni (Gene), Molly Shannon (Gail), Ken Marino (Victor), Joe Lo Truglio (Neil), Amy Poehler (Susie), Bradley Cooper (Ben)
Specs: 84 minutes; color
Genre: comedy, romance
Availability: (Universal Studios Home Entertainment)

Plot

Hilarity ensues as a group of mostly teenage counselors spend their last day at Camp Firewood trying to resolve all their unfinished business.

Background

David Wain and Michael Showalter rose to prominence as members of the State,[28] a comedy troupe whose self-titled sketch show aired on MTV between 1993 and 1995. After the show ended its run, Wain and Showalter decided to make a movie that spoofed 1980s summer camp comedies like *Meatballs* and *Gorp*,[29] but also drew on their own childhood experiences at summer camps in Maine and Massachusetts.[30] After finishing the screenplay, Wain, Showalter, and producer Howard Bernstein spent three years trying to secure funding to make the film. They managed to raise nearly $2 million,[31] and then assembled a cast comprised of up-and-coming comedians and well-known actors looking to stretch their comic muscles.

Wet Hot American Summer entered production on May 12, 2000. Camp Towanda in Honesdale, Pennsylvania, doubled for the fictional Camp Firewood, and the cast lived there throughout the entire twenty-eight-day shoot.[32] A combination of heavy rain and unseasonably cold temperatures made filming difficult for everyone involved. Nevertheless, the production ran smoothly, and principal photography wrapped on June 8, 2000. In January of 2001, Wain and his crew traveled to the Sundance Film Festival to secure a distribution deal, but most distributors rejected the film.[33] USA Films eventually purchased *Wet Hot* and released it to twenty-two theaters around the United States.[34] The film grossed less than $300,000 and received disastrous reviews.[35] *Wet Hot* disappeared from theaters soon after.

Over time, *Wet Hot* gained a devoted cult following among college kids and comedy nerds, and it launched the careers of several people who went on to be-

Coop (Michael Showalter, left) trains with Gene (Christopher Meloni, center) and Gary (A. D. Miles). *USA Films / Photofest © USA Films*

come huge stars in Hollywood.[36] The film's growing popularity inspired Wain and Showalter to reunite nearly every member of the original cast for the prequel series *Wet Hot American Summer: First Day of Camp*, which debuted on the Netflix streaming platform on July 31, 2015. Just over two years later, the *Wet Hot* crew once again teamed with Netflix to unleash *Wet Hot American Summer: Ten Years Later.*[37]

Commentary

Fans of absurdist comedy will find plenty to love in *Wet Hot American Summer*, which assaults viewers with a barrage of nonsensical gags but also includes loads of heart and razor-sharp satire. The film spoofs the tired tropes and conventions that routinely pop up in summer camp comedies, teen sex romps, and sports flicks. *Wet Hot* brilliantly satirizes well-worn clichés like the lovable loser scrambling to lose his virginity, and the scrappy misfits rallying to win the big game. At the same time, the film unleashes a torrent of irreverent and often bizarre jokes that exist independent of any context and only serve to inspire uncontrollable laughter in those who appreciate extreme silliness. However, a sense of genuine warmth lurks beneath the insanity and ironic detachment, and it soon becomes clear that Wain and Showalter hold at least some affection for their characters and the films that *Wet Hot* mocks. Thus, while the humor occasionally requires a cursory knowledge of 1980s teen flicks, *Wet Hot* features enough absurdity and earnest enthusiasm to appeal to comedy fans of all stripes, including those unfamiliar with movies such as *Meatballs*, *Hardbodies*, or *The Bad News Bears*.

In addition, *Wet Hot* celebrates and denounces nostalgia all at once, because it replicates the iconography of the 1980s but uses this imagery to expose the past as far less rosy than people remember. Comedies like *The Wedding Singer* and *Everybody Wants Some!!* offer wistful looks at the Reagan era, but *Wet Hot* mocks the idea that things were better in the so-called good old days. The film uses supremely silly humor to remind viewers that sometimes the nice guy fails to win the girl of his dreams, and it goes to some extremely dark places to reveal the sad

SPOTLIGHT: THE STATE

In 1988, New York University sophomore Todd Holoubeck formed a sketch comedy troupe with his classmates Kevin Allison, Michael Ian Black, Robert Ben Garant, Michael Patrick Jann, Kerri Kenney, Thomas Lennon, Joe Lo Truglio, Ken Marino, Michael Showalter, and David Wain. Calling themselves the State, they performed in campus drama labs and small theaters throughout downtown New York. In 1990, the group opened for comedian Dennis Miller, and two years later they made their television debut with *You Wrote It, You Watch It*, an MTV comedy series hosted by comedian Jon Stewart (host of *The Daily Show* from 1999 to 2015). From there, the group landed a six-episode order at MTV. *The State* ran from 1992 to 1995, but received dismal reviews for most of its run. Nevertheless, the show became a cult sensation, and propelled many of the performers to stardom. Members of the group later reteamed on TV shows like *Viva Variety* and *Reno 911!* and they also worked together on movies like *Wet Hot American Summer*; *The Baxter*; *Night at the Museum*; *I Love You, Man*; and more. The members of the State continue to influence comedy to this day.

truths behind those half-remembered parties that involved lots of pot and alcohol (among other things). *Wet Hot* offers up a pitch-perfect reproduction of a bygone era, but it refuses to sugarcoat the past and thereby avoids the false sentimentality that often informs period pieces like the ones mentioned earlier. Ultimately, *Wet Hot* succeeds because it captures the look and feel of the past, but employs some knowing satire and good-natured humor to skewer the idea of nostalgia itself.

See also *Putney Swope* (1969), *Rock 'n' Roll High School* (1979), *Strange Brew* (1983), *Pee-wee's Big Adventure* (1985), *UHF* (1989), *The Baxter* (2005), *They Came Together* (2014).

Appendix A

Cult around the World:
Ten Great International Cult Films

EL TOPO (1970)

Iconoclastic Mexican director Alejandro Jodorowsky serves up this surreal fable about a mysterious gunfighter who embarks on a spiritual quest across a weird Western landscape.

THE HARDER THEY COME (1972)

In Jamaican director Perry Henzell's blaxploitation classic, a hopeful young Reggae singer collides with corrupt record producers and drug pushers.

SUSPIRIA (1977)

A young American dancer travels to Germany and falls prey to a coven of witches in this excessively stylish horror film directed by Italian maestro Dario Argento.

MAD MAX (1979)

Set in a near-future dystopian landscape, Australian director George Miller's action classic tells the story of a vengeful cop who runs afoul of a violent motorcycle gang.

WITHNAIL & I (1987)

English director Bruce Robinson helms this black comedy about two unemployed actors who retreat to a quaint country cabin for an ill-fated holiday that tests their friendship.

THE KILLER (1989)

After accidentally blinding a beautiful young singer, a hit man on the verge of retirement takes one last job so that he can earn enough money to pay for the surgery that will restore her vision in director John Woo's melodramatic Hong Kong action thriller.

DELICATESSEN (1991)

French director Jean-Pierre Jeunet helms this surreal postapocalyptic black comedy, in which a handyman learns that the residents of an apartment building have decidedly killer taste in food.

RUN LOLA RUN (1998)

When a young man loses the money he owes to a vicious gangster, his girlfriend races against time to raise the cash in this innovative crime thriller from German director Tom Tykwer.

BATTLE ROYALE (2000)

In the near future, a totalitarian government deposits a group of junior high students on a deserted island and forces them to fight to the death in Japanese director Kinji Fukasaku's controversial masterpiece.

OLDBOY (2003)

After spending fifteen years imprisoned in a hotel room, a man learns that he has just five days to find his kidnapper in this darkly comic thriller from South Korean director Park Chan-wook.

Appendix B

Sex, Violence, and Everything in Between: Ten Great Exploitation Films

THE SADIST (1963)

Three people driving to a Los Angeles Dodgers game run afoul of a vicious psychopath and his crazy girlfriend in this tense thriller directed by James Landis and starring cult movie stalwart Arch Hall Jr.

THE DEVILS (1971)

A sex-starved nun accuses a priest of witchcraft in director Ken Russell's delirious retelling of an actual incident that occurred in Loudun, France, in 1634.

CAGED HEAT (1974)

Female inmates clash with a brutal warden in director Jonathan Demme's violent and sexually charged debut film.

ILSA: SHE-WOLF OF THE SS (1975)

The lustful commander of a Nazi concentration camp conducts wicked medical experiments on the prisoners in this Nazisploitation classic from director Don Edmonds.

CANNIBAL HOLOCAUST (1981)

An American professor journeys to the Amazon and discovers the shocking fate of a missing documentary crew in director Ruggero Deodato's gruesome precursor to twenty-first-century found footage horror films.

DEAD END DRIVE-IN (1986)

In director Brian Trenchard-Smith's action-packed Ozploitation satire, two lovestruck teenagers find themselves trapped in a drive-in theater that doubles as a concentration camp for society's outcasts.

KIDS (1995)

An HIV-positive teenager sets out to deflower as many virgin girls as possible in this provocative and controversial film from director Larry Clark.

RAVENOUS (1999)

A mysterious man infiltrates a remote military outpost in director Antonia Bird's slick, unconventional thriller that boasts a great anachronistic score composed by Damon Albarn (of *Blur* and *Gorillaz*).

BLACK SNAKE MOAN (2006)

A God-fearing blues musician struggles to save an emotionally damaged young woman in director Craig Brewer's searing twenty-first-century take on blaxploitation and sexploitation films.

DON'T BREATHE (2016)

Three impoverished teenagers attempt to rob a wealthy blind veteran only to discover that he hides a horrifying secret of his own in this grimy thriller from director Fede Alvarez.

Appendix C

Things That Go Bump in the Night: Ten Great Midnight Movies

BARBARELLA (1968)

A highly sexual female agent traverses forty-first-century space and encounters several bizarre individuals as she searches for the renowned scientist Durand-Durand in director Roger Vadim's campy sci-fi classic.

TARGETS (1968)

Peter Bogdanovich directs this harrowing tale of an encounter between an elderly horror film star and an unhinged Vietnam vet who embarks on a vicious shooting spree.

EQUINOX (1970)

A group of college students travel to an isolated cabin in the woods and encounter demonic forces in this inventive horror film directed by Jack Woods (with uncredited assistance from Mark Thomas McGee and Dennis Muren).

THE WICKER MAN (1973)

In director Robin Hardy's oppressively atmospheric horror film, a devoutly religious police sergeant travels to a Scottish island village in search of a missing girl, but the locals hinder his investigation at every turn.

SALÒ, OR THE 120 DAYS OF SODOM (1975)

Director Pier Paolo Pasolini serves up this controversial satire about four fascist libertines who physically and mentally abuse several young people over the course of nearly four months.

HEAVY METAL (1981)

A strange glowing sphere relates epic tales of the battle between good and evil to a terrified young girl in this animated anthology directed by Gerald Potterton.

ROAR (1981)

A pride of lions (and other big cats) terrorizes an unsuspecting family in director Noel Marshall's insane family flick, which stars his then-wife Tippi Hedren.

BASKET CASE (1982)

A pair of formerly conjoined twin brothers set out to kill the doctors who separated them years earlier in director Frank Henenlotter's comically sleazy horror film.

PINK FLOYD: THE WALL (1982)

Based on the album of the same name, this hallucinogenic film from director Alan Parker chronicles a troubled musician's slow descent into madness.

THE HAPPINESS OF THE KATAKURIS (2001)

In prolific director Takashi Miike's surreal musical horror comedy, a luckless family opens a bed and breakfast near Mount Fuji but the guests all wind up dead.

Appendix D

So Bad They're Good: Ten Great Camp Classics

SANTA CLAUS CONQUERS THE MARTIANS (1964)

Martians kidnap Santa Claus (along with two annoying kids) and force him to deliver presents to Martian children in this charmingly dopey holiday film from director Nicholas Webster.

ZARDOZ (1974)

A barbaric man from the postapocalyptic wastelands infiltrates a community of bored immortals in director John Boorman's singularly weird tale of a far-flung future world.

DEATH BED: THE BED THAT EATS (1977)

A demonically possessed bed consumes several unsuspecting victims in director George Barry's thoroughly ridiculous horror film, which was later immortalized by comedian Patton Oswalt on his 2007 album *Werewolves and Lollipops*.

ATTACK OF THE KILLER TOMATOES! (1978)

Members of a special government task force clash with mutant killer tomatoes in director John De Bello's humorous spoof of low-budget science fiction films, which spawned three sequels and a Saturday morning cartoon series.

FLASH GORDON (1980)

An American football player and his friends travel to the planet Mongo to stop the tyrannical Ming the Merciless from destroying Earth in this delightfully campy science fiction film directed by Mike Hodges and featuring a killer soundtrack by rock band Queen.

HALLOWEEN III: SEASON OF THE WITCH (1982)

In this unconventional horror sequel directed by Tommy Lee Wallace, a doctor tries to stop an evil toymaker from killing countless children on Halloween night.

HOWARD THE DUCK (1986)

A wisecracking humanoid duck teams up with a beautiful rock-and-roll singer to stop evil aliens from invading Earth in this somewhat unfairly maligned science fiction comedy from director Willard Huyck.

TROLL 2 (1990)

A family travels to a small town inhabited by vile plant-eating goblins in director Claudio Fragasso's most well-known film, which has earned the title of "Best Worst Movie."

WINTERBEAST (1992)

Possessed totem poles terrorize a small resort town in this insane shot-on-video trash masterpiece from director Christopher Thies.

DANGEROUS MEN (2005)

Iranian filmmaker Josh Rad spent twenty-six years making this gloriously nonsensical revenge tale about a traumatized woman who embarks on a bloody vendetta against all dangerous men after bikers kill her fiancé.

Appendix E

So Bad They're Bad: The Ten Worst Cult Films

ROBOT MONSTER (1953)

Phil Tucker directs this dopey dud in which a monstrous alien destroys all life on Earth except for one family, and then falls in love with one of the survivors.

FRITZ THE CAT (1972)

A sex-obsessed tomcat drops out of college and drifts through the various protest movements of the 1960s in director Ralph Bakshi's ponderous and poorly animated adaptation of Robert Crumb's satirical underground comix smash.

THE GARBAGE PAIL KIDS MOVIE (1987)

A group of disgusting alien urchins help a young antique shop employee deal with bullies and find love in this nonsensical family film directed by Rod Amateau and based on the popular trading card series.

SUPER MARIO BROS. (1993)

Two plumbers from Brooklyn travel to another dimension to rescue a princess and stop the evil King Koopa from taking over the world in this thoroughly embarrassing effort from directors Annabel Jankel and Rocky Morton.

EVENT HORIZON (1995)

A group of astronauts sent to salvage a ship that mysteriously returned from a black hole get more than they bargained for in this turgid horror flick directed by Paul W. S. Anderson.

SPACE JAM (1996)

Basketball superstar Michael Jordan joins forces with Bugs Bunny and the rest of the Looney Tunes to shill products (and defeat an alien basketball team) in this inexplicably popular turd from director Joe Pytka.

THE BOONDOCK SAINTS **(1999)**

A pair of fraternal twin brothers become vigilantes in director Troy Duffy's ugly and amateurish debut film, which features plenty of homophobic and misogynistic "humor."

REPO: THE GENETIC OPERA **(2008)**

Director Darren Lynn Bousman's daffy dystopian musical about a murderous biotech company features terrible songs, awful performances, and ugly production design straight from the clearance bin at Hot Topic.

BIRDEMIC: SHOCK AND TERROR **(2010)**

Two people find romance just as a flock of murderous mutated birds descend upon their sleepy little town in this inept and altogether absurd effort from writer/director James Nguyen.

A TALKING CAT!?! **(2013)**

A feisty talking feline brings two families together in director David DeCoteau's spectacularly incompetent family film.

Notes

INTRODUCTION

1. Ernest Mathijs and Jamie Sexton, *Cult Cinema* (Malden: Wiley-Blackwell, 2011), 234.

A

1. John L. Flynn, "Across the Eighth Dimension: Remembering the First Adventure of Buckaroo Banzai," *Sci-Fi Universe*, 1995, accessed July 19, 2017, web.archive.org/web/20070515141240/pages.towson.edu/flynn/banzai.html.

2. Lee Goldberg, "Earl Mac Rauch: Living with the Lepers of Saturn," *Starlog* 84 (July 1984): 66.

3. Flynn, "Across the Eighth Dimension"; Peter Sobczynski, "No Matter Where You Go, Here It Is: *The Adventures of Buckaroo Banzai across the 8th Dimension* Hits Blu-ray," RogerEbert.com, last modified August 17, 2016, www.rogerebert.com/demanders/no-matter-where-you-go-here-it-is-the-adventures-of-buckaroo-banzai-across-the-8th-dimension-hits-blu-ray.

4. Flynn, "Across the Eighth Dimension."

5. Ibid.

6. Sobczynski, "No Matter Where You Go."

7. Flynn, "Across the Eighth Dimension."

8. Ibid.; Sobczynski, "No Matter Where You Go."

9. Flynn, "Across the Eighth Dimension."

10. Sobczynski, "No Matter Where You Go."

11. Flynn, "Across the Eighth Dimension."

12. Danny Bowes, "Where You Go, There You Are: A Look Back at *Buckaroo Banzai*," Tor.com, last modified July 27, 2011, www.tor.com/2011/07/27/wherever-you-go-there-you-are-a-look-back-at-buckaroo-banzai/; "The Adventures of Buckaroo Banzai," Box Office Mojo, accessed July 20, 2017, www.boxofficemojo.com/movies/?id=buckaroobanzai.htm.

13. Sobczynski, "No Matter Where You Go"

14. Nisha Gopalan, "*American Psycho*: The Story behind the Film," *Guardian*, last modified March 23, 2000, www.theguardian.com/film/2000/mar/24/fiction.breteastonellis.

15. Jennifer Wood, "19 Things You Might Not Know about *American Psycho*," Mental Floss, last modified April 5, 2016, mentalfloss.com/article/63090/19-things-you-might-not-know-about-american-psycho.

16. Stuart Gordon, "Bret & Me, or How I Didn't End Up Directing *American Psycho*," Talkhouse, last modified June 10, 2016, www.talkhouse.com/bret-didnt-end-directing-american-psycho/.

17. Wood, "19 Things"; Kyle Buchanan, "Bret Easton Ellis on *American Psycho*, Christian Bale, and His Problem with Women Directors," Movieline, last modified May 18, 2010, movieline.com/2010/05/18/bret-easton-ellis-on-american-psycho-christian-bale-and-his -problem-with-women-directors/.

18. Gordon, "Bret & Me"; Kory Grow, "'*American Psycho*' at 25: Bret Easton Ellis on Patrick Bateman's Legacy," *Rolling Stone*, last modified March 31, 2016, www.rolling stone.com/culture/news/american-psycho-at-25-bret-easton-ellis-on-patrick-batemans -legacy-20160331.

19. Gopalan, "*American Psycho*"; Wood, "19 Things."

20. Gopalan, "*American Psycho*"; Lauren Duca, "*American Psycho* Could Have Starred Leonardo DiCaprio (and Been a Misogynistic Horror Film)," *Huffington Post*, last modified April 14, 2015, www.huffingtonpost.com/2015/04/14/american-psycho_n_7054104.html.

21. Wood, "19 Things."

22. Duca, "*American Psycho* Could Have Starred DiCaprio"; Gopalan, "*American Psycho*"; Dan Coz, "Casting Leo Has Harron Hesitant," *Variety*, last modified May 21, 1998, variety. com/1998/more/news/casting-leo-has-harron-hesitant-1117471132/.

23. Duca, "*American Psycho* Could Have Starred DiCaprio"; Gopalan, "*American Psycho*."

24. Gopalan, "*American Psycho*"; Wood, "19 Things."

25. Gopalan, "*American Psycho*"; Wood, "19 Things."

26. Gopalan, "*American Psycho*."

27. Ibid.

28. "*American Psycho* Cut to Appease Censors," *Guardian*, last modified February 29, 2000, www.theguardian.com/film/2000/feb/29/news.

29. Ibid.

30. Michael Fleming, "WB Aims for Pitt with 'James,'" *Variety*, last modified March 17, 2004, variety.com/2004/film/news/wb-aims-for-pitt-with-james-1117901859/.

31. Logan Hill, "Casey at the Bat," *New York Magazine*, last modified September 16, 2007, nymag.com/movies/features/37641/.

32. Emanuel Levy, "*Assassination of Jesse James by the Coward Robert Ford*," Emanuel-Levy.com, last modified February 26, 2007, emanuellevy.com/comment/assassination-of -jesse-james-by-the-coward-robert-ford-1/.

33. John Horn, "With Both Barrels," *Los Angeles Times*, last modified May 2, 2007, articles.latimes.com/2007/may/02/entertainment/et-pitt2.

34. Jack Giroux, "Casey Affleck Lovingly Reflects on *The Assassination of Jesse James by the Coward Robert Ford*," Film School Rejects, last modified December 6, 2013, film schoolrejects.com/casey-affleck-lovingly-reflects-on-the-assassination-of-jesse-james-by -the-coward-robert-ford-6561664d09b0/.

35. Horn, "With Both Barrels."

36. Stax, "Superman's New Date," IGN, last modified May 30, 2006, www.ign.com/ articles/2006/05/30/supermans-new-date.

37. Horn, "With Both Barrels."

38. "*The Assassination of Jesse James by the Coward Robert Ford*," Box Office Mojo, accessed July 11, 2017, www.boxofficemojo.com/movies/?page=weekend&id=jessejames.htm.

39. Evan Dickson, "The Films of Andrew Dominik: *The Assassination of Jesse James by the Coward Robert Ford*," Collider, last modified October 17, 2014, collider.com/the -assassination-of-jesse-james-andrew-dominik/.

40. Giroux, "Casey Affleck Reflects."

B

1. Anthony Kaufman, "Interview: Charlie Kaufman, the Man behind *Malkovich*," *IndieWire*, last modified October 27, 1999, www.indiewire.com/1999/10/interview-char lie-kaufman-the-man-behind-malkovich-82005/; Peter Kobel, "Film: The Fun and Games of Living a Virtual Life," *New York Times*, last modified October 24, 1999, www.nytimes .com/1999/10/24/arts/film-the-fun-and-games-of-living-a-virtual-life.html.

2. Adam Sternbergh, "In Conversation: Charlie Kaufman," Vulture, accessed July 13, 2017, www.vulture.com/2015/12/charlie-kaufman-anomaslisa-c-v-r.html.

3. Kobel, "Living a Virtual Life."

4. Ibid.; Robert Hofler, "Charlie Kaufman," *Variety*, last modified September 14, 1999, variety.com/1999/film/news/charlie-kaufman-1117792734/amp/.

5. Kobel, "Living a Virtual Life."

6. Benedict Carver, "Bean, Place in *Malkovich*," *Variety*, last modified August 11, 1998, variety.com/1998/film/news/bean-place-in-malkovich-1117479351/.

7. Carver, "Bean, Place"; David Rooney, "Review: *Being John Malkovich*," *Variety*, last modified September 3, 1999, variety.com/1999/film/reviews/being-john-malkov ich-1117752080/.

8. Rooney, "Review"; *Being John Malkovich*," Box Office Mojo, accessed July 13, 2017, www.boxofficemojo.com/movies/?page=weekend&id=beingjohnmalkovich.htm.

9. "*Being John Malkovich* (1999)," Rotten Tomatoes, accessed July 13, 2017, www.rot tentomatoes.com/m/being_john_malkovich/.

10. "*Being John Malkovich*," Box Office Mojo.

11. Garin Pirnia, "13 Better Facts about *Better Off Dead*," Mental Floss, February 20, 2016, mentalfloss.com/article/75810/13-better-facts-about-better-dead.

12. Joe Berkowitz, "The Long, Strange Journey of *Better Off Dead* Director 'Savage' Steve Holland," *Fast Company*, February 4, 2016, www.fastcompany.com/3055116/the -long-strange-journey-of-better-off-dead-director-savage-steve-holland.

13. Pirnia, "13 Better Facts."

14. Steven Molaro, "*Better Off Dead*—Savage Steve Holland," *The Sneeze*, March 1, 2004, www.thesneeze.com/mt-archives/000134.php.

15. Dustin Rowles, "John Cusack May Not Be the Asshole We Thought He Was," Pajiba, June 15, 2015, www.pajiba.com/career_assessments/john-cusack-has-nothing-against -better-off-dead.php.

16. Steve Spears, "30 Years Later, *Better Off Dead* Has Earned Its Two Dollars . . . and John Cusack's hatred," *Tampa Bay Times*, August 24, 2015, www.tampabay.com/blogs/80s/30- years-later-better-off-dead-has-earned-its-two-dollars—and-john/2242541.

17. "*Better Off Dead*," Box Office Mojo, accessed July 7, 2017, www.boxofficemojo.com/ movies/?id=betteroffdead.htm.

18. Berkowitz, "Long, Strange Journey."

19. Jenny M. Jones, *"The Big Lebowski": An Illustrated, Annotated History of the Greatest Cult Film of All Time* (Minneapolis: Voyageur Press, 2012), 36.

20. Ibid., 36–39.

21. Ibid.

22. Adam D'Arpino, "21 Facts about *The Big Lebowski*," Mental Floss, last modified February 2, 2016, mentalfloss.com/article/61708/21-things-you-might-not-know-about -big-lebowski.

23. Jones, *"The Big Lebowski*," 41.

24. D'Arpino, "21 Facts about *Lebowski*."

25. Jones, "*The Big Lebowski*," 43–46.

26. Ibid., 75.

27. Ibid.

28. Oliver Lyttleton, "5 Things You Might Not Know about the Coens' Cult Classic *The Big Lebowski*," *IndieWire*, last modified March 6, 2013, www.indiewire.com/2013/03/5-things-you-might-not-know-about-the-coens-cult-classic-the-big-lebowski-249015/.

29. Jones, "*The Big Lebowski*," 79.

30. Ibid., 77.

31. Ibid., 92.

32. "*The Big Lebowski*," Box Office Mojo, accessed July 11, 2017, www.boxofficemojo.com/movies/?id=biglebowski.htm.

33. Lyttleton, "5 Things."

34. Ibid.

35. James Rush, "The Dude Abides: Meet the Founder of Dudeism, the Laidback Religion Based on *The Big Lebowski* Which Now Has More Than 250,000 Followers," *Daily Mail*, last modified July 17, 2014, www.dailymail.co.uk/news/article-2695997/The-Dude-abides-Meet-founder-Dudeism-laidback-religion-based-The-Big-Lebowski-250-000-followers.html.

36. Ryan Lambie, "How Philip K Dick transformed Hollywood," Den of Geek!, last modified October 26, 2012, www.denofgeek.com/us/movies/22442/how-philip-k-dick-transformed-hollywood.

37. Paul M. Sammon, *Future Noir: The Making of "Blade Runner"* (London: Orion Media, 1996), 23; Lambie, "How Philip K Dick Transformed Hollywood."

38. Charles de Lauzirika, "Dangerous Days: Making *Blade Runner*," *Blade Runner: The Final Cut*, DVD, directed by Ridley Scott (Burbank: Warner Home Video, 2007).

39. de Lauzirika, "Dangerous Days."

40. Ibid.; "Interview with Producer Michael Deeley," IGN, last modified April 3, 2015, www.ign.com/videos/2015/04/03/the-incredible-story-behind-the-making-of-blade-runner.

41. de Lauzirika, "Dangerous Days"; Lambie, "How Philip K Dick Transformed Hollywood"; "Interview with Michael Deeley."

42. de Lauzirika, "Dangerous Days."

43. Ibid.

44. "Interview with Michael Deeley."

45. de Lauzirika, "Dangerous Days"; David Alm, "A Conversation with Hampton Fancher, Creative Genius behind *Blade Runner* and *The Minus Man*," *Forbes*, last modified May 13, 2016, www.forbes.com/sites/davidalm/2016/05/13/a-conversation-with-hampton-fancher-creative-genius-behind-blade-runner-and-the-minus-man/#688195721905.

46. de Lauzirika, "Dangerous Days"; "Interview with Michael Deeley."

47. Sammon, *Future Noir*, 211; Rob Carnevale, "No. 41: Ridley Scott," BBC News, last modified April 13, 2014, www.bbc.co.uk/films/callingtheshots/ridley_scott.shtml; "Interview with Michael Deeley."

48. de Lauzirika, "Dangerous Days"; "Interview with Michael Deeley."

49. Sammon, *Future Noir*, 98.

50. Ibid., 309.

51. Ibid., 313–15; Lambie, "How Philip K Dick Transformed Hollywood."

52. "*Blade Runner*," Box Office Mojo, accessed July 20, 2017, www.boxofficemojo.com/movies/?page=weekend&id=bladerunner.htm.

53. Ned Zeman, "Soul Men: The Making of *The Blues Brothers*," *Vanity Fair*, last modified January 2013, www.vanityfair.com/hollywood/2013/01/making-of-blues-brothers-budget-for-cocaine.

54. Ibid.

55. Ibid.

56. Ibid.; Paul Edwards, "The Making of *The Blues Brothers*," Death by Films, last modified November 29, 2013, www.deathbyfilms.com/the-making-of-the-blues-brothers.

57. Stuart Thornton, "Curtis Salgado Inspired *The Blues Brothers*, Then Survived Terminal Cancer," *Monterey County Weekly*, last modified July 31, 2008, www.monterey countyweekly.com/entertainment/music/curtis-salgado-inspired-the-blues-brothers -then-survived-terminal-cancer/article_ced717f5-c8f9-57f3-8088-9296446e9d5a.html; "The Brothers," Blues Brothers Official Site, accessed July 20, 2017, bluesbrothersofficialsite .com/p-9905-the-brothers.html.

58. Zeman, "Soul Men."

59. Ibid.

60. J. M. Kenny, "Stories behind the Making of *The Blues Brothers*," *The Blues Brothers*, 25th anniversary DVD, directed by John Landis (Universal City: Universal Studios Home Entertainment, 2005).

61. Zeman, "Soul Men."

62. Ibid.

63. Ibid.

64. Ibid.

65. Ibid.

66. Ibid.

67. Ibid.

68. Edwards, "Making of *The Blues Brothers*"; Rebecca Hawkes, "The Greatest Movie Car Stunts of All Time, and the Stories behind Them," *Telegraph*, last modified June 26, 2017, www.telegraph.co.uk/films/2016/04/20/film-car-chases-and-stunts-7-true-stories; "Stories behind the Making of *The Blues Brothers*."

69. Zeman, "Soul Men."

70. Ibid.

71. Edwards, "Making of *The Blues Brothers*"; "The Blues Brothers," Box Office Mojo, accessed July 20, 2017, www.boxofficemojo.com/movies/?id=bluesbrothers.htm.

72. Daisy Garnett, "Drugsy Malone," *Telegraph*, last modified April 30, 2006, www.tele graph.co.uk/culture/3652004/Drugsy-Malone.html.

73. Scott Tobias, "Rian Johnson," The A.V. Club, last modified April 19, 2006, www .avclub.com/article/rian-johnson-13982.

74. Garnett, "Drugsy Malone"; Tobias, "Rian Johnson."

75. Tobias, "Rian Johnson."

76. Garnett, "Drugsy Malone"; Tobias, "Rian Johnson."

77. Tobias, "Rian Johnson."

78. Garnett, "Drugsy Malone."

79. Mark Garcia, "*Brick* Gets Special San Clemente Screening," *Orange County Register*, last modified April 3, 2006, www.ocregister.com/2006/04/03/brick-gets-special-san -clemente-screening/.

80. Garnett, "Drugsy Malone."

81. Ibid.

82. "*Brick*," *Entertainment Weekly*, last modified February 10, 2006, ew.com/arti cle/2006/02/10/brick/.

83. Garcia, "*Brick* San Clemente Screening."

84. "*Brick*," Box Office Mojo, accessed July 12, 2017, www.boxofficemojo.com/ movies/?id=brick.htm.

85. Garner Simmons, *Peckinpah: A Portrait in Montage* (New York: Limelight Editions, 1998), 189.

86. Richard Harland Smith, *"Bring Me the Head of Alfredo Garcia,"* TCM.com, accessed July 17, 2017, www.tcm.com/this-month/article/209008%7C0/Bring-Me-the-Head-of -Alfredo-Garcia.html.

87. Simmons, *Peckinpah*, 189.

88. Smith, *"Alfredo Garcia."*

89. Garner Simmons, "Just the Films, Ma'am: Behind the Scenes of Peckinpah's *Bring Me the Head of Alfredo Garcia,"* *Sight and Sound*: *The International Film Magazine*, accessed July 17, 2017, www.bfi.org.uk/news-opinion/sight-sound-magazine/features/behind-scenes -peckinpah-s-bring-me-head-alfredo-garcia.

90. Ibid.

91. Ibid.; Smith, *"Alfredo Garcia."*

92. Smith, *"Alfredo Garcia."*

93. Simmons, *Peckinpah*, 196–97.

94. Ibid.

95. Ibid.

96. Ibid., 201–5.

97. Smith, *"Alfredo Garcia."*

98. Roger Ebert, *"Bring Me the Head of Alfredo Garcia,"* RogerEbert.com, last modified October 28, 2001, www.rogerebert.com/reviews/great-movie-bring-me-the-head-of -alfredo-garcia-1974.

99. "Ariel 1946–2014," AMACC, accessed July 19, 2017, amacc.mx/ver_ariel.asp?tipo =anio&anio=XVII%201975.

100. Sukhdev Sandhu, *"Bring Me the Head of Alfredo Garcia—Review,"* *Telegraph*, last modified December 29, 2008, www.telegraph.co.uk/journalists/sukhdev-sandhu/4014923/ Bring-Me-the-Head-of-Alfredo-Garcia-review.html; *"Bring Me the Head of Alfredo Garcia* (1974)," TCM.com, accessed July 19, 2017, www.tcm.com/tcmdb/title/17052/Bring-Me -the-Head-of-Alfredo-Garcia/trivia.html.

101. "Remembering the *Buffy the Vampire Slayer* Movie and Joss Whedon's First Superhero," Yahoo! Movies, last modified May 5, 2015, www.yahoo.com/movies/joss -whedon-buffy-the-vampire-slayer-118217991342.html.

102. "Remembering *Buffy the Vampire Slayer."*

103. "Vampire Pop," Movieline, last modified August 1, 1992, movieline.com/1992/ 08/01/vampire-pop/.

104. "Remembering *Buffy the Vampire Slayer."*

105. "Vampire Pop"; "Remembering *Buffy the Vampire Slayer."*

106. Tasha Robinson, "Interview with Joss Whedon," The A.V. Club, last modified September 5, 2001, www.avclub.com/article/joss-whedon-13730.

107. "Remembering *Buffy the Vampire Slayer."*

108. Robinson, "Interview"; "Remembering *Buffy the Vampire Slayer."*

109. "Vampire Pop."

110. Ibid.

111. Ibid.; "Remembering *Buffy the Vampire Slayer."*; *"Buffy the Vampire Slayer,"* Box Office Mojo, accessed July 23, 2017, www.boxofficemojo.com/movies/?id=buffythevam pireslayer.htm.

C

1. "The 1996 Summer Movie Preview: June," *Entertainment Weekly*, last modified May 24, 1996, ew.com/article/1996/05/24/1996-summer-movie-preview-june/.

2. Ibid.

3. John Sellers, "Judd Apatow Tells Us the Legend of *The Cable Guy*, the Bomb That Wasn't," Vulture, last modified March 4, 2011, www.vulture.com/2011/03/cable_guy_judd_apatow.html.

4. Nathan Rabin, "Interview with Judd Apatow," The A.V. Club, last modified March 1, 2011, www.avclub.com/article/judd-apatow-52523.

5. Robert W. Welkos, "Humor Too Dark for Its Own Good?" *Los Angeles Times*, last modified June 25, 1996, articles.latimes.com/1996-06-25/entertainment/ca-18200_1_cable-guy.

6. Ibid.

7. Ibid.

8. Ibid.

9. Rabin, "Interview with Judd Apatow."

10. Welkos, "Humor Too Dark?"

11. "*The Cable Guy*," Box Office Mojo, accessed July 23, 2017, www.boxofficemojo.com/movies/?id=cableguy.htm.

12. Dave Kehr, "Jim Carrey as the Id Unleashed a Bit before Its Time," *New York Times*, last modified February 25, 2011, www.nytimes.com/2011/02/27/movies/homevideo/27kehr.html.

13. Sellers, "The Legend of *The Cable Guy*."

14. David Chute, "Will *Cannibal! The Musical!* Be the next *Rocky Horror*?" *Los Angeles Times*, last modified June 5, 1998, articles.latimes.com/1998/jun/05/entertainment/ca-56723.

15. Ibid.

16. Trey Parker, "Commentary," *Cannibal! The Musical*, DVD, directed by Trey Parker (Long Island: Troma Entertainment, 1996).

17. Jason McHugh, "The Making of *Cannibal! The Musical*," *Cannibal! The Musical*: The Official Website, last modified January 29, 2015, www.cannibalthemusical.net/makingof01.shtml.

18. Michael Roberts, "The *South Park* Anniversary: The First Trey Parker–Matt Stone Interview," Westword, last modified August 14, 2007, www.westword.com/news/the-south-park-anniversary-the-first-trey-parker-matt-stone-interview-5858114.

19. McHugh, "Making of *Cannibal!*"

20. Ibid.

21. Ibid.

22. Ibid.

23. "*Cannibal! The Musical* (1993) Release Info," IMDb, accessed July 23, 2017, www.imdb.com/title/tt0115819/releaseinfo?ref_=tt_ov_inf.

24. Chute, "The Next *Rocky Horror*?"; "Still Hope for Trey Parker's *Cannibal: The Musical*," *Entertainment Weekly*, last modified January 30, 1998, ew.com/article/1998/01/30/still-hope-trey-parkers-cannibal-musical/.

25. Chute, "The Next *Rocky Horror*?"

26. "About the Movie," *Cannibal! The Musical*: The Official Website, last modified January 29, 2015, www.cannibalthemusical.net/about.shtml.

27. Chute, "The Next *Rocky Horror*?"

28. Charles Champlin, "The Reincarnation of *Carnival of Souls*," *Los Angeles Times*, last modified April 19, 1990, articles.latimes.com/1990-04-19/entertainment/ca-2117_1_industrial-film/2.

29. Susan Doll, "The Horror of Kansas: Herk Harvey's *Carnival of Souls*," *Streamline*: *The Filmstruck Blog*, last modified October 25, 2010, streamline.filmstruck.com/2010/10/25/the-horror-of-kansas-herk-harveys-carnival-of-souls/.

30. Herk Harvey, "Commentary," *Carnival of Souls*, Blu-ray, directed by Herk Harvey (New York: The Criterion Collection, 2016).

31. Doll, "The Horror of Kansas."

32. Champlin, "The Reincarnation of *Carnival of Souls*."

33. Ibid.

34. Charles E. Pratt Jr., "An Interview with John Clifford," *Rogue Cinema*, accessed July 10, 2017, www.roguecinema.com/an-interview-with-john-clifford-by-charles-e-pratt-jr .html.

35. Ibid.

36. Richard Crouse, "*Carnival of Souls* (1962)," in *The 100 Best Movies You've Never Seen* (Toronto: ECW Press, 2003), 37.

37. Bill Shaffer, "The Movie That Wouldn't Die: The *Carnival of Souls* Story," *Carnival of Souls*, Blu-ray, directed by Herk Harvey (New York: The Criterion Collection, 2016).

38. Harvey, "Commentary."

39. Shaffer, "The Movie That Wouldn't Die."

40. Ibid.

41. Champlin, "The Reincarnation of *Carnival of Souls*."

42. Shaffer, "The Movie That Wouldn't Die."

43. Harvey, "Commentary."

44. Kevin Polowy, "Director's Reel: Kevin Smith on the Colorful History of the Black-and-White Sensation *Clerks*," Yahoo! Movies, last modified October 19, 2016, www.yahoo .com/movies/directors-reel-kevin-smith-on-the-colorful-history-of-the-black-and-white -sensation-clerks-150509877.html.

45. Nick Keppler, "18 Black-and-White Facts about *Clerks*," Mental Floss, last modified October 17, 2015, mentalfloss.com/article/70020/18-black-and-white-facts-about-clerks.

46. Ibid.

47. Ibid.

48. Ibid.

49. "*Clerks*," Box Office Mojo, accessed July 23, 2017, www.boxofficemojo.com/ movies/?page=weekend&id=clerks.htm.

50. Ibid.

51. "The Comedy 25: The Funniest Movies of the Past 25 Years," *Entertainment Weekly*, last modified August 26, 2008, ew.com/gallery/cult-25-essential-left-field-movie -hits-83/13; ew.com/gallery/comedy-25-funniest-movies-past-25-years/5.

52. Scott Tobias, "The New Cult Canon: *Clerks*," The A.V. Club, last modified April 2, 2008, www.avclub.com/article/the-new-cult-canon-iclerksi-2239.

53. Gary Leva, "Great Bolshy Yarblockos! Making *A Clockwork Orange*," *A Clockwork Orange*, two-disc special edition DVD, directed by Stanley Kubrick (Burbank: Warner Home Video, 2007).

54. Ibid.

55. Ibid.

56. Ibid.

57. Colin Marshall, "The Making of Stanley Kubrick's *A Clockwork Orange*," *Open Culture*, last modified July 5, 2012, www.openculture.com/2012/07/the_making_of_stan ley_kubricks_ia_clockwork_orangei.html.

58. Leva, "Great Bolshy Yarblockos!"

59. Ibid.

60. Marshall, "Making *A Clockwork Orange*."

61. Leva, "Great Bolshy Yarblockos!"

62. Ibid.

63. Sean Hutchinson, "15 Things You Might Not Know about *A Clockwork Orange*," Mental Floss, last modified April 22, 2015, mentalfloss.com/article/63211/15-things-you -might-not-know-about-clockwork-orange.

64. Leva, "Great Bolshy Yarblockos!"

65. Hunter Daniels, "Malcolm McDowell and Leon Vitali Talk *A Clockwork Orange* on the 40th Anniversary," Collider, last modified May 18, 2011, collider.com/malcolm-mcdowell -leon-vitali-interview-a-clockwork-orange/.

66. Bryan Reesman, "Exclusive Q&A: Malcolm McDowell Revisits *A Clockwork Orange*," MTV.com, last modified May 30, 2011, www.mtv.com/news/2805131/malcolm -mcdowell-interview-a-clockwork-orange/.

67. Leva, "Great Bolshy Yarblockos!"

68. Alan Travis, "Retake on Kubrick Film Ban," *Guardian*, last modified September 10, 1999, www.theguardian.com/uk/1999/sep/11/alantravis.

69. Hutchinson, "15 Things."

70. "*A Clockwork Orange*," Box Office Mojo, accessed July 12, 2017, www.boxoffice mojo.com/movies/?id=clockworkorange.htm.

71. Adam B. Vary, "The Crazy Story of How *Clue* Went from Forgotten Flop to Cult Triumph," BuzzFeed, last modified December 10, 2015, www.buzzfeed.com/adamb-vary/something-terrible-has-happened-here-the-crazy-story-of-how?utm_term=.uuLOp EVvN#.ki7G0jWJE.

72. Ibid.

73. Ibid.

74. Ibid.

75. Ibid.

76. Ibid.

77. Ibid.

78. Ibid.

79. Ibid.

80. Ibid.

81. Ibid.

82. "Box Office/Business for *Clue* (1985)," IMDb, accessed July 21, 2017, www.imdb .com/title/tt0088930/business?ref_=tt_ql_dt_4.

83. Vary, "Crazy Story of *Clue*."

84. Ibid.; "*Clue*," Box Office Mojo, accessed July 21, 2017, www.boxofficemojo.com/ movies/?id=clue.htm.

85. Nick Farr, "Abnormal Interviews: *My Cousin Vinny* director Jonathan Lynn," Abnormal Use, last modified March 13, 2012, abnormaluse.com/2012/03/abnormal-interview -my-cousin-vinny-director-jonathan-lynn.html.

86. Vary, "Crazy Story of *Clue*"; Roger Ebert, "*Clue*," RogerEbert.com, last modified December 12, 1985, www.rogerebert.com/reviews/clue-1985; Janet Maslin, "Screen: *Clue*, from Game to Film," *New York Times*, last modified December 13, 1985, www.ny times.com/movie/review?res=9C05E3DE143BF930A25751C1A963948260.

87. Vary, "Crazy Story of *Clue*."

88. Ibid.

89. Mike Cecchini, "Steven E. deSouza Talks *Commando 2*, *Sgt. Rock*, the *Flash Gordon* Movie You May Never See, and Much More!" Den of Geek!, last modified December 20, 2013, www.denofgeek.com/us/movies/steven-e-de-souza/231767/steven-e-de-souza -talks-commando-2-sgt-rock-the-flash-gordon-movie-you-may-never-see-and-much-more; Ryan Lambie, "*Commando* at 30," Den of Geek!, last modified May 4, 2015, www.denofgeek .com/us/movies/commando/245957/commando-at-30.

90. Cecchini, "Steven E. deSouza."

91. Ibid.; Nick De Semlyen, "*Commando*: The Complete History," Empire, last modified March 30, 2017, www.empireonline.com/movies/features/commando-complete-history/.

92. De Semlyen, "*Commando*."

93. Jim Hemphill, "'If You Read the Script You're Not Gonna Want to Do the Movie': Mark L. Lester on *Commando*," *FilmMaker Magazine*, last modified October 1, 2015, filmmakermagazine.com/95868-if-you-read-the-script-youre-not-gonna-want-to-do-the-movie-mark-l-lester-on-commando/#.WW-TeYjyu00.

94. De Semlyen, "*Commando.*"

95. "*Commando*," AFI.com, accessed July 21, 2017, www.afi.com/members/catalog/DetailView.aspx?s=&Movie=57535.

96. Hemphill, "Mark L. Lester on *Commando.*"

97. De Semlyen, "*Commando.*"

98. Hemphill, "Mark L. Lester on *Commando.*"; "*Commando*," AFI.com.

99. "*Commando*," Box Office Mojo, accessed July 21, 2017, www.boxofficemojo.com/movies/?id=commando.htm.

100. De Semlyen, "*Commando.*"

101. Cecchini, "Steven E. deSouza.; "*Commando*," Box Office Mojo; "Commando," AFI.com.

102. Adam Markovitz, "*Commando* Remake in the Works: Who Should Take Arnold Schwarzenegger's Role?" *Entertainment Weekly*, last modified April 29, 2010, ew.com/article/2010/04/29/commando-remake-in-the-works-who-should-take-arnold-schwarzeneggers-role/.

103. Jay Fernandez, "Surprisingly, the Filmmakers Lived to Tell Their Tale," *Los Angeles Times*, last modified May 7, 2006, articles.latimes.com/2006/may/07/entertainment/ca-crank7; Kate Hubin, Todd Nickels, and Jamie Blois, "*Crank: High Voltage* production notes," Lionsgate, accessed on July 10, 2017, www.lionsgatepublicity.com/uploads/assets/pro_notes_34.doc.

104. "*Crank*," Box Office Mojo, accessed July 12, 2017, www.boxofficemojo.com/movies/?id=crank.htm.

105. Fernandez, "The Filmmakers Lived."

106. Susan King, "Up to His Old Stunts," *Los Angeles Times*, last modified August 31, 2006, articles.latimes.com/2006/aug/31/news/wk-movies31; Fernandez, "The Filmmakers Lived"; Hubin, Nickels, and Blois, "*Crank: High Voltage* Production Notes."

107. King, "Up to His Old Stunts."

108. Fernandez "The Filmmakers Lived."

109. Ibid.

110. King, "Up to His Old Stunts."

111. Ibid.

112. Ibid.

113. "*Crank*," Box Office Mojo.

114. "*Crank* (2006)," Rotten Tomatoes, accessed July 12, 2017, www.rottentomatoes.com/m/crank/.

115. Hubin, Nickels, and Blois, "*Crank: High Voltage* Production Notes."

D

1. Christopher T. Koetting, *Mind Warp! The Fantastic True Story of Roger Corman's New World Pictures* (Hailsham: Hemlock Books, 2009), 80–83.

2. Roger Corman and Jim Jerome, *How I Made a Hundred Movies in Hollywood and Never Lost a Dime* (New York: De Capo Press, 1990), 205–6.

3. Corman and Jerome, *How I Made a Hundred Movies*, 205–6

4. Roger Corman, "Playing the Game: Looking Back at *Death Race 2000*," *Death Race 2000*, special edition DVD, directed by Paul Bartel (Burbank: Buena Vista Home Entertainment, 2005).

5. Corman, "Playing the Game."

6. Corman and Jerome, *How I Made a Hundred Movies*, 205–6; "*Death Race 2000* (1975)," The Numbers, accessed July 19, 2017, www.the-numbers.com/movie/Death-Race-2000#tab=summary.

7. Corman, "Playing the Game."

8. Ibid.; Corman and Jerome, *How I Made a Hundred Movies*, 205–6.

9. Corman, "Playing the Game."

10. Corman, *How I Made a Hundred Movies*, 205–6.

11. Corman, "Playing the Game."

12. Ibid.

13. Ibid.

14. "*Death Race 2000* (1975)," The Numbers.

15. Roger Ebert, "*Death Race 2000*," RogerEbert.com, last modified April 27, 1975, www.rogerebert.com/reviews/death-race-2000.

16. "About," DeclineMovies.com, accessed July 21, 2017, www.declinemovies.com/about/.

17. "About," Decline Movies.com; Nathan Rabin, "Interview with Penelope Spheeris," The A.V. Club, last modified March 10, 1999, www.avclub.com/article/penelope-spheeris-13584; Nick Pinkerton, "Interview: Penelope Spheeris," Film Comment, last modified June 25, 2015, www.filmcomment.com/blog/interview-penelope-spheeris/.

18. Rabin, "Interview with Penelope Spheeris."

19. "About," DeclineMovies.com.

20. Rabin, "Interview with Penelope Spheeris."

21. Kory Grow, "Inside 10 Iconic *Decline of Western Civilization* Scenes," *Rolling Stone*, last modified June 16, 2015, www.rollingstone.com/movies/lists/inside-10-iconic-decline-of-western-civilization-scenes-20150616/decline-ii-sunset-strip-metalheads-dream-big-20150616.

22. Rabin, "Interview with Penelope Spheeris"; "Triple Shot of *Decline of Western Civilization* Boxed 'n' Bonus'ed!" *Goldmine*, last modified July 30, 2015, www.goldminemag.com/articles/triple-shot-decline-western-civilization-boxed-n-bonused.

23. "*The Decline of Western Civilization Part II: The Metal Years*," Drafthouse.com, accessed July 21, 2017, drafthouse.com/show/the-decline-of-western-civilization-part-ii-the-metal-years; Laura Snapes, "The Punk Director: Penelope Spheeris Revisits Her *Decline of Western Civilization* Trilogy," Pitchfork, last modified July 15, 2015, pitchfork.com/features/interview/9684-the-punk-director-penelope-spheeris-revisits-her-decline-of-western-civilization-trilogy/; Marc Spitz, "Penelope Spheeris Reissues *Decline of Western Civilization* Films," *New York Times*, last modified June 26, 2015, www.nytimes.com/2015/06/28/movies/homevideo/penelope-spheeris-reissues-decline-of-western-civilization-films.html?_r=0.

24. Rabin, "Interview with Penelope Spheeris"; "*The Decline of Western Civilization Part II: The Metal Years*," Box Office Mojo, accessed July 21, 2017, www.boxofficemojo.com/movies/?id=metalyears.htm.

25. Rabin, "Interview with Penelope Spheeris."

26. Rob Hunter, "32 Things We Learned from Neil Marshall's *Dog Soldiers* Commentary," Film School Rejects, last modified June 22, 2015, filmschoolrejects.com/32-things-we-learned-from-neil-marshalls-dog-soldiers-commentary-24d6ae302448/#.2r9alwm7e.

27. Ibid.

28. Neil Marshall, "Commentary," *Dog Soldiers*, Blu-ray, directed by Neil Marshall (Los Angeles: Shout! Factory, 2015).

29. Hunter, "32 Things."

30. Ibid.

31. Marshall, "Commentary."

32. Jonathan Bing, "*Dogs* to Bark at Bava Series," *Variety*, last modified May 29, 2002, variety.com/2002/film/markets-festivals/dogs-to-bark-at-bava-series-1117867753/.

33. Hunter, "32 Things"; "American Cinematheque Presents . . . Special Events in September," Egyptian Theatre, accessed July 12, 2017, www.egyptiantheatre.com/archive1999/2002/specialeventssept.htm.

34. Emily Buder, "An Oral History of *Donnie Darko*: Richard Kelly on the Film's Initial Failure and Ascension to Cult Classic," No Film School, last modified April 4, 2017, nofilmschool.com/2017/04/richard-kelly-interview-donnie-darko-rerelease-restoration; Phil Hoad, "How We Made *Donnie Darko*," *Guardian*, last modified December 12, 2016, www.theguardian.com/film/2016/dec/12/how-we-made-donnie-darko-jake-gyllenhaal.

35. Hoad, "How We Made *Donnie Darko*."

36. Ibid.

37. Ibid.; Adam Burnett, "'*Donnie Darko*: The Director's Cut': The Strange Afterlife of an Indie Film," *IndieWire*, last modified July 22, 2004, www.indiewire.com/2004/07/donnie-darko-the-directors-cut-the-strange-afterlife-of-an-indie-cult-film-78774/.

38. Burnett, "*Donnie Darko*: The Director's Cut'"; Gary Susman, "25 Things You May Not Know about *Donnie Darko*," Moviefone, last modified October 26, 2011, www.moviefone.com/2011/10/26/25-things-you-may-not-know-about-donnie-darko/.

39. Buder, "Oral History of *Donnie Darko*."

40. Hoad, "How We Made *Donnie Darko*."

41. Ibid.; Buder, "Oral History of *Donnie Darko*."

42. Buder, "Oral History of *Donnie Darko*"; Dave Schilling, "*Donnie Darko* Director Richard Kelly: 'Sometimes Films Need Time to Marinate," *Guardian*, last modified November 14, 2016, www.theguardian.com/film/2016/nov/14/donnie-darko-richard-kelly-donald-trump.

43. Hoad, "How We Made *Donnie Darko*."

44. Ibid.

45. Burnett, "*Donnie Darko*: The Director's Cut."

46. Buder, "Oral History of *Donnie Darko*"; Hoad, "How We Made *Donnie Darko*."

47. Buder, "Oral History of *Donnie Darko*"; Hoad, "How We Made *Donnie Darko*."

48. Burnett, "*Donnie Darko*: The Director's Cut"; Susman, "25 Things."

49. Hunter Stephenson, "Neil Marshall to Direct Hugh Jackman in *Drive*," /*Film* (blog), last modified March 20, 2008, www.slashfilm.com/neil-marshall-to-direct-hugh-jackman-in-drive; Scott Tobias, "Interview with Nicolas Winding Refn," The A.V. Club, last modified September 15, 2011, www.avclub.com/articles/nicolas-winding-refn,61788/.

50. Dennis Lim, "Cannes Q. and A.: Driving in a Noir L.A.," *ArtsBeat* (*New York Times* blog), last modified May 22, 2011, artsbeat.blogs.nytimes.com/2011/05/22/cannes-q-and-a-driving-in-a-noir-l-a/.

51. Emanuel Levy, "*Drive*: Making of Action Thriller," EmanuelLevy.com, last modified May 19, 2011, emanuellevy.com/review/drive-making-of-thriller-noir-part-one/; Tobias, "Interview with Nicolas Winding Refn."

52. Mike Fleming Jr., "FilmDistrict Drives to First Big AFM Deal," Deadline Hollywood, last modified November 3, 2010, deadline.com/2010/11/filmdistrict-drives-first-big-afm-deal-81129; Lim, "Driving in a Noir L.A."; "*Drive*," Box Office Mojo, accessed July 10, 2017, www.boxofficemojo.com/movies/?id=drive2011.htm.

53. Robert Koehler, "Nicolas Winding Refn and the Search for a Real Hero," Cinema Scope, last modified January 25, 2013, cinema-scope.com/cinema-scope-magazine/interview-nicolas-winding-refn-and-the-search-for-a-real-hero/; Tobias, "Interview with Nicolas Winding Refn."

54. Koehler, "The Search for a Real Hero"; Lim, "Driving in a Noir L.A."

55. Nicolas Winding Refn, "*Drive* without a Driver: Interview with Nicholas Winding Refn," *Drive*, Blu-ray, directed by Nicolas Winding Refn (Culver City, CA: Sony Pictures Home Entertainment, 2012).

56. Oliver Lyttelton, "Empire Big Screen '11: Nicolas Winding Refn says *Wonder Woman* a Go If He Does *Logan's Run* Right," *IndieWire*, last modified August 16, 2011, www.indiewire.com/2011/08/empire-big-screen-11-nicolas-winding-refn-says-wonder-woman-a-go-if-he-does-logans-run-right-116894/.

57. Nicolas Winding Refn. "*Drive* without a Driver."

58. "*Drive*," Box Office Mojo.

E

1. Stephen Rebello, "Grounded by *Earth Girls* and Lawyers," *American Film*, November 1988, 39.

2. Margy Rochlin, "Has Julien Temple Gone Hollywood?" *American Film*, November 1988, 34.

3. Rebello, "Grounded by *Earth Girls*."

4. Cameron Coker, "*Earth Girls Are Easy*," *Supercult Show* (blog), last modified November 5, 2013, supercultshow.wordpress.com/2013/11/05/earth-girls-are-easy/.

5. Rebello, "Grounded by *Earth Girls*."

6. Ibid.

7. Ibid.; Margot Dougherty and Michael Alexander, "*Earth Girls* Didn't Come Easy for the Unsinkable Julie Brown, but Success Has Been Topsy-Turvy," *People*, last modified June 5, 1989, people.com/archive/earth-girls-didnt-come-easy-for-the-unsinkable-julie-brown-but-success-has-been-topsy-turvy-vol-31-no-22/.

8. Rochlin, "Has Julien Temple Gone Hollywood?" 35–36.

9. Ibid.; Rebello, "Grounded by *Earth Girls*."

10. Rebello, "Grounded by *Earth Girls*."

11. Ibid.

12. Doughery and Alexander, "Unsinkable Julie Brown"; Rebello, "Grounded by *Earth Girls*."

13. Doughery and Alexander, "Unsinkable Julie Brown."

14. Rebello, "Grounded by *Earth Girls*."

15. "*Earth Girls Are Easy*," Box Office Mojo, accessed July, 21, 2017, www.boxofficemojo.com/movies/?page=weekend&id=earthgirlsareeasy.htm.

16. Colin Odell and Michelle Le Blanc, *David Lynch* (Harpenden: Kamera Books, 2007), 28.

17. K. George Godwin, "The Making of *Eraserhead*," CageyFilms, accessed July 19, 2017, www.cageyfilms.com/links/eraserhead/the-making-of-eraserhead/; Emanuel Levy, "Eraserhead: The Making of a Cult/Midnight Movie," EmanuelLevy.com, last modified January 12, 2006, emanuellevy.com/comment/eraserhead-the-making-of-a-cultmidnight-movie-1/.

18. Godwin, "Making of *Eraserhead*."

19. Ibid.; Levy, "Cult/Midnight Movie."

20. Godwin, "Making of *Eraserhead*"; Levy, "Cult/Midnight Movie"; Richard B. Woodward, "A Dark Lens on America," *New York Times*, last modified January 14, 1990, www.nytimes.com/1990/01/14/magazine/a-dark-lens-on-america.html?src=pm&pagewanted=1.

21. Godwin, "Making of *Eraserhead*"; J. Hoberman and Jonathan Rosenbaum, *Midnight Movies* (Boston: Da Capo, 1991), 215.

22. Godwin, "Making of *Eraserhead*"; Levy, "Cult/Midnight Movie."

23. Godwin, "Making of *Eraserhead*."

24. Ibid.; Woodward, "Dark Lens."

25. Sheryl Cannady, "Librarian of Congress Adds 35 Films to National Film Registry," Library of Congress, last modified December 28, 2004, www.loc.gov/item/prn-04-215/.

26. Matt Patches, "An Oral History of *Evil Dead 2*: 'We Were Like "Jackass" without Plot,'" *Hollywood Reporter*, last modified October 10, 2013, www.hollywoodreporter.com/news/evil-dead-2-oral-history-645236.

27. Matt Barone, "30 Things You Didn't Know about the *Evil Dead* Franchise," *Complex*, last modified April 4, 2014, www.complex.com/pop-culture/2013/04/evil-dead-franchise-facts/.

28. Patches, "Oral History"; Bill Warren, *The "Evil Dead" Companion* (New York: St. Martin's Griffin, 2000), 143.

29. Patches, "Oral History."

30. Ibid.

31. "Box Office/Business for *Evil Dead II* (1987)," IMDb, accessed July 21, 2017, www.imdb.com/title/tt0092991/business?ref_=tt_ql_dt_4.

32. Patches, "Oral History"; Will Murray, "Bring on the Bile: The FX of *Evil Dead II*," Essay in *Evil Dead II* Limited Edition DVD (Troy: Anchor Bay Entertainment, Inc., 2000).

33. Murray, "Bring on the Bile"; "Box Office/Business for *Evil Dead II* (1987)."

34. Patches, "Oral History."

35. Ibid.; "*Evil Dead 2*," Box Office Mojo, accessed July 21, 2017, www.boxofficemojo.com/movies/?id=evildead2.htm.

F

1. Don Stradley, "*Faster Pussycat, Kill! Kill!*: Superwomen! Belted, Buckled and Booted!" Night Flight, last modified January 5, 2017, nightflight.com/faster-pussycat-kill-kill-superwomen-belted-buckled-and-booted/.

2. Jimmy McDonough, *Big Bosoms and Square Jaws*: The Biography of Russ Meyer, King of the Sex Film (New York: Three Rivers Press, 2005), 163.

3. Ibid., 174.

4. Ibid., 163.

5. Dean Defino, "*Faster, Pussycat! Kill! Kill!*" (New York: Wallflower Press, 2014), 16.

6. Gary Morris, "Russ Meyer: An Interview," *Bright Lights Film Journal*, last modified April 1, 1996, brightlightsfilm.com/russ-meyer-interview/#.WWQ0I-mQy02.

7. David K. Frasier, *Russ Meyer—The Life and Films*: A Biography and a Comprehensive, Illustrated and Annotated Filmography and Bibliography (Jefferson: McFarland & Company, 1990), 3.

8. Morris, "Russ Meyer: An Interview."

9. Defino, "*Faster, Pussycat! Kill! Kill!*," 20.

10. Stradley, "Superwomen!"

11. Ibid.

12. Deirdra Funcheon, "*Faster Pussycat*'s Taime Downe on Sleaze Rock and 'Still Playing Every Night,'" *Miami New Times*, last modified April 20, 2015, www.miaminewtimes.com/music/faster-pussycat-s-taime-downe-on-sleaze-rock-and-still-playing-every-night-7572762.

13. Defino, "*Faster, Pussycat! Kill! Kill!*," 38.

14. Ibid.

15. Stephen Whitty, "'Pee-wee's Big Holiday' Review: I Know He Is but What Is This?" *NJ.com*, last modified March 21, 2016, www.nj.com/entertainment/index.ssf/2016/03/pee-wees_big_holiday_review_i_know_he_is_but_what.html.

16. John Waters, *Shock Value: A Tasteful Book about Bad Taste* (Philadelphia: Running Press, 2005), 192.

17. Defino, "*Faster, Pussycat! Kill! Kill!*," 31.

18. Jason Howard, "An Interview with Director Neil Breen," *Influx Magazine*, accessed July 10, 2017, influxmagazine.com/an-interview-with-director-neil-breen.

19. Ibid.

20. Josh Bell, "Local Filmmaker Neil Breen's Unique (and Terrible) Movies Earned Him a Cult Following," *Las Vegas Weekly*, last modified February 6, 2014, lasvegasweekly.com/ae/film/2014/feb/06/local-filmmaker-neil-breens-unique-and-terrible-mo/.

21. Ibid.

22. Howard, "Interview with Director Neil Breen."

23. Alan Jones, "Bad-Movie Lovers Need to Meet Neil Breen," The Dissolve, last modified June 20, 2014, thedissolve.com/features/exposition/625-bad-movie-lovers-need-to-meet-neil-breen.

24. Ibid.

25. John Naughton, "*Fight Club*: An Oral History," *Men's Health*, last modified February 2, 2016, www.menshealth.co.uk/building-muscle/fight-club-an-oral-history.

26. Sharon Waxman, *Rebels on the Backlot: Six Maverick Directors and How They Conquered the Hollywood Studio System* (New York: Harper Entertainment, 2005), 137–51; "The Blood, Sweat and Fears of *Fight Club*," *Entertainment Weekly*, last modified October 15, 1999, ew.com/article/1999/10/15/blood-sweat-fears-fight-club/.

27. Naughton, "*Fight Club:* Oral History."

28. Ibid.

29. Ibid.

30. Waxman, *Rebels on the Backlot*, 175–84; "Palahniuk: Marketing 'Fight Club' Is 'the Ultimate Absurd Joke,'" CNN.com, last modified October 29, 1999, www.cnn.com/books/news/9910/29/fight.club.author/.

31. Naughton, "*Fight Club:* Oral History."

32. Ibid.

33. "Blood, Sweat and Fears of *Fight Club*."

34. Leonard Kaldy, "Fox Holds the *Fight* to Fall," *Variety*, last modified June 17 1999, variety.com/1999/film/news/fox-holds-the-fight-to-fall-1117503196/.

35. "Blood, Sweat and Fears of *Fight Club*."; Scott Mendelson, "*Green Lantern, Fight Club*, and More Flops That Topped Their Opening Weekends," *Forbes*, last modified June 24, 2015, www.forbes.com/sites/scottmendelson/2015/06/24/green-lantern-fight-club-and-more-flops-that-topped-their-opening-weekends/#46f2a8084b32.

36. Naughton, "*Fight Club*: Oral History."

37. Mendelson, "Flops That Topped Their Opening Weekends."

38. "*Fight Club*," Box Office Mojo, accessed July 13, 2017, www.boxofficemojo.com/movies/?id=fightclub.htm.

39. Naughton, "*Fight Club*: Oral History."

40. Yannis Tzioumakis, *American Independent Cinema* (Edinburgh: Edinburgh University Press, 2006), 213–14.

41. Jack Hill, "Commentary," *Foxy Brown* DVD, directed by Jack Hill (Beverly Hills: Metro-Goldwyn-Mayer, 2001); Tzioumakis, *American Independent Cinema*, 213–14.

42. Hill, "Commentary."

43. David Walker, Andrew J. Rausch, and Chris Watson, *Reflections on Blaxploitation: Actors and Directors Speak* (Lanham: Scarecrow Press, 2009), 237.

44. Hill, "Commentary."

45. Tzioumakis, *American Independent Cinema*, 213–14.

46. Hill, "Commentary."

47. Samuel Z. Arkoff and Richard Turbo, *Flying through Hollywood by the Seat of My Pants* (New York: Birch Lane Press, 1992), 202.

48. Hill, "Commentary."

49. Erica Horhn, "*Foxy Brown* (1974)," *Women's Rights: Reflections in Popular Culture*, ed. Ann M. Savage (Santa Barbara: Greenwood, 2017), 77–78.

50. Arkoff and Turbo, *Flying through Hollywood*, 202.

51. Martin F. Norden and Madeleine A. Cahill, "Violence, Women, and Disability in Tod Browning's *Freaks* and *The Devil Doll*," *Journal of Popular Film & Television* 26, no. 2 (1998): 88.

52. Elias Savada, "The Making of *Freaks*," OlgaBaclanova.com, accessed July 9, 2017, www.olgabaclanova.com/the_making_of_freaks.htm.

53. Ibid.

54. Ibid.

55. Ibid.

56. Ibid.

57. Ibid.

58. Frank Miller, "Freaks (1932)," TCM.com, accessed July 8, 2017, www.tcm.com/tcm db/title/163/Freaks/articles.html.

59. Ibid.

60. Savada, "The Making of *Freaks*."

61. Ibid.

62. Ibid.

63. Ibid.

64. Norden and Cahill, "Violence, Women, and Disability," 89.

65. Don Sumner, "*Freaks*," in *Horror Movie Freak* (Iola, WI: Krause Publications, 2010), 184.

66. John Patterson, "The Weirdo Element," *Guardian*, last modified March 2, 2007, www.theguardian.com/film/2007/mar/02/5.

67. "And You Know This, Mannnnn: An Oral History of *Friday*," Complex, accessed July 14, 2017, www.complex.com/covers/oral-history-of-friday-20th-anniversary/.

68. Ibid.

69. Ibid.

70. Kory Grow, "Ice Cube Talks *Friday*: '"Bye Felicia" Is Such a Throwaway Line,'" *Rolling Stone*, last modified April 20, 2015, www.rollingstone.com/movies/features/ice -cube-talks-friday-bye-felicia-is-such-a-throwaway-line-20150420.

71. "Oral History of *Friday*."

72. Ibid.

73. Ibid.

74. Ibid.

75. Ibid.

76. Ibid.

77. Ibid.

78. "*Friday*," Box Office Mojo, accessed July 23, 2017, www.boxofficemojo.com/movies/?page=weekend&id=friday.htm.

79. Grow, "Ice Cube Talks *Friday*."

80. "Oral History of *Friday*."

81. Ibid.

82. Ibid.; Grow, "Ice Cube Talks *Friday*"; "Making New *Friday* Movie," TMZ, last modified April 21, 2017, www.tmz.com/2017/04/21/john-witherspoon-friday-movie-ice-cube/.

G

1. Jordan Hoffman, "*Galaxy Quest*: The Oral History," MTV.com, last modified July 23, 2014, www.mtv.com/news/1873653/galaxy-quest-oral-history/.

2. Ibid.

3. Ibid.

4. Ibid.; Michael Fleming, "Ramis Preps for Blastoff on *Galaxy Quest*," *Variety*, last modified November 1, 1998, variety.com/1998/film/news/ramis-preps-for-blastoff-on -galaxy-quest-1117488013/.

5. Ibid.

6. Ibid.

7. Ibid.

8. Ibid.

9. Ibid.

10. Kate Erbland, "20 Things You Might Not Know about *Galaxy Quest*," Mental Floss, last modified December 16, 2014, mentalfloss.com/article/60540/20-things-you-might -not-know-about-galaxy-quest.

11. "*Galaxy Quest*," Box Office Mojo, accessed July 13, 2017, www.boxofficemojo.com/ movies/?id=galaxyquest.htm.

12. Erbland, "20 Things"; Hoffman, "*Galaxy Quest*: Oral History."

13. Trent Moore, "Ouch! Fans Vote *Galaxy Quest* a Better Trek Movie Than *Into Darkness*," SyfyWire, last modified August 13, 2013, www.syfy.com/syfywire/ouch-fans-vote -galaxy-quest-better-trek-movie-darkness.

14. Fujiwara, Chris, "*Ganja and Hess*," TCM.com, accessed July 7, 2017, www.tcm.com/ this-month/article/382629%7C443275/Ganja-and-Hess.html; Brandon Harris, "Bill Gunn Surfaces at BAM," *Filmmaker Magazine*, last modified March 31, 2010, filmmakermagazine .com/6596-bill-gunn-surfaces-at-bam/#.WW_weumQy00.

15. Fujiwara, "*Ganja and Hess*"; Sergio, "Bill Gunn's Controversial and Rarely Seen Film 'Stop' to Finally See the Light of Day (Once Some Minor Problems Are Cleared)," *IndieWire*, last modified April 4, 2014, www.indiewire.com/2014/04/bill-gunns-controver sial-and-rarely-seen-film-stop-to-finally-see-the-light-of-day-once-some-minor-problems -are-cleared-160785/.

16. Fujiwara, "*Ganja and Hess*"; "The Blood of the Thing," *Ganja & Hess*, Blu-ray, directed by Bill Gunn (New York: Kino Lorber Films, 2012).

17. Fujiwara, "*Ganja and Hess*"; "The Blood of the Thing."

18. Phil Nobile, Jr., "*Ganja & Hess*: The Edge of Extinction," Birth. Movies. Death., last modified February 24, 2017, birthmoviesdeath.com/2017/02/24/ganja-hess-the-edge-of -extinction.

19. Fujiwara, "*Ganja and Hess*."

20. Fujiwara, "*Ganja and Hess*"; Brandon Harris, "Blood Couple: On Bill Gunn and Spike Lee," *n+1*, accessed July 19, 2017, nplusonemag.com/issue-22/reviews/blood-couple/.

21. "The Blood of the Thing,"; Brandon Harris, "Blood Couple."

22. Fujiwara, "*Ganja and Hess*."

23. Ibid.

24. "Making of *Ghost World*," *Ghost World*, DVD, directed by Terry Zwigoff (Beverly Hills: MGM Home Entertainment, 2002).

25. Ibid.

26. Steve Mandich, "Daniel Clowes on *Ghost World*," *Scram Magazine*, last modified June 15, 2001, scrammagazine.com/daniel-clowes-speaks; Tom Spurgeon and Michael Dean, *We Told You So*: *Comics as Art* (Seattle: Fantagraphic Books, 2016), 470.

27. "Making of *Ghost World*."

28. Ibid.

29. Ibid.

30. Emily Hall, "The Humanity of Failure: An Interview with Dan Clowes," The Stranger, last modified July 19, 2001, www.thestranger.com/seattle/the-humanity-of -failure/Content?oid=8069.

31. Hall, "Humanity of Failure."

32. Mandich, "Clowes on *Ghost World*."

33. "*Ghost World* (2001)," Rotten Tomatoes, accessed July 13, 2017, www.rottentoma toes.com/m/ghost_world/.

34. Spurgeon and Dean, *We Told You So*.

35. "*Ghost World*," Box Office Mojo, accessed July 13, 2017, www.boxofficemojo.com/ movies/?id=ghostworld.htm.

36. Joe Dante and Michael Finnell, "Commentary," *Gremlins 2*, special edition DVD, directed by Joe Dante (Burbank: Warner Home Video, 2002).

37. Ibid.

38. Drew Mackie, "25 Things You May Not Know about the *Gremlins* Movies," *People*, last modified June 12, 2015, people.com/movies/gremlins-2-turns-25-trivia-about-the -new-batch-film/.

39. "*Gremlins 2: The New Batch* (1990)," TCM.com, accessed July 22, 2017, www.tcm .com/tcmdb/title/76995/Gremlins-2-The-New-Batch/misc-notes.html.

40. Mackie, "25 Things."

41. "*Gremlins 2: The New Batch* (1990)," TCM.com.

42. Mackie, "25 Things."

43. "*Gremlins 2: The New Batch*," Box Office Mojo, accessed July 22, 2017, www.boxof ficemojo.com/movies/?id=gremlins2.htm.

44. David Crow, "Why *Gremlins 2* Is Better Than the Original," Den of Geek!, last modi- fied June 15, 2017, www.denofgeek.com/us/movies/gremlins/233074/why-gremlins -2-is-better-than-the-original.

45. Alex Zalben and Josh Horowitz, "The *Gremlins* Reboot Will Be 'a Completely Differ- ent Direction,'" MTV.com, last modified April 22, 2015, www.mtv.com/news/2141254/ chris-columbus-gremlins-reboot/.

46. Rich Johnston, "Why Bill Murray Was a Jerk to Zach Galligan on 'Nothing Lasts For- ever' and the Latest on *Gremlins 3*," Bleeding Cool, last modified December 4, 2016, www .bleedingcool.com/2016/12/04/why-bill-murray-was-a-jerk-to-zach-galligan-on-nothing -lasts-forever-and-the-latest-on-gremlins-3/.

47. "The Documentary," Grey Gardens Online, accessed July 20, 2017, greygardenson- line.com/the-documentary/; Robb Brawn, "Maysles Interview Pt 1," My Grey Gardens, accessed July 20, 2017, www.mygreygardens.com/gpage5.html.

48. "The Documentary," Grey Gardens Online.

49. Ibid.

50. Ibid.

51. Ibid.; Brawn, "Maysles Interview."

52. "The Documentary," Grey Gardens Online.

53. Ibid.

54. Ibid.; Brawn, "Maysles Interview."

55. "The Documentary," Grey Gardens Online.

56. Ibid.

57. Ibid.

58. David Coleman, "The Cult of *Grey Gardens*," Advocate, last modified March 4, 2009, www.advocate.com/arts-entertainment/television/2009/03/04/cult-grey-gardens.

H

1. Nick Dawson, *Being Hal Ashby: Life of a Hollywood Rebel* (Lexington: University Press of Kentucky, 2009), 120.

2. Ibid.

3. Ibid.

4. Ibid.

5. James A. Davidson, *Hal Ashby and the Making of "Harold and Maude"* (Jefferson: McFarland, 2016), 70.

6. Dawson, *Being Hal Ashby*, 122.

7. "Harold and Maude," American Film Institute, accessed July 12, 2017, www.afi.com/members/catalog/DetailView.aspx?s=&Movie=54046.

8. Davidson, *Making "Harold and Maude,"* 117.

9. Tara Aquino, "10 Perfectly Paired Facts about *Harold and Maude*," Mental Floss, last modified October 6, 2015, mentalfloss.com/article/69546/10-perfectly-paired-facts-about-harold-and-maude.

10. Nick Dawson and Charles B. Mulvehill, "Commentary," *Harold and Maude*, Blu-ray, directed by Hal Ashby (New York: The Criterion Collection, 2012).

11. Ibid.

12. Jason Bailey, "10 Cult Classics the Critics Got Dead Wrong," Flavorwire, last modified April 16, 2013, flavorwire.com/385192/10-cult-classics-the-critics-got-dead-wrong/6.

13. Adam D'Arpino, "11 Classic Movies That Were Box Office Bombs," MTV.com, last modified September 26, 2013, www.mtv.com/news/2817018/classic-movies-box-office-bombs/.

14. Troy Patterson, "Why *Harold and Maude* Is One of the Top 10 Cult Movies," *Entertainment Weekly*, last modified May 20, 2003, ew.com/article/2003/05/20/why-harold-and-maude-one-top-10-cult-movies/; Phil Nugent and Andrew Osborne, "The 50 Greatest Cult Movies of All Time," Nerve, accessed July 12, 2017, www.nerve.com/movies/the-fifty-greatest-cult-movies-of-all-time.

15. Nina Metz, "*Harold and Maude* Aging Gracefully," *Chicago Tribune*, last modified September 4, 2009, articles.chicagotribune.com/2009-09-04/entertainment/0909030532_1_harold-and-maude-ashby-two-films.

16. Davidson, *Making "Harold and Maude,"* 192.

17. Metz, "Aging Gracefully."

18. Adam Markovitz, "*Heathers*: An Oral History," *Entertainment Weekly*, last modified April 4, 2014, ew.com/article/2014/04/04/heathers-oral-history/.

19. Paul Rowlands, "Daniel Waters on *Heathers* (Part 1 of 2)," Money into Light, accessed July 17, 2017, www.money-into-light.com/2016/05/daniel-waters-on-heathers-part-1-of-2.html.

20. Markovitz, "Oral History."

21. Ibid.

22. Ibid.; Rowlands, "Waters on *Heathers*."

23. Markovitz, "Oral History."

24. Ibid.

25. "Box Office/Business for *Heathers* (1988)," IMDb, accessed July 21, 2017, www.imdb.com/title/tt0097493/business?ref_=tt_ql_dt_4.

26. Markovitz, "Oral History."

27. Ibid.

28. Ibid.

29. "Box Office/Business for *Heathers* (1988)."

30. Markovitz, "Oral History.

31. Ibid.; "*Heathers*," Box Office Mojo, accessed July 21, 2017, www.boxofficemojo.com/movies/?id=heathers.htm.

32. Markovitz, "Oral History."

33. Ibid.

34. Stephanie Marcus, "*Heathers* Reboot Series Is Coming to TV Land, but There's a Big Twist," *Huffington Post*, last modified March 16, 2016, www.huffingtonpost.com/entry/heathers-reboot-series-tv-land_us_56e997f2e4b0b25c918421c6.

35. Markovitz, "Oral History."

36. "*Heathers* to Get Musical Treatment," BBC News, last modified March 12, 2009, news.bbc.co.uk/2/hi/entertainment/7940156.stm; Adam Hetrick, "School's Out: *Heathers: The Musical* to Close Off-Broadway," *Playbill*, last modified July 10, 2014, http://www.playbill.com/article/schools-out-heathers-the-musical-to-close-off-broadway-com-324382.

37. Laura Nix, "Whether You Like It or Not: The Story of Hedwig," *Hedwig and the Angry Inch*, DVD, directed by John Cameron Mitchell (Los Angeles: New Line Home Entertainment, 2003).

38. Ibid.

39. David Gordon, "Word for Word: How *Hedwig and the Angry Inch* Came to Life Onstage," Theater Mania, last modified March 28, 2014, www.theatermania.com/new-york-city-theater/news/03-2014/word-for-word-how-hedwig-and-the-angry-inch-came-t_68022.html; Jennifer Wood, "Gender Bender: An Oral History of *Hedwig and the Angry Inch*," *Rolling Stone*, last modified May 7, 2014, www.rollingstone.com/movies/news/gender-bender-an-oral-history-of-hedwig-and-the-angry-inch-20140507; David Fricke, "Sex & Drag & Rock & Roll," *Rolling Stone*, last modified December 10, 1998, www.rollingstone.com/music/features/sex-drag-rock-roll-19981210.

40. Wood, "Gender Bender."

41. Nate von Zumwalt, "#TBT: *Hedwig and the Angry Inch*," Sundance Institute, last modified March 12, 2015, www.sundance.org/blogs/artist-spotlight/tbt—john-cameron-mitchells-hedwig-and-the-angry-inch; Nix, "Story of Hedwig."

42. Nix, "Story of Hedwig."

43. Ibid.

44. Ibid.

45. Scott Tobias, "*Hedwig and the Angry Inch*," The A.V. Club, last modified November 5, 2009, www.avclub.com/article/emhedwig-and-the-angry-inchem-35004; von Zumwalt, "#TBT."

46. Robert Simonson, "*Hedwig* Film Wins Awards at Sundance Festival," *Playbill*, last modified January 29, 2001, www.playbill.com/article/hedwig-film-wins-awards-at-sundance-festival-com-94636; von Zumwalt, "#TBT."

47. Dave Jones, "Hitchcock and Hedwig," *UC Davis University News*, last modified February 23, 2009, www.ucdavis.edu/news/hitchcock-and-hedwig/.

48. "*Hedwig and the Angry Inch*," Box Office Mojo, accessed July 13, 2017, www.boxofficemojo.com/movies/?id=hedwigandtheangryinch.htm.

49. Gordon, "Word for Word."

50. Adam Sternbergh, "Three Easy Steps to Comedy Stardom," *New York Magazine*, last modified July 15, 2007, nymag.com/news/features/34738/; Whitney Pastorek, "Andy Samberg Gets Stupid in *Hot Rod*," *Entertainment Weekly*, last modified July 23, 2007, ew.com/article/2007/07/23/andy-samberg-gets-stupid-hot-rod/.

51. Sternbergh, "Three Easy Steps"; Alexis Swerdloff, "Man-Child in the Promised Land," *Paper*, last modified September 27, 2007, www.papermag.com/man-child-in-the-promised-land-1425341599.html.

52. "*Hot Rod* (2007)," The Numbers, accessed July 11, 2017, www.the-numbers.com/movie/Hot-Rod#tab=summary.

53. Alex Pappademas, "The Next Sandler?" *GQ*, last modified September 14, 2006, www.gq.com/story/andy-samberg-snl-comedian.

54. Helen Earnshaw, "Exclusive *Hot Rod* Interview," Female First, last modified January 29, 2008, www.femalefirst.co.uk/celebrity_interviews/Andy+Samberg-47422-page2.html.

55. Sternbergh, "Three Easy Steps."

56. Swerdloff, "Man-Child in the Promised Land."

57. "*Hot Rod* (2007)," The Numbers.

58. Ibid.

I

1. Douglas C. Lyons, "Blacks and the New TV Season," *Ebony*, October 1990, 108.

2. Lesli Goff, "*I'm Gonna Git You Sucka* Review," *Empire*, last modified October 14, 2015, www.empireonline.com/movies/m-gonna-git-sucka/review/.

3. "Hollywood Shuffle," Box Office Mojo, accessed July 21, 2017, www.boxofficemojo.com/movies/?id=hollywoodshuffle.htm.

4. Margena A. Christian, "The First Family of Comedy," *Ebony*, April 2011, 91.

5. Amy Harrington, "Keenan Ivory Wayans," *Archive of American Television*, last modified July 8, 2013, www.emmytvlegends.org/interviews/people/keenen-ivory-wayans; "Don't Mess with Eddie Murphy's Pal Keenen Ivory Wayans: He's Making His Own Movie, Sucka," *People*, December 12, 1988, 185.

6. Sergio, "Comedy Cult Classic *I'm Gonna Git You Sucka* Coming to Blu-Ray Feb 2016," *IndieWire*, last modified October 23, 2015, www.indiewire.com/2015/10/comedy-cult-classic-im-gonna-git-you-sucka-coming-to-blu-ray-feb-2016-141214/.

7. Goff, "*I'm Gonna Git You Sucka* Review."

8. Lyons, "Blacks and the New TV Season"; Harrington, "Keenan Ivory Wayans."

9. Sergio, "Comedy Cult Classic"; Harrington, "Keenan Ivory Wayans."

10. "*I'm Gonna Git You Sucka*," Box Office Mojo, accessed July 21, 2017, www.boxofficemojo.com/movies/?page=main&id=imgonnagityousucka.htm.

11. Douglas Brode, "*Invasion of the Body Snatchers* (1956)," in *Fantastic Planets, Forbidden Zones, and Lost Continents: The 100 Greatest Science-Fiction Films* (Austin: University of Texas Press, 2015), 87.

12. Mark Mancini, "10 Facts about *Invasion of the Body Snatchers*," Mental Floss, last modified February 5, 2016, mentalfloss.com/article/74987/10-facts-about-invasion-body-snatchers.

13. Ibid.

14. Al LaValley, "*Invasion of the Body Snatchers*" (New Brunswick: Rutgers University Press, 1989), 25.

15. Christine Cornea, "'So Bad It's Good': Critical Humor in Science Fiction Cinema," in *The Last Laugh: Strange Humors of Cinema*, ed. Murray Pomerance (Detroit: Wayne State University Press, 2013), 79.

16. Mancini, "10 Facts."

17. Brode, "*Invasion of the Body Snatchers*," 88.

18. Mancini, "10 Facts."

19. Ibid.

20. "25 Films Added to National Registry," *New York Times*, last modified November 15, 1994, www.nytimes.com/1994/11/15/movies/25-films-added-to-national-registry.html?mcubz=2.

21. Richard Corliss, "1950 Sci-Fi Movies—*Invasion of the Body Snatchers*," *Time*, last modified December 11, 2008, entertainment.time.com/2008/12/12/top-ten1950s-sci-fi-movies/slide/invasion-of-the-body-snatchers-1956-3/.

22. "The Making of *The Iron Giant*," Warner Bros., accessed July 13, 2017, web.archive.org/web/20060321055611/http://movies.warnerbros.com/irongiant/cmp/production.html.

23. "Interview with Richard Bazley," Animation Artist, accessed July 13, 2017, www.animationartist.com/2000/Interviews/Animators/Richard_Bazley/RBazley.html.

24. "Making of *The Iron Giant*."

25. Louis Black, "More McCanlies, Texas," *Austin Chronicle*, last modified September 19, 2003, www.austinchronicle.com/gyrobase/Issue/story?oid=oid%3A178259.

26. "Making of *The Iron Giant*."

27. Ibid.

28. Bob Miller, "Lean, Mean Fighting Machine: How Brad Bird made *The Iron Giant*," Animation World Network, accessed July 13, 2017, www.awn.com/mag/issue4.05/4.05pages/millerbird.php3.

29. Miller, "Lean, Mean Fighting Machine"; Devan Coggan, "*The Iron Giant*: Director Brad Bird on Building a Robot with a Soul," *Entertainment Weekly*, last modified August 29, 2016, ew.com/article/2016/08/29/iron-giant-director-brad-bird/; Peter Hartlaub, "*The Iron Giant* Creators: Then and Now," *San Francisco Chronicle*, last modified September 22, 2016, www.sfchronicle.com/movies/article/The-Iron-Giant-creators-Then-and-now-9238075.php.

30. Miller "Lean, Mean Fighting Machine"; Peter Hartlaub, "Oral History of *The Iron Giant*: From Failure to Modern Classic," *San Francisco Chronicle*, last modified September 22, 2016, www.sfchronicle.com/movies/article/Oral-History-of-The-Iron-Giant-From-9237968.php.

31. Hartlaub, "Oral History"; Coggan, "*Iron Giant*."

32. Hartlaub, "Oral History."

33. Rick DeMott, "*The Iron Giant* to Air on Cartoon Network and TNT," Animation World Network, last modified January 3, 2000, www.awn.com/news/iron-giant-air-cartoon-network-and-tnt.

34. Leigh Godfrey, "*Iron Giant* Marathon on Cartoon Network," Animation World Network, last modified July 2, 2002, www.awn.com/news/iron-giant-marathon-cartoon-network; Andy Patrizio, "*The Iron Giant*: Special Edition," IGN, last modified November 2, 2004, dvd.ign.com/articles/562/562914p1.html.

J

1. Garin Pirnia, "12 Rock 'n' Roll Facts about *Josie and the Pussycats*," Mental Floss, last modified April 12, 2016, mentalfloss.com/article/78479/12-rock-n-roll-facts-about-josie-and-pussycats.

2. Nathan Rabin, "Totally Jerking Case File #147: *Josie and the Pussycats*," The A.V. Club, last modified September 30, 2009, www.avclub.com/article/totally-jerking-case-file-147-ijosie-and-the-pussy-33511.

3. Pirnia, "12 Rock 'n' Roll Facts"; Rabin, "Totally Jerking Case File."

4. Rachel Abramowtiz, "Who Will Buy 'Josie's' Big Joke?" *Los Angeles Times*, last modified April 9, 2001, articles.latimes.com/2001/apr/09/entertainment/ca-48691.

5. "*Josie and the Pussycats* (2001)," Rotten Tomatoes, accessed July 13, 2017, www.rottentomatoes.com/m/josie_and_the_pussycats/.

6. Abramowtiz, "'Josie's' Big Joke"; Pirnia, "12 Rock 'n' Roll Facts"; Rabin, "Totally Jerking Case File."

7. Pirnia, "12 Rock 'n' Roll Facts"; "*Josie and the Pussycats*," Box Office Mojo, accessed July 13, 2017, www.boxofficemojo.com/movies/?id=josieandthepussycats.htm.

8. Pirnia, "12 Rock 'n' Roll Facts"; Alex McLevy, "On the *Josie and the Pussycats* Soundtrack, Reality and Bullshit Are Inseparable," The A.V. Club, last modified November 8, 2016, www.avclub.com/article/josie-and-pussycats-soundtrack-reality-and-bullshi-244484.

9. Rabin, "Totally Jerking Case File."

K

1. "The Making of *Killer Klowns*," *Killer Klowns from Outer Space*, DVD, directed by Stephen Chiodo (Beverly Hills: Metro-Goldwyn-Mayer, 2001).

2. Kevin Carr, "22 Things We Learned from the *Killer Klowns from Outer Space* commentary," Film School Rejects, last modified October 17, 2013, filmschoolrejects.com/22-things-we-learned-from-the-killer-klowns-from-outer-space-commentary-8d6843cfc668/#.oe04jx7ir.

3. Carr, "22 Things."

4. Heather Buckley, "Exclusive: The Chiodo Brothers Talk *Killer Klowns*, Movie Making, and More!" Dread Central, last modified July 3, 2014, www.dreadcentral.com/news/54547/exclusive-the-chiodo-brothers-talk-killer-klowns-movie-making-and-more/; Mandl Nowitz, "B-List Movie of the Month: *Killer Klowns from Outer Space*," Den of Geek!, last modified November 6, 2012, www.denofgeek.com/us/movies/killer-klowns-from-outer-space/22531/b-list-movie-of-the-month-killer-klowns-from-outer-space.

5. "Box Office/Business for *Killer Klowns from Outer Space* (1988)," IMDb, accessed July 22, 2017, www.imdb.com/title/tt0095444/business?ref_=tt_ql_dt_4.

6. Buckley, "Chiodo Brothers Talk *Killer Klowns*."

7. "The Making of *Killer Klowns*."

8. Buckley, "Chiodo Brothers Talk *Killer Klowns*"; Stephen Chiodo, Edward Chiodo, and Charles Chiodo, "Commentary," *Killer Klowns from Outer Space* DVD, directed by Stephen Chiodo (Beverly Hills: Metro-Goldwyn-Mayer, 2001).

9. "*Killer Klowns from Outer Space* Film Locations," Movie-Locations.com, accessed July 22, 2017, www.movie-locations.com/movies/k/killerklowns.html#.WW1nr4jyu03.

10. Ibid.

11. Chiodo, Chiodo, and Chiodo, "Commentary."

12. Carr, "22 Things."

13. Ibid.

14. "Box Office/Business for *Killer Klowns from Outer Space*."

15. Nowitz, "*Killer Klowns from Outer Space*."

16. Adam Green and Joe Lynch, "The Movie Crypt: Episode 148: Stephen Chiodo," GeekNation, accessed July 17, 2017, geeknation.com/podcasts/the-movie-crypt-ep-148-stephen-chiodo/.

L

1. Roger Corman and Jim Jerome, *How I Made a Hundred Movies in Hollywood and Never Lost a Dime* (Boston: Da Capo Press, 1998), 63.

2. Ibid.

3. Fred Olen Ray, *The New Poverty Row: Independent Filmmakers as Distributors* (Jefferson: McFarland, 1991), 29.

4. Tom Weaver, *Return of the B Science Fiction and Horror Movie Makers: Writers, Producers, Directors, Actors, Moguls and Makeup* (Jefferson: McFarland, 1999), 387.

5. Ray, *The New Poverty Row*, 28.

6. Corman and Jerome, *How I Made a Hundred Movies*, 63.

7. Weaver, *Return of the B Science Fiction*, 388.

8. Ibid.

9. Corman and Jerome, *How I Made a Hundred Movies*, 67.

10. Ibid.

11. Ibid., 66–67.

12. Weaver, *Return of the B Science Fiction*, 389.

13. Larry Blamire, "Obey the Lost Skeleton!" *The Lost Skeleton of Cadavra*, DVD, directed by Larry Blamire (Culver City: Sony Pictures, 2004).

14. Robin, "Robin's Underrated Gems: *The Lost Skeleton of Cadavra* (2001)," The Back Row, last modified January 6, 2011, the-back-row.com/blog/2011/01/06/robins-underrated-gems-the-lost-skeleton-of-cadavra-2001/.

15. Blamire "Obey the Lost Skeleton!"

16. Robin, "Underrated Gems"; Ed Gonzalez and Jeremiah Kipp, "*The Lost Skeleton of Cadavra*," *Slant Magazine*, last modified June 9, 2004, www.slantmagazine.com/dvd/review/the-lost-skeleton-of-cadavra.

17. Blamire, "Obey the Lost Skeleton!"

18. Ibid.

19. Ibid; Robin, "Underrated Gems."

20. Blamire, "Obey the Lost Skeleton!"

21. Ibid.

22. Ibid.

23. Gonzalez and Kipp, "*Lost Skeleton.*"

24. Sam Wasson, "A Conversation with Bo Harwood," Criterion.com, last modified August 20, 2014, www.criterion.com/current/posts/3272-a-conversation-with-bo-harwood.

25. Peter Rinaldi, "'Goodbye, John': On John Cassavetes' Swan Song, *Love Streams* (1984)," *Bright Lights Film Journal*, last modified August 14, 2014, brightlightsfilm.com/goodbye-john-john-cassavetes-swan-song-love-streams-1984/#.WW-j84jyu00; Scott Tobias, "*Love Streams*," The Dissolve, last modified August 18, 2014, thedissolve.com/reviews/1007-love-streams/.

26. Wasson, "Conversation with Bo Harwood"; Dennis Lim, "*Love Streams*: A Fitful Flow," Criterion.com, last modified August 12, 2014, www.criterion.com/current/posts/3261-love-streams-a-fitful-flow.

27. Rinaldi, "'Goodbye, John.'"

28. Tobias, "*Love Streams.*"

29. "Prizes & Honours 1984," Berlinale.de, accessed July 21, 2017, www.berlinale.de/en/archiv/jahresarchive/1984/03_preistr_ger_1984/03_Preistraeger_1984.html.

30. Luke Bonanno, "*Love Streams*," DVDizzy.com, last modified September 14, 2014, www.dvdizzy.com/lovestreams.html.

31. Bill Curran, "1984: John Cassavetes' Farewell *Love Streams*," The Film Experience, last modified August 17, 2016, thefilmexperience.net/blog/2016/8/17/1984-john-cassavetes-farewell-love-streams.html; "*Love Streams*—John Cassavetes," Criterion.com, accessed July 21, 2017, www.criterion.com/films/28032-love-streams.

M

1. Daniel Griffith, Benjamin Solovey, and Rich Zunch, "Hands: The Fate of *Manos*," *Manos: The Hands of Fate*, Blu-ray, directed by Harold P. Warren (Romulus: Synapse Films, 2015).

2. Ibid.

3. Ibid.

4. Dalton Ross, "The Worst Movie Ever Made: The Long, Strange Journey of *Manos: The Hands of Fate*," *Entertainment Weekly*, last modified June 6, 2005, ew.com/article/2005/06/06/worst-movie-ever-made/.

5. Griffith, Solovey, and Zunch, "Hands: The Fate of *Manos*."

6. Ibid.

7. Ibid.

8. Ross, "Worst Movie Ever."

9. Griffith, Solovey, and Zunch, "Hands: The Fate of *Manos*."

10. Ibid.

11. Ibid.

12. Ibid.

13. Ibid.

14. Ibid.

15. Ibid.

16. Ibid.

17. Chris Morgan, "*Manos: The Hands of Fate*, or 'In Summary, *Manos, the* . . . *Hands of Fate*,'" in *The Comic Galaxy of Mystery Science Theater 3000: Twelve Classic Episodes and the Movies They Lampoon* (Jefferson: McFarland, 2015), 52–53.

18. Sean Hutchinson, "Ben Solovey on Restoring *Manos: The Hands of Fate*, the Worst Movie Ever," Inverse, last modified November 4, 2015, www.inverse.com/article/7714 -ben-solovey-on-restoring-manos-the-hands-of-fate-the-worst-movie-ever.

19. "Only the Strong Survive," *Mean Girls*, Blu-ray, directed by Mark Waters (Los Angeles: Paramount Home Media Distribution, 2009).

20. Kyle Buchanan, "*Mean Girls* Director Mark Waters Spills 10 Juicy Stories, 10 Years Later," Vulture, last modified April 30, 2014, www.vulture.com/2014/02/mean-girls -director-spills-10-juicy-stories.html.

21. Ibid.

22. Ibid.

23. David Fleischer, "Reel Toronto: *Mean Girls*," Torontoist, last modified September 9, 2008, torontoist.com/2008/09/reel_toronto_mean_girls/.

24. Buchanan "*Mean Girls* Director Mark Waters."

25. "*Mean Girls*," Box Office Mojo, accessed July 12, 2017. www.boxofficemojo.com/ movies/?id=meangirls.htm.

26. Buchanan, "*Mean Girls* Director Mark Waters."

27. Andrew Gans, "Tina Fey's *Mean Girls* Musical Will Make Premiere at Washington's National," *Playbill*, last modified March 21, 2017, www.playbill.com/article/tina-feys -mean-girls-musical-will-make-world-premiere-at-washingtons-national.

28. Daniel Fierman, "*Memento* Takes Film Noir in a New Direction," *Entertainment Weekly*, last modified March 30, 2001, ew.com/article/2001/03/30/memento-takes-film -noir-new-direction/; Anthony Kaufman, "Mindgames: Christopher Nolan Remembers *Memento*," *IndieWire*, last modified December 4, 2009, www.indiewire.com/2009/12/ decade-christopher-nolan-on-memento-55676/; Renfreu Neff and Daniel Argent,

"Remembering Where It All Began: Christopher Nolan on *Memento*," *Creative Screenwriting*, last modified July 20, 2015, creativescreenwriting.com/remembering-where-it-all -began-christopher-nolan-on-memento/.

29. James Mottram, *The Making of "Memento"* (New York: Faber, 2002), 176; Neff and Argent, "Remembering *Memento*."

30. Mottram, *Making of "Memento*," 177; Kaufman, "Mindgames."

31. Mottram, *Making of "Memento*," 106.

32. Ibid., 107–8.

33. Ibid., 125.

34. Ibid., 151–52.

35. Ibid., 125.

36. Fierman, "*Memento* Takes Noir in New Direction"; Mottram, *Making of Memento*, 62–64.

37. Fierman, "*Memento* Takes Noir in New Direction"; Scott Tobias, "Christopher Nolan," The A.V. Club, last modified June 5, 2002, www.avclub.com/article/christopher -nolan-13769.

38. Kaufman, "Mindgames."

39. "*Memento*," Box Office Mojo, accessed July 13, 2017, www.boxofficemojo.com/ movies/?page=main&id=memento.htm.

40. Mottram, *Making of "Memento*," 58.

41. For example: James Berardinelli, "Rewinding 2001: The Year in Film," Reelviews, last modified December 31, 2001, preview.reelviews.net/comment/123101.html; Eugene Hernandez, "BIZ: indieWIRE's Top Ten Lists for 2001," *IndieWire*, last modified December 21, 2001, www.indiewire.com/2001/12/biz-indiewires-top-ten-lists-for-2001-80607/.

42. "*Friends for Eternity*: The Making of *Miami Connection*," *Miami Connection*, Blu-ray, directed by Woo-sang Park (Austin: Drafthouse Films, 2012).

43. Mike Ayers, "*Miami Connection* Goes from Flop to Fame," CNN.com, last modified November 8, 2012, www.cnn.com/2012/11/08/showbiz/movies/miami-connection-film -ayers/index.html; Clark Collis, "*Miami Connection*: Ninjas, Cocaine, and Synth-Rock!" *Entertainment Weekly*, last modified November 9, 2012, ew.com/article/2012/11/09/mi- ami-connection/; Erin Sullivan, "Orlando's Grandmaster Y. K. Kim Just Wanted to Make a Good Taekwondo Movie," *Orlando Weekly*, last modified December 11, 2012, www.or landoweekly.com/orlando/orlandos-grandmaster-yk-kim-just-wanted-to-make-a-good -taekwondo-movie/Content?oid=2246254.

44. Ayers, "Flop to Fame,"; Collis, "Ninjas, Cocaine, and Synth-Rock."

45. Collis, "Ninjas, Cocaine, and Synth-Rock."

46. Ibid.; Sullivan, "Grandmaster Y. K. Kim."

47. Sullivan, "Grandmaster Y. K. Kim."

48. Collis, "Ninjas, Cocaine, and Synth-Rock."

49. Ayers, "Flop to Fame."

50. Collis, "Ninjas, Cocaine, and Synth-Rock"; Jay Boyar, "If You Can't Say Something Nice," *Orlando Sentinel*, last modified August 26, 1988, articles.orlandosentinel.com/1988 -08-26/lifestyle/0060300142_1_miami-connection-floridians-kim; Roger Hurlburt, "Dumb Ninja Saga Will Help You Kick the Habit," *Sun-Sentinel* (Broward County, FL), September 19, 1988, 7D.

51. "*Friends for Eternity*."

52. Ibid.

53. Ayers, "Flop to Fame"; Collis, "Ninjas, Cocaine, and Synth-Rock."

54. Ayers, "Flop to Fame"; Collis, "Ninjas, Cocaine, and Synth-Rock"; Sullivan, "Grand- master Y. K. Kim."

55. Abel Ferrara, "Interview with Director Abel Ferrara," *Ms .45* Blu-ray, directed by Abel Ferrara (Austin: Drafthouse Films, 2014).

56. Jack McIntyre, "Interview with Creative Consultant Jack McIntyre," *Ms .45* Blu-ray, Directed by Abel Ferrara (Austin: Drafthouse Films, 2014).

57. Ferrara, "Interview with Abel Ferrara."

58. Ibid.

59. Ibid.

60. McIntyre, "Interview with Jack McIntyre."

61. Joe Delia, "Interview with Composer Joe Delia," *Ms .45*, Blu-ray, directed by Abel Ferrara (Austin: Drafthouse Films, 2014).

62. Ferrara, "Interview with Abel Ferrara."

63. Ibid.

64. Ibid.

65. Ibid.

66. Peter M. Bracke, "The Cut List," DVDFile.com, accessed July 19, 2017, web.archive .org/web/20061019072200/http://www.dvdfile.com/software/cut_list/index_2.html.

67. Alexandra Heller-Nicholas, "*Ms. 45*" (New York: Columbia University Press, 2017), 121.

68. Jon Stobezki, "*Ms .45* Returns to Theaters This Friday," *Drafthouse Films* (blog), last modified December 12, 2013, drafthousefilms.com/blog/entry/ms-.45-returns-to-theaters -this-friday.

N

1. Brian Wilson, "George A. Romero," Senses of Cinema, last modified February 2007, sensesofcinema.com/2007/great-directors/romero/.

2. John Russo, *The Complete "Night of the Living Dead" Filmbook* (New York: Harmony Books, 1985), 7.

3. Dan Cziraky, "Oh What a 'Night': Looking Back at the *Living Dead*," *Cinefantastique*, last modified September 17, 2010, cinefantastiqueonline.com/2010/09/oh-what-a -'night'-looking-back-at-the-'living-dead'.

4. Ibid.

5. Richard Harland Smith and Jeff Stafford, "*Night of the Living Dead* (1968)," TCM .com, accessed July 11, 2017, www.tcm.com/tcmdb/title/84925/Night-of-the-Living -Dead/articles.html.

6. Ibid.

7. Kate Erbland, "26 Things We Learned from the *Night of the Living Dead* Commentary," Film School Rejects, last modified October 11, 2012, filmschoolrejects.com/26-things -we-learned-from-the-night-of-the-living-dead-commentary-1f0ef17cda1e/.

8. Ibid.

9. Ibid.

10. Jason Paul Collum, *Assault of the Killer B's: Interviews with 20 Cult Film Actresses* (Jefferson: McFarland, 2004), 3.

11. Don Sumner, "*Night of the Living Dead*," in *Horror Movie Freak* (Iola: Krause Publications, 2010), 233.

12. Jason Bailey, "10 of Hollywood's Most Surprising and Heartening Success Stories," Flavorwire, last modified August 7, 2013, flavorwire.com/408030/10-of-hollywoods-most -surprising-and-heartening-success-stories/view-all.

13. Alex Carter, "*Night of the Living Dead* and Its Dozens of Follow-Ups," Den of Geek!, last modified February 4, 2017, www.denofgeek.com/us/movies/night-of-the-living -dead/245597/night-of-the-living-dead-and-its-dozens-of-follow-ups.

14. Clark Collis, "*Night of the Living Dead*: How a 42-Year-Old Zombie Movie Refuses to Die," *Entertainment Weekly*, last modified October 28, 2010, ew.com/article/2010/10/28/walking-dead-zombies-night-of-the-living-dead/.

15. Sumner, "*Night of the Living Dead.*"

16. Kristy Puchko, "21 Things You Didn't Know about the *Nightmare before Christmas*," Mental Floss, last modified December 10, 2015, mentalfloss.com/article/60723/21-things-you-didnt-know-about-nightmare-christmas.

17. Frank Thompson, *Tim Burton's "Nightmare before Christmas"* (New York: Hyperion, 1993), 8.

18. Ibid.

19. Ibid.

20. Ibid., 11.

21. Puchko, "21 Things You Didn't Know."

22. Ibid.

23. Ibid.

24. Ibid.

25. Richard Rickitt, *Special Effects: The History and Technique* (New York: Billboard Books, 2000), 159–60.

26. Puchko, "21 Things You Didn't Know."

27. Ibid.

28. Scott Collura, "*The Nightmare before Christmas* 3-D: 13 Years and Three Dimensions Later," IGN, last modified October 20, 2006, www.ign.com/articles/2006/10/20/the-nightmare-before-christmas-3-d-13-years-and-three-dimensions-later.

29. "Tim Burton's *The Nightmare before Christmas*," Box Office Mojo, accessed July 11, 2017, www.boxofficemojo.com/movies/?id=nightmarebeforechristmas.htm.

30. Puchko, "21 Things You Didn't Know."

31. Hunter Miller, "The Haunted Mansion Is Going Full *Nightmare before Christmas* This Year," PopCulture.com, last modified August 23, 2016, popculture.com/2016/08/23/the-haunted-mansion-is-going-full-nightmare-before-christmas-thi/.

O

1. Willy Staley, "Mike Judge, the Bard of Suck," *New York Times*, last modified April 13, 2017, www.nytimes.com/2017/04/13/magazine/mike-judge-the-bard-of-suck.html?_r=0.

2. Staley, "Bard of Suck"; Roger Cormier, "20 Things You Might Not Know about *Office Space*," Mental Floss, last modified October 27, 2015, mentalfloss.com/article/61686/20-things-you-might-not-know-about-office-space.

3. Cormier, "20 Things"; Dennis Lim, "Men at Work: Finding Humor in Missteps," *New York Times*, last modified August 27, 2009, www.nytimes.com/2009/08/30/movies/30lim.html?pagewanted=all.

4. Lim, "Men at Work."

5. Cormier, "20 Things."

6. "The Fax of Life," *Entertainment Weekly*, last modified May 23, 2003, ew.com/article/2003/05/23/fax-life/.

7. Lewis Beale, "Mr. Beavis Goes to Work," *New York Daily News*, last modified February 21, 1999, www.nydailynews.com/mr-beavis-work-irreverent-animator-s-newest-target-corporate-america-live-action-film-office-space-article-1.839280; Hunter Stephenson, "The Mike Judge Interview: Part 2," /Film, last modified September 9, 2009, www.slashfilm.com/the-mike-judge-interview-part-2-gene-simmons-and-ben-affleck-in-extract-corporate-product-hilarity-in-idiocracy-and-the-kamikaze-futures-of-beavis-butt-head/.

8. Cormier, "20 Things."

9. "Fax of Life."

10. Daniel Fierman, "Mike Judge Takes on Live Action," *Entertainment Weekly*, last modified February 19, 1999, ew.com/article/1999/02/19/mike-judge-takes-live-action/; "*Office Space*," Box Office Mojo, accessed July 13, 2017, www.boxofficemojo.com/movies/?id=officespace.htm.

11. Cormier, "20 Things."

12. Ibid.

13. Brian Boone, "Why We Never Got to See *Office Space 2*," Looper, accessed July 13, 2017, www.looper.com/46912/never-got-see-office-space-2/.

14. Maya Rhodan, "Ted Cruz Spoofs *Office Space* in New Clinton Attack Ad," *Time*, last modified February 12, 2016, time.com/4219372/ted-cruz-office-space-ad-hillary-clinton/.

P

1. Meriah Doty, "Paul Reubens Turns 60: Pee-wee Herman's Origins Revealed," Yahoo! Movies, last modified August 27, 2012, www.yahoo.com/movies/bp/origins-pee-wee -herman-171518961.html; Ruth La Ferla, "The Once and Future Pee-wee," *New York Times*, last modified May 20, 2007, www.nytimes.com/2007/05/20/fashion/20peewee.html; Paul Rudd, "Paul Reubens," *Interview Magazine*, last modified October 27, 2009, www.interview magazine.com/culture/paul-reubens/#_.

2. La Ferla, "Once and Future Pee-wee."

3. Dave Itzkoff, "I, Pee-wee," *New York Times*, last modified November 7, 2004, www .nytimes.com/2004/11/07/arts/television/i-peewee.html.

4. Stacy Conradt, "15 Fun Facts about *Pee-wee's Big Adventure*," Mental Floss, last modified August 7, 2015, mentalfloss.com/article/66919/15-fun-facts-about-pee-wees -big-adventure.

5. Ibid.

6. Mark Salisbury and Tim Burton, *Burton on Burton* (London: Faber and Faber, 2008), 47.

7. "Box Office/Business for *Pee-wee's Big Adventure* (1985)," IMDb, accessed July 21, 2017, www.imdb.com/title/tt0089791/business?ref_=tt_ql_dt_4.

8. Jared Cowan, "Retracing the Steps of *Pee-wee's Big Adventure*," *LA Weekly*, last modified July 20, 2015, www.laweekly.com/slideshow/retracing-the-steps-of-pee-wee-s-big -adventure-5822291.

9. Salisbury and Burton, *Burton on Burton*, 49.

10. "Box Office/Business for *Pee-wee's Big Adventure* (1985)."

11. Kyle Anderson, "Danny Elfman on *Music from the Films of Tim Burton*, Pee-Wee and Panic," *Entertainment Weekly*, last modified July 1, 2015, ew.com/article/2015/07/01/ danny-elfman-tim-burton/.

12. Conradt, "15 Fun Facts."

13. Salisbury and Burton, *Burton on Burton*, 50.

14. Itzkoff, "I, Pee-wee."

15. John Duvoli, "'Cult' Films Spell Success for Movie-Maker," *Evening News* (Newburgh, NY), February 26, 1984, 10AA.

16. Erik Piepenburg, "Just So You Know: 'John Dies at the End,'" *ArtsBeat* (*New York Times* blog), last modified January 24, 2013, artsbeat.blogs.nytimes.com/2013/01/24/just-so-you-know-john-dies-at-the-end/?_r=0; Peter, "Month of Horror Prevues: *Phantasm*," Furious Cinema, last modified May 18, 2016, www.furiouscinema.com/mad-hell-horror -prevues-phantasm/.

17. Duvoli "'Cult' Films Spell Success"; Gina McIntyre, "Happy Birthday, Tall Man! *Phantasm* Turns 30," *Los Angeles Times*, last modified October 16, 2009, herocomplex .latimes.com/uncategorized/phantasm/; Dave Pace, "Q&A: Don Coscarelli on 'John Dies' & Independent Filmmaking for 30+ Years," Fangoria, last modified April 11, 2013, www.fangoria.com/new/qa-don-coscarelli-on-john-dies-independent-filmmaking-for -30-years/.

18. Pace, "Q&A: Don Coscarelli."

19. McIntyre, "Happy Birthday, Tall Man!"; Nate Yapp, "Reggie Bannister (*Phantasm*) Interview," Classic-Horror.com, last modified November 25, 2008, classic-horror.com/ newsreel/reggie_bannister_phantasm_interview.

20. "Box Office/Business for *Phantasm* (1979)," IMDb, accessed July 20, 2017, www .imdb.com/title/tt0079714/business?ref_=tt_ql_dt_4.

21. Marc Savlov, "Sphere of Influence," *Austin Chronicle*, last modified March 31, 2000, www.austinchronicle.com/screens/2000-03-31/76665/.

22. McIntyre, "Happy Birthday, Tall Man!"; Todd Gilchrist, "Exclusive Interview: Don Coscarelli," IGN, last modified April 10, 2007, www.ign.com/articles/2007/04/10/ exclusive-interview-don-coscarelli.

23. Savlov, "Sphere of Influence."

24. Ibid.

25. McIntyre, "Happy Birthday, Tall Man!"

26. Duvoli, "'Cult' Films Spell Success"; Savlov, "Sphere of Influence."

27. "*Phantasm*," Box Office Mojo, accessed July 20, 2017, www.boxofficemojo.com/ movies/?page=main&id=phantasm.htm.

28. Don Kaye, "*Phantom of the Paradise*: Horror's Ultimate Rock Opera?" PaulWilliams .co.uk, accessed July 19, 2017, www.paulwilliamscouk.plus.com/shiver.html.

29. Ibid.; "Production Schedule and Locations," The Swan Archives, accessed July 19, 2017, www.swanarchives.org/Production.asp.

30. Kaye, "*Phantom of the Paradise*."

31. Ibid.

32. "*Phantom of the Paradise*: De Palma's Cult Horror Musical That Got Its Second Chance to Shine," Cinephilia & Beyond, accessed July 19, 2017, cinephiliabeyond.org/phantom -paradise-de-palmas-cult-horror-musical-got-second-chance-shine/.

33. Kaye, "*Phantom of the Paradise*."

34. Ibid.

35. Doug Carlson, "Why Winnipeg? The 1975 *Phantom* Phenomenon," Phantomof theParadise.ca, accessed July 19, 2017, www.phantomoftheparadise.ca/why2.html.

36. "The 47th Academy Awards | 1975," Oscars.org, accessed July 19. 2017, www.os cars.org/oscars/ceremonies/1975; "Winners & Nominees 1975," Golden Globe Awards, accessed July 19, 2017, www.goldenglobes.com/winners-nominees/1975.

37. Carlson, "Why Winnipeg?"

38. Ibid.

39. "The Numbers Game," *Filmmaker Magazine*, accessed July 13, 2017, filmmakermaga zine.com/archives/issues/summer1998/numbers_game.php#.WWgPdIjyu01.

40. Ibid.

41. Ibid.

42. Anthony Kaufman, "An Interview with Darren Aronofsky and Sean Gullette of *Pi*," *IndieWire*, last modified January 21, 1998, www.indiewire.com/1998/01/an-interview -with-darren-aronofsky-and-sean-gullette-of-pi-83179/.

43. "Numbers Game"; Jeffrey M. Anderson, "Interview with Darren Aronofsky," Com bustible Celluloid, last modified June 25, 1998, www.combustiblecelluloid.com/daint .shtml.

44. Anthony Kaufman, "The Whiz Kid: Darren Aronofsky, Writer/Director of *Pi*," *IndieWire*, last modified July 10, 1998, www.indiewire.com/1998/07/the-whiz-kid-darren-aronofsky-writerdirector-of-pi-82736/.

45. "Numbers Game."

46. Kaufman, "Interview with Aronofsky and Gullette."

47. "Numbers Game."

48. Anderson, "Interview with Aronofsky"; Peter T. Chattaway, "Interview: Darren Aronofsky (*Pi*, 1998)," *FilmChat* (blog), last modified August 7, 1998, www.patheos.com/blogs/filmchat/1998/08/interview-darren-aronofsky-%CF%80-1998.html.

49. "Numbers Game."

50. Kaufman, "Whiz Kid."

51. "Numbers Game."

52. Kaufman, "Whiz Kid."

53. "*Pi*," Box Office Mojo, accessed July 13, 2017, www.boxofficemojo.com/movies/?id=pi.htm.

54. Cameron Beyl, "Darren Aronofsky's *Pi*," The Directors Series, last modified May 23, 2017, directorsseries.net/2017/05/23/darren-aronofskys-pi-1998/; Marc Graser, "SightSound to Netcast Franchise pix," *Variety*, last modified March 6, 2000, variety.com/2000/digital/news/sightsound-to-netcast-franchise-pix-1117779110/.

55. Emanuel Levy, "Waters, John: Pink Flamingos—Cult Midnight Movie," Emanuel Levy.com, last modified June 13, 2014, emanuellevy.com/review/featured-review/john-waters-revisited-pink-flamingos-cult-midnight-movie/; Gus Van Sant, "Timeless Trash," *Advocate*, no. 731 (April 15, 1997): 41.

56. Levy, "Cult Midnight Movie"; Alison Nastasi, "10 Low-Budget Films That Became Unexpected Hits," FlavorWire, last modified November 19, 2012, flavorwire.com/348021/10-low-budget-films-that-became-unexpected-hits.

57. Levy, "Cult Midnight Movie."

58. Ibid.

59. Ibid.; Frances Milstead, Kevin Heffernan, and Steve Yeager, *My Son Divine* (New York: Alyson Books, 2001), 66–67.

60. Levy, "Cult Midnight Movie."

61. Milstead, Heffernan, and Yeager, *My Son Divine*, 69–70.

62. Levy, "Cult Midnight Movie"; Milstead, Heffernan, and Yeager, *My Son Divine*, 69–71.

63. "Pink Flamingos," Refused-Classification.com, accessed July 19, 2017, refused-classification.com/censorship/films/p.html#pink-flamingos.

64. "Pink Flamingos," *Los Angeles Times*, accessed July 17, 2017, www.latimes.com/entertainment/lat-pinkflaming_e8g1eugw20080423122900-photo.html.

65. Levy, "Cult Midnight Movie."

66. Rudolph Grey, *Nightmare of Ecstasy: The Life and Art of Edward D. Wood, Jr.* (Portland: Feral House, 1992), 75–77.

67. Matt Singer, "The Awful, Wonderful Integrity of *Plan 9 from Outer Space*," The Dissolve, last modified June 17, 2014, thedissolve.com/features/movie-of-the-week/619-the-awful-wonderful-integrity-of-plan-9-from-outer/.

68. Grey, *Nightmare of Ecstasy*, 76.

69. Richard Harland Smith, "*Plan Nine from Outer Space* (1959)," TCM.com, accessed July 9, 2017, www.tcm.com/tcmdb/title/86783/Plan-9-from-Outer-Space/articles.html.

70. Grey, *Nightmare of Ecstasy*, 78.

71. Danny Peary, *Cult Movies* (New York: Delacorte Press, 1981), 266–70.

72. Mark Mancini, "10 Out-of-This-World Facts about *Plan 9 from Outer Space*," Mental Floss, last modified April 19, 2016, mentalfloss.com/article/78785/10-out-world-facts-about-plan-9-outer-space.

73. Ibid.

74. Matt Patches, "How *Plan 9 from Outer Space* Earned, and Lost, the Title of Worst Movie of All Time," The Dissolve, last modified June 19, 2014, thedissolve.com/features/movie-of-the-week/623-how-plan-9-from-outer-space-earned-and-lost-the-ti/.

75. Mancini, "10 Out-of-This-World Facts about *Plan 9*."

76. Sean Hutchinson, "16 Totally Awesome Facts about *Point Break*," Mental Floss, last modified January 13, 2016, mentalfloss.com/article/62432/16-totally-awesome-facts-about-point-break.

77. Ibid.

78. Ibid.

79. Adam K. Raymond, "25 Bodacious Facts about the Original *Point Break*," Yahoo! Movies, last modified December 25, 2015, www.yahoo.com/movies/25-bodacious-facts-about-the-original-1326424954028086.html.

80. Ibid.

81. Ibid.

82. Robbie Collin, "Tough Guys Have Feelings Too: The Power of *Point Break*," Telegraph, last modified February 2, 2016, www.telegraph.co.uk/film/point-break-2015/keanu-reeves-kathryn-bigelow-making-of-original/.

83. "*Point Break* Surf Training," *Entertainment Weekly*, last modified July 26, 1991, ew.com/article/1991/07/26/point-break-surf-training/.

84. "Box Office/Business for *Point Break* (1991)," IMDb.com, accessed July 22, 2017, www.imdb.com/title/tt0102685/business?ref_=tt_ql_dt_4.

85. "*Point Break*," Box Office Mojo, accessed July 22, 2017, www.boxofficemojo.com/movies/?id=pointbreak.htm; "Point Break (1991)," The Numbers, accessed July 22, 2017, www.the-numbers.com/movie/Point-Break#tab=summary.

86. Collin, "Tough Guys Have Feelings."

87. Jerry Fink, "*Point Break Live!* Wipes Out in Vegas," *Las Vegas Sun*, last modified October 9, 2008, lasvegassun.com/blogs/culture/2008/oct/09/point-break-live-wipes-out-vegas/.

88. Nathan Rabin, "*Pootie Tang*: A Look Back with Director Louis C. K.," The A.V. Club, last modified February 25, 2004, www.avclub.com/article/pootie-tang-a-look-back-with-director-louis-ck-13856; Scott Tobias, "*Pootie Tang*," The A.V. Club, last modified July 23, 2009, www.avclub.com/article/ipootie-tangi-30745.

89. Rabin, "*Pootie Tang*: A Look Back."

90. Ibid.

91. Ibid.

92. Ibid.

93. Ibid.

94. Ibid.

95. Ibid.

96. Ibid.

97. Ibid.

98. Ibid.

99. Ibid.

100. Marc Maron, "Louis C.K. Part 1," *WTF with Marc Maron*, Podcast audio, October 4, 2010, www.wtfpod.com/podcast/episodes/episode_111_-_louis_ck_part_1.

101. Rabin, "*Pootie Tang*: A Look Back"; Scott Raab, "Louis C.K.: The ESQ+A," *Esquire*, last modified May 23, 2011, www.esquire.com/entertainment/interviews/a10009/louis-ck-interview-0611/.

102. Tobias, "*Pootie Tang*."

103. Jason Bailey, *"Pulp Fiction": The Complete Story of Quentin Tarantino's Masterpiece* (Minneapolis: Voyageur Press, 2013), 32.

104. Ibid.

105. Ibid., 33.

106. Ibid.

107. Ibid., 33–34.

108. Mark Seal, "Cinema Tarantino: The Making of *Pulp Fiction*," *Vanity Fair*, last modified February 13, 2013, www.vanityfair.com/hollywood/2013/03/making-of-pulp -fiction-oral-history.

109. Bailey, *"Pulp Fiction*," 35.

110. Dale Sherman, "Chapter 10—Let's Get into Character: The Making of *Pulp Fiction*," in *Quentin Tarantino FAQ: Everything Left to Know about the Original Reservoir Dog* (Milwaukee: Applause Theatre & Cinema Books, 2015), 129.

111. Bailey, "*Pulp Fiction*," 80–81.

112. Ibid., 81.

113. Seal, "Cinema Tarantino."

114. Ibid.

115. Janet Maslin, "*Pulp Fiction*: Quentin Tarantino's Wild Ride on Life's Dangerous Road," *New York Times*, last modified September 23, 1994, www.nytimes.com/movie/ review?_r=1&res=9B0DE5DA143AF930A1575AC0A962958260&oref=slogin.

116. Glen Chapman, "Looking Back at Quentin Tarantino's *Pulp Fiction*," Den of Geek!, last modified November 7, 2011, www.denofgeek.com/movies/18296/looking-back-at -quentin-tarantinos-pulp-fiction.

117. Liz Calvario, "*Pulp Fiction*: The Inside Story of How Quentin Tarantino's Masterpiece Narrowly Avoided Censorship," *IndieWire*, last modified May 5, 2016, www .indiewire.com/2016/05/pulp-fiction-the-inside-story-of-how-quentin-tarantinos-master piece-narrowly-avoided-censorship-291191/.

118. Seal, "Cinema Tarantino."

119. Mike Cecchini, "*The Punisher*: The Bloody Legacy of Marvel's First Superhero Movie," Den of Geek!, last modified March 20, 2016, www.denofgeek.com/us/movies/ the-punisher/246961/the-punisher-the-bloody-legacy-of-marvels-first-superhero-movie.

120. "Lions Gate starting on *The Punisher* 2," Moviehole, last modified February 27, 2004, www.moviehole.net/20044077lions-gate-starting-on-the-punisher-2.

121. Eric Vespe, "AICN Exclusive: Thomas Jane Dropping Out of *Punisher* 2?!?," *Ain't It Cool News*, last modified May 15, 2007, www.aintitcool.com/node/32673.

122. Nicole Powers, "Lexi Alexander on Punisher's Behind the Scenes War Zone," SuicideGirls.com, last modified on December 4, 2008, www.suicidegirls.com/members/ nicole_powers/blog/2680069/lexi-alexander-on-punishers-behind-the-scenes-war-zone/.

123. Umberto Gonzalez, "Exclusive Scoop: We Know Who the New Punisher Is!" Latino Review, last modified July 21, 2007, www.latinoreview.com/news.php?id=2452.

124. Steve Weintraub, "Exclusive: Ray Stevenson Talks *Punisher*: *War Zone* to Help Promote the DVD and Blu-ray," Collider, last modified March 15, 2009, collider.com/ exclusive-ray-stevenson-talks-punisher-war-zone-to-help-promote-the-dvd-and-bluray/.

125. Lexi Alexander, "*Punisher: War Zone, How Did This Get Made?*" Podcast audio, October 3, 2011, www.earwolf.com/episode/punisher-war-zone/.

126. Ibid.

127. Edward Douglas, "Exclusive: Lexi Alexander on *Punisher: War Zone*," Superhero Hype, last modified December 3, 2008, www.superherohype.com/features/97853-exclu sive-lexi-alexander-on-punisher-war-zone.

128. Nix, "*Punisher*: War Zone Release Date Moved to December," Beyond Hollywood, last modified April 9, 2008, www.beyondhollywood.com/punisher-war-zone-release -date-moved-to-december/.

129. "Lexi Alexander on Shooting *Punisher*," Superhero Hype, last modified December 29, 2007, www.superherohype.com/features/95495-lexi-alexander-on-shooting-punisher.

130. "*Punisher: War Zone*," Box Office Mojo, accessed July 11, 2017, www.boxoffice mojo.com/movies/?id=punisher2.htm.

131. Lexi Alexander, "*Punisher: War Zone.*"

132. R. Emmet Sweeney, "Mad Men: *Putney Swope* (1969)," *Streamline: The Filmstruck Blog*, last modified March 28, 2017, streamline.filmstruck.com/2017/03/28/mad-men -putney-swope-1969/.

133. Ibid.

134. Ibid.

135. Michael Koresky, "Eclipse Series 33: Up All Night with Robert Downey Sr.," Criterion.com, last modified May 22, 2012, www.criterion.com/current/posts/2304-eclipse -series-33-up-all-night-with-robert-downey-sr.

136. Shipra Harbola Gupta, "Hey Filmmakers, Robert Downey Sr. Has Some Lessons for You," *IndieWire*, last modified December 7, 2014, www.indiewire.com/2014/12/hey -filmmakers-robert-downey-sr-has-some-lessons-for-you-67183/.

137. Ibid.

138. Ibid.

139. Richard Metzger, "*Putney Swope*: Most Under-Rated Cult Film of the 1960s?" Dangerous Minds, last modified December 1, 2014, dangerousminds.net/comments/put ney_swope_most_under_rated_cult_film.

140. Mike Pearl, "Revisiting *Putney Swope* with Robert Downey, Sr.," Vice, last modified December 5, 2014, www.vice.com/en_us/article/znw7k8/revisiting-putney-swope-with -robert-downey-sr; Nick Alderink, "A Quick Peek: *Putney Swope*—Things Are Changing," Michigan Theater, accessed July 12, 2017, www.michtheater.org/2017/04/10/a-quick -peek-putney-swope-things-are-changing/.

141. Edward Davis, "'What the Fuck Is Going On?' Paul Thomas Anderson & Robert Downey Sr. Talk the Criterion Box Set 'Up All Night With…,'" *IndieWire*, last modified June 4, 2012, www.indiewire.com/2012/06/what-the-fuck-is-going-on-paul-thomas-anderson -robert-downey-sr-talk-the-criterion-box-set-up-all-night-with-109948/.

142. Rick Karr, "Robert Downey Sr., Underground and Off the Cuff," NPR.org, last modified September 26, 2008, www.npr.org/templates/story/story.php?storyId=94926945.

143. Ibid.; Mike Pearl, "Revisiting *Putney Swope*."

R

1. "Stuart Gordon," *Re-Animator* Films, accessed July 21, 2017, www.re-animatorfilms .com/Bios/Gordon.html.

2. Meredith Brody, "We Killed 'Em in Chicago," *Film Comment*, February 1987, 74; Jim Hemphill, "Horror Master Stuart Gordon Talks *Re-Animator*, Lovecraft and MPAA Ratings," *Paste*, last modified July 21, 2015, www.pastemagazine.com/articles/2015/07/hor ror-master-stuart-gordon-talks-re-animator-love.html; Keith Phipps, "With *Re-Animator*, Stuart Gordon Pushed Horror and Comedy over the Line and Beyond," The Dissolve, last modified October 14, 2014, thedissolve.com/features/movie-of-the-week/785-with-re -animator-stuart-gordon-pushed-horror-and-c/.

3. Brody, "We Killed 'Em in Chicago," 74; Hemphill, "Horror Master Stuart Gordon."

4. Brody, "We Killed 'Em in Chicago," 74; "Stuart Gordon," *Re-Animator* Films.

5. Brody, "We Killed 'Em in Chicago," 74; "*Re-Animator*," Box Office Mojo, accessed July 21, 2017, www.boxofficemojo.com/movies/?id=reanimator.htm.

6. Brody, "We Killed 'Em in Chicago," 74; Hemphill, "Horror Master Stuart Gordon."

7. Brody, "We Killed 'Em in Chicago," 74.

8. Hemphill, "Horror Master Stuart Gordon."

9. Brody, "We Killed 'Em in Chicago," 74.

10. "*Re-Animator*," Box Office Mojo.

11. Roger Ebert, "*Re-Animator*," RogerEbert.com, last modified October 18, 1985, www.rogerebert.com/reviews/re-animator-1985.

12. Wheeler Winston Dixon, *A History of Horror* (New Brunswick: Rutgers University Press, 2010), 165.

13. Janet Maslin, "Screen: Stuart Gordon Directs *Re-Animator*," *New York Times*, last modified October 18, 1985, www.nytimes.com/movie/review?res=9E04EED91E39F93BA25753C1A963948260&mcubz=2.

14. Phipps, "With *Re-Animator*."

15. John Squires, "*House of Re-Animator*: The Presidential Sequel That Never Happened," Bloody Disgusting, last modified November 8, 2016, bloody-disgusting.com/news/3413822/house-re-animator-presidential-sequel-never-happened/.

16. Gina McIntyre, "*Re-Animator the Musical* Pumps New Life into Cult Favorite," *Los Angeles Times*, last modified May 3, 2011, herocomplex.latimes.com/stage/re-animator-the-musical-pumps-new-life-into-cult-favorite/.

17. Elizabeth Kramer, "'Reefer Madness' is real—and now a musical," *Naples Daily News*, last modified April 26, 2017, https://www.naplesnews.com/story/entertainment/theater/2017/04/26/reefer-madness-real---and-now-musical/100841502/.

18. Alden Ford, "Watching *Reefer Madness* for the First Time," Splitsider, last modified April 6, 2011, splitsider.com/2011/04/watching-reefer-madness-for-the-first-time/.

19. Brian Hannan, "This Joint Is Smokin': *Reefer Madness*," in *Coming Back to a Theater Near You: A History of Hollywood Reissues, 1914–2014* (Jefferson: McFarland, 2016), 262–63.

20. Eric Schaefer, *"Bold! Daring! Shocking! True!" A History of Exploitation Films, 1919–1959* (Durham: Duke University Press, 1999), 1–2.

21. Frank DiGiacomo, "The Lost Tycoons," *Vanity Fair*, last modified February 4, 2009, www.vanityfair.com/news/2009/03/new-line200903.

22. Alex Cox, "The Repo Code," essay in *Repo Man* Blu-ray, directed by Alex Cox (New York: The Criterion Collection, 2013); Alex Cox, "*Repo Man*," AlexCox.com, accessed July 21, 2017, www.alexcox.com/dir_repoman.htm.

23. Ibid.

24. Jonathan Wacks, "Repossessed," *Repo Man*, Blu-ray, directed by Alex Cox (New York: The Criterion Collection, 2013).

25. Cox, "The Repo Code."

26. Sam McPheeters, "*Repo Man*: A Lattice of Coincidence," Criterion.com, last modified April 16, 2013, www.criterion.com/current/posts/2736-repo-man-a-lattice-of-coincidence.

27. Wacks, "Repossessed."

28. Ibid.

29. Abhimanyu Das, "The Weirdest Things You Never Knew about the Making of *Repo Man*," Io9, last modified December 19, 2014, io9.gizmodo.com/the-weirdest-things-you-never-knew-about-the-making-of-1673079559.

30. McPheeters, "Lattice of Coincidence."

31. Das, "The Making of *Repo Man*."

32. Ibid.

33. Ibid.

34. Ibid.

35. Kate Fitzpatrick, "Harry Dean Stanton Is a *Repo Man*," *Brattle Theatre Film Notes* (blog), last modified September 12, 2014, www.brattleblog.brattlefilm.org/2014/09/12/harry-dean-stanton-is-a-repo-man-2358/#.WXJfJemQy00.

36. Das, "The Making of *Repo Man*."

37. McPheeters, "Lattice of Coincidence."

38. Alan Siegel, "*Road House* Is Paved with Good Intentions," The Ringer, last modified June 22, 2017, theringer.com/road-house-interview-rowdy-herrington-9f0894b29082.

39. Ibid.

40. Roger Cormier, "15 Painless Facts about *Road House*," Mental Floss, last modified May 23, 2015, mentalfloss.com/article/64233/15-painless-facts-about-road-house; Stacy Jenel Smith, "Sexy Swayze: On the Set of His First Film since *Dirty Dancing*," *Los Angeles Times*, last modified July 24, 1988, articles.latimes.com/1988-07-24/entertainment/ca-10319_1_dirty-dancing.

41. Will Harris, "Kelly Lynch on *Magic City*, John Hughes, and Playing a Drag King," The A.V. Club, last modified October 15, 2012, www.avclub.com/article/kelly-lynch-on-imagic-cityi-john-hughes-and-playin-86567.

42. Jennifer M. Wood, "The Best Fight Scenes from *Road House*," *Men's Journal*, accessed July 16, 2017, www.mensjournal.com/magazine/the-best-fight-scenes-from-road-house-20140520#ixzz3ajFq6SWi.

43. Mandi Bierly, "Patrick Swayze's *The Time of My Life*: 10 Memorable Stories," *Entertainment Weekly*, last modified September 29, 2009, ew.com/article/2009/09/29/patrick-swayze-memoir-time-of-my-life/.

44. "*Road House*," Box Office Mojo, accessed July 22, 2017, www.boxofficemojo.com/movies/?id=roadhouse.htm.

45. Siegel, "*Road House*"; "Every Patrick Swayze Film—and What It Made at the Box Office," *Datablog* (*Guardian* blog), accessed July 22, 2017, www.theguardian.com/news/datablog/2009/sep/15/patrick-swayze-films-box-office-gross.

46. Dennis Hunt, "*Road House* Looks like a Hit," *Los Angeles Times*, last modified January 18, 1990, articles.latimes.com/1990-01-18/entertainment/ca-48_1_road-house.

47. Kenneth Jones, "Mullets and Martial Arts: *Road House*, Inspired by the Movie, Starts Off-Bway Dec. 9," *Playbill*, last modified December 9, 2003, www.playbill.com/article/mullets-and-martial-arts-road-house-inspired-by-the-movie-starts-off-bway-dec-9-com-116774.

48. Cormier, "15 Painless Facts."

49. Justin Kroll, "Nick Cassavetes to Write, Direct Ronda Rousey's *Road House*," *Variety*, last modified October 12, 2015, variety.com/2015/film/news/nick-cassavetes-road-house-ronda-rousey-1201616027/.

50. Damon Martin, "Ronda Rousey: *Road House* Filming Pushed Back until at Least May," *Fox Sports*, last modified February 17, 2016, www.foxsports.com/ufc/story/ufc-ronda-rousey-road-house-filming-pushed-back-until-at-least-may-021716.

51. "Behind the Scenes of *The Rocketeer*," *Entertainment Weekly*, last modified July 12, 1991, ew.com/article/1991/07/12/behind-scenes-rocketeer/.

52. John B. Cooke and Sam Gafford, "Of Hollywood & Heroes," Comic Book Artist, accessed July 15, 2017, twomorrows.com/comicbookartist/articles/15stevens.html; Haley Tomsheck, "Looking Back at *The Rocketeer* 20 Years Later," AMC.com, accessed July 15, 2017, www.amc.com/talk/2011/07/looking-back-at-2.

53. Cooke and Gafford, "Of Hollywood & Heroes"; Tomsheck, "Looking Back at *The Rocketeer*."

54. William Gatevackes, "History of the Comic Book Film: The Rock-a-Who!?!" FilmBuffOnline, last modified August 24, 2012, www.filmbuffonline.com/FBOLNewsreel/wordpress/2012/08/24/history-of-the-comic-book-film-the-rock-a-who/; Jim Korkis, "The

Return of *The Rocketeer*," MousePlanet, last modified May 25, 2011, www.mouseplanet
.com/9630/The_Return_of_The_Rocketeer.

55. Cooke and Gafford, "Of Hollywood & Heroes."

56. Korkis, "Return of *The Rocketeer*."

57. Mike Cecchini, "*The Rocketeer*: An Adventure Movie Out of Time," Den of Geek!,
last modified Jun 23, 2017, www.denofgeek.com/us/movies/the-rocketeer/17378/the
-rocketeer-an-adventure-movie-out-of-time.

58. Tomsheck, "Looking back at *The Rocketeer*."

59. Korkis, "Return of *The Rocketeer*."

60. Daniel Schweiger, "*Rocketeer*," *Cinefantastique* 22, no. 1 (1991): 16–28.

61. Cooke and Gafford, "Of Hollywood & Heroes."

62. "Behind the Scenes," *Entertainment Weekly*.

63. Schweiger, "*Rocketeer*."

64. "Behind the Scenes," *Entertainment Weekly*.

65. Marcy Magiera, "Disney Adds to Tie-Ins," *Advertising Age*, February 11, 1991, 6.

66. Pat H. Broeske, "Summer Movie Toys and Product Spin-Offs," *Entertainment Weekly*,
last modified May 31, 1991, ew.com/article/1991/05/31/summer-movie-toys-and-prod
uct-spin-offs/.

67. Tomsheck, "Looking Back at *The Rocketeer*."

68. "*The Rocketeer*," Box Office Mojo, accessed July 23, 2017, www.boxofficemojo.com/
movies/?page=weekend&id=rocketeer.htm.

69. Borys Kit, "*Rocketeer* 20th Anniversary Reunion Causes a Stir in Hollywood,"
Hollywood Reporter, last modified June 23, 2011, www.hollywoodreporter.com/heat
-vision/rocketeer-20th-anniversary-reunion-a-205040?utm_source=feedburner&utm_
medium=feed&utm_campaign=Feed%3A+THRComicCon+%28The+Hollywood+Repor
ter+-+Heat+Vision%29.

70. Marianne Paluso, "Rediscovering a Classic: *The Rocketeer*," NerdHQ, last modified
August 6, 2012, www.nerdhq.com/rediscovering-a-classic-the-rocketeer/.

71. Borys Kit, "*The Rocketeer* Reboot in the Works from Disney," *Hollywood Reporter*,
last modified July 28, 2016, www.hollywoodreporter.com/heat-vision/rocketeer-disney
-movie-reboot-works-915037; Dave McNary, "Disney Working on *Rocketeer* Reboot," *Variety*, last modified July 28, 2016, variety.com/2016/film/news/the-rocketeer-sequel-reboot
-disney-1201825707/.

72. "Back to School: A Retrospective," *Rock 'n' Roll High School*, Rock On Edition DVD,
directed by Allan Arkush (Burbank: Buena Vista Home Entertainment, 2005).

73. Ibid.

74. Ibid.

75. Ibid.

76. Ibid.

77. Ibid.

78. Ibid.; Scott Carlson, "*Rock 'n' Roll High School*," PopMatters, last modified March 13,
2006, www.popmatters.com/review/rock-n-roll-high-school-dvd/.

79. David Konow, "*Rock 'n' Roll High School* Reunion: Do Your Parents Know You're
Ramones?" Consequence of Sound, last modified September 6, 2016, consequenceofsound
.net/2016/09/rock-n-roll-high-school-do-your-parents-know-youre-ramones/.

80. Ibid.

81. "Back to School."

82. Ibid.

83. Ibid.

84. Konow, "*Rock 'n' Roll High School* Reunion."

85. "Memory of Mt. Carmel High Kept Alive through Alumni Association," *Huffington Post*, last modified May 25, 2011, www.huffingtonpost.com/2011/03/18/memory-of-mt -carmel-high-_n_837800.html.

86. Jim Walsh, "Riff Randell Forever: P. J. Soles on *Rock 'n' Roll High School*," *MinnPost*, last modified June 27, 2013, www.minnpost.com/arts-culture/2013/06/riff-randell -forever-pj-soles-rock-n-roll-high-school.

87. Craig Sherman, "Take Three: Classic Corman film, Examined," *ArtsEditor*, last modified July 1, 2001, artseditor.com/site/take-three/.

88. Ibid.

89. "Back to School."

90. Jeff Stafford, "*Rock 'n Roll High School*," TCM.com, accessed July 18, 2017, www .tcm.com/this-month/article/150485%7C0/Rock-n-Roll-High-School.html.

91. "Back to School."

92. Kate Abbot, "How We Made: *The Rocky Horror Picture Show*," *Guardian*, last modified March 4, 2013, www.theguardian.com/stage/2013/mar/04/how-we-made -rocky-horror; Matthew Jackson, "14 Absolute Facts about *The Rocky Horror Picture Show*," Mental Floss, last modified April 11, 2016, mentalfloss.com/article/73068/14-absolute -facts-about-rocky-horror-picture-show.

93. Gregg Kilday, "Behind the Scenes with Tim Curry at 1974's *Rocky Horror* Stage Show," *Los Angeles Times*, last modified September 25, 2015, www.latimes.com/entertain ment/herocomplex/la-et-hc-tim-curry-rocky-horror-20150925-story.html; "History of the *RHS*," Rockypedia, accessed July 20, 2017, www.rockypedia.org/History_of_the_RHS.

94. "History of the *RHS*," Rockypedia.

95. Kilday, "Behind the Scenes."

96. Jackson, "14 Absolute Facts."

97. Abbot, "How We Made."

98. Ibid.

99. "History of the *RHPS*," Rockypedia, accessed July 20, 2017, www.rockypedia.org/ History_of_the_RHPS.

100. Abbot, "How We Made."

101. Ibid.

102. Ibid.; Jackson, "14 Absolute Facts."

103. "Box Office/Business for *The Rocky Horror Picture Show* (1975)," IMDb, accessed July 20, 2017, www.imdb.com/title/tt0073629/business?ref_=tt_ql_dt_4.

104. Sally Williams, "Elstree Studios," Western Mail, accessed July 17, 2017, www.the freelibrary.com/Elstree+Studios.-a0150440147.

105. "History of the *RHPS*," Rockypedia.

106. Zack Smith, "What Keeps *The Rocky Horror Picture Show* Flame Burning for More Than Two Decades in Raleigh?" *Indy Week*, last modified October 27, 2010, www .indyweek.com/indyweek/what-keeps-the-rocky-horror-picture-show-flame-burning-for -more-than-two-decades-in-raleigh/Content?oid=1753817.

107. "15 Things You Probably Didn't Know about *Romy and Michele's High School Reunion*," IFC, last modified September 22, 2014, www.ifc.com/2014/09/15-things-you -probably-didnt-know-about-romy-and-micheles-high-school-reunion.

108. Ibid.

109. Ibid.

110. Alice Vincent, "Homecoming Queens: *Romy and Michele's High School Reunion*, an Oral History," *Telegraph*, last modified April 25, 2017, www.telegraph.co.uk/films/2017/04/25/ homecoming-queens-romy-micheles-high-school-reunion-oral-history/.

111. "15 Things about *Romy and Michele*."

112. Ibid.

113. Rebecca Macatee, *"Romy and Michele's High School Reunion* Turns 20: Sorvino Looks Back—and Forward to a Possible Sequel," *E News*, last modified April 25, 2017, www.eonline.com/news/845748/romy-and-michele-s-high-school-reunion-turns -20-lisa-kudrow-and-mira-sorvino-look-back-and-forward-to-a-possible-sequel?utm_ source=eonline&utm_medium=rssfeeds&utm_campaign=imdb_topstories.

114. "Box Office/Business for *Romy and Michele's High School Reunion* (1997)," IMDb, accessed July 23, 2017, www.imdb.com/title/tt0120032/business?ref_=tt_ql_dt_4.

115. *"Romy and Michele's High School Reunion* (1997)," Rotten Tomatoes, accessed July 23, 2017, www.rottentomatoes.com/m/romy_and_micheles_high_school_reunion.

116. *"Romy & Michele's High School Reunion,"* Box Office Mojo, accessed July 23, 2017, www.boxofficemojo.com/movies/?id=romymichelleshighschoolreunion.htm.

117. Melissa Grego, "ABC Greenlights *Reunion* Prequel," *Variety*, last modified August 26, 2002, variety.com/2002/scene/markets-festivals/abc-greenlights-reunion-pre-quel-1117871916/.

118. Dennis Harvey, "Seattle Theater Review: *Romy and Michele's High School Reunion,* the Musical," *Variety*, last modified June 20, 2017, variety.com/2017/legit/reviews/romy -and-micheles-high-school-reunion-review-musical-1202471730/.

119. Nate Jones, "How *The Room* Became the Biggest Cult Film of the Past Decade," *Vulture*, last modified June 27, 2013, www.vulture.com/2013/06/the-room-10th-anniversary -history.html.

120. Ned Lannamann, "Tommy Wiseau: The Complete Interview(s)," *Portland Mercury*, last modified August 13, 2009, www.portlandmercury.com/portland/interview -with-tommy-wiseau/Content?oid=1573119; Will Sloan, "The Varsity Interview: Tommy Wiseau," *Varsity*, last modified April 27, 2011, thevarsity.ca/2011/04/27/the-varsity -interview-tommy-wiseau/.

121. Jones, "The Biggest Cult Film of the Decade."

122. Elina Shatkin, "LAist Interviews Tommy Wiseau, the Face behind the Billboard," *LAist*, last modified on April 27, 2007, laist.com/2007/04/27/laist_interviews_tommy_ wiseau_the_face_behind_the_billboard.php.

123. Steve Heisler, "Tommy Wiseau," The A.V. Club, last modified June 24, 2009, www .avclub.com/article/tommy-wiseau-29598.

124. Conor Lastowka, "RiffTrax Interview with *The Room*'s Greg Ellery," RiffTrax, last modified June 12, 2009, blog.rifftrax.com:80/2009/06/12/rifftrax-interview-with-the -rooms-greg-ellery/.

125. Sloan, "Interview: Tommy Wiseau."

126. Lastowka, "Interview with Greg Ellery"; Shatkin, "LAist Interviews Tommy Wiseau."

127. Shatkin, "LAist Interviews Tommy Wiseau."

128. Clark Collis, "The Crazy Cult of *The Room,"* *Entertainment Weekly*, last modified December 12, 2008, ew.com/article/2008/12/12/crazy-cult-room/.

129. Shatkin, "LAist Interviews Tommy Wiseau."

130. Jones, "The Biggest Cult Film of the Decade."

131. Sloan ""Interview: Tommy Wiseau."

132. Collis, "The Crazy Cult of *The Room."*

133. Collis, "The Crazy Cult of *The Room"*; Jones, "The Biggest Cult Film of the Decade."

134. Jones, "The Biggest Cult Film of the Decade"; Dave McNary, "James Franco Comedy *The Disaster Artist* Gets Awards-Season Release from A24," *Variety*, last modified May 15, 2017, variety.com/2017/film/news/james-franco-disaster-artist-release -date-1202427741/.

135. Brian Formo, *"Bottle Rocket* at 20: Can Wes Anderson Go Home Again?" *Collider*, last modified February 21, 2016, collider.com/bottle-rocket-movie-wes-anderson-owen -wilson-retrospective/.

136. Laura Winters, "An Original at Ease in the Studio System," *New York Times*, last modified January 31, 1999, http://www.nytimes.com/1999/01/31/movies/film-an-origi nal-at-ease-in-the-studio-system.html.

137. Patrick Goldstein, "Carving Out His Niche," *Los Angeles Times*, last modified January 29, 1999, articles.latimes.com/1999/jan/29/entertainment/ca-2676/2.

138. Winters, "An Original at Ease in the Studio System."

139. Ibid.; Jeff Giles, "A Real Buddy Picture," *Newsweek*, December 7, 1998, 72.

140. Giles, "Real Buddy Picture."

141. Matt Zoller Seitz, *The Wes Anderson Collection* (New York: Abrams Brooks, 2013), 83.

142. Winters, "An Original at Ease in the Studio System."

143. Chris Willman, "The 1998 Telluride Film Festival," *Entertainment Weekly*, last modified September 18, 1998, ew.com/article/1998/09/18/1998-telluride-film-festival/; Dan Cox, "*Rushmore* Buzz Mounts," *Variety*, last modified September 8, 1998, variety .com/1998/film/news/rushmore-buzz-mounts-1117480184/.

144. Giles, "Real Buddy Picture."

145. Winters, "An Original at Ease in the Studio System."

146. "*Rushmore*," Box Office Mojo, accessed July 13, 2017, www.boxofficemojo.com/ movies/?id=rushmore.htm.

147. "*Rushmore*," Alamo Drafthouse, accessed July 13, 2017, drafthouse.com/show/ rushmore; "*Rushmore* Awards + Nominations," Fandango, accessed July 13, 2017, www .fandango.com/rushmore_40733/awards.

S

1. Sean Hutchinson, "15 Things You Probably Didn't Know about *Scott Pilgrim vs. the World*," Mental Floss, last modified November 19, 2014, mentalfloss.com/article/60108/15 -things-you-probably-didnt-know-about-scott-pilgrim-vs-world.

2. Clark Collis, "The Making of *Scott Pilgrim vs. the World*: Edgar Wright and Michael Cera Describe How They Brought Us the Year's Most Hard-to-Describe Movie 'Epic,'" *Entertainment Weekly*, last modified August 10, 2010, ew.com/article/2010/08/10/scott -pilgrim-cera-wright-making-of/.

3. Dan, "An Epic Conversation with Edgar Wright and Michael Cera of *Scott Pilgrim vs. the World*," Geekadelphia, last modified August 16, 2010, www.geekadelphia .com/2010/08/16/an-epic-conversation-with-edgar-wright-michael-cera-of-scott-pilgrim -vs-the-world/.

4. Collis, "The Making of *Scott Pilgrim*."

5. Ibid.

6. Dan, "An Epic Conversation"; Collis, "The Making of *Scott Pilgrim*."

7. Johanna Schneller, "Hollywood Goes Toronto," *Globe and Mail*, last modified August 23, 2012, www.theglobeandmail.com/news/national/hollywood-goes-toronto/arti- cle1150576/; Nicole Villeneuve, "*Scott Pilgrim vs. the World* (Just Not Toronto)," Torontoist, last modified April 8, 2009, torontoist.com/2009/04/scott_pilgrim_vs_toronto/.

8. Peter Sciretta, "*Scott Pilgrim* Set Interview: Edgar Wright, Michael Cera, and Jason Schwartzman," /*Film* (blog), last modified May 25, 2010, www.slashfilm.com/scott-pil grim-set-interview-edgar-wright-michael-cera-and-jason-schwartzman/; Edgar Wright, "The Making of *Scott Pilgrim vs. the World*," *Scott Pilgrim vs. the World*, Blu-ray, directed by Edgar Wright (Universal City: Universal Studios Home Entertainment, 2010).

9. Margaret Heidenry, "The Little-Known Story of How *The Shawshank Redemption* Became One of the Most Beloved Films of All Time," *Vanity Fair*, last modified September 22, 2014, www.vanityfair.com/hollywood/2014/09/shawshank-redemption-anniversary-story.

10. Ibid.

11. Ibid.

12. Ibid.

13. Ibid.

14. "Box Office/Business for *The Shawshank Redemption* (1994)," IMDb, accessed July 23, 2017, www.imdb.com/title/tt0111161/business.

15. Robin Rauzi, "Doing *Redemption* Time in a Former Prison," *Los Angeles Times*, last modified December 1, 1993, articles.latimes.com/1993-12-01/entertainment/ca-62788_1_ohio-reformatory.

16. Heidenry, "Little-Known Story."

17. Ibid.

18. Ibid.

19. "Box Office/Business for *The Shawshank Redemption* (1994)."

20. Ibid.

21. Ibid.

22. Ibid.

23. "*The Shawshank Redemption*," Box Office Mojo, accessed July 23, 2017, www.boxofficemojo.com/movies/?id=shawshankredemption.htm.

24. Heidenry, "Little-Known Story."

25. Ibid.

26. Ibid.

27. Samuel Fuller, Christa Lang Fuller, and Jerome Henry Rudes, *A Third Face: My Tale of Writing, Fighting, and Filmmaking* (New York: Applause Theatre & Cinema Books, 2002), 403.

28. Ibid.

29. Ibid., 242–43.

30. Ibid., 403.

31. Robert Polito, "*Shock Corridor*: Lindywood Confidential," Criterion.com, last modified January 18, 2011, www.criterion.com/current/posts/1716-shock-corridor-lindywood-confidential.

32. Fuller, Fuller, and Rudes, *A Third Face*, 403.

33. Ibid.

34. Ibid., 404.

35. Ibid., 412.

36. Ibid.

37. Bruce Dancis, "Two Lurid Classics from Filmmaker Samuel Fuller," *Reading Eagle*, last modified January 26, 2011. http://www2.readingeagle.com/article.aspx?id=281999.

38. Ibid.

39. Brian Raftery, "*Slacker*: 15 Years Later," *Salon*, last modified July 5, 2006, www.salon.com/2006/07/05/slacker/.

40. Ibid.

41. Ibid.

42. Bill Higgins, "When Richard Linklater Took *Slacker* to Sundance in 1991," *Hollywood Reporter*, last modified January 22, 2015, www.hollywoodreporter.com/news/richard-linklater-took-slacker-sundance-764847; Raftery, "15 Years Later."

43. Raftery, "15 Years Later."

44. Ibid.

45. Ibid.

46. Marc Savlov, "Slack to the Future," *Austin Chronicle*, last modified January 21, 2011, www.austinchronicle.com/screens/2011-01-21/slack-to-the-future/.

47. Higgins, "When Linklater Took *Slacker* to Sundance."

48. Raferty, "15 Years Later."

49. Marjorie Baumgarten, "Slack Where We Started," *Austin Chronicle*, last modified June 29, 2001, www.austinchronicle.com/screens/2001-06-29/82235/; Kevin Smith, *An Evening with Kevin Smith*, DVD, Destination Films, 2002.

50. Baumgarten, "Slack Where We Started"; Raftery, "15 Years Later."

51. Baumgarten, "Slack Where We Started"; Raftery, "15 Years Later."

52. Dion, "Ultra Rare *Sorcerer* Screening, Followed by Director William Friedkin Q&A," *The Podwits*, last modified May 10, 2013, www.podwits.com/2013/05/10/ultra-rare-sorcerer-screening-followed-by-director-william-friedkin-qa.

53. Paul Shirey, "The Best Movie You Never Saw: William Friedkin's *Sorcerer*," JoBlo, last modified June 6, 2014, www.joblo.com/movie-news/the-best-movie-you-never-saw-sorcerer.

54. Dion, "Ultra Rare *Sorcerer* Screening."

55. Shirey, "Best Movie You Never Saw."

56. Dion "Ultra Rare *Sorcerer* Screening"; "William Friedkin on Roy Scheider," *Entertainment Weekly*, last modified February 17, 2008, ew.com/article/2008/02/17/william-friedkin-roy-scheider/.

57. Shirey, "Best Movie You Never Saw."

58. William Friedkin, "Director William Friedkin on How He Conjured 1977's *Sorcerer*," *Variety*, last modified May 13, 2016, variety.com/2016/voices/columns/director-william-friedkin-1201770806/.

59. Shirey, "Best Movie You Never Saw"; "*Sorcerer*," American Film Institute, accessed July 20, 2017, www.afi.com/members//catalog/DetailView.aspx?s=&Movie=55890.

60. Friedkin, "Friedkin on *Sorcerer*"; Adam Pockross, "*Sorcerer*: The Film That *Star Wars* Buried Rises Again," Yahoo! Movies, last modified April 25, 2014, www.yahoo.com/movies/sorcerer-the-film-that-star-wars-buried-rises-84177275157.html.

61. Friedkin, "Friedkin on *Sorcerer*."

62. Ibid.; Andrew L. Urban, "Friedkin, William: *Sorcerer*," Urban Cinefile, last modified December 5, 2002, www.urbancinefile.com.au/home/view.asp?a=6832.

63. Pockross, "*Sorcerer*."

64. Urban, "Friedkin, William."

65. Shirey, "Best Movie You Never Saw."

66. Friedkin, "Friedkin on *Sorcerer*"; Shirey, "Best Movie You Never Saw"; Bryan Reesman, "Inside the Forgotten Movie Masterpiece *Sorcerer*," *Esquire*, last modified April 30, 2014, www.esquire.com/entertainment/movies/a28501/sorcerer-william-friedkin/.

67. Shirey, "Best Movie You Never Saw."

68. Brett Arnold, "How a 1977 Box-Office Bomb Became a Cult Classic 35 Years Later," *Business Insider*, last modified October 6, 2014, www.businessinsider.com/sorcerer-movie-popular-35-years-later-2014-9.

69. "*Speed Racer* to Become a Film," *Chicago Tribune*, last modified September 3, 1992, articles.chicagotribune.com/1992-09-03/features/9203200425_1_speed-racer-art-houses-silver-pictures.

70. Michael Fleming and Pamela McClintock, "Sibs Built for *Speed*," *Variety*, last modified October 31, 2006, variety.com/2006/digital/news/sibs-built-for-speed-1117953047/.

71. Rebecca Murray, "Producer Joel Silver Talks *Speed Racer*," About Entertainment, last modified April 3, 2007, http://web.archive.org/web/20071211085555/movies.about.com/od/thereaping/a/silver040107.htm.

72. Hugh Hart, "Oscar-winner John Gaeta Explains *Speed Racer* effects," *Wired*, last modified May 10, 2008, www.wired.com/2008/05/oscar-winner-jo/; "*Speed Racer*: Car-Fu Cinema," *Speed Racer*, Blu-ray, directed by Lana Wachowski and Lilly Wachowski (Burbank: Warner Home Video, 2010).

73. Ed Meza, "New Film Funds Gets Up to *Speed*," *Variety*, last modified April 29, 2007, variety.com/2007/film/news/new-film-funds-gets-up-to-speed-1117963955/.

74. Olly Richards, "Emile Hirsch Talks *Speed Racer*," Empire, last modified October 8, 2015, www.empireonline.com/movies/news/emile-hirsch-talks-speed-racer-2/.

75. "*Speed Racer*: Car-Fu Cinema."

76. Murray, "Joel Silver Talks *Speed Racer*."

77. "*Speed Racer*: Car-Fu Cinema."

78. Meza, "New Film Funds."

79. "*Speed Racer*," Box Office Mojo, accessed July 10, 2017, www.boxofficemojo.com/movies/?id=speedracer.htm.

80. Jon Humbert, "In Defense of *Speed Racer*," *Hollywood Reporter*, last modified April 1, 2017, www.hollywoodreporter.com/heat-vision/speed-racer-defense-2008-wachowskis-movie-990512; Emily Asher-Perrin, "*Speed Racer*: An Overlooked Masterstroke That's Good Enough to Eat," Tor.com, last modified June 16, 2016, www.tor.com/2016/06/16/speed-racer-an-overlooked-masterstroke-thats-good-enough-to-eat/; Chris Wade, "*Speed Racer*, the Wachowskis' Masterpiece," *Browbeat* (*Slate* blog), last modified October 25, 2015, www.slate.com/blogs/browbeat/2012/10/25/speed_racer_the_wachowskis_masterpiece_is_underrated.html.

81. Geek Dave, "1997: 10 Things You Might Not Know about *Starship Troopers*," Warped Factor, last modified January 30, 2017, www.warpedfactor.com/2017/01/1997-10-things-you-might-not-know-about.html.

82. Alex Simon, "Great Conversations: Paul Verhoeven," *Huffington Post*, last modified June 12, 2016, www.huffingtonpost.com/alex-simon/great-conversations-paul_b_7566170.html.

83. Geek Dave, "10 Things."

84. Jeff Wells, "15 Fun Facts about *Starship Troopers*," Mental Floss, last modified November 11, 2015, mentalfloss.com/article/71119/15-fun-facts-about-starship-troopers.

85. Daniel Podgorski, "Poking Fun at Militarism: How Paul Verhoeven's Cult Classic *Starship Troopers* Willfully Discards Robert Heinlein's Novel," *Gemsbok*, last modified February 4, 2016, https://thegemsbok.com/art-reviews-and-articles/thursday-theater-starship-troopers-paul-verhoeven-robert-heinlein/; Adam Smith and Owen Williams, "Triple Dutch: Paul Verhoeven's Sci-Fi Trilogy," Empire, last modified August 31, 2016, www.empireonline.com/movies/features/paul-verhoeven/.

86. Benjamin Svetkey, "*Starship Troopers* Relys on Nazi Imagery," *Entertainment Weekly*, last modified November 21, 1997, ew.com/article/1997/11/21/starship-troopers-relys-nazi-imagery/.

87. Smith and Williams, "Triple Dutch."

88. Bruce Fretts, "Jake Busey on *Justified*, Getting Splattered, and Dear Old Dad," *Esquire*, last modified February 11, 2015, www.esquire.com/entertainment/tv/interviews/a33088/jake-busey-justified/.

89. Smith and Williams, "Triple Dutch."

90. "*Starship Troopers*: Federal Network Visual Effects and Computer Graphics," Banned from the Ranch, accessed July 13, 2017, vfxhq.com/bftr/projects/starship.html.

91. Paul Verhoeven and Ed Neumeier, audio commentary for *Starship Troopers* DVD (Burbank: Buena Vista International, 1998).

92. Calum Marsh, "'*Starship Troopers*: One of the Most Misunderstood Movies Ever," *Atlantic*, last modified November 7, 2013, www.theatlantic.com/entertainment/archive/2013/11/-em-starship-troopers-em-one-of-the-most-misunderstood-movies-ever/281236/.

93. "*Starship Troopers*," Box Office Mojo, accessed July 13, 2017, www.boxofficemojo.com/movies/?id=starshiptroopers.htm.

94. Marsh, "One of the Most Misunderstood Movies."

95. Ibid.

96. Kenneth Plume, "Interview with Dave Thomas," IGN, last modified February 10, 2000, www.ign.com/articles/2000/02/10/interview-with-dave-thomas-part-1-of-5.

97. Ibid.

98. Sean Hutchinson, "12 Frosty Facts about *Strange Brew*," Mental Floss, last modified March 1, 2016, mentalfloss.com/article/76398/12-frosty-facts-about-strange-brew; Erin Hanna, "Second City or Second Country? The Question of Canadian Identity in *SCTV*'s Transcultural Text," *Cineaction*, 78 (2009): 52.

99. Plume, "Interview with Dave Thomas."

100. Ibid.

101. Ibid.

102. "Box Office/Business for *Strange Brew* (1983)," IMDb, accessed July 20, 2017, www.imdb.com/title/tt0086373/business?ref_=tt_ql_dt_4.

103. David Fleischer, "Where the Cult Classic *Strange Brew* was Filmed in Toronto," *Torontoist*, last modified September 29, 2016, torontoist.com/2016/09/where-strange-brew-was-filmed-in-toronto/.

104. Frank Peebles, "Short Stuff Returns with a Whallop," *Prince George Citizen*, last modified May 14, 2011, www.princegeorgecitizen.com/news/local-news/short-stuff-returns-with-a-whallop-1.1090844.

105. "Box Office/Business for *Strange Brew*."

106. "*Strange Brew* (1983) Release Info," IMDb, accessed July 20, 2017, www.imdb.com/title/tt0086373/releaseinfo?ref_=tt_ql_dt_2.

107. Hanna, "Second City."

108. "*Strange Brew*," Box Office Mojo, accessed July 20, 2017, www.boxofficemojo.com/movies/?id=strangebrew.htm.

109. Hutchinson, "12 Frosty Facts."

110. Ibid.

111. J. Hoberman, "Paradise Regained," Criterion.com, last modified September 3, 2007, www.criterion.com/current/posts/568-paradise-regained.

112. Theo Alexander, "*Stranger Than Paradise*," *Unsung Films*, last modified December 16, 2011, www.unsungfilms.com/1436/stranger-than-paradise/.

113. Alexander, "*Stranger Than Paradise*"; Hoberman, "Paradise Regained."

114. Alexander, "*Stranger Than Paradise*."

115. Ibid.

116. Hoberman, "Paradise Regained."

117. Roger Ebert, "*Stranger Than Paradise*," *Chicago Sun-Times*, last modified January 1, 1984, www.rogerebert.com/reviews/stranger-than-paradise-1984.

118. "*Stranger Than Paradise*," Box Office Mojo, accessed July 21, 2017, www.boxofficemojo.com/movies/?id=strangerthanparadise.htm.

119. Sergio, "Melvin Van Peebles' Groundbreaking *Sweet Sweetback's Baadasssss Song* Coming to (Finally) Blu-Ray This Year," *IndieWire*, last modified April 1, 2015, www.indiewire.com/2015/04/melvin-van-peebles-groundbreaking-sweet-sweetbacks-baadasssss-song-coming-to-finally-blu-ray-this-year-155219/.

120. Ibid.

121. Roger Ebert, "Baadasssss!" in *Roger Ebert's Four Star Reviews—1967–2007* (Kansas City: Andrews McMeel, 2007), 54; Robert E. Weems, *Desegregating the Dollar: African American Consumerism in the Twentieth Century* (New York: New York University Press, 1998), 82.

122. Mark Bould, "Watermelon Man," in *Directory of World Cinema: American Independent*, vol. 1, ed. John Berra (Chicago: Intellect Books, 2010), 60.

123. Sergio, "*Sweet Sweetback* Coming to Blu-Ray"; Daniel McNeil, *Sex and Race in the Black Atlantic: Mulatto Devils and Multiracial Messiahs* (New York: Routledge, 2010), 94.

124. Erin Kimmel, "An Introduction to *Sweet Sweetback's Baadasssss Song*," Ballroom Marfa, last modified June 12, 2013, ballroommarfa.org/archive/an-introduction-to-sweet-sweetbacks-baadasssss-song/.

125. Ibid.

126. Richard K. Rein, "Broadway's *Baadasssss*, Melvin Van Peebles, Won't Fold His Play and Just Go Away," *People*, last modified February 15, 1982, people.com/archive/broad ways-baadasssss-melvin-van-peebles-wont-fold-his-play-and-just-go-away-vol-17-no-6/.

127. Sergio, "*Sweet Sweetback* Coming to Blu-Ray."

128. Kimmel, "Introduction to *Sweet Sweetback*."

129. Julie Hinds, "DIA Hosts Melvin Van Peebles, *Sweet Sweetback* Return," *Detroit Free Press*, last modified February 25, 2016, www.freep.com/story/entertainment/2016/02/25/melvin-van-peebles-sweet-sweetback-baadasssss-song-independent-film-burnt-sugar -arkestra-detroit-institute-of-arts/80612538/.

130. Todd Boyd, "Blaxploitation's Baadasssss History," The Root, last modified April 21, 2011, www.theroot.com/blaxploitations-baadasssss-history-1790863642.

131. Stephen Holden, "Film View; *Sweet Sweetback*'s World Revisited," *New York Times*, last modified July 2, 1995, www.nytimes.com/1995/07/02/movies/film-view-sweet -sweetback-s-world-revisited.html?mcubz=2.

T

1. Yoram Allon and Hannah Patterson, *Contemporary North American Film Directors: A Wallflower Critical Guide* (New York: Wallflower Press, 2002), 246.

2. John Bloom, "They Came. They Sawed," *Texas Monthly*, last modified November 2004, www.texasmonthly.com/articles/they-came-they-sawed/; Tobe Hooper, "Tobe Hooper Interview," *The Texas Chainsaw Massacre*, DVD, directed by Tobe Hooper (Orland Park: Dark Sky Films, 2006).

3. Bloom, "They Came."

4. Ibid.

5. Ibid.

6. Ibid.

7. Ibid.

8. Gunnar Hansen, "A Date with Leatherface," *Texas Monthly*, last modified May 1985, www.texasmonthly.com/articles/a-date-with-leatherface/; Stefan Jaworzyn, "*The Texas Chainsaw Massacre*" *Companion* (London: Titan Books, 2012), 63.

9. Bloom, "They Came."

10. Ibid.; "*The Texas Chainsaw Massacre* (1974)," The Numbers, accessed July 19, 2017, www.the-numbers.com/movie/Texas-Chainsaw-Massacre-The#tab=summary; "The Calm, Peaceful Life of Leatherface," CNN.com, last modified June 10, 2004, archive.li/atkZS.

11. "Box Office/Business for *The Texas Chainsaw Massacre* (1974)," IMDb, accessed July 19, 2017, www.imdb.com/title/tt0072271/business?ref_=tt_ql_dt_4.

12. Bloom, "They Came."

13. Jaworzyn, "*Texas Chainsaw*" *Companion*, 40.

14. Stephen Vaughn, *Freedom and Entertainment: Rating the Movies in an Age of New Media* (New York: Cambridge University Press, 2006), 58.

15. Don Sumner, "*The Texas Chainsaw Massacre*," in *Horror Movie Freak* (Iola: Krause Publication, 2010), 109.

16. Bloom, "They Came."

17. "*The Texas Chainsaw Massacre*," Box Office Mojo, accessed July 19, 2017, www.box officemojo.com/movies/?id=texaschainsaw.htm; "*The Texas Chainsaw Massacre* (1974)," The Numbers.

18. Bloom, "They Came"; "Screen 'Video Nasty' Hits Channel 4," *BBC News*, last modified October 16, 2000, news.bbc.co.uk/2/hi/entertainment/974619.stm.

19. Bloom, "They Came."

20. Stuart Cohen, "The Writers B.C. (Before Carpenter)," *The Original Fan* (blog), last modified January 21, 2012, theoriginalfan.blogspot.co.uk/2012/01/writers-b-c-before-carpenter.html.

21. Ibid.

22. Ibid.; Simon Abrams, "John Carpenter Talks about His Storied Filmmaking Career, Creative Differences, and the Term 'Slasher,'" Vulture, last modified September 26, 2015, www.vulture.com/2014/09/john-carpenter-halloween-directing-storied-career-transcript.html.

23. Cohen, "The Writers B.C."

24. Ibid.

25. Ibid.

26. Ibid.

27. Stuart Cohen, "The Screenplay," *The Original Fan* (blog), last modified February 13, 2012, http://theoriginalfan.blogspot.com/2012/02/screenplay.html.

28. Ibid.

29. Stuart Cohen, "When The Thing Became John Carpenters' *The Thing*," *The Original Fan* (blog), last modified June 25, 2013, http://theoriginalfan.blogspot.com/2013/06/when-thing-became-john-carpenters-thing.html.

30. "Box Office/Business for *The Thing* (1982)," IMDb, accessed July 20, 2017, www.imdb.com/title/tt0084787/business?ref_=tt_ql_dt_4; "The Thing (1982)," Box Office Mojo, accessed July 20, 2017, www.boxofficemojo.com/movies/?id=thing.htm.

31. James L. Menzies, "13 Fascinating Facts about *The Thing*," Mental Floss, last modified June 25, 2017, mentalfloss.com/article/68365/13-fascinating-facts-about-thing; Michael Nordine, "*The Thing* Making-of Documentary: John Carpenter, Kurt Russell & More Go Deep on the Cult Classic," *IndieWire*, last modified June 22, 2016, www.indiewire.com/2016/06/the-thing-making-of-documentary-john-carpenter-kurt-russell-1201692015/.

32. Karl French, "The A-Z of *Spinal Tap*," *Guardian*, last modified September 21, 2000, www.theguardian.com/books/2000/sep/22/film.film; Steve O'Brien, "Mock Rock," The Fan Can, accessed July 12, 2017, www.thefancan.com/fancandy/features/moviefeatures/spinal.html.

33. Rob Nixon, "The Big Idea behind *This Is Spinal Tap*," TCM.com, accessed July 12, 2017, www.tcm.com/this-month/article/467146%7C0/This-Is-Spinal-Tap.html.

34. French, "A-Z of *Spinal Tap*"; Jennifer M. Wood, "15 Things You Might Not Know about *This Is Spinal Tap*," Mental Floss, last modified March 3, 2014, mentalfloss.com/article/55369/15-things-you-might-not-know-about-spinal-tap.

35. French, "A-Z of *Spinal Tap*"; O'Brien, "Mock Rock."

36. Wood, "15 Things"; Rob Nixon, "*This Is Spinal Tap* (1984)," TCM.com, accessed July 12, 2017, www.tcm.com/tcmdb/title/92967/This-Is-Spinal-Tap/articles.html.

37. Wood, "15 Things."

38. French, "A-Z of *Spinal Tap*."

39. O'Brien, "Mock Rock"; Wood, "15 Things."

40. Wood, "15 Things."

41. Lloyd Kaufman and James Gunn, *All I Need to Know about Filmmaking I Learned from "The Toxic Avenger": The Shocking True Story of Troma Studios* (New York: Berkley Boulevard Books, 1998), 160–61.

42. Ibid., 161–63.

43. Ibid., 165–68.

44. Ibid., 168–72.

45. Ibid., 176–77.

46. Ibid., 181.

47. Jim Knipfel, "*The Toxic Avenger*: A Brief History of Troma's Superhero Franchise," Den of Geek!, last modified April 11, 2017, www.denofgeek.com/us/movies/toxic-avenger/254308/the-toxic-avenger-a-brief-history-of-tromas-superhero-franchise.

48. Ibid.

49. Matt Barone, "The Scary-Good Afterlife of *Trick 'r Treat*, the Movie That Should Be Halloween's Answer to *A Christmas Story*," Complex, last modified October 28, 2013, www.complex.com/pop-culture/2013/10/trick-r-treat-movie; Kevin Woods, "Cool Horror Videos: Michael Dougherty's Season's Greetings: The Short That Inspired *Trick 'r Treat*," *Arrow in the Head* (JoBlo blog), last modified October 23, 2013, http://www.joblo .com/horror-movies/news/cool-horror-videos-michael-doughertys-seasons-greetings -the-short-that-inspired-trick-r-treat.

50. Barone, "The Scary-Good Afterlife of *Trick 'r Treat*."

51. Ibid.

52. Ibid.

53. William Penix, "How *Trick 'r Treat* became the newest, most unlikely, Halloween tradition," Popoptiq, last modified November 6, 2015, www.popoptiq.com/trick-r-treat -2007-became-newest-unlikely-halloween-tradition/.

54. Barone, "The Scary-Good Afterlife of *Trick 'r Treat*."

55. Brad Miska, "*Trick 'r Treat* Hits the Road in July, DVD/Blu-ray in October!" Bloody Disgusting, last modified June 6, 2009, bloody-disgusting.com/news/16407/trick-r-treat -hits-the-road-in-july-dvdblu-ray-in-october/.

56. "2009 Fright Meter Award Winners," *Fright Meter Awards*, accessed July 11, 2017, www.frightmeterawards.com/past-winners-of-fright-meter.php?sYr=2009.

57. Barone, "The Scary-Good Afterlife of *Trick 'r Treat*."

58. Larry Carroll, "*Trick 'r Treat* Horror Maestro Planning Sequel, Knows Ending and Villain," MTV News, last modified October 8, 2009, www.mtv.com/news/2433905/trick -r-treat-horror-maestro-planning-sequel-knows-ending-and-villain/.

U

1. Cap Blackard, "'Weird Al' Yankovic and Jay Levey: 25 Years of *UHF*," Consequence of Sound, last modified November 11, 2014, consequenceofsound.net/2014/11/weird-al -yankovic-and-jay-levey-25-years-of-uhf/; Sean O'Neal, "We Got It All on *UHF*: An Oral History of 'Weird Al' Yankovic's Cult Classic," The A.V. Club, last modified March 23, 2015, www.avclub.com/article/we-got-it-all-uhf-oral-history-weird-al-yankovics—215579.

2. O'Neal, "Oral History."

3. Ibid.

4. Ibid.

5. Ibid.

6. Ibid.; Wayne McCombs, "A Little History of KFML 1050 AM," *Tulsa TV Memories*, accessed July 16, 2017, tulsatvmemories.com/kfmj.html; Rob O'Hara, "*UHF*: My 15-Year Pilgrimage," Robohara.com, accessed July 16, 2017, www.robohara.com/uhf/.

7. Blackard, "25 Years of *UHF*"; O'Neal, "Oral History."

8. O'Neal, "Oral History."

9. Ibid.

10. Ibid.

11. Ibid.

12. Ibid.; "*UHF* (1989)," Metacritic, accessed July 22, 2017, www.metacritic.com/movie/uhf.

V

1. *Freedom Forever! Making "V for Vendetta*," *V for Vendetta*, two-disc special edition DVD, directed by James McTeigue (Burbank: Warner Home Video, 2006).

2. Ibid.

3. Hilary Goldstein, "*V for Vendetta*: Comic vs. Film," IGN, last modified March 17, 2006, www.ign.com/articles/2006/03/18/v-for-vendetta-comic-vs-film.

4. Rob Carnevale, "Joel Silver and James McTeigue: *V for Vendetta*," BBC News, last modified September 24, 2014, www.bbc.co.uk/films/2006/03/10/silver_and_mcteigue_v_for_vendetta_2006_interview.shtml; Dave Itzkoff, "The Vendetta behind *V for Vendetta*," *New York Times*, last modified March 12, 2006, www.nytimes.com/2006/03/12/movies/the-vendetta-behind-v-for-vendetta.html; Sam Jordison, "*V for Vendetta*: Reading the Film," *Guardian*, last modified November 21, 2011, www.theguardian.com/books/2011/nov/21/v-for-vendetta-film.

5. John Hiscock, "Why *V for Vendetta* Spells C for Controversy," *Telegraph*, last modified March 10, 2006, www.telegraph.co.uk/culture/film/3650833/Why-V-for-Vendetta-spells-C-for-controversy.html.

6. Brian B., "Producer Joel Silver and Director James McTeigue Talk *V for Vendetta*," Movieweb, last modified March 14, 2006, movieweb.com/producer-joel-silver-and-director-james-mcteigue-talk-v-for-vendetta/.

7. Hiscock, "C for Controversy"; "How E Got the V in *Vendetta*," *Guardian*, last modified March 23, 2006, www.theguardian.com/film/2006/mar/23/news.

8. "*V for Vendetta*," Box Office Mojo, accessed July 11, 2017, www.boxofficemojo.com/movies/?id=vforvendetta.htm.

9. "*V for Vendetta* (2006)," Rotten Tomatoes, accessed July 11, 2017, www.rottentomatoes.com/m/v_for_vendetta/.

10. Sarah Warn, "Review of *V for Vendetta*," After Ellen, last modified March 20, 2006, http://www.afterellen.com/movies/4499-review-of-v-for-vendetta.

11. Rosie Waites, "*V for Vendetta* Masks: Who's behind Them?" BBC News, last modified October 20, 2011, www.bbc.com/news/magazine-15359735.

W

1. Erin McCarthy, "20 Hilarious Facts about *Waiting for Guffman*," Mental Floss, last modified January 31, 2017, mentalfloss.com/article/91688/20-hilarious-facts-about-waiting-guffman.

2. Ibid.

3. John Kenneth Muir, *Best in Show: The Films of Christopher Guest and Company* (Winona: Applause Theatre and Cinema Books, 2004), 60–62.

4. Ibid.

5. Christopher Guest and Eugene Levy, "Commentary," *Waiting for Guffman*, DVD, (Burbank: Warner Home Video, 2001).

6. Muir, *Best in Show*, 109.

7. "*Waiting for Guffman*," Box Office Mojo, accessed July 23, 2017, www.boxofficemojo.com/movies/?id=waitingforguffman.htm.

8. Ibid.

9. Alex Cohen, "Amid the Humor, Dewey Cox's Music Is for Real," NPR.org, last modified December 7, 2007, www.npr.org/templates/transcript/transcript.php?storyId=17002243.

10. Ibid.

11. Brian Hiatt, "The Next *Spinal Tap*?" *Rolling Stone*, August 9, 2007, 20.

12. Brian Collins, "*Walk Hard*: Better Than the Movies It's Parodying," Birth. Movies. Death., last modified August 12, 2015, birthmoviesdeath.com/2015/08/12/walk-hard-better-than-the-movies-its-parodying.

13. Ibid.

14. *"Walk Hard: The Dewey Cox Story* (2007)," Rotten Tomatoes, accessed July 11, 2017, www.rottentomatoes.com/m/walk_hard/.

15. *"Walk Hard: The Dewey Cox Story,"* Box Office Mojo, accessed July 11, 2007, www.boxofficemojo.com/movies/?id=walkhard.htm.

16. Eric Ducker, "New York Mythology," The Fader, last modified October 3, 2005, www.thefader.com/2005/10/03/new-york-mythology/; Jennifer M. Wood, "'Can You Dig It?' *The Warriors,* 35 Years Later," *Esquire,* last modified February 19, 2014, www.esquire.com/entertainment/movies/interviews/a27499/the-warriors-walter-hill-interview/; "The Making of *The Warriors,*" *The Warriors* Movie Site, accessed July 20, 2017, warriorsmovie.co.uk/production.

17. "The Making of *The Warriors.*"

18. Ducker, "New York Mythology."

19. "The Making of *The Warriors.*"

20. Ducker, "New York Mythology"; Wood, "'Can You Dig It?'"

21. Ducker, "New York Mythology"; "The Making of *The Warriors.*"

22. Ducker, "New York Mythology."

23. Ibid.

24. Ibid.; Jackson Connor, "Remember *The Warriors*: Behind the Chaotic, Drug-Fueled, and Often Terrifying Making of a Cult Classic," *Village Voice,* last modified September 8, 2015, www.villagevoice.com/2015/09/08/remember-the-warriors-behind-the-chaotic-drug-fueled-and-often-terrifying-making-of-a-cult-classic/.

25. Ducker, "New York Mythology"; "The Making of *The Warriors.*"

26. Ducker, "New York Mythology."

27. Ibid.

28. Clark Collis, *"Wet Hot American Summer*: The Crazy Story behind the Cult Classic," *Entertainment Weekly,* last modified June 24, 2011, ew.com/article/2011/06/24/wet-hot-american-summer-crazy-story-behind-cult-classic/.

29. Scott Tobias, "The New Cult Canon: *Wet Hot American Summer,*" The A.V. Club, last modified June 11, 2008, www.avclub.com/article/the-new-cult-canon-iwet-hot-american-summeri-2341.

30. Collis, "The Crazy Story"; Clark Collis, *"Wet Hot American Summer* 10th Anniversary: David Wain, Michael Showalter, and Joe Lo Truglio Remember Their Days at Camp Firewood," *Entertainment Weekly,* last modified on August 2, 2011, ew.com/article/2011/08/02/wet-hot-american-summer-david-wain/.

31. Collis, "The Crazy Story."

32. Ibid.

33. Ibid.; Collis, *"Wet Hot American Summer* 10th Anniversary."

34. Collis, "The Crazy Story."

35. Collis, "The Crazy Story"; Tobias, "New Cult Canon."

36. Collis, *"Wet Hot American Summer* 10th Anniversary."

37. Nellie Andreeva, *"Wet Hot American Summer: Ten Years Later* Sequel Series Ordered by Netflix," Deadline, last modified on April 27, 2016, deadline.com/2016/04/wet-hot-american-summer-ten-years-later-sequel-series-netflix-1201742946/; Ryan Reed, "Watch Hilarious *Wet Hot American Summer: 10 Years Later* trailer," *Rolling Stone,* last modified June 22, 2017, www.rollingstone.com/tv/news/watch-hilarious-wet-hot-american-summer-10-years-later-trailer-w489139.

Index

About the Author

Christopher J. Olson is a PhD student in the Media, Cinema, and Digital Studies Program at the University of Wisconsin–Milwaukee English Department. He is coeditor of *Making Sense of Cinema: Empirical Studies into Film Spectators and Spectatorship* (2016) and *Heroes, Heroines, and Everything in Between: Challenging Gender and Sexuality Stereotypes in Children's Entertainment Media* (2017). Olson is also coauthor of *Possessed Women, Haunted States: Cultural Tensions in Exorcism Cinema* (2016).